Thinking Through Twentieth-Century Architecture

W0013468

Thinking Through Twentieth-Century Architecture connects the practice of architecture with its recent history and its theoretical origins – those philosophical ideas that lay behind modernism and its aftermath. By analyzing in straightforward and jargon-free language the genesis of modernism and the complex reactions to it, the book clarifies a continuing debate. It has been specifically written to connect issues of theory, history and contemporary practice and to allow students to make these connections easily.

This is a history of twentieth-century architecture, written with close critical attention to the theories that lie behind the works described. Importantly, unlike other historical accounts, it does not take sides and urge the reader to identify with one strand of thinking or style of architecture at the expense of others, but it presents a dispassionate view, with persuasive arguments on behalf of different positions. It pursues the history of European and American architecture chronologically, but the history is interwoven with the philosophical ideas that informed both writers and architects and are essential for its understanding.

The book is relevant to current issues of contemporary practice and education, showing that philosophical issues are fundamental and those relating to design decisions never go away. It includes 200 illustrations and will appeal to all those interested in twentieth-century architecture and to architectural students.

Nicholas Ray, currently a Visiting Professor at the University of Liverpool, practised and taught at Cambridge for more than 40 years, where he is an Emeritus Fellow of Jesus College. Previous publications include monographs on Alvar Aalto and Rafael Moneo and co-authored books and articles with Christian Illies, a German philosopher.

Thinking Through
Twentieth-Century Architecture

Nicholas Ray

Routledge
Taylor & Francis Group

LONDON AND NEW YORK

Cover image: © Johnny Hebblethwaite

First published 2023
by Routledge
4 Park Square, Milton Park, Abingdon, Oxon OX14 4RN

and by Routledge
605 Third Avenue, New York, NY 10158

Routledge is an imprint of the Taylor & Francis Group, an informa business

British Library Cataloguing-in-Publication Data
A catalogue record for this book is available from the British Library

Library of Congress Cataloging-in-Publication Data
Names: Ray, Nicholas, author.
Title: Thinking through twentieth-century architecture / Nicholas Ray.
Description: Abingdon, Oxon : Routledge, 2023. | Includes bibliographical
    references and index.
Identifiers: LCCN 2022022300 (print) | LCCN 2022022301 (ebook) |
    ISBN 9781032156118 (hardback) | ISBN 9781032156125 (paperback) |
    ISBN 9781003244943 (ebook)
Subjects: LCSH: Modern movement (Architecture) | Architecture, Modern—20th
    century—Philosophy.
Classification: LCC NA682.M63 R39 2023 (print) | LCC NA682.M63 (ebook) |
    DDC 724/.6—dc23/eng/20220603
LC record available at https://lccn.loc.gov/2022022300
LC ebook record available at https://lccn.loc.gov/2022022301

ISBN: 978-1-032-15611-8 (hbk)
ISBN: 978-1-032-15612-5 (pbk)
ISBN: 978-1-003-24494-3 (ebk)

DOI: 10.4324/9781003244943

Typeset in Minion
by Apex CoVantage, LLC

Printed in the UK by Severn, Gloucester on responsibly sourced paper

MIX
Paper from
responsible sources
FSC
www.fsc.org   FSC® C022174

In memoriam G.O.
and to Sarah and our grandchildren

For Sonny

xxx

Papa Nick.

Contents

Introduction   1

1 A philosophical framework   6
   Introduction   6
   1.1   Logic   7
   1.2   Epistemology   9
   1.3   Ethics   10
   1.4   Aesthetics   11
   1.5   Metaphysics   14
   1.6   Three broad metaphysical distinctions: Idealism   16
   1.7   Three broad metaphysical distinctions: Scepticism
          or nominalism   18
   1.8   Three broad metaphysical distinctions: Pragmatism   20
   1.9   The Enlightenment split   22
   1.10   Implications for architectural education and practice   24

2 Origins of modernism – the European picture   26
   2.1   Mechanization   26
   2.2   The problem of the city   31
   2.3   The cultural issue of a modern style   35
   2.4   Respect for the past   39
   2.5   Moral criteria   42
   2.6   Art Nouveau as the first manifestation
          of modernism   45
   2.7   Aesthetics, ethics and politics: some broader
          questions   51

3 *Fin-de-siècle* Vienna as a paradigm of modernism   55
   3.1   Historical and cultural background   55
   3.2   Sitte and Wagner – two views of the city   57
   3.3   Politics and philosophical thinking   60
   3.4   Literature and psychology   61
   3.5   Music   62
   3.6   Furniture and painting   63

3.7   Architecture – Wagner and Loos   64
3.8   Relevance   77

4   The modernist canon: The Bauhaus, Le Corbusier
    and CIAM   79
    4.1   Gropius and the Bauhaus   79
    4.2   Gropius' later career   81
    4.3   Le Corbusier   85
    4.4   The inherited problem of the city   86
    4.5   CIAM's solution to the problems of the city   87
    4.6   Functional and formal disciplines   92
    4.7   A first critique: decorated diagrams   98
    4.8   The campus as a CIAM city   101
    4.9   Philosophy and politics: the Bauhaus in its
          German context   105
    4.10 Conflicted positions in Le Corbusier   107

5   Positive scepticism – Alvar Aalto as an alternative
    modernist   110
    Introduction   110
    5.1   The Finnish context   111
    5.2   Neo-classical beginnings   112
    5.3   Paimio, Villa Mairea and Aalto's own house   114
    5.4   Baker House, some of the post-war brick
          buildings and Finlandia Hall   120
    5.5   Some underlying themes   126
    5.6   The philosophical nature of Aalto's scepticism   128

6   Ideals and their representation: Louis Kahn   134
    Introduction   134
    6.1   Education and early work   134
    6.2   Yale Art Gallery extension and Trenton
          Community Center   135
    6.3   Richards Research Laboratory   140
    6.4   Rochester Unitarian Church   141
    6.5   Salk laboratories   144
    6.6   Philips Exeter Academy   145
    6.7   The Kimbell Museum and Mellon Gallery
          for British Art   145
    6.8   Kahn's primary concerns, strengths and
          weaknesses   154

7   Humanizing modernism – Team Ten and the Dutch   158
    Introduction   158
    7.1   Say leaf, say tree   158
    7.2   Ralph Erskine – a Sweden-based member
          of Team Ten   161
    7.3   British contributors to Team Ten   165

7.4	Aldo van Eyck	166
7.5	Herman Hertzberger	171
7.6	The architectural contribution of Team Ten	175
7.7	The philosophical context of the Team Ten critique	178

8 Postmodernism: Irony and inclusiveness — 180

	Introduction	180
8.1	Venturi's critique	181
8.2	Mother's House and a Lutyens precedent	183
8.3	Ducks and decorated sheds	189
8.4	Irony as the only truthful response to twentieth-century conditions	192
8.5	Michael Graves and a referential architecture	194

9 The typological critique — 203

	Introduction	203
9.1	No describable public space	203
9.2	Un-nameable objects	206
9.3	Absence of hierarchy	208
9.4	Architectural typology	210
9.5	The argument for typology in the twentieth century	213
9.6	Aldo Rossi	215
9.7	The slide into historical pastiche	219
9.8	A Kantian apologist for the continuing relevance of the classical language and pragmatic responses	224
9.9	Legacy	228

10 Conflicting existential ideals — 231

	Introduction	231
10.1	Some consequences of the destruction of a post-Kantian world-view	232
10.2	Embracing the conditions of a changed world: Rem Koolhaas	235
10.3	Embracing the conditions of a changed world: Bernard Tschumi	239
10.4	Resisting the conditions of a changed world: a phenomenological critique	242
10.5	Architectural interpretations of a phenomenological position	245
10.6	Understanding history from a phenomenological perspective	251

11 Conclusions – twenty-first century hindsight — 253

11.1	Twentieth-century post-Enlightenment thinking	253
11.2	Critical perspectives from the twenty-first century: racial inclusivity	257

11.3   Critical perspectives from the twenty-first
       century: gender inclusivity   259
11.4   Critical perspectives from the twenty-first
       century: sustainability   260
11.5   Implications in the search for a language of form   261
11.6   Some architects and writers on architecture
       who accept its contingent nature   263
11.7   Further implications for architectural education   265
11.8   A Humean position   269

Acknowledgements   271
Select bibliography   273
List of plates and credits   285
Index   289

INTRODUCTION

On 21 May 1956, the architectural historian John Summerson delivered a lecture at the Royal Institute of British Architects in London entitled "The Case for a Theory of Modern Architecture".[1] He pointed out that modern architecture, by which he meant the architecture of the twentieth century and most particularly the architecture that came out of Europe in the first half of that century and by 1956 had been adopted worldwide, was different from all previous architecture: it was founded on the principle that the function of the building provided "the source of unity". Previous styles of architecture were precisely that: styles. Buildings might have been "born of utility" as the Renaissance architect Leon Battista Alberti claimed, but they were also consciously "dressed" in some way – or "decorated" – so as to endow them with the appropriate degree of dignity, or "decorum". Indeed *decor*, or propriety, had been one of the principles the Roman architect Vitruvius had listed in the first book of his ten-book treatise *De Architectura*, written in the first century BC, stressing the importance of the 'proper' expression for different types of buildings.[2] In modernism a theory existed, Summerson claimed, in that the way in which the architect met the programme, or functional brief, had become the source of unity. But the 'language' the architecture used to speak was missing, and "it is quite possible that the missing language will remain missing".[3] In 1963, Summerson went on to employ this analogy extensively – treating architecture as capable of communicating meanings by non-verbal means in the same way that language does – in a set of six lectures on the BBC's *Third Programme*, which were collected the following year into his book *The Classical Language of Architecture*.[4] The analogy is useful even if, as Summerson himself acknowledged, architecture could be shown to predate language: buildings can be 'articulate' or 'illiterate' in any given style, 'poetic', 'grammatically correct' and so on.[5] But modernist apologists explicitly declared that modernism was not a style, which poses the problem he referred to of a "missing language".

Summerson's provocative lecture raised a fundamental issue of expression that was to face architects through the second half of the twentieth century and beyond. That issue is a principal theme of the present book, which explores the variety of responses by architects, illustrated in what they designed and built and in what they said or wrote about architecture. It also takes into account the histories of the period written by architectural historians as apologists or critics: treating modernism as a heroic campaign, for instance, or as an aberration, as an irrelevance given the material and economic circumstances of the twentieth

1 Summerson 1957, pp. 307–313, originally given at the RIBA on 21 May 1956. There was a vote of thanks by Jacob Bronowski, seconded by Michael Patrick. Comments were printed from Reyner Banham, Peter Smithson, W.A. Eden and G.E. Wickham, with a brief response by Summerson. The lecture, but not the vote of thanks or discussion, is reprinted in Summerson 1990, pp. 257–266.
2 In Vitruvius 1960 (original translation 1914), Morgan uses the word "propriety". In *Vitruvius* 1999, p. 25, Roland, Howe and Dewar translate *decor* as "correctness" and contextualize their interpretation on pp. 150–151.
3 Adrian Forty lists six ways in which architecture might intersect with language, predicting that, unsatisfactory though they are, linguistic metaphors will continue to be employed productively (Forty 2000, pp. 63–85).
4 Summerson 1980. The book was reprinted several times with improved illustrations and is still in print and widely read.
5 Bernard Tschumi, whose writings and work will be discussed in Chapter 10, suggested that architecture is like language in another way, as a mask that hints at the meanings it might be trying to express. Tschumi 1996, pp. 93–94.

DOI: 10.4324/9781003244943-1

century or as a frustrated technical project yet to be fulfilled.[6] And one could think of more.

As a historian of modernism who most clearly celebrated its heroic mission, we might instance Sigfried Giedion, who explained:

> I have attempted to establish, both by argument and by objective evidence, that in spite of the seeming confusion there is nevertheless a true, if hidden, unity, a secret synthesis, in our present civilisation.[7]

and argued:

> The contemporary movement is not a "style" in the 19th century meaning of form characterization. It is an approach to the life that slumbers unconsciously within all of us.

Modernism, for Giedion, was the inevitable and irresistible consequence of changed material circumstances and was forging its way to a bright future. But for David Watkin, modernism was a complete aberration. In his *Morality and Architecture* he sought to show that anybody exercising dispassionate aesthetic judgment, or taste, would be unmoved by arguments by people like Giedion that the 'spirit of the age' demanded new forms, and he saw modernism as a perverted faith that produced ugly buildings:

> One of the developments we shall be tracing in the following pages is the consequence of the belief that modern man should build a new collectivist society based on a universally accepted moral and social consensus, in which architecture would be an unassailably "genuine" and "universal" truth no longer marred by the "individual" and "inventive" traits of the old world in which individual taste and imagination were regarded as important.[8]

Bill Riseboro, as a Marxist critic, would regard such an emphasis on taste as irrelevant in view of the economic differentials at work in the world. An increasing proportion of global development is in the so-called 'informal' sector, and architects are not involved at all. Whether a building is stylistically neo-classical, 'high-tech' or postmodern is completely beside the point:

> Material conditions – that is social systems, political institutions and culture in general including art and architecture – are dependent ultimately on the way a society earns its living. Modern architecture and design must thus be seen in the context of, and defined by, the modern economic system.[9]

A similar argument could be mounted from the perspective of environmental sustainability. This was an issue architects in the mid-twentieth century hardly considered, but now, in the light of the consequences of carbon emissions, one could argue that there are more important things to worry about than the aesthetic decisions of privileged architects.

6 Not all historians are as partisan. For generally thoughtful and balanced accounts see Curtis 1982 and Frampton 1980, though naturally those two authors reveal their own positions by what they choose to emphasise or suppress.
7 Giedion 2008.
8 Watkin 1977.
9 Riseboro 1982. The book illustrates 'vulgar Marxism', from which more sophisticated Marxist critics such as Manfredo Tafuri (see Tafuri 1990) would distance themselves, but is a useful summary of the position.

But others, including Martin Pawley, agreed with Reyner Banham, who, in *Theory and Design in the First Machine Age*, had described the aesthetic prejudices that prevented an authentic technically efficient modernism from emerging.[10] (He had concluded his book with the American engineer Buckminster Fuller's project for a "Dymaxion House" as a better model.) In *Theory and Design in the Second Machine Age*, Pawley waxed lyrical about future possibilities:

> Architecture, which is now nothing more than an occult world of ignorance and magic shot through with individual acts of achievement, could become a mega-technology. . . . If an ideological certainty equal to that of the Modern Movement could be achieved for the new architecture of technology transfer, architects, freed of the tyranny of history for the second time in a century, could concentrate on design by assembly, identifying the availability of new materials and techniques, and if necessary "specifying them into culture" with a squeeze on the joystick button.[11]

We might not agree wholeheartedly with any of these positions, but there is surely something to each of them. With hindsight, it is difficult not to see some cultural consistency in the architecture of certain periods, even if we do not choose to describe it as a 'secret synthesis'. We might object to the tone of Watkin's remarks but see why he thought it was necessary to re-establish the idea of individual judgment and taste in the face of some twentieth-century polemic. Without subscribing to Marxist doctrine, it is clear, for instance, that the economics of Neo-Liberalism had a major effect on the form of cities and buildings in the latter half of the twentieth century. At the same time, while not necessarily seeing technological developments as the single most important factor, architects of whatever persuasion undeniably had to take account of them, and surely practitioners in the discipline will continue to do so.

Summerson's concern – for a lost language of architectural expression – is 'epistemological' in philosophical terms, but I shall be arguing that behind epistemological concerns lie metaphysical views of the world that philosophy can help to reveal. The first chapter is therefore dedicated to explaining the terms (such as 'epistemological') used throughout the book to describe ways of thinking that derive initially from Greek antiquity and were reframed at two significant stages, the Renaissance and the Enlightenment, and during the twentieth century were to determine thinking not only in Europe but throughout the world. My thesis is that the practice of architecture and its critical understanding are dependent on views of the world that can be examined philosophically. Just as historians of modernism came from different philosophical positions, so did the architects who practised during the period, whether or not they acknowledged it. The chapter contains the names of numerous philosophers because that allows a comprehensible shorthand in those that follow ('Hegelian', for instance), though naturally I cannot cover their thinking in detail. The second chapter is more straightforward

10 Banham 1980.
11 Pawley 1990.

historical – an abbreviated summary of the context from which the movement emerged that came to be known as 'modernism'. The third is a case study of a particular city, Vienna, where the genesis of modernism can be seen in all the arts. In Chapter 4, I concentrate on the two most frequently cited representatives of modern architecture, Walter Gropius and Le Corbusier, introducing critiques of their positions that emerged while they were still practising. The seven succeeding chapters examine reactions to the perceived inadequacies of architectural modernism by individual architects or groups of architects. Whether the architects concerned approved of the description or not (and usually they didn't), critics have described much of their work as "postmodern", adopting a term that was applied initially to literature but later to many other disciplines. The case studies to which I refer are necessarily highly selective; the final chapter draws conclusions from what has been discussed and thereby aims to be more general and to acknowledge, with hindsight, the problems we have in understanding theory and practice in the last century. It is clear that, unlike easel painting, architecture of any scale cannot be created without collaborators – consultants as well as architectural colleagues. Conventionally, buildings are identified with a particular architect. So we talk about "the work of James Stirling". But at different periods he was in partnership with James Gowan and, later, with Michael Wilford. The problem is especially acute when the contribution of women is suppressed: this is an issue to which I shall return in the final chapter. Each of the architects or practices that I discuss was distinguished in its time and contained truly talented individuals. But just as every philosophical position can be criticized, so can their work: there are no unambiguously 'right' answers in either discipline.

The format of the historical chapters does not attempt to be rigorously consistent – first setting out relevant philosophical ideas and then identifying architectural examples, for instance, which is appropriate in some cases – because different architects, or groups of architects, seem to demand different treatments. In Chapter 5, I therefore discuss many examples of the work of Alvar Aalto (an architect who was sceptical of the benefits of theoretical descriptions compared to the direct experience of his buildings) before suggesting what ideas lie behind his practice. It will be clear that, in providing both an abbreviated history of an extended period and trying to summarize complex arguments in few words, this book contains numerous simplifications and can only serve as an introduction to more detailed historical and theoretical writings: I refer to many of these in the sidenotes and bibliography.

Architectural theory has developed in recent decades as an independent discipline with its own distinguished practitioners. Sometimes they are tempted to describe an unbuilt project, rendered in drawings, or even their own contributions to the discourse as 'architecture'.[12] That is not the position taken in this book, which is similar to that advanced by Rafael Moneo:

> I believe that in the crude reality of built works one can see clearly the essence of a project, the consistency of ideas. I firmly believe that

12 In a recent article (Burrow 2021), a literary critic warned against the potential for aggrandizement of those critics who argue that creation is no more than "criticism widened and deepened": ". . . critics do need to remember, I think, that creation requires something other and beyond criticism. In saying this, I believe I have God on my side, since 'Let there be light' is not a critical statement. The implied prior act of criticism ('I'm getting a bit sick of all this darkness') requires the additional power of creation to make something new. Once that power has done its stuff God becomes a critic again, and sees that it is good. But it's the bit in between – the making – that matters most, even though it might pain a critic to confess it". For an architectural example, see, for instance, an interview with Mark Wigley: www.youtube.com/watch?v=107m4d_07yw.

architecture needs the support of matter; that the former is insep-
arable from the latter. Architecture arrives when our thoughts about
it acquire the real condition that only materials can provide.[13]

But might theory, written discourse, supersede architecture and render it mute and incapable of symbolizing anything beyond perhaps the
means of its own fabrication? Such an anxiety, for architects, is hardly
new. In Victor Hugo's 1831 novel *Notre-Dame de Paris*, the archdeacon
had famously suggested as much: "*ceci tuera cela*".[14] Even those philosophers whose work seems to be most relevant to architecture were
mostly concerned with language: frequently they use architecture as a
metaphor for the complexities of linguistic communication, whereas
architects use linguistic metaphors to describe how architecture can be
expressive.

The theoretical ideas discussed are not an end in themselves but, by
furthering an understanding of twentieth-century theory and practice, are intended as a means to an end: the design of thoughtful buildings, as well as the appreciation of works of architecture that reveal
such thoughtfulness. Just as it was a mistake in the twentieth century
to ignore what was good in the architecture of the nineteenth, so it is
important that in the twenty-first century, as well as being quite properly critical of aspects that we now find questionable (or, in some cases
wholly unacceptable), we seek to understand its best work and try and
come to a balanced judgment. Problematic issues would include most
prominently attitudes to colonialism and race,[15] changed attitudes to
gender and the environmental problems that have been caused by a
generally irresponsible attitude to environmental sustainability; these
questions are discussed on pp. 257–261 of the Conclusions. The process of coming to a 'balanced view' itself involves taking a philosophical
position: if discrimination is generally to be avoided, for instance, how
far is it proper to engage in *positive* discrimination?[16] This is among the
questions philosophers have always debated, as we shall see in the next
chapter.

13 From a talk originally delivered as the Kenzo Tange Lecture in Harvard, 9 March 1985, reprinted in Moneo 1989. Peter Zumthor takes a similar view (Zumthor 1998, pp. 11–12).
14 See Levine 1982.
15 See, for instance, Cheng, Davis and Wilson 2020.
16 We need to consider this question not only in relation to the treatment of historically disadvantaged people globally, but also inter-generationally in more privileged societies. In view of their behaviour in previ-ous decades in exploiting the world's resources, how far should the comfort of older generations be compromised in favour of those who are inheriting the resulting problems?

1

A PHILOSOPHICAL FRAMEWORK

Introduction

This chapter establishes some of the philosophical terms I shall use in the chapters that follow when discussing architects, their buildings and statements about their work. Whereas European schools conventionally include lessons on broad philosophical issues at secondary level, British education has mostly avoided them: students might study comparative religion but wouldn't usually be familiar with philosophical distinctions unless they chose to study the topic at sixth form level. When an education in the classics was more common, a student might have read Cicero's speeches, or even dipped into Plato's *The Republic*, but that is now a minority pursuit, so many British students at undergraduate level would probably subscribe to a sceptical empiricism without being aware of the terms that describe their position.

Philosophy is a lifelong study, however, and one might argue that to attempt to summarize a long history of thinking is bound to lead to superficiality. Nevertheless, I believe the attempt is a necessary one since my purpose is to show that the (frequently unacknowledged) positions architects hold can have a profound influence on how they design. Moreover, the very way that architectural students are taught at university level, and the criteria that are used in judging their work, imply some philosophical standpoint. If that is so, it is a subject that should be discussed much more broadly, and the hope is that those who find the subject interesting and relevant will pursue it further and be able to refine (and challenge) the inevitable generalizations that I shall make.[1]

It should also be clear that for the purposes of this book, which relates to twentieth-century modernism in Europe and America, I am referring to the Western philosophical tradition. That is the tradition which lay behind the work of the architects under discussion and remains the tradition on which most teaching in British universities depends, whether or not that is made explicit.[2] The philosophers mentioned in this chapter are those that can be said to have established the paradigmatic pre-twentieth-century framework. So many recent interesting European thinkers, for example, Jean François Lyotard (1924–1998) or Julia Kristeva (1941–), are mentioned only briefly, if at all. In England, Elizabeth Anscombe, Iris Murdoch, Mary Midgley and Philippa Foot (all graduating from Oxford) were instrumental in countering extreme forms of logical positivism.[3] The thinking of that generation, whether

1 There is much information on the web, some of it quite misleading, so there is no real substitute for reading the original texts of philosophers, preferably in their original language. The most reliable general articles in English, fairly regularly updated, are in the Stanford Encyclopedia of Philosophy. 2 For a detailed article on the relation between Western and Chinese philosophical traditions, see: http://plato.stanford.edu/entries/comparphil-chiwes/. Some argue that "Chinese philosophy is 'wisdom' literature, composed primarily of stories and sayings designed to move the audience to adopt a way of life or to confirm its adoption of that way of life. Western philosophy is systematic argumentation and theory", and that therefore they may be incommensurable; others see useful parallels. See also Wang 2017, reviewed in Botz-Bornstein 2017. 3 Two books were recently published about their contribution within a few months of each other: Lipscomb 2021; Mac Cumhaill and Wiseman 2022.

DOI: 10.4324/9781003244943-2

male or female, was self-consciously dependent on the Western tradition, and their contribution cannot be understood without a sense of the ground from which they sprang and which they in turn critique. An unfortunate consequence is that most of those I refer to as establishing the philosophical terms in common use are men.

It could be said of philosophical problems that they never go away, so those I discuss are hardly new, though in each generation what seems most important changes, and the emphasis is always shifting. Some explain insolubility by saying that philosophy by its nature is the home for problems for which we have no method of solution; others say that philosophical problems do sometimes turn out to be soluble, but as soon as we see them as soluble we assign them to other disciplines. If we decided, for instance, that insulating existing buildings to the maximum was the over-riding priority, regardless of its effect on appearance, the issue becomes technical: how to do it most effectively. But we know there are reasons we might not always adopt that course. The attitude adopted here is to acknowledge that there are arguments for and against design decisions, and disagreements depend on the philosophical framework within which they are set; I try to present them evenly, even if that ambition itself reveals a certain bias.

Western philosophy has been conventionally divided into logic, epistemology, ethics, aesthetics and metaphysics, and these are briefly discussed in that order.

1.1 Logic

Logic is the study of the structure and principles of reasoning and sound argument. It depends on our acceptance that certain facts, such as that $2 + 2 = 4$, are axiomatically correct. Logic examines how deductions are made from the facts. (As we shall see later, objectivity in itself can be challenged at a metaphysical level.) Deductive logic derives a conclusion that is inevitable once we accept assumptions. An obvious example for an architectural student would be when a visiting critic remarks: "you have said you wish to encourage sunshine into the living spaces of the building you have designed for a site in Liverpool, yet you have made all the habitable rooms face north". The student accepts the assumption that in Liverpool the sun will continue to shine (when it does so) from the south rather than the north and the conclusion is inescapable – the design does not meet the claims that the student has made for it.

Logic at its most rigorous is quite technical and mathematical and has been developed into newer fields such as modal logic, though these aspects are likely to have a minimal application to architectural issues. As we shall see, some have sought to end the 'artistic' side of architectural design, by postulating methods that would remove or minimize it, but they are usually forced to acknowledge that there is a limit to the application of logic to architecture. The starting point of a design ('inspiration') might appear to be quite arbitrary, though ideas do depend on the imagination of individuals, which can be more or less informed; in their development architects can also take wayward decisions. But the testing of the design's performance against accepted criteria can be properly objective. In a response to comments made at his 1956 lecture, referred to in the Introduction of this book, John Summerson said:

> Where forms come from, as any art historian knows, is a very great mystery indeed. They come from the artist's personality, his totality of experience, and how they come is a problem of the psychology of art which I cannot go into and of which astonishingly little is known. Certainly Mr. Smithson touches on a very important point there.[4]

So only when the general idea for a design is established (since its genesis might be quite personal) can one truly engage in objective evaluation. Ideally, one should be able to model the consequences of a design decision in order to start that process. Yet it is a well-known problem that architectural works frequently have to act as prototypes, since there is no opportunity to test full-scale the particular conjunctions of locations, forms and materials in the way that there is with some industrial products. If exhaustive modelling of a building's anticipated performance is seldom possible, that makes 'post-occupancy evaluation' all the more important, to test whether the claims made for it at design stage are fulfilled.

So far, I have mentioned deductive logic only. Inductive logic involves claims for the general or future performance of particular objects, materials or structures based on their past performance. Implied in the earlier deductive example is the induction that the sun *will* rise tomorrow because it has risen in the past. That's a premise we normally accept without demur, but other inductions might be questioned more easily. When we try to draw general conclusions from specific instances, this is more problematic: a claim, for example, that the town square an architect has designed will promote convivial behaviour because it has the same geometrical configuration and orientation as that of the Piazza del Campo in Siena. And the reverse is true: designers are on shaky ground when they attempt to argue for one particular design as the inevitable form arising out of their solution to technical problems. A famous twentieth-century instance was the architect Hannes Meyer's claims for his League of Nations competition proposal (**Figure 1.1**). As Kenneth Frampton has pointed out, following Meyer's statement that the form of his 1927 proposal for the League of Nations was entirely determined by answering functional problems and "symbolizes nothing", he went on to explain that a twentieth-century architect could not possibly

> . . . cram such a novel social organization into the straitjacket of traditional architecture. No pillared reception rooms for weary monarchs but hygienic workrooms for the busy representatives of their people. No back corridors for backstairs diplomacy but open glazed rooms for public negotiation of honest men.[5]

4 Summerson 1957, p. 313. For Peter Smithson, the British architect and member of Team Ten who had raised the point, see p. 168.
5 Quoted in Frampton 1980, p. 134.

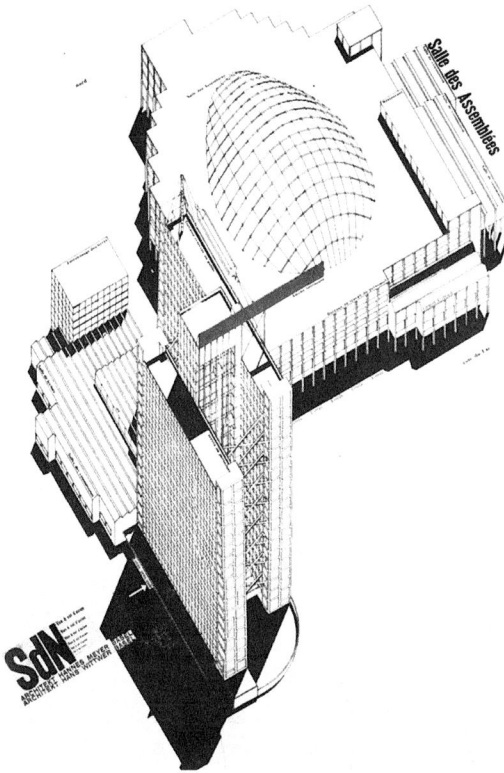

Figure 1.1 Hannes Meyer: League of Nations competition entry, 1927

It is easy to show that Meyer's claim that the forms he has invented are entirely determined by functional considerations cannot be the case. First, we could question his premises – whether he had sufficiently defined all the criteria that should be met. Even if we agreed that his criteria were adequate and sufficient, we would certainly be able to discover other forms that met them. His further statements reveal the symbolism behind the forms and materials he had chosen and thereby lead us to question his belief that it is possible to create buildings which symbolize nothing.[6]

There is another way in which logic might appear: architects could devise a formal system, a mathematical set of proportions or procedures for example, which creates a discipline against which other forms or formal developments could be judged. Some architects have explored this approach, as we shall see. Others would regard it as a trivial formalism or even dangerous because of its self-referential internalized character.

1.2 Epistemology

Epistemology is the theory of knowledge, and in particular theories of how knowledge is derived. Rationalists, like Plato (428–347 BC) and René Descartes (1596–1650), assert that ideas of reason that are intrinsic

6 For the complex history of the meanings of transparency in modernism, see a brief summary in Forty 2000, pp. 286–288; Rowe and Slutzky 1963 & 1971; Vidler 1992, pp. 217–225.

to the mind are the only source of knowledge. Empiricists, such as John Locke (1632–1704) and David Hume (1711–1776), claim that all knowledge is ultimately derived from experience: the motto of the Royal Society (of which Christopher Wren was a founding member) is *Nullius in Verba* – "(rely) on the words of no one".[7] It has frequently been observed – as I suggested earlier – that most Britons subscribe to a sceptical empiricism.[8] In other words, the British seem predisposed to be suspicious of continental theory.

The work of one of the most influential Western philosophers, Immanuel Kant (1724–1804), consisted in trying to reconcile these two ways we encounter and conceive of the world. He believed there was a real world out there but conceded that we cannot know about it as it is but only as we understand it to be. He agreed that there were two types of knowledge: 'sense', which is gained by experience, and 'understanding', thus constituting an irreducible duality that is 'transcendental' in that human beings necessarily engage with both types. Understanding involves both those things that are true in themselves, by definition, and can therefore (he claims) be known a priori, and those things that can be argued for 'synthetically' on the basis of such an a priori understanding. Moreover, Kant argues that it is only thanks to a priori knowledge that we can make sense of our perceptions in the first place. Everyone agrees on Kant's importance, and in some sense all Western philosophy since his time can be seen as a reaction in one way or another to his theories, but some would say his elaborate construction was nevertheless a magnificent failure.[9]

As we shall see in the chapters that follow, certain philosophical movements have sought to rebalance epistemological thinking, and this can have a profound effect on the way architects think about design.

1.3 Ethics

Much philosophy has little to do with everyday life: we tend just to get on with living it, rather than wondering what it really means to know something. But ethics, the study of what it is right or proper to do, does have implications.[10] An initially attractive position is to say it is right to promote the greatest happiness for the greatest number of people, in which an architect's role would be a modest one as the servant of society. This is called utilitarianism. But would architects in that case have any duty to their art over and beyond their duty to their public? It is extremely difficult to reconcile differing values in practice, and some philosophers would accept that engaging in any social activity (like architecture) necessarily involves such conflicts. Architects, in particular, are likely to have a duty to their clients (who pay for their services, after all) as well as a duty to the wider public who experience their buildings daily.[11]

Just as you might point out that dividing philosophical problems into five categories is somewhat arbitrary, the division that follows of ethical positions into three can be questioned. Nevertheless, it is useful and has become the convention. 'Deontological ethics' is duty or principle-

7 For an examination of Wren's thinking, see "The Mind of Wren" in Summerson 2013.

8 This is of course a generalization; between about 1870 and 1920 there were some serious British idealists, such as Bosanquet and Bradley, who built on the German Hegelian tradition.

9 The phrase is Bernard Williams'. He was most critical of Kant's over-systematized ethical theory, taking too little account of the actual dilemmas people face in everyday life. See Williams 1973; Chappell and Smyth 2018.

10 Even if professional philosophers sometimes deny it. Broad 1930 begins with a characteristically careful disclaimer of any usefulness. Some philosophers would say that it is naïve to suppose that philosophical ideas in general have any practical consequences; it hardly needs to be stressed that this is not the position taken in the present book.

11 These and similar issues are discussed in Spector 2001; Ray 2005b.

based, 'consequentialist' ethics privileges the likely outcome and 'virtue ethics' is concerned with the nature of the agent. Each position carries its own problems and arguably needs to draw from the others. A 'deontological' position would hold that there are absolute rules, such as 'you must never tell a lie', which was one of Kant's 'categorical imperatives'. (If there was widespread untruthfulness, society would break down.) A well-known difficulty, which Kant acknowledged, is known as the axe-man problem. If a man wielding an axe came to your door and asked you where your friend was, you would be duty bound to tell the truth, even if it meant that your friend might die. A 'consequentialist' position accepts that if, for instance, you dissimulated so as to give yourself time to alert others and prevent a murder, that better outcome can be justified. But retrospective justification also gets us into a tricky position.[12] To use an architectural example, architects might be commissioned to design a building for a purpose they did not believe in, such as prison. Should they accept the commission? It would be principled if they refused, certainly, but an architectural practice might take the view that any prison it designed would be better than those others could design, and although they would prefer to be designing opera houses, prisons are necessary institutions in a civil society and deserve proper consideration: the consequence for the prisoners and wardens would be better if a skilful practice agreed to act as architect.

Virtue ethics takes a wider view and refers more to persons and the way they seek to live their lives than to any one activity: is this an action, we would ask, that a virtuous person would take? Its strength is that it promises an over-riding principle yet acknowledges that what might be regarded as right in one age may be disapproved of in another: just as nowadays we disapprove of slavery, we are in the process of revising our attitudes to gender in general and not only in the architectural profession. A weakness of virtue ethics, however, is that it is unlikely to provide guidance in any particular situation.

Another way in which ethics might intersect with architecture is when architects and critics claim that buildings should be 'truthful' in their expression, particularly their structural expression, or 'truthful' to their age and the spirit of their time. One of the nineteenth-century critic John Ruskin's "Seven Lamps" was the lamp of truth.[13] His claims were ridiculed in the 1920s by Geoffrey Scott in *The Architecture of Humanism* as the "ethical fallacy".[14] The twentieth-century architectural historian David Watkin, whose views have already been mentioned, engaged in a similar attack on the notion of the 'spirit of the age' and the sense that architects should be required to conform to it.[15] He would claim the whole discussion, which will return in a number of the examples investigated later, confuses ethical and aesthetic judgments.

1.4 Aesthetics

Aesthetics, as a relatively independent philosophical study of art, only emerges with any clarity in the eighteenth century. It is the branch of philosophy that appears to relate most strongly to architecture, or at

12 See Williams 1981; Nagel 1979
13 Ruskin 1849 and 2010
14 Scott 1999.
15 Watkin 1977.

least to its appreciation, so it will occupy a larger proportion of this chapter than the others.

Applying the distinctions already outlined, Rationalists would argue that certain canons (like systems of proportion) lie behind all art we describe as beautiful: the quality of beauty is inherent in the object – what is true is also beautiful. Empiricists, on the other hand, might just begin with an approximate definition (say, of what people have judged to be beautiful in the past). This can then act as a kind of convention and, in turn, assist in determining its extension to other examples. In such a view, we would presumably require an infinite number of examples of the beautiful in order to define beauty precisely, or simply subscribe to a view that what most people now regard as beautiful is so. A sceptical solution, as ever, is to regard nothing as proven: the theory is merely a hypothesis which is good only so long as it is not falsified.

Empiricists claim in any case that it is the effect of the object, not the object itself, that is important. David Hume derides the mathematician who:

> took no pleasure in reading Virgil but that in examining Aeneas' voyage by means of the map . . . He knew, therefore, everything in the poem: But he was ignorant of its beauty.[16]

The whole point of the poetry, Hume says, is its effect on the reader. The mathematician understood quantitative matters but not qualitative. In the same way, architects, arguing for the integrity of their conception, which they believe people will benefit from aesthetically, sometimes accuse their quantity surveyors, or unsympathetic clients, of knowing the price of everything but the value of nothing – they do not take account of what cannot be measured, but that does not mean that those qualities do not exist or are not worthwhile.[17]

Epistemological scepticism has a long history, beginning in the fifth century BC, in distinction to the position of Stoics, who emphasized formal logic, so that seventeenth- or eighteenth-century debates are prefigured in the discussions that took place both before and after the death of Socrates (c. 470–399 BC), whose thinking summarized that of his predecessors. Our chief access to Socrates' thinking is through Plato (427–347 BC), who recorded it in a number of *Dialogues*. Whereas the later Stoics thought that Socrates showed a way to gain knowledge, or become wise, Sceptics doubted that was possible – all that could be done was to "subject all claims to the kind of dialectical scrutiny Socrates had subjected them to".[18] It was a debate that became 'academic' in the worst sense of the word and survived throughout the Middle Ages. Not until the Renaissance did a renewed idealism reassert itself in the form of a revived Neo-Platonism.

Immanuel Kant typically tried to maintain a balance: he held that aesthetic judgment is unlike theoretical (logical) judgment or practical (moral or ethical) judgment in that it is affected solely by the subject. But

16 Hume 1975.
17 "Not everything that counts can be counted and not everything that can be counted, counts" is a statement frequently, though probably inaccurately, attributed to Albert Einstein.
18 Frede 1983.

though aesthetic judgments cannot be objective, he argued, they should be scientifically disinterested, and that is what makes them potentially generalizable rather than merely private and 'sensual'. Thus, we could say, Kant seeks to rescue unruly taste into the orderly world of culture.[19]

Others argue that moral and aesthetic judgments are not indistinct versions of analytical ones. Unlike analytical judgments, they do not adhere to systemic criteria such as non-contradiction and so cannot be computed in advance. They are humanistic and conventional rather than absolute. On the analogy of British case law (rather than Roman Law), aesthetic judgment, though it should be guided and informed, would more properly be like a trial by jury than an oracular judgment issued by persons with special training.[20] But such an empirical attitude to aesthetics might be regarded as peculiarly British. A Rationalist would say it just deflects the argument from the court to the jury room because members of the jury would necessarily be appealing to questions of principle in their deliberations, as well as to the circumstances of the case itself.

A subjective response does not necessarily imply total arbitrariness because we share similar experiences (or at least we believe we do): it may be natural to empathize with certain forms or even buildings. Empathy is now a much-used term, but it was German art historians working on the reception of architecture who introduced the concept as part of aesthetic theory: Robert Vischer (1847–1943), Theodor Lipps (1851–1914), August Schmarsow (1853–1936) and the Swiss Heinrich Wölfflin (1864–1945). The idea influenced Gestalt psychologists, scholars at the Warburg Institute in London and some of the teachers at the Bauhaus. In the twentieth century, ideas of psychoanalysis were applied with some degree of success to aesthetics: the very experience of birth as a passage, for example, suggests that architecture is much older than language, which as we have seen is often used as an analogy when talking of architectural expression. Sigmund Freud (1856–1939), the Viennese thinker whose work is described in Chapter 3, is usually regarded as the father of psychoanalysis; though he did not say much about architecture, the writings of his erstwhile collaborator Carl Jung (1875–1961) or pupil Melanie Klein (1882–1960) as interpreted by the aesthete Adrian Stokes are often cited to reinforce aesthetic judgments.[21] Others, following the philosophy of Maurice Merleau-Ponty (1908–1961), point out that the sense of touch is fundamental to architectural appreciation.[22] And some would claim that more recently the discovery of 'mirror neurons' justifies the aesthetic theories of nineteenth-century psychologists.[23]

Alain de Botton (1969–), in *The Architecture of Happiness*, suggested that buildings communicated in an empathetic way and that there was an analogy between aesthetic and ethical debate:

> Arguments about what is beautiful emerge as no easier to resolve, but then again no harder, than disputes about what is wise or right. We can learn to defend or attack a concept of beauty in the same

19 There is a vast literature on subjectivity and objectivity in aesthetic judgment and architectural design. For a recent argument by an architect in favour of a post-Kantian position derived from Schopenhauer, see Lyons 2018.
20 See Roberts 2005.
21 See Stokes 1972.
22 Rasmussen 1964; Pallasmaa 2012 both emphasize 'haptic' experience, which the poet and polymath Johann Goethe (1749–1832), who was acutely sensitive to architecture, had also stressed; see Goethe 1970.
23 See Mallgrave 2013. Most neuroscientists would be cautious of this claim: we can certainly experience empathy but exactly how we do so, or why, remains to be explained.

way we might defend or attack a legal position or an ethical stance. We can understand, and publicly explain, why we believe a building to be desirable or offensive on the basis of the things it talks about.[24]

But the phrase "on the basis of the things it talks about" is metaphorical.[25] It either implies that there is some universal, as yet not fully understood, language behind all architectural expression, perhaps based on psychology, or else it suggests that there should be some generally accepted set of conventions, such as those provided within the classical style which Summerson had treated as a 'language'; but it remains uncertain, without such agreed stylistic conventions, what this language might be.

1.5 Metaphysics

Metaphysics is the core of philosophy, dealing with fundamental issues about what exists, at the most general level of classification. This might include our most profound beliefs – whether we think the world is meaningful or not. The disciplines described previously each have a 'meta' component: if ethics, for example, is broadly about how we ought to behave, 'meta-ethics' would ask: "what is the meaning of 'right' in the moral context?" Some hold that metaphysical thinking is doomed to failure because, for instance, it has to express itself in language, which is inevitably culturally and historically conditioned.

If, as I claimed, as soon as a problem is soluble, it ceases to be philosophical, amongst philosophers only Gottfried Leibniz (1646–1716) perhaps seems to have thought that exhaustive intellectual definition was possible; but positivism, the view that the application of rational technique will eventually solve all the problems of the world, remains a powerful belief. The cosmologist Stephen Hawking, author of *A Brief History of Time*, did not have much respect for philosophers and declared he was a positivist. But, when asked on "Desert Island Discs" (on 25 December 1992) whether this meant there was no space for God, he replied:

> All that my work has shown is that you don't have to say that the way the universe began was the personal whim of God. But you still have the question: why does the universe bother to exist? If you like, you can define God to be the answer to that question.

In the second half of the twentieth century one of the philosophers whose metaphysical thought had a most profound influence on architectural theory was Martin Heidegger (1889–1976), although he tended to deny that his thinking was metaphysical. His starting point was the phenomenology of his teacher Edmund Husserl (1859–1938).[26] Heidegger regarded the split between the objectivity of science and the subjectivity of art as a kind of schizophrenia, which only arrived with the post-Socratic philosophers of Ancient Greece and believed the true subject of philosophy was the understanding of 'Being'. His late essays refer to the idea of the "fourfold": the earth, the heavens, mortals and

24 De Botton 2007, p. 73.
25 Lakoff and Johnson 2003 seek to demonstrate, with numerous examples, the pervasive and mostly unacknowledged use of metaphor in everyday speech. They argue that metaphor is not merely a matter of language, but structures human thought.
26 Husserl summarized his phenomenology in 1913 as "the science of the essence of consciousness . . . in the first person": see Husserl 1983. His approach was methodical in comparison to Heidegger's later more poetic vein.

deities. It is the primary task of architecture to make us feel at home in the world, since 'dwelling' is the very essence of 'being'.[27] That is not to say that Heidegger's inheritance is not problematic in a number of ways, as will become evident later in this book.

In the next section, I suggest three broad metaphysical categories that I will be referring to as a useful shorthand. Since one of philosophy's enduring (epistemological) problems is that of agreeing the meanings of the words that are employed, a preliminary clarification may be useful. I have already found it necessary to use some of them:

- **Idealism** privileges the universal over the particular: architects would have a duty to ensure their work conformed to wider ideals since how they did so would ensure general positive benefits. Maintaining the strength of the idea, both formally and ideologically, is more important than meeting a particular need.[28]

- **Scepticism** denies or questions the validity of universals in favour of a concentration on the particular, which is after all how the client's brief to an architect might be framed, as a matter of 'problem-solving'. Architects could suspect any universal principle and there can even be no clear implication as to an ethical position.

- **Pragmatism** holds in abeyance the validity of universals but nevertheless believes it to be part of architects' task to make the world a better place, which is of course in some sense an 'ideal'. It therefore mediates between the two other positions, maintaining a neutral stance on fundamental questions.

These terms are proposed as a useful handle, specifically for thinking about architecture, and are treated in more detail later. Others would categorize things differently and have done so in the past. In 1903 the German philosopher Wilhelm Dilthey (1833–1911) celebrated his 70th birthday and in his speech suggested that every philosopher would hold a "world-view" (*Weltanschauung*) conditioned not just by their historical context but by the region or nation state in which they grew up (its climate and geography) and also by their psychological temperament (optimistic or pessimistic).[29] He also proposed three types. Antagonistic terms were 'Subjective Idealism' or the 'Idealism of Freedom' versus 'Naturalism' – where "God, immortality and the invisible order of things are only phantoms of [our] wishful thinking". His favoured position, however, was what he called 'Objective Idealism', reconciling the two positions. As Dilthey himself acknowledged, all such metaphysical generalizations are conditioned by their author's background. The purpose of the distinctions I have suggested is not to insist that the reader sees things in that way. Indeed, with Dilthey, I tend to believe that every reader will form their own 'world-view' which will be affected by the context within which they grew up and is likely to modify over time, just as Summerson suggested an architect's ideas would be conditioned by "the artist's personality, his totality of experience".

27 Heidegger's most important work is *Being and Time* (Heidegger 2010). His most relevant post-war essays for architects are usefully collected in Heidegger 1993.
28 It is possible to see Marx's philosophy of history as a form of political idealism (as does Popper 2002b): in order for the inexorable laws of capitalism to ensure a classless society the rights of individuals are necessarily compromised and sometimes denied.
29 His lecture was published in Dilthey 1911. Dilthey is more remembered now for the influence his metaphysical generalizations had on the emerging disciplines of cultural anthropology and sociology (particularly of Max Weber) than as a thinker in his own right.

30 Plato's influence can hardly be exaggerated: the British philosopher A.N. Whitehead remarked that the European philosophical tradition consisted in "a series of footnotes to Plato" (Whitehead 1978).

31 Explained most clearly in the *Timaeus*. The world was created by a divine being imposing mathematical order on chaos. See Waterfield 2008.

1.6 Three broad metaphysical distinctions: Idealism

In the past, two broad attitudes have often been distinguished, associated with Plato, whom we have already encountered, and his pupil Aristotle (384–332 BC).[30] They occupy centre stage in Raphael's 1509–1511 *School of Athens* in the Vatican (**Figure 1.2**).

Idealists, like Plato, believe that there is a world of ideas beyond the world of things (there are "properties or universals over and above particulars") – that is how we can talk about such abstract notions as 'Goodness' or 'Architecture'. Individual objects in the world reflect in a shadowy way the fundamental ideas. Famously, in his book *The Republic*, Plato used the image of the cave as an allegory of the human condition: mortals crouched within are condemned to see only the shadows of images created by the light from a fire (which we could interpret as the sun) but not perceive the light itself, or the world outside the cave. Only a chosen few would be able to emerge and do that (philosophers, perhaps), but Plato's ideal world can be approached by intellectual disciplines such as mathematics.[31] The reason we may be moved by art is because it aspires to, or is mimetic of, this higher ideal.

A majority of people are probably idealists in some form or another. We have become accustomed, for instance, to the extraordinary success of science in all areas, so we send people into space, we communicate across the ether, we listen to digitized musical recordings of Beethoven's symphonies as we drive cars and when we fall ill we can hope that remote keyhole surgery might come to our aid. All of these technologies ultimately depend on abstract calculations; they apply to practical ends the findings of science, which relies on research that proceeds by isolating, or abstracting, problems for

Figure 1.2 Raphael: *Disputa*, or *School of Athens*, 1509; detail, Plato points to the heavens, the 'ideal' world; Aristotle's hand is stretched out to embrace the 'particulars' of the world we occupy

solution within a theoretical model that can predict how the world behaves. But there are well-known problems. One is epistemological: how we know about the world. A common illustration is the problem of left-handed and right-handed leather gloves – we all know they are different, but you cannot tell the difference unless you 'situate' yourself in relation to them. Some would claim that time illustrates a similar problem: the concept of 'the past' depends on a standpoint (of somebody) in time. There always seems to be an irreducible residue of particularity left. Other illustrations of apparently intractable problems would be paradoxes like that of the Cretan Liar[32] or Kurt Gödel's incompleteness theorem. The irreducibility problem does not rule out an idealist position, since many people who acknowledge it are idealists, Kant to start with. But these are illustrations of difficulties that have to be struggled with. There's a more fundamental doctrine of Idealism, which would hold that only minds exist (while an extreme version – Solipsism – asserts that only *my* mind exists). Plato, in comparison, is a 'realist' as well as an 'idealist': like Kant he does believe there are real things in the world.

When we consider architects, I shall argue that Le Corbusier and Louis Kahn, for instance, were idealists of the Platonic kind, though both were complex characters, and their thinking was multi-layered. As we shall see in Chapter 4, Le Corbusier's polemic in his *Vers une Architecture*, which was stylistically iconoclastic, relies on constant appeals to a return to Platonic order. His house for his mother in Switzerland places the *idea* of the house before the site. Even Villa Savoye is seen as a 'type' which could be reproduced in multiple in Rio de Janeiro. I will suggest in Chapter 6 that Louis Kahn's description of architectural invention, as well as what he built, illustrates his idealist position.

The idealism of Georg Hegel (1770–1831) is especially relevant for two reasons. First, he believed every age had its own character, necessarily reflected in the thinking, the art and the architecture of its time. Therefore, in order to make successful buildings architects would be required to build in accordance with the spirit of the age. Secondly, his influence on architectural historians has entered our everyday interpretations. He saw history as a tripartite dialectical process: thesis, antithesis and synthesis. Classical architecture can be understood as going through such phases: the High Renaissance work of Bramante represents a thesis (calm and ordered); Mannerism is its antithesis (disturbed and contradictory); the Baroque synthesizes the two to create an enriched, sometimes overblown, style, where parts and whole cohere. This in turn becomes a new thesis, and neo-classicism, as a return to a purer sensibility, is its antithesis. For Hegel, this process is inevitable: as we saw in the Introduction, Sigfried Giedion subscribed to the historical inevitability of modernism; David Watkin's response was 'anti-Hegelian'.

32 Traditionally ascribed to Epimenides, a Cretan who declared all Cretans were liars. A logical statement thereby seems to lead to an insoluble paradox. See *Stanford Encyclopedia of Philosophy*, "Liar Paradox".

33 Popper 2002b.
34 The description which
follows illustrates the way
Aristotle was interpreted
until the mid-twentieth
century. Some more recent
readings have argued for a
closer relationship to Plato's
thought.
35 Aristotle 1999. A parallel issue occurs in legal
judgment: absolute rules are
insufficient and have to be
modified in some way by a
principle of Equity.
36 Pevsner 1990.
37 Gombrich 2007. The art
historian Ernst Gombrich
(1903–2001) was a close
friend of Karl Popper, who is
best known as a philosopher
of science, and they fre-
quently credited each other
for insights into their own
discipline.
38 Goodman 1976. Such
a definition, for instance,
allows without difficulty for
the 'ready-mades' of an artist
like Marcel Duchamp: a
urinal placed in a gallery can
be seen as an art work. See
Capdevila-Werning 2014;
Goodman 1976. A book
that outlines a nominalist
position across a very broad
field, from a highly 'anthropocentric' point of view, is
Frayn 2007.

In the political sphere, some have argued that there is a distinct tendency towards totalitarianism in Idealism: the philosopher Karl Popper (1902–1994) accused Plato, Hegel and Karl Marx (1818–1883) of
this tendency.[33] In *The Republic* Plato had argued that art, as imitation,
is twice-removed from the ideal (there is an original conception of a
table, an idea which a carpenter imitates in making a particular table; a
painter's representation is an imitation of that imitation). Poets are also
imitators and revel in emotions, which rational persons should aim to
suppress: according to Plato, poets should therefore be banned from the
ideal society or only tolerated if their art is useful to the state. Similarly,
given the historical inevitability of changed circumstances or architectural styles, people should be educated to accept their consequences
because, in the end, temporary personal discomfort will be justified by
general improvement. We will observe in Chapter 4 how some remarks
by Walter Gropius reflect that position.

1.7 Three broad metaphysical distinctions: Scepticism or nominalism

Aristotle was sceptical about a world of independent ideas (or universals) that could be distinguished from instances (or particulars). For the
moment we shall postpone a discussion as to what sort of Scepticism he
can be said to have subscribed.[34] There may be no such thing, or essence,
as 'Architecture', for instance – it is just the name we happen to use, conventionally, for the product of what architects and others design. That is
not to say that Aristotle (a champion of 'virtue ethics') did not believe in
'goodness' as an aspiration for us all: he questioned the necessity for an
abstracted *idea* of 'the good'. As it happens, in the *Nicomachaean Ethics*,
Aristotle uses the example of building to illustrate his notion of what
we mean by 'good': since ethics is a practical science, we would study
"not to know what goodness is, but how to become good men". "The
causes and means that bring about any form of excellence" are therefore
a result of practice: "Men will become good builders as a result of building well, and bad ones as a result of building badly".[35]

Sceptics would therefore question the twentieth-century architectural
historian Nikolaus Pevsner's statement, at the very beginning of his
Outline of European Architecture, that Lincoln Cathedral is a piece of
architecture but that a bicycle shed is a building – sometimes, depending on the context, a bicycle shed can surely be a work of architecture or be seen as such.[36] This view of the world is echoed in Ernst
Gombrich's celebrated anti-Platonic first two sentences in his *Story of
Art*: "There is really no such thing as Art. There are only artists".[37] If
there is no Art, there cannot be rules about art, merely conventions
(or names – hence 'nominalism') that apply: these could be arbitrary
in origin but may be sanctioned by persistent use. The attempt that
some twentieth-century idealists make to define art (and distinguish
it from craft) is therefore futile and a more real question than "what is
art?", as the philosopher Nelson Goodman (1906–1998) suggested, is
"when is art?"[38]

A problem for Nominalists could be: if there's nothing beyond or behind the physical world, if the world is all surface and no substance, what is there left to believe in? Perhaps nothing: this is the melancholic position ('romantic despair') held by thinkers such as Walter Benjamin (1892–1940). Melancholy, which Benjamin uses in the context of seventeenth century art, is the view that God is radically absent from this world. Whereas Platonist art is basically optimistic about the power of our rationality to account for existence, melancholic art necessarily questions this optimism.

The extreme form of Melancholy is Nihilism. The philosophy of Friedrich Nietzsche (1844–1900) illustrates this position in the nineteenth century, as perhaps (in architecture) the architecture of Bernard Tschumi and Rem Koolhaas, discussed in Chapter 10, might in the twentieth. Nietzsche valued art very highly because, metaphysically, he believed existence was absurd; art, uniquely, could perhaps manage to assist in rendering bearable "the terror and horror of existence".[39] Nietzsche refined his position throughout his life, but his early essay *The Birth of Tragedy* anticipates his later thought in a number of respects. He distinguished between the 'Apollonian' and 'Dionysian' strands of Greek art – Apollo being associated with ideal harmonic proportion (Figure 1.3) and Dionysus (Bacchus in Roman mythology) with revelry and ecstasy. (**Figure 1.3** and **Figure 1.4**). Nietzsche ridiculed as one-sided the de-sexed distanced appreciation of art by neo-classicist apologists

39 Unsurprisingly there are different interpretations of Nietzsche's nihilism. He claims that nihilism is the only honest position to hold, yet his idea of the *Übermensch* (superman) suggests that it could be overcome by heroic individuals – but even that must remain doubtful, since it could never be a substitute for a metaphysics that was irretrievably lost.

Figure 1.3 Nicolas Poussin: *Et in Arcadia Ego*, 1637–1638; illustrating Nietzsche's idea of the Apollonian ideal in Greek art

Figure 1.4 Titian:
Bacchus and Ariadne,
1520–1523; illustrating
Nietzsche's idea of the
Dionysian in Greek art

like Johann Winckelmann (1717–1768, discussed in the next chapter) and, anticipating Freud, introduces a 'psychological' reading to philosophy, asking what kind of person would it be that requires such obsessive rules as "there should be no poets in the Republic"? Thus Nietzsche questions the absolute truth of the ancients by seeing them in context. Just as we would no longer subscribe to all their social views (such as the acceptance of slavery), so we understand that their analysis of the true and the beautiful is relative not absolute. Nietzsche's later writing continued to be fascinatingly provocative, while also being troublingly misogynist, sexist and even racist.[40]

1.8 Three broad metaphysical distinctions: Pragmatism

Pragmatism (literally 'what works') is the view that Platonic idealism may be untenable, but melancholic scepticism is not compelling. It suspends judgment about any relationship between rationality and the reality of the world but insists that rational conclusions are not to be disregarded simply on the grounds that they may be no more than provisional. Aesthetically, art is not the imitation of transcendental structures, nor their despairing rejection, but an affirmation that human constructions are nonetheless real for being merely human. Art then involves (among other things) the expression of aspirations that are utopian but may be secular. In Chapter 5 I shall suggest that the work of the architect Alvar Aalto (who referred

40 Nietzsche's *Will to Power* was published posthumously and edited by his sister, who may be partly responsible for its anti-Semitism.

to the need for 'positive scepticism'), as well as that of many other lesser architects, might illustrate this position; usually the case is not made very articulately and can descend into sentimentality. Sometimes people use the word pragmatic pejoratively to describe action in the absence of any principle. Another way of seeing it is to say that a pragmatic approach leaves in abeyance epistemological problems (such as how we know what we think we know or how we would determine the beautiful) and says the real issue is how to get on with dealing with the world as we find it.

Though Pragmatism has its articulate advocates, William James (1842–1910), John Dewey (1859–1952) and Richard Rorty (1931–2007) amongst them, many find it difficult to suspend a belief in a world of ideas beyond the actualities. An attempt to do this appears in Richard Hill's book *Designs and their Consequences*.[41] Most architects conceive of the design process as starting with an idea for a building, which they then represent, in various ways, by means of drawings or models. The drawings attain more precision as instructions to builders who then realize the architect's idea with varying degrees of accuracy depending on their skill and the circumstances of construction. Plato, had he concerned himself with architecture, would have recognized this description: as in the example of a table, buildings are reflections, or copies, of an ideal, which can be portrayed in other ways, by illustrations, for example, or by mathematics. But Richard Hill argues that this is a misleading description: what architects do when they design is to draw (necessarily incomplete) pictures of a building which they intend; what is eventually produced, requiring an act of imaginative recreation by the builder, is an object in itself, not the model of an idea, and it is the object itself we appreciate aesthetically. The closest analogy with the other arts is theatrical: the building as an aesthetic object is in fact a consequence of a complicated and lengthy performance on site. The benefit of Hill's approach is that it gives the practice of constructing architecture its proper place; the problem is that we may wonder whether it is possible to formulate an architectural *intention* that is not an *idea*.

The Spanish architect Rafael Moneo (1937–) has applied a broad distinction between idealist and nominalist approaches to the question of architectural typology, discussed in more detail in Chapter 9. It will be clear by now that Aristotle's scepticism is far from extreme, yet the distinction of his thought with Plato's remains fruitful:

> The notion of type implies the recognition of common features that allow us to identify those works of architecture that share the same formal structure, leading us, again, to the age-old question of universality. The side one chooses to be on – Plato versus Aristotle – is crucial in defining the concept of type. While for Platonists a type is the eternal representation of the original idea, regardless of specific examples, for Aristotelians it is the common denominator that can be perceived through the careful observation of a series of works that maintain the principle of continuity through which history unfolds. These two approaches lead to clearly differentiated theories in architecture.[42]

41 Hill 1999. The argument leans on Wollheim 1980.
42 Moneo 2010. A more extended discussion of Moneo's position can be found in González de Canales and Ray 2015.

Moneo, a thoughtful architect, was discussing one of his own buildings. He also taught, all his career, in Barcelona, in Madrid and at the Graduate School of Design in Harvard. The two approaches (with the middle way – a weak idealism, you could say, or a 'positive scepticism') surely have implications for architectural understanding and for the education of architects, and it is part of the purpose of this book to suggest that they should be made explicit.

1.9 The Enlightenment split

Such metaphysical distinctions might seem rather theoretical, however. A more obvious split which we all experience is that between the 'arts' and the 'sciences'. When students write personal statements as to why they want to read architecture at a university, they may well say that it was one of the few courses on offer that seemed to combine 'sciences' and 'arts'. Secondary education makes that distinction, and they may have been asked to choose between them at sixth form level, if not before. Such a distinction may be embedded in ancient Greek post-Socratic philosophy, or it could be endemic to the human condition generally.[43] But it was certainly exacerbated in the Enlightenment. The Roman architect Vitruvius had made no distinction between science and art – between astronomy, for example, and astrology – and even the scientist Isaac Newton (1642–1727) was intensely concerned with alchemy and theological debate.[44]

René Descartes, whose epistemology we mentioned earlier, began with the radically sceptical question: "how can I be sure of anything at all, including my own existence?" He is usually credited with initiating an extreme distinction between science and art (or, more fundamentally, between objective and subjective descriptions of the world) and laying down the foundations for rationalism. His famous three-word aphorism *Cogito ergo sum* ("I think, therefore I am") encapsulates his conclusion: even the process of doubting one's own existence must involve thinking, so the inevitable conclusion is that I exist as a thinking being – more precisely, as a mind embedded in a body.[45] He therefore distrusted perception per se as the origin of knowledge; knowledge can and should be studied and pursued as an independent discipline. Since material body and the immaterial mind are distinct, that allows for (indeed, for Descartes, requires) the existence of a deity: although he acknowledged that a wicked demon of some kind might have been responsible, he concluded that only God could have endowed humans, uniquely, with a rational mind or a soul. 'Cartesian dualism' lies behind the development in the arts we call Romanticism: when the world of science threatens to take over, we take refuge for our finer feelings in a world of poetry and romance. As a concept it only really became foundational in the eighteenth century, coinciding with the advent of that category of philosophy defined earlier as aesthetics and represented in England by the work of Edmund Burke (1729–1797).

A continuing critique of post-eighteenth-century artefacts is therefore that they reveal this disjunction all too clearly. An architect like Karl Friedrich Schinkel, for example, skilful though he undoubtedly is, exhibits all the precision of a scientist in some of his buildings but also illustrates idealized projects in a dreamy romantic landscape (**Figure 1.5**, **Figure 1.6**). And in the twentieth century this characteristic became ever more extreme. In an influential essay, *Typology and Design Method*, the British architectural critic Alan Colquhoun (1921–2012) described the "picture in the general body of doctrine embedded in the Modern Movement" as follows: "It consists of a tension between two apparently contradictory ideas – biotechnical determinism on the one hand and free expression on the other".[46]

46 Colquhoun 1985, p. 46. See Chapter 9 for a fuller discussion.

Figure 1.5 A painting by Karl Friedrich Schinkel: Gothic cathedral by the water

Figure 1.6 Karl Friedrich Schinkel: etching of Alte Nationalgalerie in Berlin, 1825–1830

The determinism Colquhoun cites is positivistic: on the one hand an appeal to 'nature', identified as a resource for mankind to exploit, combined with a belief in science. 'Free expression', on the other hand, is the licence for artists to do whatsoever they please: 'Art for Art's sake'. Can such a schizophrenic dilemma between subjectivity and objectivity be resolved? Kant, as we saw, had argued that fundamental structural features of the world that we perceive (such as space, time or causal relations) were artefacts of our subjective cognitive faculties rather than properties or relations of things in themselves. But if you are a Realist, you believe that 'temperature', for instance, exists, even if we are not around to measure it, and its measurement can be objective:

> We cannot measure temperature with a thermometer unless there is a certain constancy in the results of such measurement. But that doesn't mean that temperature is nothing but a phenomenon of agreement among thermometer readings. It would exist even if there were no thermometers, and we can explain the actual agreement among thermometers by the uniform effect on them of temperature. In giving this explanation we use the concept of temperature, and a condition of our having the concept of temperature that we have is that we can measure it. But that doesn't make the explanation circular, any more than a lecture on the operation of the larynx is circular. To use something that one is trying to explain is not to explain it in terms of itself.[47]

But this, one might say, leads us back to a form of Cartesian dualism, which for many is unacceptable. As we saw, the attraction to architects of Heidegger's or Merleau-Ponty's phenomenology, which will be discussed in Chapter 10, was that it promised to reconcile this split, though some would say that it does not effect a resolution so much as value poetics over rationality.[48]

1.10 Implications for architectural education and practice

That the discipline of architecture sits uneasily between the arts and sciences causes difficulties for a university, where most schools of architecture are embedded. It is possible to study the subject academically, like history or cosmology, but for many it leads to professional qualification and thence to practice, with the ethical dilemmas that involves. I return to this issue in the Conclusions (p. 265): a restrictive approach may be seen as the consequence of a positivist legacy, wherein 'practice' appears as a puzzling anomaly. If practical knowledge is construed as 'knowledge of the relationship of means to ends', given an agreement about ends the question 'How ought I to act?' could be reduced to a merely instrumental issue about the means best suited to achieve one's ends. The answer to the question becomes 'scientific' since the best means can be selected by the use of science-based technique. But that question – "how

47 Nagel 1986. As Thomas Nagel explains in his introduction: "This book is about a single problem: how to combine the perspective of a particular person inside the world with an objective view of that same world, the person and his viewpoint included".
48 See pp. 242–245. For a neuro-scientific exploration of 'right brain' intuitions compared to 'left brain' measurable argumentation, see McGilchrist 2009. Following Nietzsche, he mounts a comprehensive argument that an imbalance has grown, ever since the post-Socratic philosophers, between the left-sided hemisphere of the brain and the right-sided one, and that this imbalance accounts for much of our current cultural distress.

ought I to act?" – is properly philosophical, or ethical, and cannot be reduced in this way.

This chapter has begun to raise a few of the many philosophical complexities involved in the practice of architecture, or a consideration of its practice, as well as pointing to philosophers whose thinking may be relevant. In the chapters that follow, we shall see numerous illustrations of how they arise and the attempts that were made to resolve them.

2

ORIGINS OF MODERNISM – THE EUROPEAN PICTURE

This chapter examines the origins of architectural modernism in the context of Western Europe and North America. In the following chapter, I look more closely at a particular example, the city of Vienna, as a means of relating the genesis of architectural modernism to wider cultural issues.

If we consider the origins of any architectural period, there are clearly several factors which can lead to a shift in the prevailing paradigm – technical innovations, social and economic forces, changes in philosophical thinking.[1] Some authors, when describing the origins of European Gothic architecture in the twelfth century, for example, privilege the technical inventions of the rib vault and flying buttress and the ability to create large areas of glass; others concentrate on the wealth of the monasteries and the emergent economy of the Middle Ages; yet others ask why people sought large areas of glass in the first place and consider the transcendental meaning of light in the theology of the period.[2] So it is with the origins of modernism. Kenneth Frampton's study of modern architecture talks of Cultural Transformations, Territorial Transformations and Technical Transformations.[3] This chapter begins by describing the influence of technology, before discussing the problem of the city, aesthetic consequences – the problem of style – and the concurrent shifts in economic and political thought. As will become clear, these themes are necessarily intertwined.

2.1 Mechanization

The successes of science from the seventeenth century onwards are hard to exaggerate. The foundations of biology, physics, chemistry and astronomy were established, and notions derived from the ancient Greeks were shown to be fallacies. Once people could calculate the anticipated outcome of experiments, useful applications could follow: the creation of cast iron, and later steel, to make machines and to use for construction purposes and the steam engine which enabled their transportation across long distances. The same process that extruded the railway tracks that began to cover Europe and bring far apart cities within convenient journey times could make structurally efficient I-beams. Prefabrication could ensure both economy and speed of construction. The Industrial Revolution was, of course,

1 Paradigm was the term popularised by the philosopher of science Thomas Kuhn to talk about the progress of science; it has subsequently been used by architects to talk about the stylistic framework within which architects work conventionally (Kuhn 2012). In one of his 'scrapbooks', the eighteenth-century German scientist Georg Lichtenberg had made a similar observation.
2 In a similar way, archaeologists argue about the Epipalaeolithic and Aceramic Neolithic periods: do cultural changes precede or follow technological advance? See Watkins 2011.
3 Frampton 1985.

DOI: 10.4324/9781003244943-3

Figure 2.1 Joseph
Paxton: Crystal Palace,
1851

underpinned by the remarkable efficiency of its primary fuel, coal, compared to wood or charcoal, which was superseded in the twentieth century by oil and gas.

The most convincing and closely-studied example of the effect of mechanization on architecture is that of the Crystal Palace of 1851 (**Figure 2.1**). It was designed in just eight days by Joseph Paxton (1803–1865), modelled on greenhouses he had constructed at Chatsworth in Derbyshire, and erected in four months; no traditional construction system could possibly have met this timetable. The 8 ft module (2.400 mm, roughly), repeated throughout the building, allowed for rationalizing the fabrication of the glass. The repetitive purlins also acted as gutters, and the cast-iron columns also acted as rainwater downpipes. The building had deficiencies: numerous leaks in the glazing that the putty available at the time could not solve and a generally uneven environmental performance. Despite its external awnings and a system of louvres and perforated floors, the pavilions overheated on warm days. These were not critical defects in a temporary exhibition building but indicated problems that were to persist later into the twentieth century. Seduced by the economy, speed of construction and efficiency of developing technologies, architects were tempted to discount technical teething problems, reassuring their clients that they would be soluble shortly (with the development

Figure 2.2 Adler and Sullivan: Carson Pirie Scott building, Chicago, 1899

of more effective mastics, for example). If that seemed uncertain, they argued that buildings should have a shorter life than traditional constructions: they could be disposable, rather like motor cars. Moreover, with the advent of air conditioning and the promise of cheap energy, architects could afford to forget about environmental issues; not until the end of the twentieth century, with the realization of the effects of fossil fuels on global warming, did many architects begin to take them as seriously as structural rationalization.[4]

Buildings like the Crystal Palace, however, and the railway stations that were being constructed all over Europe, challenged the authority of the stylistic precedents to which traditional architecture referred. The requirements of speed and economy were urgent, and architects had to adapt themselves to the new technologies. By the last quarter of the nineteenth century, the locus for the most thoroughgoing re-examination of the relation between architecture and engineering was Chicago, the Midwestern American city that was undergoing a huge expansion following a catastrophic fire in 1871. It saw the birth of what became known as the skyscraper, initially built using traditional methods. The 16-storey Monadnock building, constructed in two phases from 1891, is the tallest load-bearing brick structure in the world, expressing its loads by the swelling of the masonry base to nearly 2 metres.[5] It was

4 For a history of architecture concentrating on the way fuel costs and availability have driven architectural development and the consequences for the planet, see Calder 2021.
5 The architects for the first, less decorated, phase (and hence more readily admired by modernists) were Burnham and Root; the second phase two years later was by Holobird and Roche.

braced internally against wind by cast and wrought iron. The second phase already made use of a steel frame, but the first of the skyscrapers to express the skeletal nature of steel, so the façade had a much more open horizontal layering, was the Carson Pirie Scott building by Dankmar Adler and Louis Sullivan[6] (**Figure 2.2**). They developed the fireproofed steel frame from elements that had been used for engineering constructions like bridges. High-rise construction was absolutely dependent on the elevator, originally invented by Elisha Graves Otis in 1854 – immediately quadrupling the number of floors that could be accessed economically.[7]

Louis Sullivan was not only one of the most successful of the Chicago architects, but he was a thoughtfully self-conscious designer and author of two books and several articles. He was proud of Chicago's achievements and boasted that architects of "the East" (namely New York) had nothing to contribute to the development of the high-rise office typology, though he worried, aesthetically, about how to deal with the ordering of such large-scale constructions. His Whitmanesque *Autobiography of an Idea* describes his life and ambitions in the most romantic terms.[8] He is most famous for a passage in which he apparently articulates the doctrine of functionalism:

> It is the pervading law of all things organic and inorganic, of all things physical and metaphysical, of all things human, and all things super-human, of all true manifestations of the head, of the heart, of the soul, that the life is recognizable in its expression, that form ever follows function.[9]

As we have seen, in Chicago, it was the development of new technologies such as steel and the elevator that made it possible to cater for the function of housing office workers in ever more efficient buildings. Improved technologies were required as a response to the demands of developers to maximize their profits: not only could there be more floors, but steel frames took up less area than masonry walls so on each floor there was a greater proportion of lettable space. The resultant external proportions of high-rise buildings were unprecedented, so the problem of architectural expression became acute. Sullivan and his contemporaries worried how far the traditional tripartite classical ordering of base or plinth, shaft and capital (in a column), or plinth course, wall plane and cornice (in a building façade) could be stretched and still make sense.

The anxiety that traditional architects felt at the enlarged aesthetic licence was reflected in the Chicago Columbian Exhibition of 1893, which was an extraordinary contrast to the Crystal Palace of 42 years earlier. Its masterplan was designed by Daniel Burnham, one of the architects of the Monadnock building. With the exception of Sullivan's Transportation Building, the temporary pavilions, designed by distinguished architects with a traditional training, were dressed in classical costume (**Figure 2.3**). Sullivan declared that it had set back the cause of modern architecture in America by 40 years.[10] One of the architects

6 The Carson Pirie Scott building had a complex history of phased proposals and changes of mind. The first building to use a steel frame was William Le Baron Jenney's Home Insurance building (designed 1884; demolished 1931).
7 More precisely, Otis invented the brake mechanism, which for the first time ensured elevators could operate safely.
8 Sullivan 1924. The book is full of the romance of the boundless space of America. In a beautiful passage, Sullivan describes arriving in Liverpool and taking a train to London, amazed at the "finished land" he observed through the windows: small scale tended fields so different from the boundless prairie of the Midwest.
9 Sullivan 1896.
10 Sullivan 1924, p. 325.

Figure 2.3 Daniel Burnham: Chicago World's Fair, 1899

who accepted that they would inevitably make use of new technologies and were to have an important influence on modernism was the young Frank Lloyd Wright, formerly a pupil of Louis Sullivan. He delivered a lecture in 1901 to the Chicago Arts and Crafts Society, later published as "The Art and Craft of the Machine".[11] This important article will be discussed in more detail in Chapter 4.

By contrast to advocates for modernism in America such as Wright, the reaction to the technological inventions that came out of the Industrial Revolution in England was much less positive. William Morris, for whom his friend Philip Webb designed the Red House in 1889, was unambiguous:

> As for an iron architecture, there never was and never could be such. Every improvement in the art of engineering made the use of iron more ugly, until at last they had that supreme expression of ugliness, the Forth Bridge.[12]

In parallel with the development of the steel frame in America, was the increasing sophistication of reinforced concrete, mainly in the hands of French engineers: François Coignet, Joseph Monier, François Hennebique, Auguste Perret (with whom Le Corbusier worked briefly) and later Eugène Freyssinet and Robert Maillart. Their refinements (such as the use of pre-stressing) were mostly to be seen in engineering works such as bridges, but these new techniques also allowed for large-scale

11 Wright 1901.
12 This was Morris' reported response to a lecture in Edinburgh by the Arts and Crafts architect Edward Prior on the subject of "Texture as a quality of art and a condition for architecture". Prior replied by saying that "he did not quite agree . . . that they never could have iron architecture, but they did not have it and did not seem likely to have it for many centuries". Reproduced in Valinsky 2014.

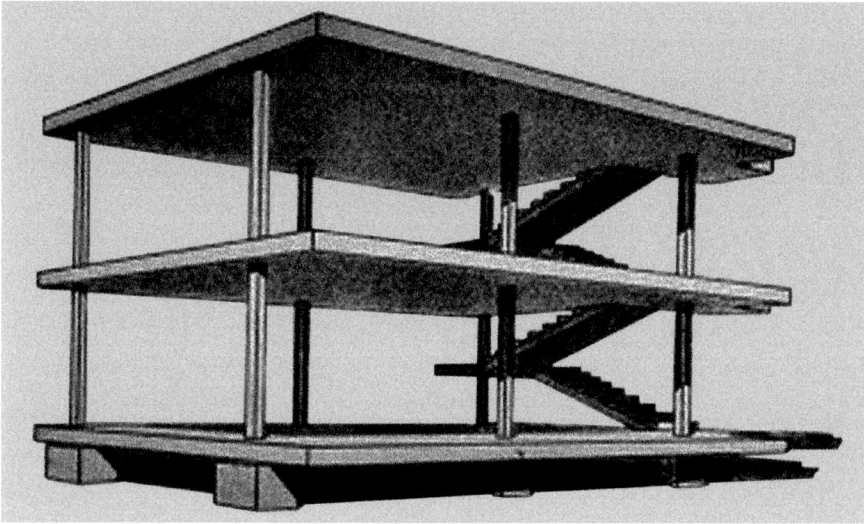

**Figure 2.4 Le
Corbusier: diagram of
Dom-Ino system, 1914**

buildings such as the German architect Max Berg's 1913 Jahrhundert-
halle in Breslau. Domestic architecture seldom required such overt
technical expression. Auguste Perret, who worked with his two broth-
ers almost exclusively in concrete, developed a system of visible vertical
posts and horizontal beams – that is trabeated elements; a building such
as his 1903 apartment building at 25 bis Rue Franklin, Paris, retained
links with a stripped neo-classical aesthetic. The exposed frame ordered
the façade, retaining the proportional discipline of traditional classicism but with the decoration omitted. To the end of his life Perret
remained aesthetically convinced by more traditional ordering systems.
He was the architect for the post-war rebuilding of Le Havre following
its destruction by allied bombing, using rationalized concrete frames
and refined pre-cast concrete cladding to create a remarkably coherent
urban fabric.[13] It had widespread influence in the Soviet Union, unfortunately without Perret's sophisticated material or urban understanding.
As we shall see in Chapter 4, it would be left to Le Corbusier to recognize that just as a concrete frame allowed non-load-bearing partitions
to be arranged at will, so, by keeping the framed structure back from
the line of the façade, architects could also arrange the façade freely: he
saw it as his task to formulate principles that could recall the new technology, which was clearly capable of many forms, to some kind of new
aesthetic order (**Figure 2.4**).

2.2 The problem of the city

With the invention of machines for mass-production, the Industrial
Revolution and a rapid increase in population came the unprecedented
expansion of European cities. In England, the terrace house, which had
proved such a flexible and effective housing form in the eighteenth century, was reproduced across thousands of square miles. The etchings of
Gustave Doré illustrate how gardens became paved yards and smoke

13 See Britton 2010 for a
comparison between Le Corbusier's and Perret's attitude
to concrete.

Figure 2.5 Etching by Gustave Doré: London housing conditions, 1872

14 A clear account of the development of twentieth century planning remains in Benevolo 1971. Rykwert 2000 provides an abbreviated description.

pollution from the many chimneys poisoned the air (**Figure 2.5**). One consequence of overcrowding and inadequate drainage was outbreaks of typhoid and tuberculosis. As the first country to experience the Industrial Revolution, Britain was the first to react against it. Engels and Marx (whose thinking will be discussed in more detail later) wrote of its economic and social consequences, while William Morris, also a convinced socialist, resisted the advent of machine technology, as we have seen, and dreamt of a return to what we might term a more sustainable world today based on idealized medieval precedents. His vision, enshrined in his 1891 *News from Nowhere*, was partly a reaction to Edward Bellamy's 1888 *Looking Backward*. Whereas Bellamy's utopia was idealistic in a Platonic sense, prescribing the way its inhabitants were to behave, Morris' aspiration was closer to the political anarchism of Peter Kropotkin. Ebenezer Howard, the initiator of the Garden City movement in England, was influenced by both Bellamy and Morris and admired Kropotkin and transcendental philosophers like Henry George and Emerson. The first edition of his 1898 book *Tomorrow, a Peaceful Path to Real Reform* was soon revised and republished as *Garden Cities of Tomorrow*. Garden Cities, Howard claimed, could combine the social benefits of cities with the healthy virtues of rural living if towns could be limited in population and planned around parks[14] (**Figure 2.6**). A central city containing 60,000 people would be ringed by satellites of 30,000 people each. The density he proposed was 30 people per acre, or 73 per hectare. In architectural

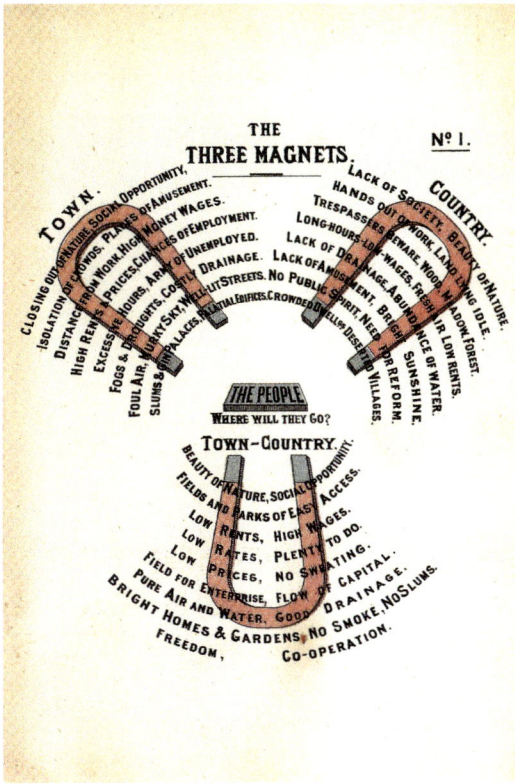

Figure 2.6 Ebenezer Howard: diagrams from *Tomorrow a Peaceful Path to Real Reform*, 1898

and planning terms, his proposals followed the model villages established for their workers by enlightened manufacturers like Arkwright and Wedgwood. One architectural practice working at Letchworth, the first Garden City established on Howard's principles, was Parker and Unwin; they had already built a model village at New Earswick, near York, for the Rowntree family. Raymond Unwin's article "Nothing Gained by Over-crowding" of 1912 was to prove the most influential housing manifesto in England for the next century. He advocated densities equivalent to Howard's of no higher than 12 dwellings to the acre, and this became the pattern not only for the garden cities and suburbs but also for the new towns around London after the Second World War.[15]

Stylistically, Unwin's and Parker's buildings were Arts and Crafts, inheritors of that reaction to rigid machine-made products that imitated Gothic or Renaissance styles. A skilled practitioner in this manner who built at Letchworth was M.H. Baillie Scott, whose houses aspire to a timeless quality: it is difficult to date them because they are intentionally designed as an apparently natural product of an indigenous culture – a highly self-conscious artefact that aims at unselfconsciousness. As a typical plan shows, Baillie Scott conceived of his houses as absolutely at one with their settings: indeed his two books, in 1906 and 1933, were both entitled *Houses and Gardens*[16] (**Figure 2.7**). Areas within the garden were treated as rooms, and they merged ambiguously with lesser spaces like the kitchen court, arbours and garden rooms into the house proper,

15 For an argument for the health-promoting effects of Garden Cities, see McFadyen 1938. Norman McFadyen was Letchworth's first medical officer of health and chair of the Town and Country Planning Association from 1929–1944.
16 Baillie Scott 1906; Baillie Scott and Beresford 1933.

Figure 2.7 M.H. Baillie Scott: illustration to "A Cottage in the Country" article, 1904

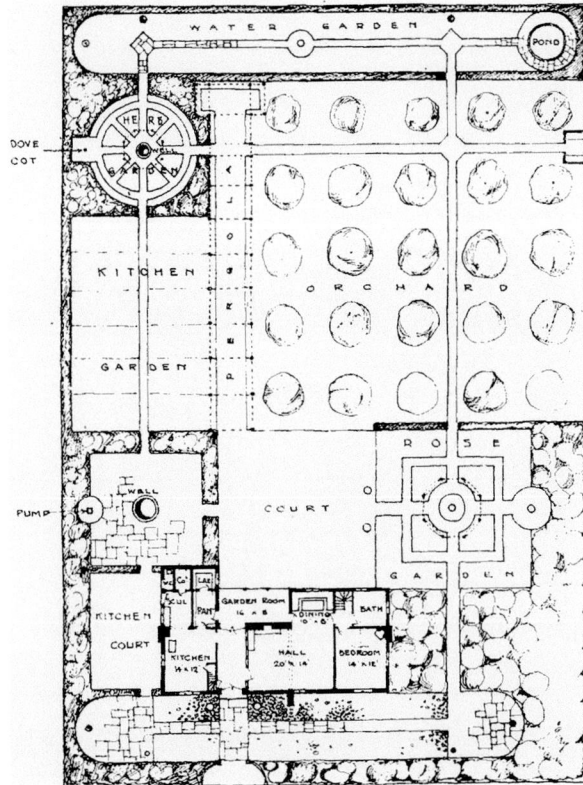

the rooms of which are in turn articulated with ingle nooks and sitting bays.[17] Yet, according to Nikolaus Pevsner, the stylistic origins of modernism are to be found in the English Arts and Crafts, a claim to which we shall return.

So there is a very powerful anti-urban strand in the origins of modernism at a planning scale: the lowering of densities leads towards Frank Lloyd Wright's Broadacre City, discussed in Chapter 4, and eventually to the phenomenon of car-dependent suburbs, particularly in America. If the ideal 'solution' to the manifest problems associated with the nineteenth century was anti-urban, what was to be done about existing cities? They had to adapt to deal with changed circumstances. Circulation was rationalized, and urban extensions planned specifically to allow for more rapid forms of transport by tram and carriage, originally horse-drawn but soon to be motorized. In Paris, to tackle its dense slums and to create an efficient circulation system which could also be useful in controlling riots, Baron Haussmann cut boulevards through the traditional quarters, much of them on a medieval street pattern, and placed a ring road around the perimeter. When Barcelona expanded, the Spanish engineer Idelfonso Cerdá conceived a project based on a repetitive grid with generous pavements and improved drainage that allowed for different kinds of development within a uniform city block; Cerdá can also be credited with the invention of the term urbanism, in his 1867

17 Kornwolf 1972 tries to claim Baillie Scott as a proto-modernist, comparing the relationship of his indoor and outdoor spaces to those of Mies van der Rohe, but his spatial planning is much more cellular and depends not on a flow of space but a double reading of indoor and outdoor rooms.

Teoria General de la Urbanización. Amsterdam provided the chance in 1901 for the great father of Dutch modernism, Hendrik Berlage, to plan an ideal extension at Amsterdam South, eventually realized from 1917. And, as we shall see in Chapter 3, with the construction of the Viennese Ringstrasse, a new opportunity arose for a sequence of monumental institutions and for the urban projects of Otto Wagner. Some of the apartment buildings that lined these boulevards, avenues and ring roads were to be designed in a version of the style known as Art Nouveau – the first manifestation of modernism – discussed further in this chapter. But first, we have to consider the soil within which this new style was sown and flourished, albeit briefly.

2.3 The cultural issue of a modern style

During the eighteenth century, the authority of the classical style, which had been accepted with few exceptions throughout Europe for important buildings since the Renaissance, broke down. Nineteenth-century architectural eclecticism was affected by both sides of the Enlightenment split between objective science and artistic romance. Architects made precise measurements of the orders of the surviving Greek temples so that it was possible to be archaeologically correct by accurately reproducing their proportions and profiles and no longer relying on 'debased' versions, which the Romans had employed and Vitruvius had described. The most famous of the architectural archaeologists was the German Johann Winckelmann, whose 1764 *History of Ancient Art* could be said to have initiated the academic discipline of art history in a normative sense. His example was followed by many others who observed that in a Greek temple the columns were load-bearing, as they needed to be in a trabeated construction. Roman architecture had involved massive walls employing arches to make openings and vaults to cover significant spaces. The orders were transformed so that they became merely decorative symbols that could be attached as required. As the partly-ruined Roman Colosseum illustrated very clearly, you could strip off the orders and the structure would survive perfectly satisfactorily. The architects of the Italian Renaissance had refined and developed this principle, most clearly articulated by Alberti and illustrated by buildings like his Palazzo Rucellai in Florence. But from the sixteenth century onwards, decoration had been piled upon decoration resulting in what were considered to be the excesses of the Baroque and Rococo. Neo-classicism represented a return to a 'truthful' and rational use of the orders, and its principles were established most famously by the Abbé Laugier (1713–1769) and swiftly adopted all over Europe. His appeal to the primitive hut, as the authentic origin of architecture, echoes Vitruvius' claim that wooden buildings formed the basis of the classical style.[18] In the frontispiece to the second edition in 1755 of Laugier's *Essai sur l'architecture*, the figure in the foreground gestures towards the structure that is formed of separate elements that are either vertical or horizontal or lean together to create a triangular pediment, the basic vocabulary of classicism.[19] William Chambers' illustrations of an even simpler trabeated hut

18 See Rykwert 1981 for a poetic description of the enduring appeal of this idea. But see also a critical review of the book by Ernst Gombrich, reprinted in Gombrich 1987.
19 Laugier's *Essai* criticised not only pilasters and columns that are engaged with the wall but also irrational column bases and incorrect proportions. It chimed with Jean-Jacques Rousseau's broader notion of the virtues of the primitive: humans are born in a state of innocence, and only as they gather together in larger groups are they introduced to the complexities of society.

Figure 2.8 William Chambers: illustration from his *Treatise of Civil Architecture*, 1768

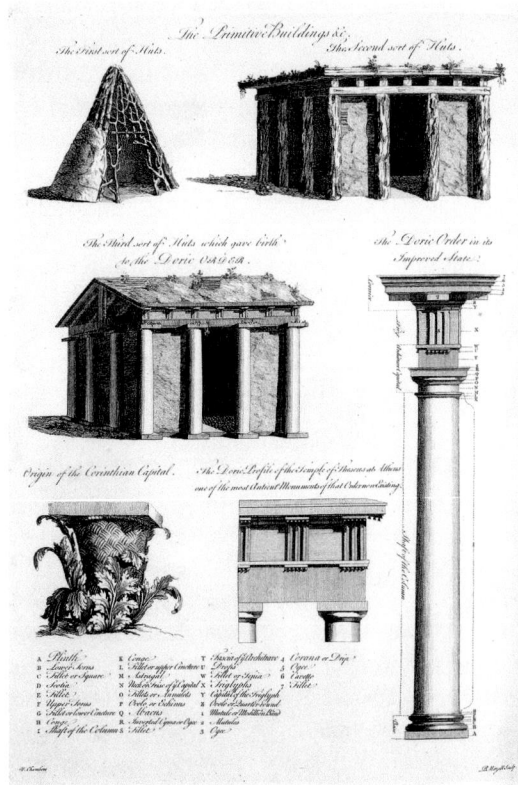

20 There are other theories of the derivation of symbolic elements such as triglyphs and metopes; for a minority view, see Wilson-Jones 2014.
21 Numerous books and articles from within the phenomenological tradition tend to begin their critique of modernism with the deficiencies of Cartesian thought, proceed to the arguments for a rational neoclassicism, and thence to its debasement as a system. See Rykwert 1984, which deals specifically with the eighteenth-century origins of Modernism, and pp. 211–12.
22 This worry, in poetry, was to be crystallized in 1973 in a famous book by the literary critic Harold Bloom, *The Anxiety of Influence, a Theory of Poetry*. The concern of artists and architects of this period was nuanced: they distinguished between mere copying and imitation, which was creative work inspired by antique models. See Honour 1968, pp. 107–114.

show how elements of the most primitive Doric order (triglyphs) can be derived from the projecting ends of timber beams[20] (**Figure 2.8**). The campaign, for that is what it became in the hands of enthusiastic adherents, represented a powerful and apparently rational 'recall to order', but when it became systematized it could lead to treating the elements of architecture as a highly reduced kit of parts – an attitude that arguably lies behind certain kinds of modernism.[21]

The other half of the Enlightenment divide – the romance of nature and of the past – is illustrated by the paintings of artists such as Caspar David Friedrich and beautifully represented in an etching by Henri Fuseli entitled "The artist moved to despair at the grandeur of antique fragments" (**Figure 2.9**). How could contemporary culture even approach the magnificence of the decayed civilization evident in the artefacts that were being discovered?[22] Neo-classicism could be both classical and romantic – a rational response to the inherited traditions recalling architecture to order and simultaneously an aspect of a heightened aesthetic sensibility.

Behind the classical tradition, whether Renaissance, Baroque or neo-classical lay pattern books that were produced in Italy by influential architects such as Andrea Palladio and Sebastiano Serlio (**Figure 2.10**). In continental Europe, particularly in France, the tradition had been reinforced and codified by teaching at the École des Beaux-Arts and the

Figure 2.9 Henry Fuseli: "The artist moved to despair at the grandeur of antique fragments", 1778–1779

annual Prix de Rome, the winners of which went to Italy and sometimes on to Greece to study the antique and publish their findings. Often they questioned previous orthodoxy: Henri Labrouste (1801–1875), for example, architect of the Bibliothèque Sainte Geneviève and the Salle Labrouste in the Bibliothèque Nationale in Paris, was one of those whose research showed that Winckelmann's view of Greek architecture as pure and white was erroneous: the temples had been polychromatic.[23] Beaux-Arts' teaching principles involved monthly competitions between students who followed a sequential process of design development.[24] Perhaps the most influential French teacher was Jean-Nicolas-Louis Durand (1760–1834), who taught a highly simplified version of the method at the École Polytechnique from 1797 to 1833, and the effects of his teaching will be referred to in subsequent chapters. Faced with any particular brief, students would produce a rapid sketch or *esquisse*, encompassing their conceptual idea, on a small enough format to be carried about or placed in a pocket – *poché*. Some would be eliminated at this stage because their choice of formal organization – their *parti* – was inappropriate. The next stage was for the finalists to work up their schemes to describe the project in more detail: the *projet*. The final stage involved the laborious process of drawing up the project in detail. Students would be *en charrette* (literally meaning on a wagon, the vehicle that would carry them with their drawings for final presentation) but

23 Winckelmann's preference for whiteness was consistent: in his *History of Ancient Art* he declared that "a beautiful body will . . . be the more beautiful the whiter it is". The implications are racial as much as aesthetic.
24 See essays by Annie Jacques and Neil Levine in Middleton 1982 for detailed descriptions of Beaux-Arts teaching and practice.

Figure 2.10 The proportions of the five orders in Serlio's *Book IV* of 1537

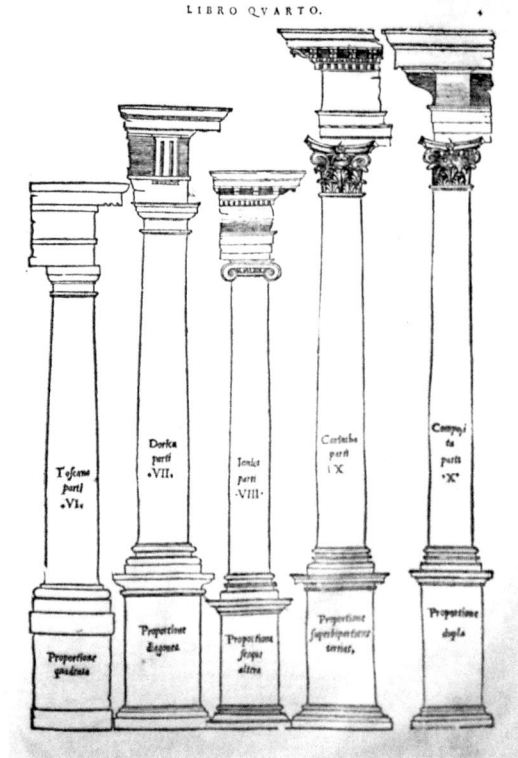

the term was later taken to signify in general the significant work they needed to undertake, often working night and day. Students had begun by a study of the orders and learnt to draw them with correct skiagraphy – the casting of shadows at 45° – but more importantly they had learnt how to organize their buildings: generous and coherent sequences of space formed the central route (or *marche*) through the building with principal volumes symmetrically disposed on either side. There was no need for what is today called wayfinding because for any visitor it was clear which spaces were important and which subsidiary – partly because of the extravagance of circulation in relation to useful space. Although a classical discipline need not pertain in many neo-Gothic buildings, composition in this way had become the norm so that earlier examples of neo-Gothic – even London's Houses of Parliament – obeyed similar principles.[25] In the United Kingdom, there was no equivalent teaching to the Beaux-Arts; architects gained their knowledge of classical architecture on the grand tour and of Gothic architecture by visiting and sketching churches and cathedrals; they were trained by apprenticing themselves to a practice, as both Philip Webb and William Morris had done in the office of George Edmund Street. The most successful large practices nevertheless developed formidable skills in the organization of complex briefs, as is clear, for example, in entries to the competition for the Law Courts in the Strand, which Street won, and which occupied him for many years.[26]

25 The building's layout was designed by the classically-trained Charles Barry; A.W.N. Pugin provided the decorative Gothic detail.
26 See Wilson 1992, pp. 198–203, for a wry comment on the way Street was treated by his clients, and see pp. 206–226 for a description of Alfred Waterhouse's competition entry.

2.4 Respect for the past

Another aspect to the reconsideration of the styles of the past was to have repercussions throughout the twentieth century – the value we place on the buildings we inherit. The investigation of various historic styles led to an increasingly sophisticated understanding of their development and resulted in cataloguing them and giving them names. Thomas Rickman, for instance, divided Gothic architecture into three periods: Early English, Decorated and Perpendicular. In his *Outline of European Architecture* and his comprehensive county-by-county survey *The Buildings of England*, the anglophile Nikolaus Pevsner adopted Rickman's taxonomy (abbreviated to EE, Dec and Perp). There were others: early enthusiasts for Gothic such as Pugin tended to prefer the earlier or mid periods, which he called "middle pointed". When old buildings were not entirely replaced but restored, architects had no compunction in demolishing degenerate later additions in favour of the purest manner. Accounts of the history of our attitude to the preservation of ancient buildings, and how we might add to them, usually begin in the United Kingdom with William Morris and the foundation in 1877 of the Society for the Protection of Ancient Buildings (SPAB). The great nineteenth-century historian and critic John Ruskin, however, had already argued in his *Seven Lamps of Architecture* that because the monuments of the past are too precious to lose, we have no right to alter them:

> it is again no question of expediency or feeling whether we shall preserve the buildings of past times or not. We have no right whatever to touch them. They are not ours. They belong partly to those who built them, and partly to all the generations of mankind who are to follow us.[27]

A few paragraphs earlier, Ruskin had made clear his position on restoration:

> Neither by the public, nor by those who have the care of public monuments, is the true meaning of the word *restoration* understood. It means the most total destruction which a building can suffer: a destruction out of which no remnants can be gathered; a destruction accompanied with false description of the thing destroyed. Do not let us deceive ourselves in this important matter; it is *impossible*, as impossible as to raise the dead, to restore anything that has ever been great or beautiful in architecture.[28]

Distinguishing between the notion of irresponsible restoration and necessary repair is the thrust of William Morris' famous argument that became SPAB's manifesto.[29] He explained that

> the civilised world of the nineteenth century has no style of its own amidst its wide knowledge of the styles of other centuries. From this lack and this gain arose in men's minds the strange idea of the Restoration of ancient buildings; and a strange and most fatal idea, which by its very name implies that it is possible to strip from a building this, that, and the other part of its history – of its life that is – and

27 Ruskin 1849, Ch VI ("The Lamp of Memory"), para. XX.
28 Ruskin 1849, Ch VI ("The Lamp of Memory"), para. XVIII.
29 See www.spab.org.uk/about-us/spab-manifesto.

30 For the essay on
Strasbourg Cathedral, "On
German Architecture",
originally published in 1772,
see Goethe 1994. The *Italian
Journey* was written in two
parts, in 1816 and 1828–1830,
recording his sojourn in
1786–1788: Goethe 1970.

then to stay the hand at some arbitrary point, and leave it still historical, living, and even as it once was.

In early times this kind of forgery was impossible, because knowledge failed the builders, or perhaps because instinct held them back.
If repairs were needed, if ambition or piety pricked on to change,
that change was of necessity wrought in the unmistakable fashion
of the time; a church of the eleventh century might be added to or
altered in the twelfth, thirteenth, fourteenth, fifteenth, sixteenth,
or even the seventeenth or eighteenth centuries; but every change,
whatever history it destroyed, left history in the gap, and was alive
with the spirit of the deeds done midst its fashioning. The result of
all this was often a building in which the many changes, though
harsh and visible enough, were, by their very contrast, interesting
and instructive and could by no possibility mislead.

So well-meaning restorers enhanced the fabric in an inauthentic manner:

of all the Restorations yet undertaken, the worst have meant the
reckless stripping a building of some of its most interesting material
features; whilst the best have their exact analogy in the Restoration
of an old picture, where the partly-perished work of the ancient
craftsmaster has been made neat and smooth by the tricky hand of
some unoriginal and thoughtless hack of today.

Summing up, he says "in short, a feeble and lifeless forgery is the final
result of all the wasted labour". Architects should therefore

resist all tampering with either the fabric or ornament of the building
as it stands; if it has become inconvenient for its present use, to raise
another building rather than alter or enlarge the old one; in fine to treat
our ancient buildings as monuments of a bygone art, created by bygone
manners, that modern art cannot meddle with without destroying.

Nineteenth-century eclecticism is frequently referred to as the battle
of the styles. Sometimes the taste of sensitive critics changed over
time: after his stay in 1770–1771, Goethe had famously enthused over
the medieval cathedral in Strasbourg, but his *Italian Journey*, the first
part of which is subtitled "Et in Arcadia Ego", records a rediscovery
of classic art, along with much else.[30] Architects often borrowed from
several styles, as we have already seen – Karl Friederich Schinkel
being one of the most fluent and successful eclectic architects. His
classical Altes Museum (**Figure 1.6**) and his Gothic Friederichswer-
desche Kirche were built in Berlin simultaneously. William Wilkins
built a Gothic screen to match the adjacent chapel for King's College,
Cambridge, but did not succeed in re-cladding the classical Fellows
Building by James Gibbs in Gothic costume or in constructing a
neo-classical library for the university (**Figure 2.11**). If the city was a
kind of theatre, the task of the architect was to provide appropriate settings, and even costume, to assist in staging the spectacle. In England,
later in the century, the arguments became more polarized, no longer
just a suit of clothes, but a conviction: George Gilbert Scott (a passionate Goth) was famously required to build the Foreign Office

Figure 2.11 William Wilkins: proposals for King's College and the University in Cambridge

Figure 2.12 George Gilbert Scott: Midland Grand Hotel, St Pancras, 1865

in London in classical dress in order to retain the commission and was uncomfortable in doing so. Scott's Midland Hotel at St Pancras used the style and many of the details he would have preferred to have employed on the Foreign Office[31] (**Figure 2.12**). But the real issue was to become whether architecture, whatever precedents it might draw upon, was required to symbolize anything more than its means of construction. There is an extreme contrast between the styled-up

31 For a vivid description of the debate surrounding Scott's appointment at the Foreign Office and the appropriate style for the building, see Heffer 2013, pp. 735–751. In his autobiography, Gilbert Scott worried that he might be accused of a pragmatic lack of principle in adopting a style in which he did not believe but argued that he could do a better job than most in any case: Scott 1995.

**Figure 2.13 W.H.
Barlow: St Pancras
train station junction
with the George
Gilbert Scott Midland
Grand Hotel, 1865**

hotel on the front and the structurally inventive St Pancras train
shed behind by the engineer William Henry Barlow (**Figure 2.13**) –
a collision of an architecture fashioned predominantly in relation
to association and an engineer's aesthetic deriving from the experiments at the Crystal Palace and other large-scale structures. Both
hotel and station were equally dependent on the efficient transportation of material across the country (the hard red bricks of the hotel,
resistant to the soot of the city, came from Leicestershire factories);
the difference was that the station was seen as aesthetically utilitarian whereas the hotel was 'architecture', acting as a grand gateway to
the wild romantic North. By the middle of the twentieth century, for
most critics the train shed represented an authentic expression and
the hotel was deceitful; it was only in the last quarter of that century
that the question was most widely and forcibly raised again of how far
a celebration of engineering technique could constitute the entirety
of architectural expression.

2.5 Moral criteria

The word "deceitful" used in the previous section suggests moral criteria for the use of style. How did such a notion arise? That architectural
expression should principally be a question of association had become

visible first in mid-eighteenth-century garden ornaments, or follies. Landowners in their classical country houses might enjoy the frisson of seeing a Gothic ruin in the landscape in which they could imagine some anchorite scraping a living. From 1747 the dilettante Horace Walpole (at Strawberry Hill, **Figure 2.14**) and from 1796 the eccentric William Beckford (at Fonthill, Wiltshire, **Figure 2.15**) built whole country houses in the Gothic style.[32] The associations they summoned up were designed, respectively, to amuse or to provoke a pleasurable frisson of terror.

That the choice of style should rest primarily on taste and association, however, seemed plainly unsatisfactory. A.W.N. Pugin's primary argument for Gothic was sociological and religious. In his polemical texts *Contrasts* of 1836 and *The True Principles of Pointed or Christian Architecture* of 1841, he had introduced a moral criterion: Gothic was more truthful to the culture, ethos and climate of the British Isles (**Figure 2.16**). Ruskin followed Pugin in advocating Gothic architecture. Amongst his many arguments is that classical architecture, designed on the drawing board by a separate professional, necessarily condemned the builders to a subservient role, as mere executors of a preconceived design. He claimed the workmen on the great cathedrals, within the more fluid aesthetic of Gothic, could vary motifs and elaborate the buildings at will. As William Lethaby, the architect who was the founder and first

32 Walpole's father was the first British Prime Minister, Sir Robert Walpole. Beckford's fortune was inherited from his father, who was said to have owned 3,000 slaves working on his sugar plantations in Barbados. Both wrote "Gothick" novels: Walpole *The Castle of Otranto*, and Beckford *Vathek*, reflecting their different tastes.

Figure 2.14 Horace Walpole with Richard Bentley: Strawberry Hill, 1749

FONTHILL ABBEY.

VIEW OF THE WEST, & NORTH FRONTS.

Figure 2.15 William Beckford with James Wyatt: Fonthill Abbey, 1796–1813

principal of the Central School of Art and Design in London, somewhat poetically put it: a Gothic cathedral was "a thousand men deep"[33]. So the argument introduces an ethical component into aesthetics, which some would say should be kept completely separate.[34] Yet styles can have implications. The demand for precision (implied in classical architecture that requires absolute symmetry, for instance) does entail the suppression of individual fancy, and that has consequences for the personal satisfaction of those engaged in the act of building. The same kinds of arguments pertain in the alienating nature of mass-production, when workers do not get to see the results of their handiwork and must be content with the team spirit that comes from an achievement in which everyone has participated.

Many nineteenth-century architects yearned for a rationale that would allow a new manner to emerge. Both Pugin and Ruskin had marshalled an argument for Gothic as more structurally efficient than classical architecture, but the crucial rationalist theorist of modernism, though an unskilled and clumsy designer, was the Frenchman Eugène Viollet-le-Duc (**Figure 2.17**). In his 1863–1872 *Discourses*, he argues for a contemporary manner:

33 See Lethaby 1956.
34 Watkin 1977, for instance, already quoted in the Introduction, would ridicule such an idea.

Suppose that an architect of the twelfth or thirteenth century were to return among us and that he were to be initiated into our modern

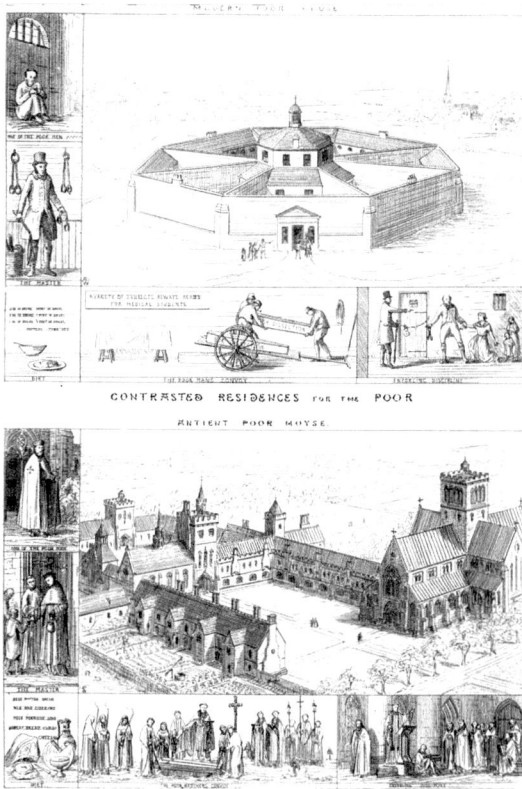

Figure 2.16   A.W.N. Pugin, plate from *Contrasts*, 1836

ideas; if one put at his disposal the perfections of modern industry, he would not build an edifice of the time of Philip Augustus or
St Louis, because this would be to falsify the first law of art, which is
to conform to the needs and customs of the times.[35]

Arising from the advances of technology, the moral arguments for
Gothic and the rationalism of the neo-classicists, it seems there were
grounds for the emergence of a new style in architecture. Its first manifestation appears in what was termed Art Nouveau: in the best examples of this briefly popular international style, the combination of more
recently developed materials such as cast iron and traditional masonry,
which is so awkward in Viollet-le-Duc's projects, becomes something
elegant and refined.

2.6 Art Nouveau as the first manifestation of modernism

Art Nouveau offered a way out from the false choice between classical
and Gothic (or the employment of more exotic styles) by adopting a
principle of articulating structure per se and decorating it with motifs
derived from nature rather than pre-existing styles. The linear decorative style first emerged in book illustrations and the drawings of 'deca-
dent' artists like Aubrey Beardsley but swiftly appeared in architecture

35 Viollet-le-Duc 1959, cited
in Curtis 1982, p. 14.

Figure 2.17 Eugène Viollet-le-Duc: illustration from *Entretiens*, 1863–1872

all over Europe and also in America (as part of the solution to Louis Sullivan's problem of how to order tall buildings, for instance). In the new rationalized boulevards of European capital cities, nature softened the raw technology that built the apartments occupied by the bourgeoisie. Victor Horta and Henry Van der Velde, in Brussels, Hector Guimard in Paris and Antoni Gaudí in Barcelona (though his sensibility is of course particularly Catalan) all contribute to the new style (**Figure 2.18**). In Germany the parallel movement went by the name of *Jugendstil*. The remarkable Glasgow School of Art (built in two phases, 1897–1909), by Charles Rennie Mackintosh, is one of the masterpieces of the period.[36] With his wife, Margaret Macdonald, and partly influenced by Japanese taste, he demonstrated how, in the hands of skilled designers, powerful compositions could be sensitively detailed to make people feel thoroughly at home in them. The style anticipated modernism, in being international, but maintained regional characteristics.

Mackintosh was also acutely aware of environmental issues, especially the treatment of natural light which is so important in an art school.[37] Art Nouveau buildings are often technically sophisticated, integrating the handling of natural and artificial light and hot water heating within the construction and fluently using iron and steel structural techniques. The grand private houses (*hôtels*) designed by Victor Horta (1861–1947) are masterpieces in their handling of light and of slender metal

36 Mackintosh's masterpiece was severely damaged by two fires in May 2014 and June 2018. It is to be thoroughly repaired but can only ever be a simulacrum.

37 Lawrence 2020.

Figure 2.18 Antoni Gaudí: Casa Batlló, detail, 1904

construction, the lines of which merge into decorative motifs on walls, ceilings and floors (**Figure 2.19**). Often the components are finished on site by the contribution of a craftsman or even through the interventions of the architects themselves. Mouldings on the external stonework, which might recall classical details, merge organically with the wall plane, while metal lintels are frankly expressed but elegantly handled (**Figure 2.20**).

Fluid organic forms were certainly one means by which to fill the vacuum left when traditional stylistic motifs were jettisoned. Architects continued to wonder, however, whether it would not be possible to derive the formal expression from meeting the buildings' functional and technical requirements without imposing a style of any kind. That idea of stylelessness – building without recourse to stylistic precedent – had been explored in British domestic architecture, as we saw when looking at the cottages employed at low densities that aimed to solve the slum conditions of the cities. Eventually it is that attempted stylelessness that can best explain their importance for the development of modernism. In a German competition in 1901 for a "House for an Art Lover", Charles Rennie Mackintosh's elegant Art Nouveau solution was ruled out because he submitted some of his interior sketches late (**Figure 2.21**). No first prize was awarded, and Baillie Scott's cruder Arts and Crafts 'butterfly' design was given second place (**Figure 2.22**). Baillie Scott was one of the

Figure 2.19 Victor Horta: Hotel Tassell, 1892–1893

Figure 2.20 Victor Horta: stone and metal detailing in Brussels Hotels

Figure 2.21 Charles Rennie Mackintosh: House for an Art Lover competition, 1901

architects particularly admired by Hermann Muthesius, an important figure in the promulgation of the idea of a rational domestic architecture. In 1896 Muthesius was appointed as a technical attaché to the German embassy in London. He and his wife rented a house in Hammersmith, close to Kelmscott House, where William Morris (who died that year) had lived. Muthesius understood Morris' importance and regarded his first house, the 1859 Red House, designed by his friend Philip Webb, as harbinger of the new manner. In 1904 Muthesius published *Das Englische Haus*, a comprehensive historical survey of the development of British domestic architecture, which culminates in buildings by Arts and Crafts architects such as Baillie Scott and Edward Prior.[38] He praised the way plans were manipulated to catch the sunshine by indentations

38 Muthesius 2007, vol 2, pp. 118–139.

Figure 2.22 M.H. Baillie Scott: House for an Art Lover competition, 1901

and protrusions such as bay windows. Baillie Scott's House for an Art Lover and Edward Prior's house The Barn both have a 'butterfly' form. And Muthesius' own Freudenberg House is similarly composed, seeking maximum solar penetration to the living spaces.[39]

Muthesius' book and his subsequent career provided Nikolaus Pevsner with justification for his claim that the Arts and Crafts movement was one of the originators of European modernism.[40] Muthesius, who became the designer and first professor at the Grand Ducal School of Fine Art in Weimar, was a founder, with Peter Behrens and the Art Nouveau architect Henry van der Velde, of the Deutsche Werkbund Society in 1907. One of its most important developments was a new settlement – not unlike an Arts and Crafts Garden Suburb – at Hellerau, near Dresden, which became an artistic magnet for the middle classes: a cultural initiative based there with wide influence was the school of dance and its annual festivals organized by Émile Dalcroze. The theatre was designed by Heinrich Tessenow, a talented architect in a manner that was inspired both by vernacular buildings and neo-classicism; he later taught at the Berlin-Charlottenburg Institute of Technology. The Werkbund's most famous achievement was an exhibition it mounted in 1914, which is rightly celebrated as illustrating the prototypical forms of twentieth-century modernism. Walter Gropius and Adolf Meyer, both of whom had worked in Behrens' office, designed a conservatively planned steel-framed model factory with glass stair towers: conventional symmetry but novel materials. Van der Velde's softly rounded concrete theatre was more overtly artistic, clearly within the formal vocabulary of Art Nouveau or Jugendstil, but anticipating the more adventurous fluidity of post First World War Expressionism[41] (**Figure 2.23**). Within the Werkbund, Muthesius argued for the rational and systematic, while van der Velde maintained that the architect was at root an artist. With

39 A British precedent for the butterfly form was Chesters, a house by Norman Shaw of 1891–1893, but Alan Colquhoun points out that a plan of a *hôtel particulier* by Viollet-le-Duc, published in his 17th *Discourse*, anticipates this form (Colquhoun 1985, pp. 167–168 and 207; Viollet-le-Duc 1959).
40 Pevsner 1936, 1960.
41 Many of the most influential Jugendstil architects also practised in Munich and Darmstadt, south of Frankfurt.

Figure 2.23 Henry Van de Velde: Werkbund Theatre, 1913–1914

the post-war foundation of the Bauhaus, this argument was to continue, under Gropius' leadership, oscillating between an artistic expressionism and a scientific concern for rational fabrication systems. The most satisfactory pre-war resolution of the conflict is to be found in the product designs of Peter Behrens for AEG – everyday pieces of equipment that can be understood in the terms that Le Corbusier was later to employ as *objet-types*.

2.7 Aesthetics, ethics and politics: some broader questions

Although we might be sceptical that there are ethical reasons for the adoption of a particular style because it is more truthful, as Pugin and Ruskin suggested, the choices architects make in relation to aesthetic expression may yet carry ethical implications. If we accept that typically architects have aesthetic aims in view, are there more or less responsible positions they should take?

In eighteenth-century architectural aesthetics, the theories of an Englishman, Edmund Burke, author of *A Philosophical Enquiry into the Origin of our Idea of the Sublime and the Beautiful*, written in 1757–1759, were particularly influential.[42] As his title suggests, Burke aimed to distinguish between two qualities that we might appreciate aesthetically. In the *Enquiry*, this is how Burke defines the *sublime*:

> Whatever is fitted in any sort to excite the ideas of pain and danger, that is to say whatever is any sort terrible, or is conversant about terrible objects, or operates in a manner analogous to terror, is in a

42 Burke 2008.

sense sublime; that is it is productive of the strongest emotion which the mind is capable of feeling. I say the strongest emotion, because I am satisfied the ideas of pain are much more powerful than those which enter on the part of pleasure.

Ruskin's later admiration for the 'savageness' of Gothic may come to mind. In moving on to describe beauty, Burke turns to the question of sexual reproduction to illustrate how, in the act of love in humans, a brute animal passion is replaced by "a mixed passion which we call love", and the object of this mixed passion is beauty.[43] The aesthetic distinctions which Burke draws between the sublime (huge, rough, awesome, natural, overwhelming) and the beautiful (petite, smooth, highly fashioned and seductive) can be read psychoanalytically, economically and politically.[44] We already saw the contrast between two neo-Gothic houses, Fonthill Abbey and Strawberry Hill, which were designed to summon up contrasted associations (**Figure 2.18**). In Burke's terms, the two projects are *sublime* and *beautiful*, respectively.

Nietzsche's 1872 *Birth of Tragedy*, with its distinction between the Dionysian and Apollonian, mentioned in the previous chapter, could be said to draw upon a similar distinction, so that we could see Burke's idea as pre-figuring a challenge to the complacent tastefulness of the eighteenth century. David Hume, in the enlightened city of Edinburgh where the New Town was under construction from 1767, had been clear that good taste was a convention to which every educated individual would subscribe:[45] the nineteenth century was very different. But Edmund Burke disconcerted many of his admirers with his book written in 1790, *Reflections on the Revolution in France*, which drew back from the wider implications: he had sympathized with the cause of American independence, but he could not support a bloody revolution as a consequence of his admiration of the sublime.

Aesthetic issues thus merge with the political. When Ruskin argued for the retention of ancient buildings or complained that classical architecture made slaves of its workmen, in comparison with the Gothic manner, his concern was not merely aesthetic but was at one with his passionate belief in the rights of the craftsman (assumed to be male) to be fulfilled, most clearly set out in essays published in *Cornhill* magazine between 1860 and 1862 and emerging as *Unto This Last*. He railed against the inequalities of nineteenth-century society and proposed a graduated income tax to ameliorate them. But in common with many (though not all) of his contemporaries, he was also clear that cultured Europeans were a superior race: they deserved their empires and had a moral duty to govern them well.

> We are rich in an inheritance of honour, bequeathed to us through a thousand years of noble history, which it should be our daily thirst to increase with splendid avarice, so that Englishmen, if it be a sin to covet honour, should be the most offending souls alive.

43 We might expect to find combinations of the qualities of the sublime and the beautiful in every work of art, but Burke himself avoids the naming of any third intermediate term (later to be called *picturesque*) – he is content to describe differences. For an excellent discussion of these issues, see Macarthur 2007.

44 For a close reading of both the *Enquiry* and Burke's *Reflections on the Revolution in France*, see Furniss 1993.

45 "A building, whose doors and windows were exact squares, would hurt the eye by that very proportion; as ill adapted to the figure of a human creature, for whose service the fabric was intended". Hume 1998, Section 5, para. 1.

> The England who is to be mistress of half the earth cannot remain herself a heap of cinders, trampled by contending and miserable crowds; she must yet again become the England she was once, and in all beautiful ways more; so happy, so secluded, and so pure . . . She must guide the human arts, and gather the divine knowledge, of distant nations, transformed from savageness to manhood, and redeemed from despairing into peace.[46]

We could take the Chhatrapati Shivaji Terminus in Mumbai, India, as indicative of the architectural consequences of imperialism: it was designed in a broadly Gilbert Scott neo-Gothic manner by a British architect Frederick Stevens and originally named Victoria Terminus after the British Queen, who was Empress of India. Under construction for ten years from 1878, and just as dependent on the transportation systems and new manufacturing techniques, it was much larger than St Pancras – awe-inspiring in its scale, technical achievement and the richness of its material and decoration. The awe it was intended to induce included a proper reverence for the imperial power that brought the fruits of European culture to the colonies.

For Karl Marx (1818–1883), colonialism was not the fundamental cause of oppression, it was the economic system itself, capitalism, which effectively made slaves of ordinary people all over the globe. He was to be one of the two or three most influential thinkers for the twentieth century, informing attitudes to history, economics, sociology and philosophy, including much twentieth-century critical theory applied to architecture, which often arises out of a conjunction of his theories and those of Sigmund Freud (discussed in the next chapter). Marx was born in Trier, in what is now Germany, where he studied before going to Berlin and came under the influence of Hegel. He moved to London in 1849, where he was based for the rest of his life. As I suggested in Chapter 1, Marx's dialectical materialism can be seen as a secular form of Hegel's idealism, with a further significant difference in relation to his view of history: rather than being confident in the inexorable progress towards a better form of society under a wise ruler, Marx believed it would require a revolution to create the communist society he sought. In fact, revolution was unavoidable once capitalism, an economic system that inevitably led to extreme differentials between the wealthy bourgeoisie and the impoverished workers – the proletariat – had reached a certain point. The historical irony turned out to be that those countries that successfully engaged in revolutions in the twentieth century were not advanced capitalist societies but nations that had economically under-developed, substantially agrarian economies. With the Russian revolution of 1917, an experimental architecture became imaginable (before it was suppressed in the Stalinist era) and projects were prepared, for which the technology was inadequate in that country, that were later to be influential in France and Germany. We shall also see in subsequent chapters how Marxist theory lay behind some strands of modernist polemic in the earlier years of the twentieth

46 The excerpt is from Ruskin's 1870 *Inaugural Lecture*, given on 8 February 1870, as the Slade Professor of Fine Art at Oxford on his 51st birthday, cited in Shea and Whitla 2014.

47 The conjunction of the thinking of Marx and Freud was particularly influential. Its effect on Deleuze and Guattari, for example, is illustrated in Bogue 1987.
48 With the exception of the Russian empire, always both Asian and European, reappearing in expanded form after the Revolution as the USSR and still retaining significant power after its refashioning in 1989.

century and how critical thinking on architecture and urbanism later in the century continued to draw on it.[47]

Western European empires were to collapse in the twentieth century,[48] which saw two devastating internal wars that involved nearly every nation on earth. Confidence in rational progress, sustained by the objectivity and dispassion that is central to a scientific attitude, was hard to maintain. The arts could hardly fail to reflect the anxiety that resulted. Besides, if, as Nietzsche held, it is part of the task of the artist to disturb and to summon up the strongest emotions, this would be intrinsic to their role. The City of Vienna at the dawn of the twentieth century, formerly capital of the Austria-Hungarian empire, to which we turn next, provides a particularly rich illustration of the consequences.

3

FIN-DE-SIÈCLE VIENNA AS A PARADIGM OF MODERNISM

The cultural context in Vienna at the dawn of the twentieth century is both characteristic of discussions that are still current about the roles of continuity and revolution in all the arts and, because of the city's particular history, uniquely complex. As Carl Schorske summarized it in 1980, Vienna:

> provides one of the most fertile breeding grounds of our century's a-historical culture. Its great intellectual innovators – in music and philosophy, in economics and architecture, and, of course, in psychoanalysis – all broke, more or less deliberately, their ties to the historical outlook central to the nineteenth-century liberal culture in which they had been reared.[1]

3.1 Historical and cultural background

In the sixteenth century, Vienna became capital of that part of the Habsburg empire which stretched from the Danube to Trieste. A paradoxical result was that the city lost its autonomy. Unlike cities like Nuremberg or Strasbourg, Vienna was less concerned to celebrate its own civic traditions and as compensation moved to a gradual liberalization in all the arts, with the exception, in general, of literature. The somewhat complacent and comfortable culture that resulted, named "Biedermeier" after a fictional German schoolmaster, survived until 1848. What we now think of as one of its golden periods began from the time of political catastrophe when the Austro-Hungarian empire collapsed with defeats at Solferino in 1859 and Königgrätz, Bohemia, in 1866. The emperor Franz Joseph had already ordered the demolition of the city walls on Christmas Eve 1857 and inaugurated a grandiose ring road in place of the 'glacis' – a park that had existed since the 1880s acting as a kind of green belt (**Figure 3.1**). As in Haussmann's later campaign in Paris, part of the task of the 65-metre wide Ringstrasse was to allow for ease of troop movements to ensure safety in the face of future uprisings; in fact a barracks was one of the first buildings planned. Abandoning imperial ambitions, the city should be "Strong through Law and Peace", though the 1860 Ringstrasse map clearly shows that Vienna was to be embellished by art: finally the city would assume its role as a *Weltstadt* or truly cosmopolitan city. The architecture, as we

1 There is extensive literature on *Fin de siècle* Vienna. In addition to general histories of Modern Architecture (Frampton 1985; Curtis 1982; Colquhoun 2002), see also Schorske 1980; Spiel 1987; Kandel 2012; Eva Branscombe, Murray Fraser and Michael Gnehm, "Central Europe (Germany and Austro-Hungarian Empire) 1815–1914" in Fraser and Gregg 2019.

DOI: 10.4324/9781003244943-4

Figure 3.1 Plan of Vienna's walls up until Franz Joseph's 1857 decree

Figure 3.2 Parliament Building on the Ringstrasse

might expect of the period, was eclectic: the Town Hall was Gothic; the State Opera House was a somewhat stilted Baroque; the university was Renaissance; and the Parliament was Greek (**Figure 3.2**). It was also theatrical in character. In each case, the choice of style was determined by the appropriate associations: Gothic represented the indigenous pre-modern foundation of the city; Baroque was the quint-essential theatrical manner; Renaissance celebrated the rebirth of learning; Greek, naturally enough, referred to the origins of democracy. Between the monumental civic buildings were apartment blocks, four to six storeys high, modelled on bourgeois-aristocratic precedents which were already springing up beyond the fortifications and 'glacis' – commercial space on the ground floor, grand apartments on first and sometimes second floors and more modest flats above.[2] Textile entrepreneurs and minor nobility often lived in the grander apartments of the buildings, of which they might own the freehold, or a long lease, and let out smaller flats. The buildings could therefore be divided into separate blocks and occupied by different functions or classes of society, but they were still fashioned to appear as a single monumental composition, and their façades and grand staircases were deliberately detailed to resemble those of palaces.

3.2 Sitte and Wagner – two views of the city

The two principal critics of the Ringstrasse were Camillo Sitte (1843–1903) and Otto Wagner (1841–1918) – but the nature of their criticism differed. Camillo Sitte was the author of what was to become an influential book: *City Planning according to Artistic Principles*;[3] in England Raymond Unwin was one of his admirers. Sitte deprecated the systematic commercial nature of the Ringstrasse development, invoking Aristotle to contrast it with the organic and aesthetic ideals of the past. He had no quarrel with the historical styles of the individual buildings but regretted the absence of "the agora, the forum and the marketplace": outdoor squares should serve as the "theatre of the common life", as they did in medieval cities he had analyzed (**Figure 3.3**), whereas the spaces the Ringstrasse created were "heartlessly utilitarian". He claimed that "a free-standing building remains forever a cake on a platter".[4] As we shall see, this perception (that urban spaces are more important for the character of a city than individual buildings conceived as objects) eventually passed into the orthodoxy of urban design in the last quarter of the twentieth century, having been revived in anti-modernist critiques by Colin Rowe, Léon Krier and others in the 1970s and 1980s.

Otto Wagner's criticism turned out to be the reverse. He had won the competition for the expansion of Vienna with a proposal based almost entirely on rational circulation involving a series of ring roads, of which the already constructed Ringstrasse would be the first (**Figure 3.4**). He argued that the "only possible point of departure for our artistic creation is modern life".[5] Wagner himself was a highly successful architect-entrepreneur: he built on the Ringstrasse in a free Renaissance style and conceived public proposals, such as the Artibus museum project of 1880, while his scheme of 1891 for a cathedral in Berlin was on a truly monumental scale. In his mixed-use blocks, he stripped the inner utilitarian courts of ornament, but otherwise the architecture is conventionally classical. In response to particular contexts, however, he was a subtle designer. His project for the Stadtmuseum in Vienna, for instance, negotiates its awkwardly shaped site in relation to pre-existing buildings with consummate skill in a way that creates outside spaces as coherent as the

2 Much of the existing city inside the fortifications, occupied by the aristocrats and former political elite, was surprisingly cramped, which partly accounts for the popularity of the coffee house culture described later.
3 Sitte 1922, 2013.
4 Sitte 1922, quoted in Schorske 1980, p. 64.
5 Wagner 1914, quoted in Schorske 1980, p. 74.

Figure 3.3 Sitte's critique of the Ringstrasse

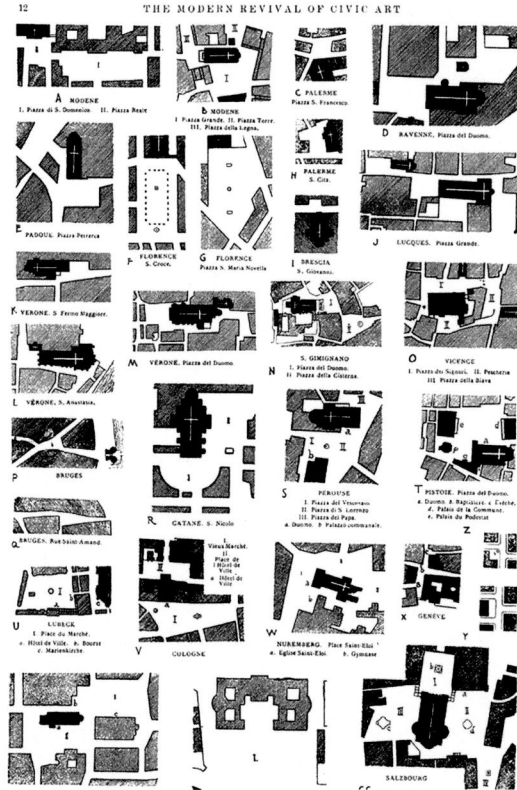

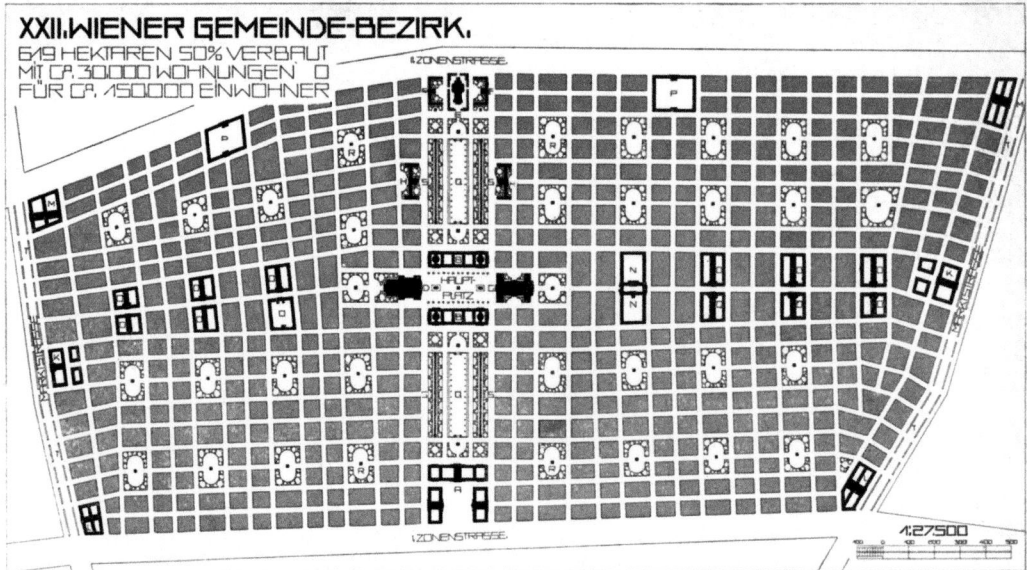

Figure 3.4 Otto Wagner: plan for the XXII sector of Vienna's city expansion, 1910–1911

indoor volumes (**Figure 3.5**). As is often the case, a sensitive architect can take a polemical position that in the hands of those less talented could result in a highly impoverished environment.

As City Architect from 1894, Wagner was in charge of massive engineering works, including viaducts, bridges, tunnels, locks and 30 stations in which he began to incorporate the expression of modern materials such as iron and cast aluminium into his architecture. That same year he was also appointed Professor of Architecture at the Academy of Fine Arts (beating Sitte to the post) and in 1895 summarized his position in *Modern Architecture*: architects should seek inspiration in the modern metropolis rather than in Rome. In 1897 he was instrumental in setting up the *Secession* – the Viennese Art Nouveau group. Its motto, coined by the art critic Ludwig Hevesi, was "To the age its art; to art its freedom"; and amongst its members was Gustav Klimt (1862–1918), whose paintings Wagner especially admired. Though his architecture, as we shall see, was grounded in the classical tradition, Wagner claimed that modernity as it would be reflected in the discipline should be essentially rational and efficient, while art works could be personal and erotic, as Klimt's were.

For different reasons, both Sitte and Wagner may have had contradictory views on the way cities should be fashioned but were united in their admiration for a project by Gottfried Semper in 1869, which was never completed, for a majestic new *Burgplatz* – a major civic forum – on the Ringstrasse. Semper is now much more highly regarded for his theories on the origins of architecture than he is as a designer, and later I mention how these are reflected in the way Wagner detailed his buildings.

Figure 3.5 Otto Wagner: Kaiser Franz Josef Stadtsmuseum project, 1903

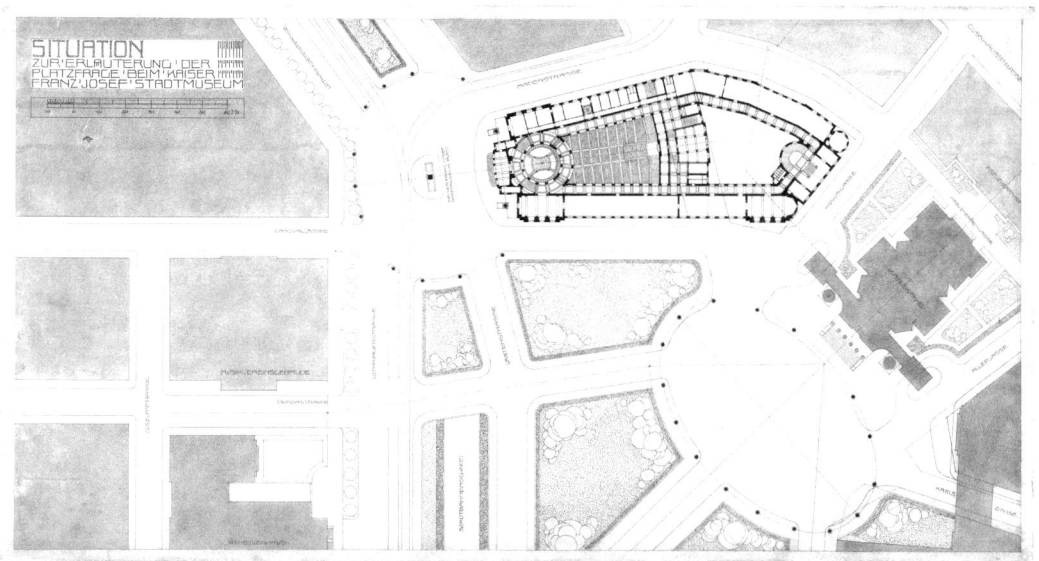

3.3 Politics and philosophical thinking

Vienna was always a melting pot of nationalities: Germans, Czechs, Croats, Bohemians, Moravians, Slovaks, Turks, Italians, Greeks, Macedonians and Romanians. As was the case all over Europe, Jews were periodically driven out.[6] The Viennese dialect reflects this multiethnicity: Bavarian is mixed in with Yiddish (itself a conflation of German and Hebrew), and there are traces of the languages of all its inhabitants. It may be that the peculiarly contradictory and inconsistent character of Viennese culture is a result – an irresolution that borders on schizophrenia: everyday pleasure (*Gemütlichkeit*) was always tinged with melancholy and even deep despair.

A significant proportion of the Viennese population was Czech in origin, and there was long-standing pressure on the emperor to grant more autonomy to their homeland regions of Bohemia and Moravia. Vienna witnessed a Pan-Germanic movement led in the 1880s by the disagreeable Georg von Schönerer. He was simultaneously antisocialist, anti-capitalist, anti-Catholic, anti-liberal, anti-Habsburg and fervently anti-Semitic. Karl Lueger led the Christian Socialists in the following decade: friend and patron of Otto Wagner, a zealous Catholic but equally anti-Semitic, he was mayor of Vienna until his death in 1910. Both were admired by Adolf Hitler, who was living in Stumpergasse in 1908, having been twice refused admission to the Kunsthistorische Akademie. The year before, Victor Adler, who had Marxist sympathies and had met Friederich Engels in Switzerland, led a rational and secular Social Democracy to electoral victory; he retained his influence until his death in 1918. Meanwhile Theodor Herzl founded a Zionist newspaper in Vienna and campaigned energetically for a Jewish State. For him, Great Britain was a model politically and educationally, and he was well received in the East End of London in 1896, the year in which he published his *Der Judenstaat*. A mesmeric speaker, he sought to further his cause all over Europe; Israel named an annual memorial day after him. Later, Vienna was to be famous for its socialist housing programmes, analyzed in some detail by Manfredo Tafuri and others in the 1980s.[7]

The Viennese attitude to religion was ambiguous. The Catholic faith had the most adherents: the great journalist Hermann Bahr remarked of them that they "were able to indulge while renouncing, to be ascetically opulent and piously to sin".[8] But there were also Greek, Serbian, Romanian, Russian and Bulgarian Orthodox Christians, Calvinists and Lutherans. Islam was officially recognized from 1908.

While, culturally, Vienna appeared to be extremely conservative, the city paradoxically fostered artistic experiments of the most radical kind. The café was the most important institution – an inheritance perhaps from Turkish practice, reflected also in its pastries, such as the middle-eastern *Kipfurl* in the shape of a crescent moon.[9] The first café opened in 1863, and its many imitators were to become the focus for political discussion and the home of satirists like Karl Kraus. His work has a reputation for untranslatability because of its wit, irony, puns and obscure references.

Aged only 25, he attacked all his contemporaries mercilessly in his peri-odical *Die Fackel* (The Torch), launched in 1899; it lasted 31 years and numbered 921 issues. Personally charismatic, he influenced his many disciples all their life. For architects his most famous quotation runs: "All that Loos and I have done, he literally, I verbally, was to show that there is a difference between an urn and a chamber-pot and that only in this difference does culture find room to play".[10] He refers to the Vienn-ese architect Adolf Loos, whose buildings are discussed later, and to the idea that it was inauthentic to overvalue the everyday. A chamber pot should not be celebrated in the way that a sacred vessel, such as an urn, should be: its authentic expression would be mute. In a similar way, the Vienna-born Ludwig Wittgenstein, regarded by many as the most important and influential philosopher of the twentieth century, was concerned all his life with the limitations of what language can, or should, express.[11] Wittgenstein, as it happens, understood architec-ture as a difficult enterprise for a perfectionist like himself because he designed his own two-storey wooden house by a Norwegian lake and participated in the design of a house for his sister in Vienna by a pupil of Loos. He claimed "All architecture celebrates something. Where there is nothing to celebrate there can be no architecture".[12] Wittgenstein had begun by studying aeronautical engineering and then undertook a PhD in philosophy in Cambridge, returning there to lecture after some years. Unsurprisingly, critics have been intrigued by the relations between his thinking and architecture which will be discussed in more detail in Chapter 10.

3.4 Literature and psychology

Vienna was also the birthplace of Sigmund Freud (1856–1939), usually regarded as the founder of psychoanalysis.[13] Freud, who saw his activity as scientific – the careful unravelling of the effect of the subconscious on the lives of individuals and societies – always acknowledged that the subjective perceptions of imaginative writers had anticipated the con-clusions of his laborious researches. Arthur Schnitzler's famous 1897 play *Reigen* (more commonly known by its French title *La Ronde*), for instance, is a kind of sexual merry-go-round in ten scenes and was published privately in 1900, the same year as Freud's *Interpretation of Dreams*, though not performed in Vienna until after the First World War.[14] Freud argued that dreams revealed primal urges (the *id*), invar-iably of a sexual nature, which the *superego* sought to repress.[15] Such repression inevitably caused individual neurosis. The most well-known example is what Freud called the Oedipus Complex, following the Greek legend: the repressed desire, which he claims every small boy harbours, to murder his father and sleep with his mother. For Freud, art was essentially a sublimation – a substitute for sexual fulfilment – and here we can detect the influence of Nietzsche. He described the develop-ment of sexuality in children as going through three phases: oral (when they test everything by attempting to taste it), anal and genital; so that in Freudian terms architects might be seen as stuck in an anal phase, fixated on littering their surroundings with their excrement, which they

10 See Wilson 1992, pp. 54–65.

11 For an excellent biogra-phy, see Monk 1991. Monk 2021 is an accessible article to celebrate the centenary of the publication of Wittgen-stein's *Tractatus*, summa-rizing key aspects of his thought.

12 Wittgenstein 1980. See Sarnitz 2017 for one of the more detailed accounts of Wittgenstein's house for his sister, illustrating a more nuanced understanding of Viennese cross-cultural connections than Schorske, as an "outsider", provides.

13 For a general introduc-tion to his thinking, see Freud 2012.

14 Schnitzler had trained in medicine in Vienna at the same time as Freud and worked with Charcot in Paris. There's evidence in a letter from Freud to him in 1922 that Freud was aware of his superior understanding of women and somewhat jealous of him: see Kandel 2012, pp. 77–89.

15 Some neurophysiologists, such as Mark Solms, have sought to integrate Freud's hypotheses with recent discoveries in neuroscience. See Kandel 2012, pp. 375–377; Solms 2002.

seek to manipulate obsessively. As it happens, Freud wrote some interesting articles about art but little about architecture. He was not well served by English translators, who sought to emphasize his scientific credentials by translating such everyday concepts as slips of the tongue (which we now term "Freudian slips") as *parapraxes*.[16] In fact, many of his other examples are of apparently quite ordinary anxieties, such as the fear of missing trains.[17]

Freud was not alone in his investigations: an important colleague was Karl Bühler, who taught at the University of Vienna and stressed the desire of humans to fulfil themselves creatively, rather than just overcome their psychic disorders. Few now subscribe wholeheartedly to Freud's theories: for a start, he concentrated almost entirely on the male ego and, unlike Schnitzler, seemed to have had little understanding of female sexuality. Yet the terms he introduced and his insights into subconscious repressed desires have profoundly affected our thinking.[18] Indeed the theoretical discourse of many of the most frequently consulted thinkers in the latter part of the twentieth century is dependent on his work. Our descriptions of Freud's own deficiencies often tend to be couched in Freudian terms so that, faced by those who resist his formulations most strenuously, we ask ourselves what is causing their resistance. Freud's colleagues and pupils, a number of whom broke away from his group, included the mystical Carl Jung (1875–1961, inventor of the distinctions between extroverts and introverts and champion of the archetype), Alfred Adler (1870–1937, who focused on the will to power) and the brilliant but ultimately unhinged Wilhelm Reich (1897–1957).

3.5 Music

Vienna had held a central place in musical development in the late eighteenth and early nineteenth centuries as either the home or the city offering the most prestigious location for performance for Haydn, Mozart, Beethoven and Schubert. Johannes Brahms lived there from 1862 until his death in 1897, but by the end of the nineteenth century the city preferred music that reflected a complacent and comfortable culture (the waltzes of Johann Strauss the younger and on to the operettas in the twentieth century of Franz Lehár). Yet it also acted as the birthplace of the most extreme form of modernist composition – the serial technique of Arnold Schönberg (1874–1951). Gustav Mahler, the composer and conductor at the Vienna Court Opera from 1897, confessed to Freud, who undertook "a kind of lightning analysis", that it was after fleeing a terrible row between his parents that he encountered a hurdy-gurdy player in the street, and this cemented "the bond between the tragic and the trivial" that is so characteristic of his music, and which "possibly prevented him from reaching the highest rank of creativity".[19] The extreme contrasts, evident in Mahler's nine completed symphonies and increasingly appreciated by music lovers in the later twentieth and twenty-first centuries, are particularly Viennese.

But was such unconstrained expression sufficient? Arnold Schönberg's early music is lusciously romantic and was indebted to Richard Wagner

16 See Bettelheim 2001.
17 Karl Kraus remarked that psychoanalysis was "the disease for which it takes itself to be the cure" (*Die Fackel*, 376/377, 30 May 1913, p. 21), quoted in Rée 2019, p. 518. Rée suggested the same barbed comment could be applied to the philosophical argument in the *Tractatus* by Wittgenstein, who admired Kraus and would probably have agreed with him.
18 A persuasive case has been made for his indirect influence not only on account of his books and the spread of his ideas internationally, organized by his pupils and collaborators, but also thanks to his nephew Edward Bernays (1891–1995), widely credited as the most important pioneer of public relations and propaganda. The link between his techniques and those of Anna Freud (which were not identical with her father's) were described in a 2002 documentary by Adam Curtis, *The Century of the Self*. See also Malcolm 1984 for a particularly dramatic series of criticisms of Freud's work from within the psychoanalytical tradition.
19 Quoted in Spiel 1987, p. 163.

as well as to Mahler and Richard Strauss, who retreated from his more adventurous music such as the 1909 *Elektra* to compose the nostalgic *Der Rosenkavalier* in 1911 and the most sugary of Vienna ballets, aptly named *Schlagobers* or "Whipped Cream", in 1921. We can trace the development of Schönberg's own style, in the other direction as it were, by comparing his 1899 *Verklärte Nacht* with the *Five Orchestral Pieces* of ten years later and the *Variations for Orchestra* of 1928. *Verklärte Nacht* is an exceptionally romantic programme-piece, following the tale of a woman confessing to her husband that she is pregnant by another man – he forgives her, and the many shifting harmonies of the music are resolved in a shimmering tonal conclusion. The abstract *Five Orchestral Pieces* abandons the conventions of tonality so that the composition is completely free of harmonic discipline and depends for its coherence on identifiable sequences with distinct rhythms and character. The *Variations for Orchestra* completes Schönberg's journey from the sensuous to the stringently intellectual, employing his dodecaphonic technique, whereby key signatures are abandoned and replaced by the composition of a tone row, which uses all 12 notes of the scale and becomes the basis of each piece.[20] It was a system "as pure in its rationality as a house by Adolf Loos".[21] Schorske suggested that Schönberg's music represented a "humanism unfamiliarly mixed with nihilism": Schönberg was a "subverter of the garden of beauty", in favour of a nihilistic wilderness but later showed "to those who could listen . . . how it might be organized in sound to replace the garden he had done so much to destroy". For our purposes, the way in which he felt compelled to seek a new ordering principle, to compensate for the loss of the traditional tonal language that he felt had lost its authority, represents an interesting parallel to the dilemmas architects faced when conventional architectural styles were abandoned and forms could be imagined at will.[22] Bearing in mind psychoanalytical analysis, we can ask ourselves why he *needed* to pursue the path he did: the critic Hans Keller, who was one of the most fervent advocates of Schönberg's music, admitted there was no necessity to abandon tonality.[23]

3.6 Furniture and painting

The garden in Schorske's comment refers to the pervasive vegetative iconography of Art Nouveau. As in Brussels and Barcelona, the sinuous Art Nouveau style found its way into furniture and fabric design. In 1903, partly inspired by the work of the Glaswegian Charles Rennie Mackintosh and the English Arts and Crafts furniture maker Charles Ashbee, the Wiener Werkstätte was founded, and its own furniture was invariably decorated with floral and vegetal motifs. It survived until 1932, with branches in other European cities and in New York, and its influence was substantial. The Art Nouveau manner could be employed for the design of fabrics, furniture and chinaware, making for a consistent appearance in the interior of private houses: the most fully realized being a grand house in Brussels by Josef Hoffmann. Hoffmann was one of Otto Wagner's pupils, had won the Prix de Rome before joining his practice in 1897 and was one of the founders of the Wiener Werkstätte.

20 The serial technique was actually the invention of an untalented composer, Josef Matthias Hauer, who first proposed the idea to Schönberg of a 12-tone series as the basis for composition. Intriguingly, the interior monologue, the *sine qua non* of modernist literary composition, employed by James Joyce and Virginia Woolf, was also invented by an obscure writer, Édouard Dujardin, in his novel *Les lauriers sont coupés*. It is those who are able to make creative use of such inventions who are true geniuses.
21 Schorske 1980, p. 362.
22 This is a comparison that has been frequently made.
23 See Garnham and Woodhouse 2019, p. 347.

24 Schorske 1980, p. 271.
Exhibitions of the work of
Klimt and Schiele, such
as that in London's Royal
Academy in 2018–2019,
reveal the reciprocal influence each had on the other.
25 Alma's affair with
Gropius began in 1910, the
year before Mahler died.
They married in 1915 and
separated four years later.

His marble-clad Palais Stoclet is a *Gesamtkunstwerk* – a total work of art – a concept that may have been derived from the work of the composer Richard Wagner, who had written the librettos for his operas and designed both the stage sets and the theatre in Bayreuth in which they would be performed. That an architect, working with colleagues from various other disciplines, could determine the complete character of a building from its overall form down to its tableware became the ambition for members of the Bauhaus in Germany and also for Nordic architects, as we shall see in Chapter 5 in the case of the Finnish master Alvar Aalto.

In the Dining Room of the Palais Stoclet, the most prominent decorative features were the mosaics by Gustav Klimt. Before he was 30, Klimt had enjoyed huge success for his decorations of theatres on the Ringstrasse in a conventional style, but he was young enough to be identified as one of *Die Jungen*, and, in 1897, to lead the foundation of the *Secession* with its journal *Ver Sacrum*. Klimt's three murals for the University of Vienna, *Philosophy*, *Medicine* and *Jurisprudence*, caused scandal because of their explicit sexuality, but his later work was stylized and self-indulgent: as Schorske puts it he "passed irrevocably from the roles of history, time and struggle to that of aesthetic abstraction and social resignation".[24] The work of Klimt's young friend and rival Egon Schiele (1890–1918) was even more overtly neurotic and sexually explicit, and the expression of neurosis reached a climax in Oskar Kokoschka's 1914 self-portrait showing himself entwined with his lover, Alma Mahler, widow of the composer and briefly wife of the architect Walter Gropius (**Figure 3.6**).[25] To add to these interconnections, we should realize that the composer Arnold Schönberg was also a talented painter (**Figure 3.7**) and that his gifted pupil Alban Berg later dedicated his 1935 violin concerto (widely regarded as the masterpiece of the Second Viennese School) to the memory of Alma's daughter Manon Gropius, who had died of polio.

3.7 Architecture – Wagner and Loos

Having seen some aspects of the complex interrelations between the arts in Vienna, we can return to the question of architecture as a further example, and in particular to a comparison between the positions of Otto Wagner and Adolf Loos, as revealed in their writings and their buildings. We already saw how Wagner apparently embraced a modernist philosophy in his planning principles, yet began his career designing in an overtly classical manner. And we also saw Wagner's role in helping to set up the Vienna *Secession*. Its exhibition building is another illustration of how the lives of all the individuals in the city of Vienna were interconnected (**Figure 3.8**). It was funded by Karl Wittgenstein, father of the philosopher Ludwig and paterfamilias of the second wealthiest family in Vienna. The architect was one of Wagner's pupils, J.M. Olbrich, who created a flexible interior space that could house the erotic masterpieces of artists like Gustav Klimt. Externally it was decorated with gilded foliage and inscriptions.

Figure 3.6 Oskar Kokoschka: portrait of himself and Alma Mahler

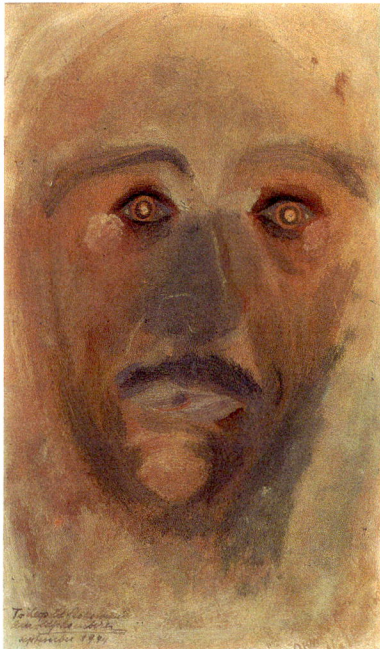

Figure 3.7 Arnold Schönberg: self-portrait

Figure 3.8 J.M. Olbrich: front façade of Vienna Secession building, 1897

Wagner's 1898–1899 apartment buildings, such as the three well-known Linke Wienzeile Buildings, of which the Majolica House, number 48, is the most famous, dramatize the separation of functions (commerce below, living above) but decorate the flat façades with foliage: the clearest and most florid demonstration in Vienna of the widespread Art Nouveau project to soften the effect of urban speculation by vegetation (**Figure 3.9**). The interiors, as in the hôtels of his Belgian contemporary Victor Horta and Hoffmann's Palais Stoclet, carry the sinuous decorative motifs into details such as the staircase balustrades and lift enclosures. Wagner's later work is more overtly functional and less decorative. At Steinhof, just outside Vienna, he provided the master plan for a psychiatric hospital though he had no hand in its buildings except for the Church of St Leopold. As Leopold Bauer pointed out, in the address he gave at Wagner's funeral, the genesis of the design was classical, not romantic:

> Absolutely foreign to Wagner was the mystical element of architecture. His architecture completely dispensed with the manipulation of mood; the mysterious consecration of medieval church rooms, the confusing web of Gothic tracery, the wonderful surfaces of high steep church roofs – this was a chapter of art for which the master had little understanding. I know from his own mouth that he never felt comfortable in Gothic churches, and he often criticized such buildings in an uncomfortable way.[26]

26 Bauer 1919, author's translation.

Figure 3.9 Otto Wagner: Majolikahaus (left), junction with Linke Wienzeile building, 1898–99

But classic sensibility was modulated by a close concern for functional considerations: the floor was slightly sloped so the congregation could get a better view, surfaces were hygienic and easily cleaned and the luminous character of the space is achieved by the generous light that floods the building through high-level clear glass windows, supplemented by limited decorative elements – the gilded cupola over the altar, which reflects the form of the dome above, and stained glass by Koloman Moser.[27]

Wagner's 1904–1906 Postal Savings Bank, located on the Ringstrasse, illustrates his mature style: the granite and marble external cladding is anchored by visible aluminium bolts, as it had been at Steinhof, which with some figures on the skyline constitute the decoration (**Figure 3.10**). It is a hybrid structure: a concrete frame but with load-bearing external walls.[28] Inside the main top-lit hall there is no decoration, the effect being solely dependent on the tasteful proportioning of functional elements, such as the glass-block floors, the free-standing hot air outlets and the elegant furniture designed especially for the building (**Figure 3.11**, **Figure 3.12**, **Figure 3.13**). In his funeral address quoted earlier, Leopold Bauer was disconcerted by Wagner's progressive abandonment of classical motifs, and particularly by his teaching to that effect, because lesser talents, without a background in designing within the discipline of classicism, could take that teaching to heart and produce a lifeless abstraction.

27 Wagner's decorative effects can appear to reflect a quasi-Byzantine character.
28 The visible aluminium-capped bolts are therefore locating devices and predominantly decorative, or illustrative, because the profiled granite is bonded to the wall by cement.

**Figure 3.10 Otto
Wagner: Postal Savings
Bank 1904–1906, cut-
away elevation and
section**

Figure 3.11 Otto Wagner: Postal Savings Bank, 1904–1906, main staircase

Figure 3.12 Otto Wagner: Postal Savings Bank, 1904–1906, post hall with glazed roof and glass block floor

Wagner is one of many architects whose work illustrates such a progression and also one whose written polemics often contrast with his practice. By accommodating himself to changing fashions he certainly continued to attract commissions. In his *Die Grossstadt* (*Metropolis*) of 1911, as we saw, Wagner had proposed modular suburban districts with

**Figure 3.13 Otto
Wagner: Postal Savings
Bank, 1904–1906, stool**

a regular grid of streets, even if the neighbourhood's character would presumably be modulated and decorated by consumerist glitter. His final completed project, the Neustiftgasse 40 apartment block (1909–1910), in which he occupied an apartment himself, appears thoroughly abstract and modern. Decoration is confined to some black glazed tiling, but it still exhibits Wagner's classically-derived compositional skill and fastidious attention to detail (**Figure 3.14**). Wagner continued to teach until retiring in 1912; amongst his last pupils was Rudolph Schindler (1887–1953) who emigrated to California and, along with Richard Neutra (1892–1970), who had also studied in Vienna, brought European ideas into the West Coast modernism that Wright had already helped to forge.[29]

Adolf Loos (1870–1933), nearly 30 years younger than Wagner, was an architect of a different persuasion. Although he admired Wagner's skill, he could not accept the lack of principle that he felt Wagner's domestic work exhibited. His own practice mostly depended on private houses, and he believed a dwelling was not a work of art: it was more like a domestic utensil or useful object. There was a difference, moreover, between the inside and the outside. This is the philosophy expressed in Loos' notorious satirical essay *Ornament and Crime*: only the bodies of savages and prisoners are defaced by tattoos.[30] Loos acknowledged that one of the purposes of art was to challenge accepted conventions and

29 In 1969, Neutra provided an appreciative Foreword to a well-illustrated book on Wagner, originally published in Salzburg and translated into English in Geretsegger and Peintner 1979.

30 Loos 2019.

Figure 3.14 Otto Wagner: Neustiftgasse Apartments, 1909–1910, perspective drawing

discomfort people; Kokoschka's paintings could therefore be entirely personal, raw and sensuous. But the purpose of architecture, particularly domestic architecture, was precisely the reverse: it should promote comfort, above all, which could be provided, or even 'celebrated', by fine materials lining the walls, by cozy ingle-nook fireplaces (as in the English Arts and Crafts houses he admired) and by personal belongings like paintings (**Figure 3.15**). But the outside had nothing to say: architects such as Wagner, who decorated their apartment blocks with vegetation, trivialized the discipline, and (in Karl Kraus' terms) confused the urn with the chamber pot. The mechanistic functionalism of Gropius' Bauhaus, discussed in the next chapter, would prove equally inappropriate to Loos and here a remark by Schönberg in 1928 is revealing:

> I can't complain, not everything has gone badly for me. Not only have I always had as friends men like Adolf Loos, but I have always had as enemies men like Walter Gropius.[31]

Adolf Loos' concern above all was to fashion an authentic 'culture' of architecture. Just as Schönberg attempted in music, he wanted to compensate for the loss of a traditional language that had lost its authority.

Loos' houses of the 1920s have complicated three-dimensional interlocking spaces but externally they are quite mute (**Figure 3.16**). Windows

31 Arnold Schönberg, *Aphorismen, Anekdoten, Sprächte: Texte zu Kanous*, Vienna 1928, quoted in Gravagnuolo 1982, p. 78.

Figure 3.15   Adolf Loos: Müller House, Prague, 1929, upper sitting room recess

Figure 3.16   Adolf Loos: Moller House, Vienna, street view

are simple openings in walls, and his houses have nothing comparable to the Corbusian planar free plan with its emphasis on the tectonic
expression of the frame.[32] The interior volumes interlock on half and
quarter levels and are therefore difficult to read on a plan (**Figure 3.17**),
establishing subtle relationships between small, interconnected areas
that overlook each other.[33] For public buildings he was less strict. Loos'
1909–1911 building on Michaelerplatz distinguishes between the finely
clad commercial premises for Goldman and Salatsch (**Figure 3.18**)
and the apartments with their undecorated window surrounds above –
though he was compelled by the authorities to add window boxes.
Like his writings, however, some of his projects are highly ironic: his
competition entry in 1922 for the *Tribune* newspaper office in Chicago
caricatured American capitalist hubris by fashioning the whole building
as a gigantic Doric column (**Figure 3.19**).

By contrast, Wagner's work is never ironic. Its decorative effects, both
inside and out, are mostly achieved by elaborating on the construction
and environmental mechanisms of his buildings, as is evident in the
beautiful handling of material from the heaviest engineering elements
to the lightest metal roofs of his Lock Keeper's house (**Figure 3.20**,

32 See Risselada 1988. This
book, which originated as an
exhibition at the Univer-
sity of Delft in 1987, has a
number of excellent essays
comparing the work of Loos
and Le Corbusier.
33 See Beatriz Colomina,
"The Split Wall: Domestic
Voyeurism", in Colomina
1992.

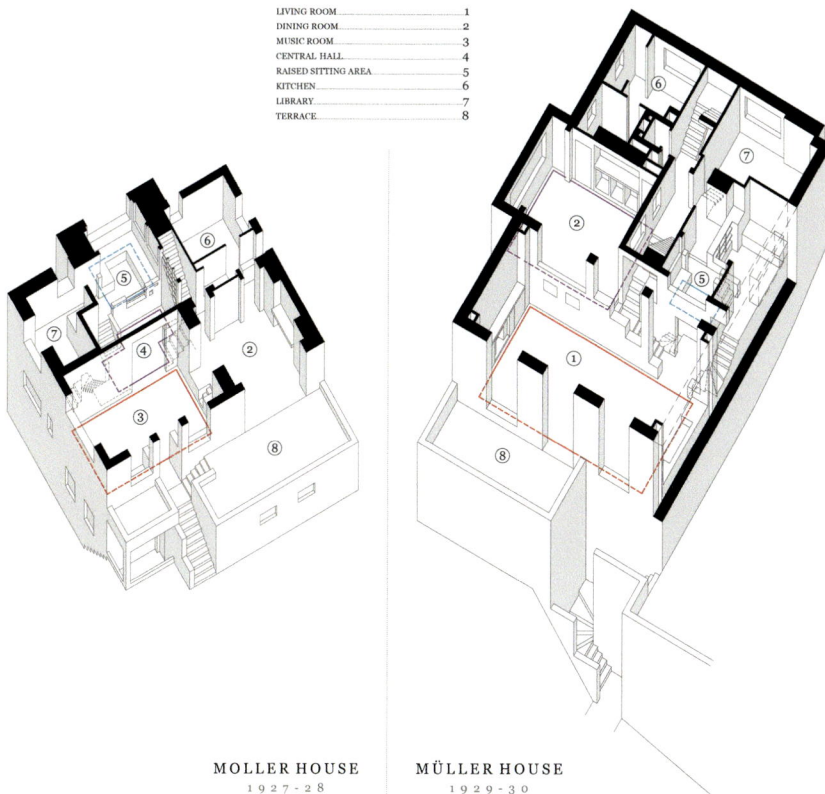

LIVING ROOM	1
DINING ROOM	2
MUSIC ROOM	3
CENTRAL HALL	4
RAISED SITTING AREA	5
KITCHEN	6
LIBRARY	7
TERRACE	8

MOLLER HOUSE
1927-28

MÜLLER HOUSE
1929-30

**Figure 3.17 Adolf Loos: Moller House, Vienna and Müller House, Prague,
axonometrics**

Figure 3.18 Adolf Loos: Goldman & Salatsch building, Michaelerplatz, Vienna, 1910

Figure 3.19 Adolf Loos:
***Chicago Tribune* Tower**
competition entry

Figure 3.21) or the panelled walls of his stations or indeed at the sophisticated Postal Savings Bank. Yet in one respect the attitudes of Wagner and Loos to decoration was not so dissimilar. The aesthetic theory behind Wagner's use of decoration is often ascribed to Alois Riegl (1858–1905). Alan Colquhoun summarizes his theory as follows:

Figure 3.20 Otto Wagner: Lock Keeper's house, view across the lock

Figure 3.21 Otto Wagner: Lock Keeper's house, detail of metalwork, Vienna

According to Riegl, the decorative arts were the origin of all artistic expression. Art was rooted in indigenous culture, not derived from universal natural law. This idea ... stood in stark contrast to the idea (derived from the Enlightenment) that architecture should align itself with progress, science, and the Cartesian spirit.[34]

34 Colquhoun 2002, p. 27. Riegl was also an influential champion of Expressionism, arguing that art, to be true to its age, should not strive to be beautiful but to express the inner life of its subjects.

35 Semper 1989.
36 See Semper 2004; Mall-
grave 2018.

Here another figure is important: the German architect Gottfried Sem-
per, already mentioned as the architect, at the end of his life, of the
Burgplatz project on the Ringstrasse, was admired by both Sitte and
Wagner. Semper suggested that the fundamental components of architecture were the hearth, an earthwork or mound, a framework (which
includes the roof) and finally an enclosing membrane (**Figure 3.22**).
The wall can be conceived of as originally non-load-bearing fabric:
"The beginning of building coincides with the beginning of textiles".[35]
Semper's approach is anthropological as much as architectural: he is
interested in the customs and rituals of former civilizations which had
developed the sophisticated decorative patterns that he, along with so
many others, had admired at the 1851 Great Exhibition, held in Paxton's
Crystal Palace.[36] The end of the nineteenth century saw not only the
birth of anthropology, but also of sociology, in the figure of Max Weber
(1864–1920); both these disciplines use a dispassionate analysis of society's customs and hypothesize theoretical frameworks to account for the
phenomena that have been observed and recorded. Weber was friends
with many architects and visited the artistic settlement Hellerau. He was
troubled by the subsequent rationalization of architecture as a purely
technical discipline, which he saw as symptomatic of a society that was
increasingly secular and in danger of being dominated by the unstopp-
able forces of capitalism. This is a critique that continues to be levelled

**Figure 3.22 Gottfried
Semper: *Style in the
Technical or Tectonic
Arts or Practical
Aesthetics*, 1860–1863,
Indian hut from
Trinidad**

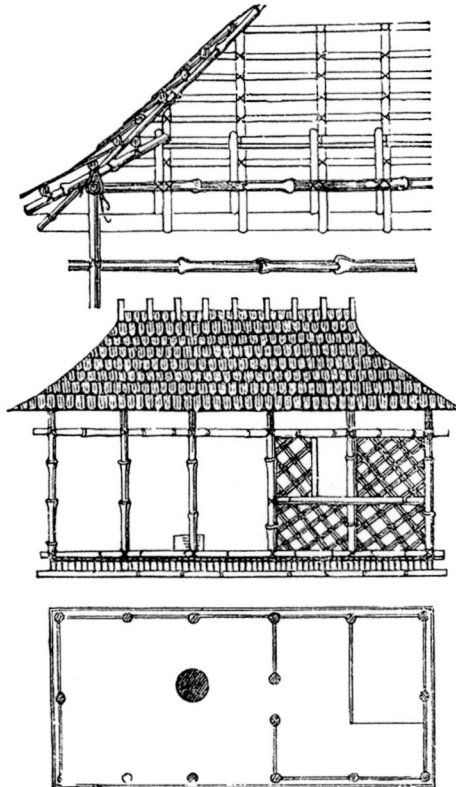

by those disciplines on the work of architects, which displays all too clearly the social context within which their buildings are constructed.

Semper's theories of the origins of architecture allow for appropriate decoration. In this respect, Wagner and Loos are united in following a Semperian theory though they clearly disagree as to the propriety of decoration – what it is appropriate to say.[37] Such a notion contrasts with the moral idea that Enlightenment neo-classicism had embraced, where decoration is suspect per se. That strand of theory, following Laugier and illustrated in the work of architects such as the nineteenth-century theorist Eugène Viollet-le-Duc, expounded the primacy of the tectonic (albeit from a Gothic position, as we saw in Chapter 2) and was in turn inherited by Le Corbusier. In the mid-twentieth century, the tectonic idea lies behind ethical reasoning for styles such as 1960s Brutalism. If Laugier's tectonic frame or aedicule[38] is the origin of architecture, then its articulate and truthful expression must be the aim of architects; if, on the other hand, Riegl and Semper are to be believed, the expressive task is somewhat more complex. Architects can enjoy the display of 'fictive structure', as Alberti had in his Palazzo Rucellai, and the express-ive and decorative hierarchy of materials in works like Wagner's Lock Keeper's House or the Post Office where the stone is expressed as a drape (**Figure 3.23**). The question Loos raises is: when is it proper to do so?[39]

3.8 Relevance

At an architectural level, in the later twentieth century there was a com-pelling technical reason for a revived interest in someone like Semper and the interpretation of his ideas in building: increasingly, cladding had to be seen as separate from structure. This is because much higher

37 Loos' essay *The Principle of Cladding* elaborates on his position; his subtle theory allows for a proper respect for tradition, but also, in the right context, a radically modern expression. See Loos 1988.

38 Literally: a little house. Roman shrines and Gothic altarpieces, which are sym-metrical framed structures can be seen as miniature versions of a domestic space.

39 Ed Ford expressed their difference well: "It was Wag-ner who saw the potential of a theory of cladding in the modern era, it was Adolf Loos who saw its dangers. And if Wagner recognised that modern processes of building made possible a language of architecture that was largely analogous and symbolic in expression of structure, Loos recognised that it made possible a lan-guage of Kitsch" (Ford 1990, p. 225).

Figure 3.23 Otto Wagner: Postal Savings Bank, 1904–1906, stone expressed as cladding fixed to a frame

degrees of thermal insulation were required, and it was foolish to expend fossil fuels by heating space inefficiently. Building regulations in most countries with cold climates began to proscribe 'cold bridges', or fabric that connects inside and outside. Walls then are perforce skins, which can be decorated or not according to taste. Semper's theory of representation or some variation of it, such as that which Loos attempted in *The Principle of Cladding*, necessarily became more influential than that of Laugier.

At a philosophical level, the rupture with nineteenth-century culture that *Fin-de-siècle* Vienna exhibits continues to fascinate us. We recall the thinking of Friedrich Nietzsche who believed that art was uniquely capable of helping us render "the terror and horror of existence" bearable and anticipated Freud in seeing art as a sublimation, a socially acceptable way of expressing the primitive urges that individuals need to repress in order to participate in society. Such melancholy has not lost its relevance in our own times. At any rate, we are compelled in each generation to reassess our position in relation to the authority of inherited traditions, the role of invention within our culture, and whether individuals, with their acknowledged neuroses, can feel at home in an ever more complex world. Vienna, a city with a uniquely rich historical and cultural history, could be said to provide particularly expressive answers to the ethical question raised earlier: the reconciliation between romantic subjectivism and the objectivity and dispassion that is central to the scientific attitude. In addressing the problem of the Enlightenment split, *Fin-de-siècle* Vienna displays artistic expressions that range from the trivial to the profound and attitudes from the idealistically optimistic to the deeply melancholic. This is evident in all aspects of its culture, from music to philosophy, from psychoanalysis to painting. Its architects revealed their positions from the scale of the city to the scale of an aluminium bolt.

4

THE MODERNIST CANON

The Bauhaus, Le Corbusier and CIAM

The two figures who dominate the discussion in this chapter, Walter Gropius and Le Corbusier, are treated in some detail because they were, in different ways, the most influential voices in early modernism and are frequently invoked in subsequent debates for and against what they stood for – or have been accused of standing for. Needless to say, there were many talented and skilful architects practising during the period whose reputations have fluctuated.[1] There were also energetic modernist movements in other countries – Futurism in Italy and Constructivism in Russia. Some of their principal participants migrated to the Bauhaus, however, and both Gropius and Le Corbusier absorbed much of the thinking and the formal inventions associated with these movements. The chapter concludes with examples of European and American university campus design to illustrate some of the consequences.

4.1 Gropius and the Bauhaus

Walter Gropius became director in 1919 of the combined Weimar institutes: the *Grossherzogliche Sächsische Kunstgewerbeschule* and the *Grossherzogliche Sächsische Hochschule für Bildende Kunst* (the Saxon Grand Duke's School of Applied Arts and Fine Arts, respectively). He named the resulting multi-disciplinary school the *Staatliche Bauhaus* recalling somewhat the *Bauhutte*, a term used to describe the builders of cathedrals in the Middle Ages. It lasted until 1933 but had a much longer international influence on all aspects of design. The Bauhaus, as it quickly came to be known, aimed to teach all the crafts of which the culmination was architecture, though architecture itself did not figure in the curriculum until 1927, only a few months before Gropius ceased to be its director. During those eight years, he ran the school in parallel with his private practice in partnership with Adolf Meyer, and its buildings were presented as illustrative of the school's architectural ideals.

Even over that brief period of Gropius' headship the focus of the school shifted markedly, as is also evident in the buildings emerging from his office; one of the first was a thoroughly folk-inspired building constructed of logs, the Sommerfeld House (**Figure 4.1**). The first sentence of the April 1919 *Bauhaus Manifesto* read "The ultimate goal of all arts is the building!" and it went on:

> Architects, sculptors, painters, we all must return to the crafts! For art is not a "profession." There is no essential difference between

1 Two of the many who are now receiving long overdue attention are the Munich architect Hans Döllgast and Fernand Pouillon in France, both of whom were more cautious aesthetically than those who were influenced by Le Corbusier or the Bauhaus but whose best work is in some respects exemplary.

DOI: 10.4324/9781003244943-5

Figure 4.1 Walter Gropius and Adolf Meyer: Sommerfeld Haus, 1920–1922

Figure 4.1 Walter Gropius and Adolf Meyer: Sommerfeld Haus, 1920–1922

Figure 4.2 Lyonel Feininger: image for the cover of the *Bauhaus Manifesto*, 1919

Figure 4.2 Lyonel Feininger: image for the cover of the *Bauhaus Manifesto*, 1919

the artist and the craftsman. The artist is an exalted craftsman. . . . Together let us desire, conceive, and create the new structure of the future, which will embrace architecture and sculpture and painting in one unity and which will one day rise toward heaven from the hands of a million workers like the crystal symbol of a new faith.

The manifesto's cover, by Lyonel Feininger, one of the first Bauhaus teachers, illustrated this "crystal symbol of a new faith" with a shattered image that simultaneously reflected the modernist techniques of cubism, evoked a Gothic cathedral spire and expressed an evident excitement at future prospects (**Figure 4.2**). It echoed the tone of the more polemical texts of avant-garde movements elsewhere in Europe, such as the Futurists in Italy before the First World War. But the vision conveyed both graphically and in the text was thoroughly romantic, and there was no mention of the effect that the machine might have on architecture and design.

The celebrated "Bauhaus Vorkurs" (introductory course) taught by Johannes Itten (1888–1967) introduced students to elementary principles of form and colour theory based on principles that were entirely abstract, though by no means objective. Itten was inclined towards mysticism and influenced by Zoroastrianism. Indeed the theories that lay behind Bauhaus teaching varied considerably, depending on who was doing the teaching. Itten had invited the Swiss artist Paul Klee (1879–1940) to join the faculty, and he remained there for ten years. He was as mystical, in his own way, as Itten, as we can see in the notebooks that record his teaching, but he was also adept at translating his personal perceptions into principles that could be communicated to his students.[2]

By 1922–1923, the school's ethos had shifted, largely as a result of the influence of new staff and Itten's resignation. László Moholy-Nagy had taken over the Vorkurs and the emphasis was on what was called the 'new objectivity' (*Neue Sachlichkeit*), reflecting an artistic movement that was a reaction to more overt romantic expressionism, though the *Neue Sachlichkeit* itself contained members of different persuasions. The Russian painter Wassily Kandinsky, whose work was moving from a free-form abstract and expressionistic style towards something much more precise and mechanical, and the Dutch artist Theo van Doesburg, a friend of Piet Mondrian, the most austerely abstract painter of the *De Stijl* movement, had joined the faculty.[3] And in 1923 Gropius, who was now engaged in negotiations with representatives of German industry, declared, "we want an architecture adapted to our world of machines, radios and fast cars".[4] In 1925 the school moved from Weimar, where it had occupied the van der Velde designed studios, to a new purpose-built complex in Dessau designed by Gropius' practice (**Figure 4.3**). It is a careful abstract composition, making full use of the most recent industrially produced components.[5] Gropius invited the left-wing Hannes Meyer to teach at the school, and he was to inaugurate the architecture programme and to succeed Gropius as head of the school when he resigned early in 1928. Meyer furthered the connections with industry and built within the city of Dessau, but, as an extreme functionalist, dismissed members of staff who still clung to aesthetic ideals – in Chapter 1 we already saw his justification of his League of Nations competition. Meyer was deposed in 1930, and in 1931 the Nazi party, by now in control of Dessau city council, shut the school there. It had a brief afterlife under its new head, Mies van der Rohe, in Berlin before finally closing in 1933.[6] But its influence lived on.

4.2 Gropius' later career

Walter Gropius' particular genius was his ability to hold together a group of extraordinarily talented individuals and allow them to flourish in extreme economic and political times. It is astonishing that he was

2 See Klee 1961.
3 Van Doesburg was a complex character since he also participated in Dadaism. See Joseph Rykwert's essay "The Dark Side of the Bauhaus" in Rykwert 1982.
4 Quoted in Curtis 1982.
5 Typically for its time, it took little account of environmental comfort or energy usage. The fully-glazed workshops were particularly problematic: see Barber 2020.
6 Mies' particular form of idealism and its influence on his architecture deserves a much fuller treatment for which there is inadequate space here. See an illuminating discussion of his Villa Tugendhat in Düchs 2021.

Figure 4.3 Walter Gropius and Adolf Meyer: Bauhaus building, Dessau, 1925, view

7 Colin Rowe was particularly scathing: "The persistence of the mystique of Walter Gropius is very hard to understand. For, as both architect and educator, Gropius was surely inept. With the Bauhaus almost a symbol of the Weimar Republic, he came to the United States as the widely advertised emancipator. Not only here but in Europe it was supposed that Gropius was a supreme Moses-figure, preparing and illuminating the way, but then when the way turned out to be no more than relentless kitsch catastrophe, the mystique still survived and it continues to plague architectural education to this day" (Letter to Roger Conover, November 1982, in Rowe 2016).

8 Gropius 1935.

9 The Nazis had accused the Bauhaus of 'cultural bolshevism'. Perhaps more relevantly, Gropius had married the Jewish Ilse Frank in 1923, and from early 1933 persecution of the Jews intensified.

able to keep the whole enterprise afloat. In the subsequent diaspora, many of them went on to teach and thereby influenced the education of artists, designers and architects worldwide. A version of Bauhaus teaching became the orthodoxy that everywhere superseded that of the Beaux-Arts. As a designer, Gropius is not highly regarded by architects in general: nearly all of his buildings were as a result of collaboration with others and (partly because he did not draw himself but invariably used his colleagues' work to illustrate his ideas) it is difficult to pin down his personal contribution.[7] In this, he could hardly present a greater contrast to Le Corbusier, who divided his time between painting and architecture. But Gropius also offered his thoughts on the aims of the Bauhaus in a book published in 1935 entitled *The New Architecture and the Bauhaus*.[8] He had fled Hitler's Germany in 1933[9] and was in North London, living at Lawn Road, one of the few Bauhaus-inspired blocks of flats in the United Kingdom, and in practice with Maxwell Fry. It was mainly Jack Pritchard, responsible for the development of Lawn Road, and his friends Herbert Read, Philip Morton Shand (translator of his book) and Frank Pick (who provided the Introduction) who had persuaded him to write it. *The New Architecture and the Bauhaus* was widely praised when it appeared, cementing Gropius' reputation as one of the key figures in international modernism.

In his book, Gropius went out of his way to explain that what was important at the Bauhaus was its approach. It was the Bauhaus' concentration on the design of technical products, he wrote, that "gave rise to the erro-neous idea that the Bauhaus had set itself up as the apotheosis of ration-alism".[10] It was more concerned with "the intellectual purpose" of art "at the focal point where civilization and culture meet". The basic uni-formity of the designs that emerged was therefore the result of a com-mon intellectual outlook not an imaginary Bauhaus style. Importantly, Gropius explained that in the Vorkurs, "The first task was to liberate the pupil's individuality from the dead weight of conventions". As we shall see, the idea that historical precedents could be completely ignored in teaching design, and that individual students' imaginative experiences should be evacuated, was one of the principal aspects of Bauhaus teach-ing that was to come under attack.[11]

Gropius failed to find substantial patronage in Britain and in 1938 emi-grated to America, where he had been invited to become the Chair of the Graduate School of Design at Harvard. It was rumoured that all of the books in the library relating to architectural history were removed in preparation for his arrival. He practised within TAC (The Architects Collaborative): their many buildings included the 1957–1969 develop-ment plan for the University of Baghdad (**Figure 4.4**). With Pietro Bel-luschi and Emery Roth he was also responsible for the insensitive 1963 Pan Am Building in New York. More influential was his teaching: his pupils were of the generation of American modernist architects who went on to build worldwide; perhaps foremost amongst them was the Chinese-American architect I.M. Pei (1917–2019).

In 1956, Gropius' Charles Eliot Norton lectures were collected to form his second book *The Scope of Total Architecture*.[12] Much of the mat-erial repeated topics (and sometimes even sentences) from *The New Architecture and the Bauhaus*. Some of the themes were new, however, and related to contemporary American practice: he deplored the low

10 Gropius 1935, p. 60.
11 Gropius 1935, p. 47. On pp. 52–53, however, he acknowledges that in music there does seem to be room for understanding some previous formal conventions: "Even today a knowledge of counterpoint is essential to a musical composer".
12 Gropius 1956.

Figure 4.4 Walter Gropius and The Architects Collaborative: Baghdad University masterplan

13 Gropius 1956, pp. 117–130, "Houses, walk-ups or High-Rise Apartment Blocks?"

salaries of architects, for instance, and clients' preference for package deals that might not involve architects at all. But other chapters suggested Gropius' thinking had not moved on: that on housing referred to his pre-war research into the optimum distances of slab blocks and how these could be determined by light angles. Acknowledging that the results had not always met with public approval, he wrote "only practice can conquer the prevailing mentality, and we must fight in all countries in favour of the construction of high-rise apartment blocks". Historically, he explained, legal codes had been necessary to get rid of the "terrible light-well apartments of the late nineteenth century", which in turn needed to be updated to encourage parallel rows of apartment blocks and avoid "unsatisfactory corner solutions, with overshadowed apartments". But he added in a footnote: "we have progressed today to a much more unorthodox and varied grouping . . . the optimum of orientation has to be compromised sometimes to avoid dull regularity at all costs".[13] In a similar way, he described a problem in the development at Harvard Yard, on which his practice TAC was engaged, where the context demanded some kind of courtyard formation (**Figure 4.5**). It was essential that the blocks should be made of "repetitive standard parts", but he explained that TAC "strove to break the monotony which might have resulted from repetitive fenestration by changing the direction of the dormitory blocks as well as the design of their ends and links". Gropius possessed neither the natural compositional fluency of an architect like Otto Wagner nor the rigorous intellectual capacity of Adolf Loos; although he realized that some kind of softening of the logic of modernism was required, he was unable to explain what principles would be brought to bear in order to achieve this. As we shall see, it was this kind of uncertainty in the thinking of one of the most prominent representatives of modernism that led to stringent critiques of the following decades, which questioned the very premises on which the modern movement had relied.

Figure 4.5 Walter Gropius and The Architects Collaborative: extensions to Harvard Yard

4.3 Le Corbusier

Le Corbusier was born Charles-Édouard Jeanneret in 1887 and brought up in La Chaux de Fonds, a provincial town in Switzerland, where his inspiring art teacher introduced him to Ruskin's work and encouraged his study of nature. Highly talented and ambitious, he believed himself destined for greatness, which is why, after extensive travel in his twenties, he moved permanently to Paris in 1917, the European city with the liveliest artistic culture. He worked there with the painter Amédée Ozenfant, jointly editing a magazine called *L'Ésprit Nouveau*, and producing 'purist' paintings.[14] Purism, the movement they founded, represented a retreat from the extreme experiments of Picasso and Braque's cubism, where forms are shattered and disaggregated, by using clear outlines and profiles of engineering projections as the basis for the flattened forms that appear in their still lives. Le Corbusier's architecture, which in Switzerland had begun with villas in an Arts and Crafts manner, was similarly purged of romantic associations. It was not that he was unable to absorb exotic influences, such as those he had encountered in his travels through Europe and the Middle East, but he possessed the ability to distil them, abstract them and make them his own.[15] A brief stint working with Peter Behrens in Germany had taught him what he needed to know about rationalized product design, and with Auguste Perret in France he had learnt the potential of concrete. His Parisian architectural practice was established initially by building studios and apartments for the artistic community, where he was able to experiment with new materials and the aesthetic that he believed those materials demanded.[16]

Le Corbusier collected his own articles from *L'Ésprit Nouveau* into a volume entitled *Vers une Architecture* – translated into English by Frederick Etchells as *Towards a New Architecture* – which became the most influential piece of propaganda for architectural modernism in the twentieth century.[17] It is by no means a straightforward polemic, and it is easy to misinterpret its message by selective quotation. At a certain point, for example, he declares "a house is a machine for living in",[18] and he frequently draws the attention of his readers to the dispassionate analysis undertaken by engineers and to the products of technology from aeroplanes to ocean liners and grain silos.[19] So he can be accused of a thoroughly mechanistic positivism. Elsewhere he makes it clear that such objective analysis of the changed conditions of the twentieth century is only the starting point:

> Finally, it will be a delight to talk of ARCHITECTURE after so many grain-stores, workshops, machines and skyscrapers. ARCHITECTURE is a thing of art, a phenomenon of the emotions, lying outside questions of construction and beyond them. The purpose of construction is to HOLD THINGS TOGETHER; of architecture TO MOVE US.[20]

His message, in a nutshell, was first that architects had to acknowledge the profound social, economic and technical changes that had

14 See http://arti.sba. uniroma3.it/esprit/. It was Ozenfant who suggested the pseudonym Le Corbusier. In his many writings, Le Corbusier consistently refers to himself in the third person, using this name.

15 For William Curtis, this is the principal quality of Le Corbusier's genius. See Curtis 1992.

16 Le Corbusier's cousin, Pierre Jeanneret, who had much more practical knowledge of construction, worked with him intermittently from the office's foundation in 1922.

17 Le Corbusier 1923, 1946. The British architect Denys Lasdun would not have been alone in his claim to know the book off by heart.

18 Le Corbusier 1946, p. 89.

19 He was by no means original in his choice of grain silos: Gropius had illustrated them in a lecture in 1911 on "Monumental Art and Industrial Building". What distinguished Le Corbusier's book was its forceful propagandistic expression and wide circulation.

20 Le Corbusier 1946, p. 23. The capitalization is typical of the emphatic tone of the book, where key points are hammered home in brief summaries at the start of each section.

21 The *Philebus* is one of
Plato's last dialogues, in
which pure forms symbolize
the highest ideals. For the
thesis that Le Corbusier's
forms were influenced by
the simplified geometries of
French neo-classicism, see
Kaufmann 1933.
22 Jencks 1987 argues for
this interpretation of Le
Corbusier.

taken place and could not afford to play games with inherited styles
that no longer made any sense. But then a 'recall to order' (*rapell
à l'ordre*) was required: the new purified forms had to be manipulated by people with aesthetic sensibility – architects, who at root
are artists even if they deal with buildings or whole parts of cities,
rather than with the arrangement of objects on a table as painters
do. Philosophically, we could claim that Le Corbusier was an
idealist – he frequently appeals to mathematics, for instance, and the
Platonic pure forms of the Phileban solids.[21] At the same time, he
viewed himself, in a way that Nietzsche would have recognized, as
one who was tragically destined to fulfil the destiny of those who, in
the absence of a deity to whom we can all subscribe, have the highest
duty, namely to create the great works of art of their time.[22] In relation to providing exquisite houses and private institutions for the
rich, such a philosophy served him well, and his masterpieces are as
moving as any in the period; at the scale of the city, the consequences
could be catastrophic.

4.4 The inherited problem of the city

As we saw in Chapter 2, the conditions inherited by those who wished to
address the problems of cities were appalling. Even before the invention
of the motorcar, cities had become congested with traffic of all kinds
mixing with people and children; sewage treatment was primitive, and
the gutter was often an open foul drain. In Liverpool and Manchester
and many other manufacturing cities in the United Kingdom, mortality from smallpox, measles, scarlet fever and whooping cough was four
times as high as in the surrounding countryside, and mortality from
convulsions was ten times as high.

We saw that in Britain the reaction to the consequences of the Industrial
Revolution took the form of Ruskin's attack on mechanization and the
medieval Romanticism of William Morris, inspiring the Garden City
movement. In America, the machine was more acceptable: architects in
Chicago developed a new typology – the high-rise office building – in
response to the requirements of the rapidly expanding city and making
full use of technical inventions. It is worth examining Frank Lloyd
Wright's justification for mechanization as potentially liberating in his
important essay of 1901, already mentioned, "The Art and Craft of the
Machine":

> Now let us learn from the Machine. It teaches us that the beauty of
> wood lies first in its qualities as wood; . . . that all woodcarving is apt
> to be a forcing of the material, an insult to its finer possibilities as a
> material having in itself intrinsically artistic properties, of which its
> beautiful markings is one, its texture another, its color a third.
>
> The machine, by its wonderful cutting, shaping, smoothing, and
> repetitive capacity, has made it possible to so use it without waste
> that the poor as well as the rich may enjoy to-day beautiful surface

Figure 4.6 Frank Lloyd Wright: Robie House interior, showing use of machined wood

treatments of clean, strong forms that the branch veneers of Sheraton and Chippendale only hinted at, with dire extravagance, and which the middle ages utterly ignored.

> The machine has emancipated these beauties of nature in wood; made it possible to wipe out the mass of meaningless torture to which wood has been subject[23] (**Figure 4.6**).

Wright's architecture and ideas were to have a major influence in Holland and Germany following the publication of a portfolio of his drawings in 1910 by Ernst Wasmuth. When it came to urban theory, however, Wright, who practised from the leafy Chicago suburb of Oak Park, fully espoused Garden City ideals and was not enamoured of the city's downtown. He worked on a scheme for what he called Broadacre City from 1932 onwards; a model was exhibited three years later, and he continued to elaborate the project until his death in 1959 (**Figure 4.7**). Its extremely low densities prefigured the suburban sprawl that was to become the norm at the periphery of every American city. Movement is entirely by car or private helicopter.

4.5 CIAM's solution to the problems of the city

By contrast, Le Corbusier's vision seems positively urban, although it involved entirely re-casting the idea of a city. His utopian 1922 project for a City for Three Million laid out an idealized Cartesian grid with office towers in the centre around which were housing apartment blocks, and, well separated from the city itself, an industrial quarter (**Figure 4.8**). Le Corbusier believed that earlier cities would necessarily have to adapt in order to survive economically, and this would involve their wholesale redevelopment. It was foolish romanticism to believe otherwise. In the hands of a talented architect, the necessary ruthlessness could approach

23 Wright 1901.

**Figure 4.7 Photograph
of Wright and two
assistants with a model
of Broadacre City**

**Figure 4.8 Le
Corbusier: City for
Three Million, 1922,
aerial perspective of
central towers with
airport**

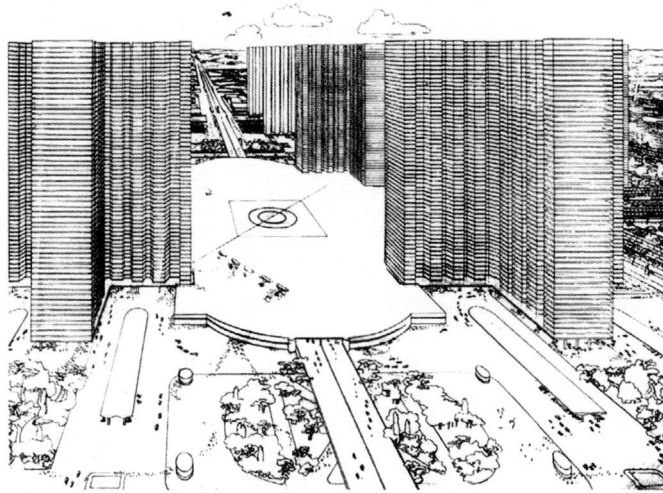

the sublime, as illustrated in his 1925 Voisin Plan for Paris (**Figure 4.9**).
First, here is his criticism of the existing context:

> The definition of the street which has held good up to the present
> day is "a roadway that is usually bordered by pavements, narrow
> or wide as the case may be". Rising straight up from it are walls of
> houses, which when seen against the sky-line present a grotesquely
> jagged silhouette of gables, attics, and zinc chimneys. At the very
> bottom of this scenic railway lies the street, plunged in eternal
> twilight. The sky is a remote hope far, far above it. The street is no more
> than a trench, a deep cleft, a narrow passage. And although we have
> been accustomed to it for more than a thousand years, our hearts are
> always oppressed by the constriction of its enclosing walls.

Figure 4.9 Model
of central Paris with
Le Corbusier's Plan
Voisin proposal
superimposed

In his vision of the new city, the office buildings would be entirely of glass.

> A sheet of glass and three partition-walls make an ideal office: this type of construction holds good when a thousand have to be provided. So from top to bottom the façades of the new city's office-buildings form unbroken expanses of glass. These colossal structures evince no vestige of masonry. All that remains visible is glass . . . and proportion. The architect has discarded brick and stone.

And he concludes:

> What you have just been shown was the city's 'City', its feverishly active business centre. The idea of realizing it in the heart of Paris is no Utopian flight of fancy. There are cold figures to substantiate this thesis. The enormous increase of land-values that must result would yield a profit to the state running into milliards of francs – for to acquire the central part of Paris and redevelop it in accordance with a coordinated plan means the creation of an immense fresh source of wealth.
>
> Then the street as we know it will cease to exist. And the old makeshift expedient of canyon-like cross-roads would no longer be tolerated in residential and dormitory districts.[24]

When Le Corbusier described the idea of a "city of towers" in his 1923 *Vers une Architecture* (**Figure 4.10**), it's instructive that in the caption to an illustration of the sixty-storey cruciform buildings he appears to change his mind about their function:

> A project for Apartments or Flats . . . It is evident such buildings would necessarily be exclusively devoted to business . . . Family life would hardly be at home in them. The figures are terrifying, pitiless but magnificent.[25]

24 Le Corbusier and Jeanneret 1964, pp. 118–119. For a fuller treatment, see Le Corbusier 1987.
25 Le Corbusier 1946.

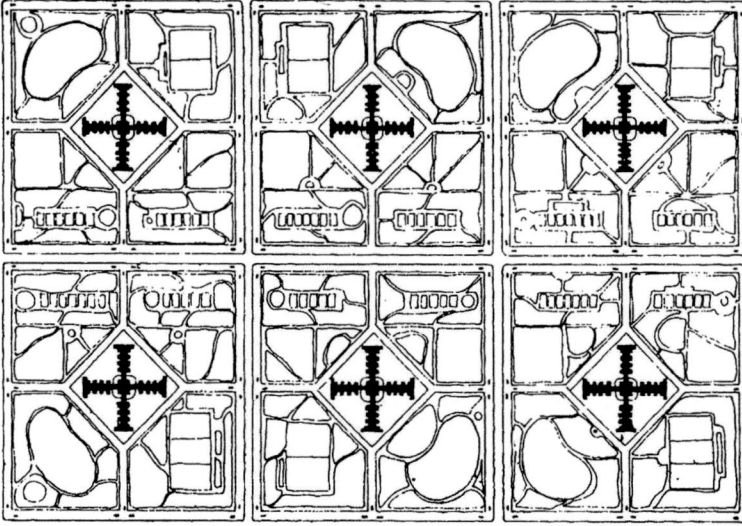

LE CORBUSIER, 1920. A CITY OF TOWERS

A project for Apartments or Flats, built as towers of 60 storeys and rising to a height of 700 feet ; the distance between the towers would be from 250 to 300 yards. The towers would be from 500 to 600 feet through their greatest breadth. In spite of the great area devoted to the surrounding parks, the density of a normal town of to-day is multiplied many times over. It is evident that such buildings would necessarily be devoted exclusively to business offices and that their proper place would therefore be in the centre of great cities, with a view to eliminating the appalling congestion of the main arteries. Family life would hardly be at home in them, with their prodigious mechanism of lifts. The figures are terrifying, pitiless but magnificent : giving each employee a superficial area of 10 sq. yds., a skyscraper 650 feet in breadth would house 40,000 people.

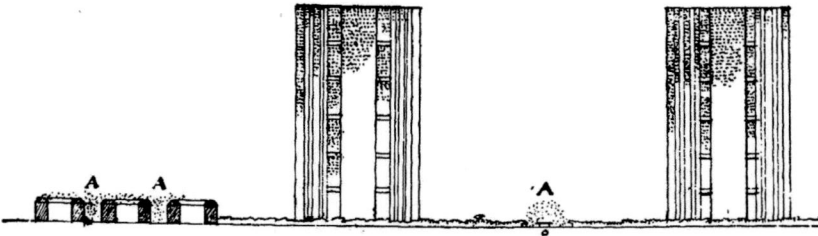

A CITY OF TOWERS

This section shows on the left how dust, smells, and noise stifle our towns of to-day. The towers, on the other hand, are far removed from all this and set in clean air amidst trees and grass. Indeed the whole town is " verdure clad."

Figure 4.10 A page from the English edition of Le Corbusier, *Vers une Architecture*, 1923

Le Corbusier believed architects could meet the "terrifying" architectural challenge offered by the problem of the twentieth-century city and that the result itself could be magnificent, while at the same time admitting that high-rise buildings are not a suitable form for housing families: they would be accommodated in *maisons à redents* – four-storey maisonette blocks "with set-backs". It is therefore unfair to blame Le Corbusier personally (unlike Gropius) for the ubiquitous high-rise housing tower blocks and slabs of the later twentieth century that were designed to accommodate families, even though the accusation is understandable in view of his contradictory polemic. It was not until his later post-war *Unité d'habitation* blocks that he was able to find a form that embedded mixed uses in a high-rise building allowing family housing to be provided above four storeys: the blocks were conceived to be more like ocean liners, with all facilities on board.[26] More problematic is his ready acceptance that architects should treat mass housing, and whole cities, as an aspect of the aesthetic sublime.

Some have argued that Le Corbusier's urban theories were not prescriptions but predictions: this is how cities were going to be in any case, and architects needed to get a handle on how to compose them or the results would be catastrophic. They claim the subsequent phenomenon of urbanization all over the world, most visible first in Japan and then China, justifies that argument. Others would say that it was partly because architects, along with everyone else, were prepared to accept the brute realities – relishing them rather than furnishing an alternative vision of some kind – that we find ourselves in such a position.[27]

In 1933 members of CIAM, the *Congrès Internationaux d'Architecture Moderne*, met on the steamship *Patras II* in Marseilles, and sailed to Athens and back. CIAM was a self-appointed avant-garde of progressive European architects, and this was their fourth meeting. They discussed the idea of the city, and the results of their deliberations were enshrined in a manifesto, the *Charter of Athens*, published ten years later.[28] Le Corbusier was both the dominant influence on board and edited the subsequent publication, which reflected their prescriptions in 95 categorical pronouncements. Number 27 forbade the creation of streets by buildings that would form a line along them; Number 29 advocated high-rise buildings. Number 77 contained an extraordinarily reductive definition of the city as consisting of only three functions – habitation, work and recreation – which would be joined together by circulation, and Number 78 was positively dictatorial in stressing their autonomy. These prescriptions could hardly be called merely predictions.

The influence of CIAM's thinking was considerable and nowhere more than in road engineering. As volumes of traffic increased, techniques were developed to measure anticipated passenger car units quite precisely and plan out the implications of catering for them. The transportation engineer Colin Buchanan's 1963 *Traffic in Towns* showed the consequences of absorbing the motorcar into towns and cities in the United Kingdom (**Figure 4.11**).[29] Kenneth Browne, an artist who worked on *The Architectural Review*, provided the graphic images, illustrating

26 The *Unité* blocks are about six times larger than their most famous British imitations, the slabs at Roehampton West. The first and most famous *Unité*, in Marseilles, is now predominantly occupied by architectural aficionados. It is unfortunately the case that many of Le Corbusier's surviving buildings have become museums of some kind or another to be enjoyed by a select minority who have learnt to appreciate their aesthetic quality.
27 See for instance the many writings of Lewis Mumford (1895–1990), notably Mumford 1961.
28 Le Corbusier 1973.
29 Buchanan 1961.

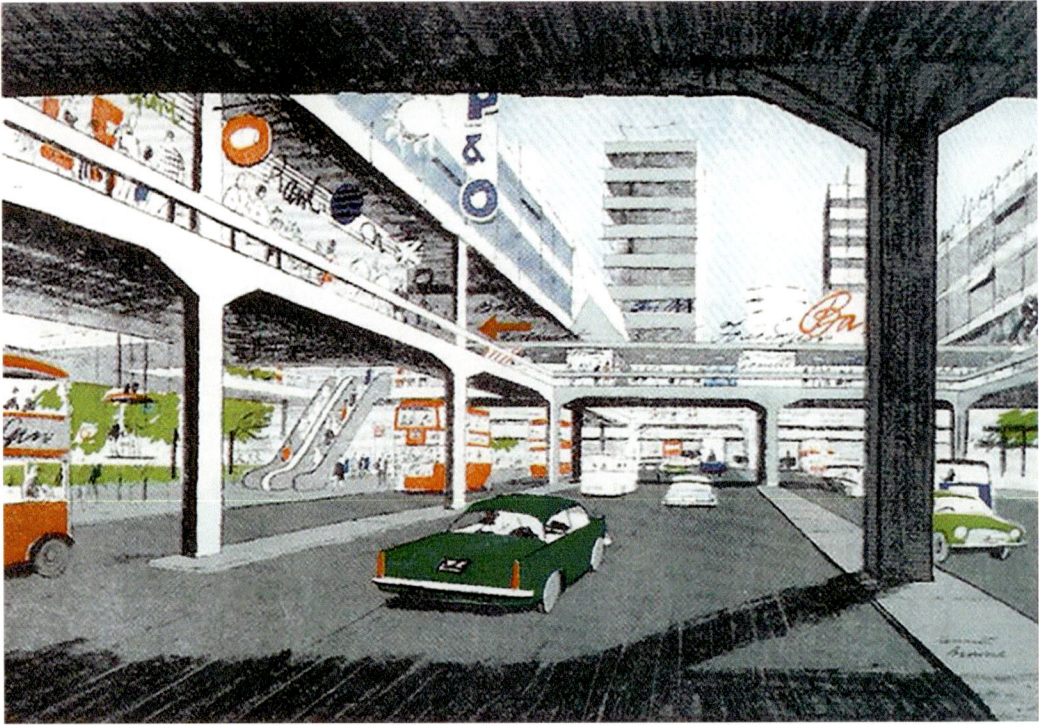

Figure 4.11 Illustration by Kenneth Browne from *Traffic in Towns*, 1963

how pedestrians would be confined to decks and vehicular roads given priority. Buchanan offered a choice: you did not *have* to cater for motor cars. But people were clearly going to. All over Europe similar projects were promoted, although many of them only proceeded a certain way, as the truncated upper-level walkways around the Barbican in the City of London indicate.

4.6 Functional and formal disciplines

Having briefly examined the urban prescriptions of Le Corbusier and CIAM, we can turn to the implications for architectural style. Now that references to historic precedent had been abandoned or could no longer be sanctioned, a formal vacuum appeared. Imagery had to come from somewhere, however, and sometimes it seemed to have been absorbed from the fantasies of comic book artists. In the 1950s, Frank Hampson and his successors – talented artists of "Dan Dare", a strip in *The Eagle* – needed to portray the architecture of the future (**Figure 4.12**). Their images perhaps reflected Wright's illustrations for Broadacre City or those of the Italian Futurists. Buildings were streamlined; corners were rounded; the air was full of transport devices. Very similar imagery occurred in the planning proposals of the 1960s: Bakema and van de Broek's proposal for Amsterdam East is a typical example (**Figure 4.13**).[30]

30 More extreme and eventually more influential examples were the graphic fantasies of the British group *Archigram*. The notion that services and circulation would themselves constitute the expression of a building found its fulfilment in Piano and Rogers' winning competition entry for the Pompidou Centre in Paris in 1971.

Figure 4.12 Illustration from *The Eagle* children's comic in November 1950

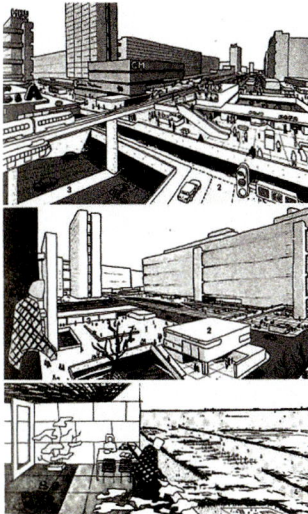

Figure 4.13 Bakema & van den Broek: planning proposals for Amsterdam East, 1965

As John Summerson had pointed out, the idea – obvious as it might seem to us now – that the function of the building could provide the starting point and the source of unity in an architectural design, was the revolutionary contribution of modernism. In its most extreme

31 Blundell-Jones 2002.

form, this philosophy was embraced by the German architect Hugo Häring (1882–1958), who engaged in a famous debate with Le Corbusier at the initiation of CIAM in June 1928. Le Corbusier, as we have seen, believed that what distinguished architecture from engineering was art: the architect in fact was essentially an artist, albeit of a particular kind, manipulating the forms of the twentieth century (which were certainly the product of technology) in order to "touch our hearts". Thus Le Corbusier's buildings, and also his utopian town planning proposals, were clearly not conditioned by an exclusive concern for function but by formal prejudices, such as the Cartesian grid to which his skyscrapers conform in the Voisin plan for Paris. In an article of 1926, Häring had criticized the urban projects of Ludwig Hilberseimer and Le Corbusier for subordinating the lives of their inhabitants to abstract geometrical principles. It should be the other way round, he argued: the organic unfolding of human life itself should generate form without aesthetic preconceptions.

In his book on Häring, Peter Blundell Jones used the term "coincidental form" to describe the way in which Häring's carefully considered plans bend and inflect to accommodate particular functions internally, but simultaneously address other external functions, like the geometry of vehicular turning circles[31] (**Figure 4.14**). Häring himself talked of *Leistungsform* – performance form – a term that lies at the heart of his conception of organic architecture. Häring failed to build on a substantial scale, but a close examination of his house plans shows the careful way in which he considered the experience of the individual arriving, disposing of coats and proceeding towards a variety of welcoming spaces: ingle nooks or curved built-in sofas. The overall composition is nothing more or less than the aggregation of these episodes. His largest built project was for a farm complex, Gut Garkau, near Lübeck, where Häring was equally concerned for the welfare of the animals, in the milking parlour for instance, so that the sequence of activity was always smoothed and modulated. The external appearance was the result of the forms which emerged: sometimes it can be striking, sometimes merely clumsy. The buildings of his contemporary Hans Scharoun, who did attract larger commissions, often succeed in meeting the crucial needs of the brief, such as the excellent acoustics of his Berlin Philharmonie, but at the expense of a somewhat incoherent external expression. One can hardly imagine a city entirely composed of such objects – at least that was a criticism to be levelled at these kinds of compositions by a later generation.

Whereas in the nineteenth century the adjective 'organic' was most often used in arguments on behalf of the natural Gothic style, in antithesis to the artificial disciplines of classical architecture, for Häring it became not so much the reflection of biological form as the symptom of an integrated approach to design that approaches the mystical. The 'beingness of building' made formal demands on architects to which they had to respond. But Le Corbusier (who was just as inclined, in

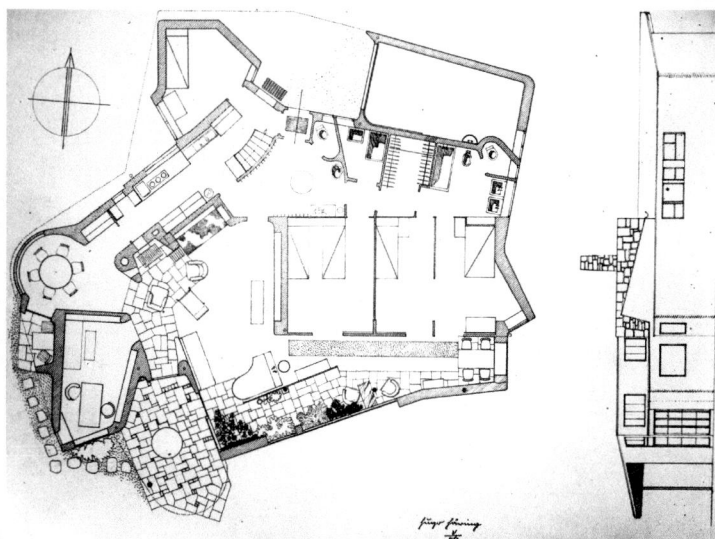

Figure 4.14 Hugo Häring: theoretical house plan, 1946

a different way, to the poetic and mystical) believed in abstract composition in a quite conventional sense, even though the elements of such composition, dictated by modern technology and his preference for pure forms, would be architecturally unconventional. It is clear that Le Corbusier's compositional method owes much to the forms of Purist painting, to which he devoted half his working life. His plans were conceived of as a series of layers lying on top of each other, sometimes cut away to reveal double or triple-height voids. In a similar way, his façades are the foremost layer of a number of frontal planes running back through the building. As we have seen, it is a very different technique from that employed by Adolf Loos, which consisted of half and quarter levels nested within each other to form ambiguous volumes. In four didactic diagrams Le Corbusier illustrated the tensions embodied in his villa designs (**Figure 4.15**). The first shows a free assembly of different volumes (it is a diagram of his Maison La Roche of 1923–1925). Even though it is much more disciplined than a Häring project, this clearly failed to satisfy him, and he reminded himself of the coherence of a simple rectangular box. The third diagram shows his resolution of the problem: a free plan form embedded within a disciplined regular grid of columns, and the fourth is based on his 1928–1931 Villa Savoye, which incorporated open space (the raised first floor terrace) within the overall near-square composition.

It would be left to critics and theorists to try and discern the formal principles that lay behind modernist composition in more detail, and

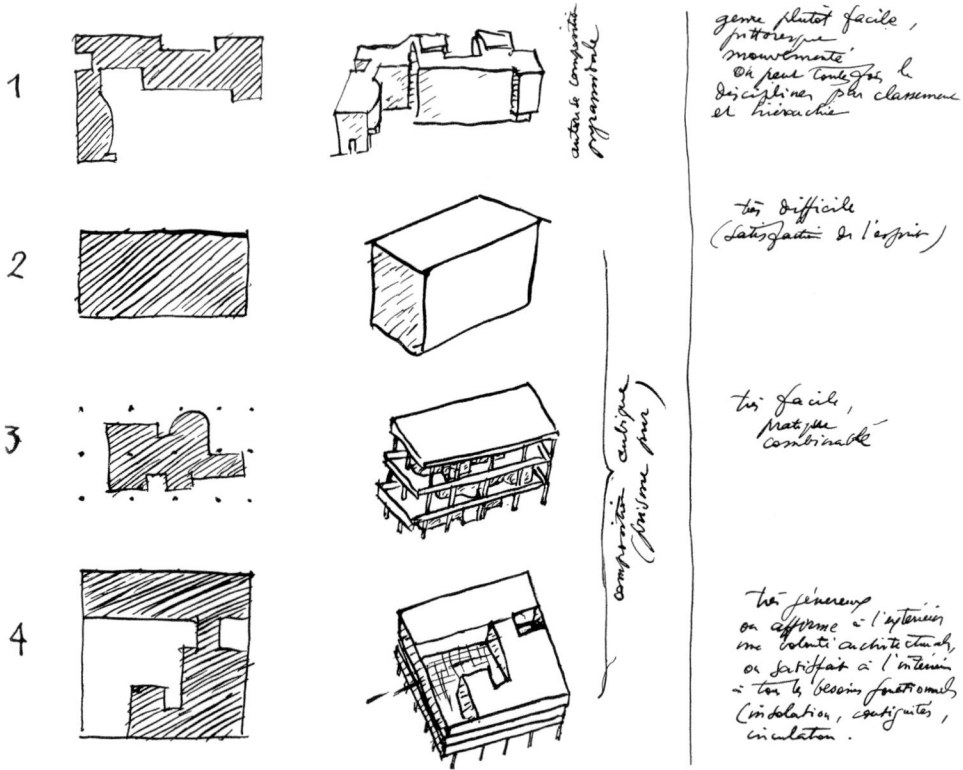

Figure 4.15 Le Corbusier: diagrams to illustrate the development of his *plan libre*

32 Reprinted in Rowe 1982.
33 Published, after many years of circulation in Xeroxed copies, as Eisenman 2018.

as we might expect, they found Le Corbusier's work the most fruitful to study. One of the first articles to suggest there could be a coherent formal basis for modern design was "The Mathematics of the Ideal Villa", written by Colin Rowe in 1947.[32] Surprisingly, it compared Le Corbusier's Villa at Garches to Palladio's Villa at Ema, the so-called Malcontenta (**Figure 4.16**). The article discussed the nature of the villa as a type, and its origin in the dreams of the Roman poet Virgil (in his *Eclogues* and *Georgics*), but its most influential aspect was the way in which Rowe felt able to describe the composition of buildings from two such different architectural traditions. He had been working at the Warburg Institute under the émigré scholar Rudolf Wittkower (1901–1971), whose *Architectural Principles in the Age of Humanism* was to contain a formal 'ur-diagram' that he argued lay behind Palladio's villa typology.

Rowe in turn taught the young Peter Eisenman whose 1963 Cambridge PhD thesis was entitled *The Formal Basis of Modern Architecture*.[33] Eisenman was quite explicit that, in the absence of a conventional ordering system such as the classical orders, or stylistic revivals such as

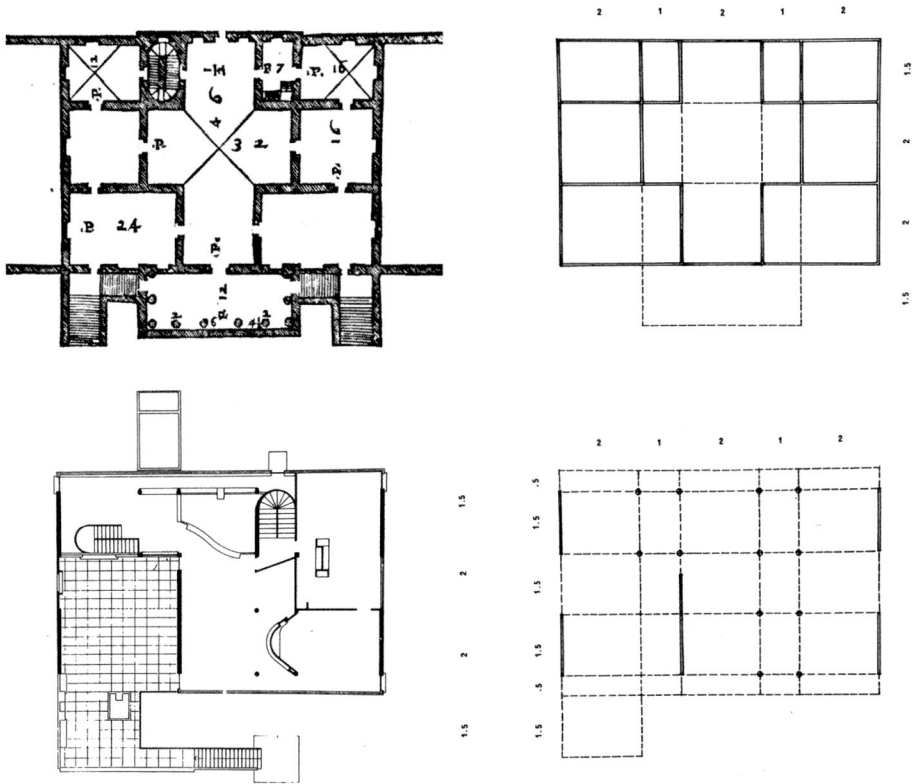

Figure 4.16 Colin Rowe: comparison of Palladio's *Villa Foscari* (Malcontenta) and Le Corbusier's *Villa at Garches*, in *Mathematics of the Ideal Villa*, 1947

neo-Gothic, all that the architect could call upon was geometry. He pro-posed a distinction between generic forms (for Eisenman only three, in principle: centroidal, linear or spiral), and specific forms, which would be the forms that we encounter in particular buildings as modifications of generic forms to meet the given circumstances. Later critics built on Eisenman's procedures though they found sources for legitimate adjust-ment wider than circulation and orientation.[34] For a building such as Le Corbusier's Pavillon Suisse, a hostel for university students in Paris, Eisenman provided a compelling formal analysis accounting for its many subtle inflections (**Figure 4.17**, **Figure 4.18**). Le Corbusier had distinguished the common facilities (to the north) from the accom-modation (raised on concrete columns or *pilotis*) and the circulation (the entrance hall, lift and stairs). The expression of the building runs from the formal urban frontal plane back to a rustic wall on the rear. The whole composition bends at the point of entry, displacing columns and twisting the stair obliquely in the process.

Eisenman continued his analysis down to many levels of detail in this and other examples. His thesis was most persuasive when

34 See, for example, Baker 1996 or Ching 2015.

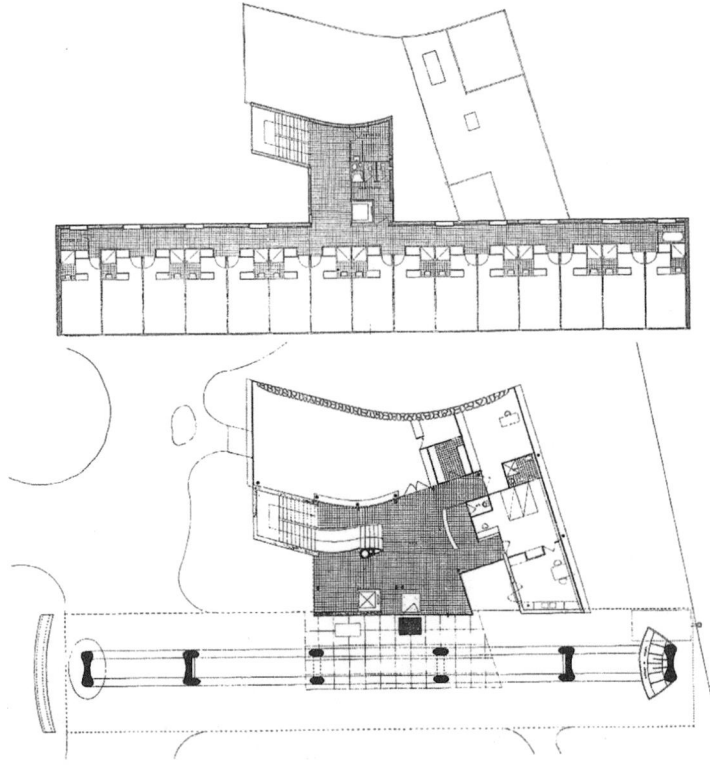

35 Herdeg 1983.

applied to the work of the Italian architect Giuseppe Terragni, but Eisenman even extended his analytical method to less assimilable examples such as Aalto's Säynätsalo civic centre, described in Chapter 5. Although Eisenman claimed to use a similar procedure himself in producing his own designs, it is clear that such a formal analysis is no more than that – it can hardly be a prescription in the way that the conventions of traditional styles, such as the orders, were. It offers itself rather as a methodology to assess whether the formal arrangement of a particular design tends towards coherence, and can be illuminating in demonstrating the sophistication of skilful designers.

4.7 A first critique: decorated diagrams

In his 1983 book *The Decorated Diagram, Harvard Architecture and the Failure of the Bauhaus Legacy*, Klaus Herdeg set out to demonstrate the limitations of modernist composition, as it had been taught in Walter Gropius' time as the Chair at the Harvard Graduate School of Design.[35] The cover of his book displayed an image from Gropius' *Scope of Total Architecture*, which indicated Gropius' positivistic philosophy in comparing the eye to a camera and Ed Larrabee Barnes' SUNY campus in comparison to Jefferson's at the University

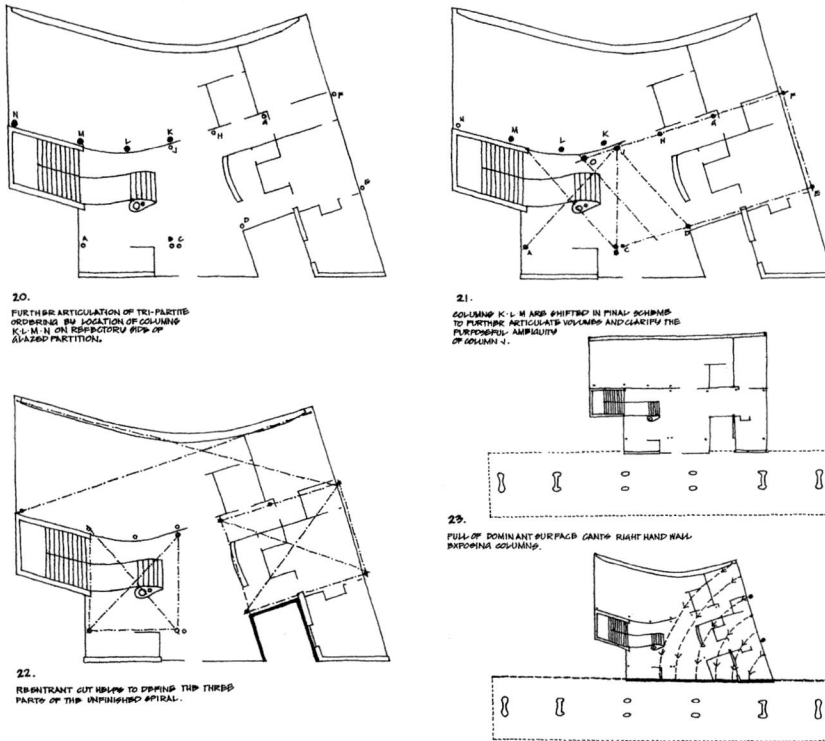

Figure 4.18 Part of an analysis by Peter Eisenman of Le Corbusier's Pavillon Suisse

of Virginia (**Figure 4.19**). Indeed, Gropius had explicitly stated, "The human eye is built very similar [*sic*] to a camera".[36] One of Herdeg's examples to show the poverty of the design principles taught during Gropius' time at Harvard was I.M. Pei's Herbert F. Johnson Museum of Art for Cornell University (**Figure 4.20**, **Figure 4.21**). The floor areas of the building may have been derived from following the client's brief fastidiously, but the form that resulted was a gratuitous piece of sculpture – the problem (since that is how the resolution of the brief was seen) could have been solved in any number of other ways. Broadly, Herdeg accuses Gropius and his colleagues of teaching a design methodology that consisted of generating architectural forms from functional diagrams, assembling them in relation to convenient adjacencies and then decorating them according to prevalent taste. Their complete ignorance of history made for a vacuous architecture. This was perhaps not the most compelling example to choose, however. Pei was a talented architect and not afraid to make bold gestures, as in his 1984 glass pyramid design at the Louvre in Paris. He was given a prominent site at Cornell and a conventional building would have blocked a distant view. The peculiar form of

36 Walter Gropius, "Is there a Science of Design" in Gropius 1956, pp. 35–49. This misleadingly positivistic view of human perception will be discussed in some detail in Chapter 11.

Figure 4.19 Book cover
of Klaus Herdeg, *The
Decorated Diagram*,
1983

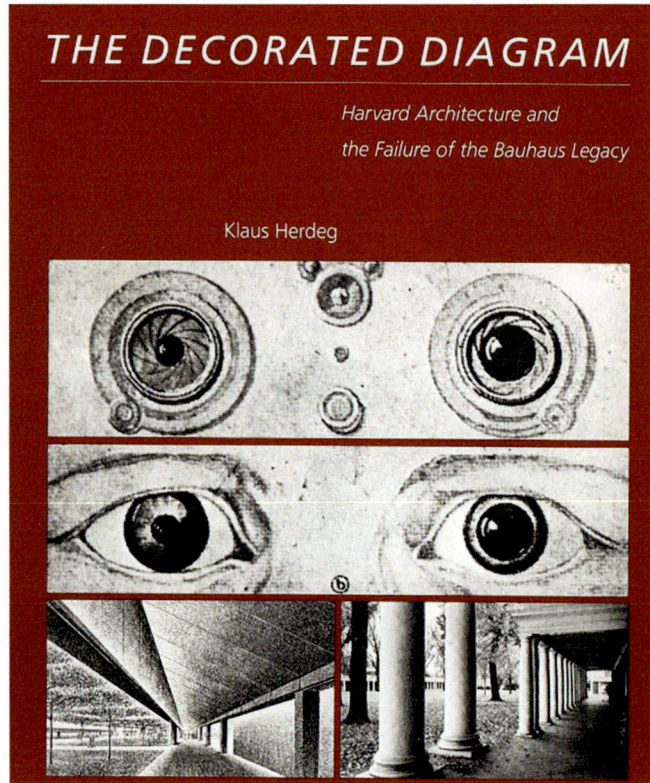

Figure 4.20 I.M. Pei:
Johnson Museum of
Art, Cornell, section

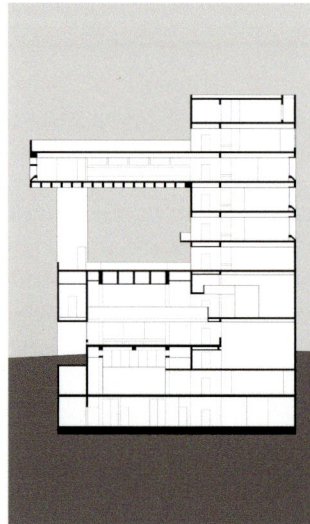

the gallery, held aloft over a massive void, was justified by maintaining and framing that vista. A later extension was constructed mostly underground to retain the idea. Residents of Ithaca have

Figure 4.21 I.M. Pei: Johnson Museum of Art, Cornell, view

grown fond of this idiosyncratic sculptural object, one of many now in the menagerie of iconic signature buildings that have been added to university campuses throughout the United States. One lesson might be that the absence of theory, or an inadequate one, need not necessarily lead to poor architecture provided the architects are skilful enough. Le Corbusier, brilliant sculptor that he was, illustrated in his famous church at Ronchamp how he could manipulate form and light to fashion a masterpiece (**Figure 4.22**). That this was an inadequate prescription for those of lesser talent is illustrated by the project in the following decade by his cousin and indefatigable assistant, Pierre Jeanneret, for the Gandhi Bhawan at the University at Chandigarh (**Figure 4.23**).

4.8 The campus as a CIAM city

In the era after the Second World War, the university campus was the place where principles of modernist planning and the manipulation of architectural form can be seen most clearly. Architects hoped for opportunities to design whole cities, but they seldom arose – Chandigarh in North India and Brasilia being well-known exceptions – and campuses were the closest approximation. Two British examples of their design will serve as illustrations.

In 1958 Chamberlin, Powell & Bon, later to be architects of the Barbican in London, were appointed to prepare a development plan for the University of Leeds "with fresh and independent minds", superseding Lanchester, Lucas and Lodge, who had been the university's architects since 1927.[37] They thoroughly researched the anticipated numbers of students, the space requirements of the various departments and their

37 Chamberlin, Powell and Bon 1960 Wright 1974.

inter-relationship, which were clearly crucial issues. In relation to what they described as "factors determining the physical grouping" of the component parts, two were pre-eminent: the site's proximity to the city centre, and its pronounced slope. The diagrams that illustrated the strength of connections and therefore relative importance of circulation patterns between departments formed the basis of the topological arrangement. An efficient stacking diagram for lecture theatres became the framework for the perspective illustrating the sculptural free-standing block proposed. Together with such compositional freedom when traditional styles were abandoned came the opportunities offered by new technologies and what seems to us now a naïve optimism about their effectiveness. The problem of the progressive expansion of the library, for example, was to be solved by using a Swiss system for multi-storey car parks, which could be jacked up from below when additional layers were required. This extraordinary proposal indicates the faith in innovative techniques prevalent at the time, and unsurprisingly the vertically stacked library was not built in this form. Nor were the lecture theatres built as first proposed. But the lecture block as constructed does illustrate clearly the way in which the stacking diagram and the ventilation ducts created the façade: the overt expression of these functional components undertook the task previously allocated to

Figure 4.22 Le Corbusier: Notre Dame du Haut, Ronchamp, 1954

a referential honorific language (**Figure 4.24**). Architects and critics of the next generation, as we shall see, were to protest that this was simply an inadequate way to derive the external expression of a building. In Herdeg's terms, the architects had used functional determinants to fashion the buildings' layouts and forms and decorated them merely as they fancied.

At Churchill College, Cambridge, the 1958 competition-winning scheme by Richard Shepherd, Robson and Partners separated out the library (work), the common spaces (recreation) and the residential courts (living) and linked them with covered ways (circulation), thereby obeying precisely CIAM's prescriptions for a city (**Figure 4.25**). The TAC proposals for the University of Baghdad had done just the same (**Figure 4.4**). The buildings worked effectively, but people wondered whether they created something more like a conference centre than a college. Oxbridge colleges have a complex history as independent institutions that combine accommodation, teaching and research and communal activities such as formal dining and religious observance. Churchill did contain a chapel but it was located well away from the rest of the buildings since the foundation was determinedly modern and wanted to be seen as secular. The opportunities for iconographic celebration

Figure 4.23 Pierre Jeanneret: Ghandi Bhawan, Chandigarh, 1962

Figure 4.24 Chamberlin, Powell & Bon: University of Leeds lecture block as constructed

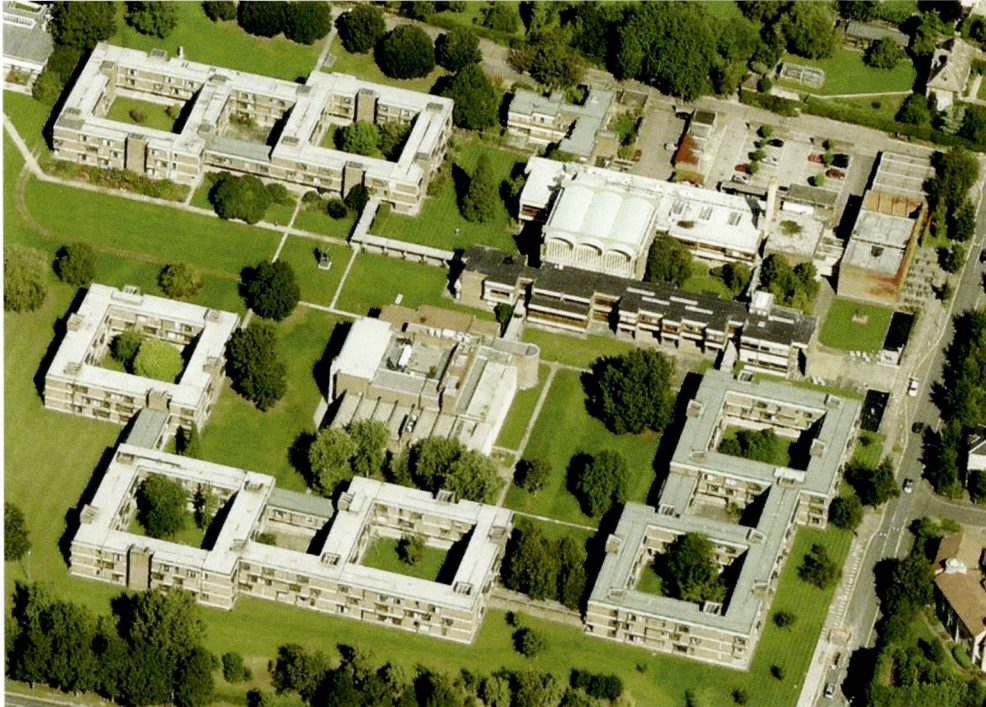

Figure 4.25 Richard Sheppard, Robson & Partners: Churchill College aerial view

Figure 4.26 Richard Sheppard, Robson & Partners: Churchill College, Cambridge, view of dining room block

compared to traditional buildings were thereby reduced.[38] At Churchill, although the single-use residential courts were fully enclosed (something that we saw TAC avoided at Harvard) they were raised on chunky brick walls and piers, rather than slender Corbusian *pilotis*, encouraging the free flow of space which is a hallmark of modernist aesthetics and associated with the democratization of the public realm.[39] In the detailed treatment, heroic sculptural expression of in situ and pre-cast concrete, supported on the brick walls, dramatized the truthfulness of the construction as the principal aesthetic message (**Figure 4.26**). As in the University of Leeds buildings, and indeed in most of the Brutalist architecture of the 1960s, this comes at the expense of forming 'cold bridges' between internal and external fabric – a consequence, as we noted in the previous chapter, of an inherited ethic of construction.[40]

4.9 Philosophy and politics: the Bauhaus in its German context

To clarify the context within which Gropius' views of architecture developed, we need to understand the regional nature of German philosophy and politics and how it intersected with and paralleled architectural positions. We saw how Gropius' own views shifted, depending on the ideas he encountered: the mission of architecture (and for Gropius it was always a mission) moved from that of recovering a spirit of medieval crafts to the embracing of abstraction and privileging of the machine as a means to achieve a better world. What united all German thinking

38 It is interesting that Robinson College, founded at Cambridge in the 1980s, reverted to a deliberately pre-modern pattern, mixing all the traditional functions around a court, as the architects called it, though it is more like a raised deck.
39 This has subsequently been compromised by security screens, a common manifestation of a different attitude to public space in the twenty-first century. Whether the modernists were naïvely optimistic or later generations too prepared to submit to an ethos of privatisation remains a matter for debate.
40 Reyner Banham's book on Brutalism is subtitled "ethic or aesthetic?" (Banham 1966).

between the wars was the shared sense that Germany, besides suffering defeat in the First World War with all its economic consequences, also faced a cultural crisis that needed to be addressed. Oswald Spengler, in his deeply pessimistic *The Decline of the West*, which appeared in 1918, blamed in eschatological terms a fixation on the benefits of improved technology for a general moral decline. Spengler was essentially a propagandist, but at the same time German philosophers were engaged in re-reading in different ways Kant's careful balancing of subjective sense and objective understanding, which had been studied anew from the 1870s onwards. While not going so far as to endorse completely the metaphysics of Dilthey's *Weltanschauung* (p. 15), which privileged national or regional character and acknowledged irrational subjectivity, a group of thinkers in Heidelberg and Freiburg (the 'south-western school') sought an interpretation of Kant that would allow philosophy to contribute to the interpretation of history, including cultural history and aesthetics. More generally, there was also a new emphasis on philosophical anthropology, associated principally with Max Scheler (1874–1928). By contrast, philosophers associated with the Marburg school emphasized Kant's orientation towards scientific objectivity, even as it might be applied to aesthetics: philosophy for them should be more like a science (*Wissenschaft*). In the precarious years of the Weimar Republic, attempting to hold a balance between extremes, those associated with the south-western school tended to the political right and, as the Nazis gradually gained ascendancy, were prepared to make accommodations with the new regime, whereas the Marburg school was more sympathetic to Lenin's October 1917 revolution and communism. Ernst Cassirer (1874–1945), who will reappear in Chapter 10, tried to mediate between these positions in a way that was entirely symptomatic of the fragile liberalism of the Weimar regime.

Architectural differences had a similar regional character. By the mid-1920s there were several schools of architecture associated with differing principles: Munich and Dresden for instance, or the Berlin-Charlottenburg Institute of Technology, at which Heinrich Tessenow taught. Among the most prominent was the Stuttgart school, where one of its two heads, Paul Schmitthenner, developed a rationalized timber-frame system for housing which he proved was cheaper to construct and made dwellings that were a good deal more comfortable than the awkward industrialized systems being developed by the Bauhaus. His aesthetic, however, was thoroughly conservative, continuing somewhat in the manner of Tessenow and others at Hellerau (see p. 50) by employing steep pitched roofs and traditional shuttered windows. Schmitthenner was a member of the Werkbund but, like Tessenow, refused to participate in the 1927 *Weissenhofsiedlung* that Mies van der Rohe organized, even though it was on his doorstep; he argued that its forms, such as flat roofs, were neither constructionally nor functionally necessary, but merely an arbitrary formalist preference. (Mies would probably have sought to veto his participation in any case, as he had that of Hugo Häring.) Politically, Schmitthenner was a member of the National Socialist Party and remained working in Germany throughout the Second World War,

41 Speer was one of Tessenow's least talented pupils; in his *Spandau Diaries* it's clear that he remained fond of his teacher. Speer occasionally acknowledged his own limited skills and also revealed a deep ethical confusion as to his role as Hitler's architect: would he have preferred the life of a provincial architect to the opportunities he was given? "My head reels when

though it seems he failed to be awarded major projects because he had criticized the grotesque and overblown neo-classical work of Albert Speer, Hitler's favoured "Reich Minister of Building".[41]

Gropius' Bauhaus, on the other hand, as it embraced the machine, became ever more committed to a belief in the triumph of rationalism and proscribed any kind of attachment to traditional sentiment or forms that were reminiscent of earlier styles. In welcoming émigré modernists from Russia, such as El Lissitzky, the Bauhaus moved to the left, which was one of the reasons it could not survive the Nazi regime, even though Mies van der Rohe (who had designed the monument to Rosa Luxembourg, thanks to his friendship with the communist Eduard Fuchs) tried to compromise. As a result of its assiduous promotion by Sigfried Giedion, the *Weissenhofsiedlung* was a principal focus of the highly influential 1932 Museum of Modern Art exhibition in New York, "The International Style". Once Gropius had moved to Harvard, his reform of architectural education was swiftly adopted in schools all over the country. Since it promised lower costs, the rationalization of building construction methods that he recommended was welcomed by industry, by developers and even by the estates directors of universities. Tom Wolfe, in his satirical *From Bauhaus to Our House*, lamented the importation of German ideas for *existenzminimum* dwellings into a prosperous capitalist economy, but it seemed irresistible, not least because it symbolized modernity, and America wanted above all to be seen as modern.[42] Americans forgot their own more balanced contributors, such as Louis Sullivan and even Frank Lloyd Wright, whose later work was much less influential than his earlier.[43] Eventually, as part of the cultural 'Cold War' with the USSR, America actively promoted the work of modernist European émigré artists, authors, composers and architects.[44]

4.10 Conflicted positions in Le Corbusier

It will have become clear that Le Corbusier's views cannot be assigned to a simple set of philosophical principles. Unlike Gropius, he was a lone figure: never tempted to work collaboratively, he simply dominated any group of which he became a member. Although it is possible to chart a stylistic development from his Arts and Crafts or Art Nouveau Swiss work to the purism of the 1920s and 1930s, towards the freer more sculptural manner of the later buildings,[45] his thinking reflected an extraordinarily diverse set of influences. He was always as moved by Ruskin's prose about nature as by the sight of grain silos or aeroplanes. In Paris he studied the Beaux-Arts rational analyses of Auguste Choisy at the same time as reading Nietzsche's *Also Spracht Zarathustra*. He saw differences between French artistic pre-eminence, which he associated with its rationalism, and Germany's 'productive' strength, which promised a liberation of the forces of technology.[46]

By 1933, Emil Kaufmann had already proposed that Le Corbusier was the inheritor of an Enlightenment rational tradition, evident in the way

I pose this question. Certainly I cannot answer it at all" Speer 1976, pp. 404–407.

42 Wolfe 1981. Excerpts of the book reached a wide audience in *Harper's Magazine*, June & July 1981. Wolfe used the phrase "The Silver Prince", a nickname given to him by Gropius' Bauhaus colleagues, to describe his irresistible attraction to American patrons. Wolfe was far from the first to complain of European modernism being imported uncritically into America. See Mallgrave 2009, pp. 336–367, who refers to the April 1953 issue of *House Beautiful*.

43 Most architects saw a serious decline in the quality of Wright's work in the 1950s, perhaps as a result of members of his office who went on to found Taliesin Associated Architects, but Robert Twombly made a case for Wright's own performance growing "more dazzling as his death grew nearer" (Twombly 1979). Much of it remained domestic, but he also conceived a 528-storey tower, "Mile High Illinois", which must have seemed fantastic at the time but is less improbable from a twenty-first century perspective.

44 In 1950 the American CIA created the Congress for Cultural Freedom (CCF) specifically to counter the USSR's Cominform.

45 Even that is problematic: during the 1930s, when he was supposedly fixated by machines, he also planned rustic earth-bound dwellings such as the Maison de Week-End (1935), whose themes were to be recapitulated in the 1951–1954 Jaoul houses and 1951–1955 Villa Sarabhai in Ahmedabad.

46 As is evident in the report he prepared, published in *La Chaux de Fonds* in 1912 as "Étude sur le mouvement de l'art décoratif en Allemagne".

his architecture ruthlessly eliminated detail.[47] His 1914 'Dom-Ino' house diagram (**Figure 2.4**), which appears to be an idealized distillation of the barest structural necessities, was aesthetically rather than structurally determined and difficult to build at the time, since he prohibited drop beams or any enlargement of the columns at their junction with the horizontal slab.[48] In September 1907 the young Jeanerret had been profoundly moved by a Carthusian monastery at Ema, near Florence, and though never subscribing to a faith, he retained that austere vision as an ideal all his life. Individual dwellings in his city layouts have the character of monastic cells, while their planner (in William Curtis' description) would be "given an inordinate amount of influence over the lives of others – rather like Plato's philosopher king who visualizes the constitution of the ideal state and paints a picture of it in an ideal city plan".[49] In the late 1920s Le Corbusier had flirted with Syndicalism, a movement then in decline in France, but his 1935 *Ville Radieuse*, where functions were even more ruthlessly separated than in the 1922 City for Three Million, was dedicated "To Authority" and at various times he sent the project to Stalin, Mussolini, Pétain and Nehru.

Reflecting artistic movements in Paris, however, Le Corbusier was equally attracted by the primitive, anarchic and surreal – though we may recall from Chapter 2 how the neo-classicism of Laugier could be both classical and romantic, a rational response to debased inherited traditions, recalling architecture to order, and simultaneously an aspect of a heightened artistic sensibility and appreciation of the 'primitive'. Le Corbusier drew and painted figures (for instance his 1929 *Two Seated Women with Necklaces*) and oxen, a perennial personal theme, as well as still lives. Later he worked with the sculptor Josef Savina and created a private *Cabanon*: a log cabin for himself and his wife at Cap St Martin, where he could be a "noble savage" on vacation.[50] Le Corbusier's most surreal work was the Beistegui penthouse apartment of 1929–1931, which contained an electronic device on its roof-garden enabling a hedge to be manipulated and reveal the Arc de Triomphe beyond.[51] In his essay "Architecture, Painting and Le Corbusier", John Summerson suggested the inversions to conventional order that Le Corbusier proposed, such as making the ground floor the lightest element rather than the heaviest and placing planting on the roof, were themselves deliberate subversions of our expectations, and therefore surreal.[52]

Le Corbusier was a man of immense charisma, especially for other architects (if not for Aalto's assistant Nils-Gustav Hahl, who wrote back from the steamship *Patras II* that "his eyes have the confidence of the unshakeable fanatic"[53]). He was assiduous in self-promotion to anyone who would listen, but it was to a pair of British architects, Maxwell Fry and Jane Drew, that he owed his personal recommendation to Nehru and employment in 1950 for the new city of Chandigarh.[54] His achievement continues to divide those who write about him into fervent admirers, as many become after unprejudiced encounters with his finest work, and vociferous critics who "associate him directly with the ugliness and banality of many modern townscapes as if he had single-handedly invented the worst aspects of industrialism".[55]

47 Kaufmann 1933.
48 He was dependent on the engineer Max Dubois. See Eleanor Gregh, "The Dom-Ino Idea," in *Oppositions*, winter-spring 1979, 61–87, cited in Mallgrave 2009, pp. 253–254.
49 Curtis 1992, p. 63–64.
50 See Vogt 2000, who investigated this side of his character, proposing the continuing influence of the Swiss lake dwellings on his architecture, particularly his obsession with *piloti*.
51 From another viewpoint, the Arc de Triomphe sits like an ornament on the mantelpiece of a fake Rococo fireplace.
52 Summerson 2013, pp. 177–194.
53 Schildt 1986, p. 93.
54 He took over the role from the Polish architect Matthew Nowicki (who had died in a plane crash) and his planning partner Albert Mayer, and determined revisions to their plan in a matter of a few weeks. See Evenson 1966.
55 Curtis 1992, p. 233.

Figure 4.27 Le Corbusier: diagram to accompany *La Maison des Hommes*

Both Gropius and Le Corbusier were adept at promoting themselves and benefited from the powerful support of Sigfried Giedion, who acknowledged that his historical writings followed Hegel in seeking to uncover the "spirit of the age": for him they were unquestionably the two most important figures in architectural modernism. While Gropius was the ultimate 'Committee Man', brilliant at welding together the advocates of widely disparate positions, Le Corbusier was a loner: he summed up the two sides of his nature (and perhaps all our natures – Apollonian and Dionysian, in Nietzschean terms) in a powerful diagram he prepared for his 1942 book *La Maison des Hommes* (**Figure 4.27**). The wider ethical question his career posed was how far the visions of individuals, seeing themselves as great artists, should be allowed to determine not just single dwellings or institutions but whole cities.[56]

In the following chapters, we shall explore the criticisms of CIAM and its methodologies in more depth: by a second-generation modernist, Louis Kahn; by postmodernists, concerned to enrich an apparently impoverished formal vocabulary; by members of a younger generation within CIAM itself and by those who argued for a deeper tradition – a typological basis for design. But first we turn to Alvar Aalto, an architect firmly within the first generation of modernists but a significant member of an alternative tradition, who were critical from the start of the limitations of orthodox modernism.

56 Which is not to say that utopian visions may not serve a purpose as long as they are understood as just that: see Blewitt 2018, pp. 244–273.

5

POSITIVE SCEPTICISM – ALVAR AALTO AS AN ALTERNATIVE MODERNIST

Introduction

The work of a single architect is described in each of the next two chapters, not simply because of its intrinsic quality but because it illustrates alternative views on how they saw the task of an architect in the second half of the twentieth century. Alvar Aalto[1] was born in 1898 in a small provincial town in central Finland and died in 1976; he was widely viewed internationally as one of the foremost contemporary architects: his image appeared on the bank notes of the national currency – the Finnmark – before Finland joined the EU and adopted the Euro. Much as the Finnish composer Jean Sibelius established such a reputation that he eclipsed all of his musical contemporaries in the international imagination, so Alvar Aalto has dominated our understanding of Finnish architecture.

He was an extraordinarily gifted architect, practising within the period of heroic modernism yet clearly offering an alternative approach if you examine his work in detail or what he said in his many lectures. Aalto taught briefly at MIT and humorously described the experience:

> My students wanted to learn, preferably everything. They asked, among other things, how one creates good art. I replied 'I don't know'. The consequences were shattering. One fine day the parents of one of my former students appeared at a meeting with the professor. The first thing they said was: "We're shelling out $700 per term for our talented son's education and his professor says 'I don't know'". It was, judging by everything, the end of my short teaching career.[2]

The uncertainty he expresses is characteristic; but, in their absence, we cannot verify his position by discerning principles from the recollections of his pupils. Unlike Le Corbusier or Walter Gropius, Aalto never wrote a book, famously declaring that paper was meant for drawing on and that if people wanted to know what he thought about architecture they should visit his buildings. But transcriptions of the many lectures he gave reveal an architect who thought deeply about the activity and held strong opinions.[3] In a contribution to the fourth Alvar Aalto

1 This chapter draws on my book *Alvar Aalto* (Ray 2005a), as well as the many sources listed therein; it was intended as a brief introduction to the work of an architect who demands, and rewards, much more extended study.
2 *Arkkitehti*, No. 1–2, 1958, reprinted in a slightly different translation in Schildt 1998, pp. 263–264. Göran Schildt was Aalto's close friend and biographer.
3 "An architect is a person who has to deal with form and material and what they say does not mean a damn thing. What counts is what they do. What I think about architecture you can see in my work, and what I say you can just forget" (Schildt 1998, p. 184). See also Schildt 1985.

DOI: 10.4324/9781003244943-6

symposium in Jyväskylä in 1988, Alvaro Siza, a Portuguese architect who has undoubtedly been influenced by Aalto's work, referred to his remark about the misuse of paper when he said:

> it would be impossible to make good buildings without a strong theoretical base; and I would say that Alvar Aalto must have had a very good theoretical base. Maybe when he spoke about misusing paper, he was reacting to some preconceptions about architecture and exaggerated. As far as I understand Aalto's personality, he may also have been joking.[4]

I first follow Aalto's career chronologically and then pick out five themes that seem to constitute the character of his architecture: landscape and place-making; his careful accommodation of functions; his avoidance of formalization; his view of the proper place of art; and his compositional method of balancing order and freedom. These pave the way for a discussion of 'creative scepticism', particularly in relation to Aalto's church architecture, as the philosophical position which I shall argue lies behind the themes, and indeed of his work as a whole.

5.1 The Finnish context

Finland had a population of five and a half million in the second half of the twentieth century – about the same as the combined populations of Liverpool and Greater Manchester – more than double what it was in 1898. But its area is roughly twice that of Great Britain, making it the most sparsely populated country in the European Union. Until the beginning of the nineteenth century it was dominated politically by Sweden, but from then until the twentieth century it was part of the Russian Empire, only achieving independence in 1917, when it was swiftly engulfed in civil war. The north of Finland is above the Arctic Circle, and the whole country experiences extremes of light and temperature between winter, when there are long nights and little daylight, and summer when the sun barely sets. Aalto's work frequently capitalizes on the characteristic low sun angles, so that housing on a south-facing slope in Jyväskylä continues to catch light late into a summer evening, and the vertical curved ceramic tiles on his Town Hall building in Seinäjoki create dazzling reflections on an April morning when the ground is still covered in snow (**Figure 5.1**).

Finnish architecture was dominated historically by timber building, with stone used only for castles and churches. But in the early nineteenth century, Carl Ludvig Engel constructed the centre of its capital, Helsinki, along neo-classical lines, like a miniature St Petersburg. By later in the century, many Finnish architects worked in a 'National Romantic' style, in common with architects in other northern European countries and indeed with those of an earlier generation in North America, such as Louis Sullivan's contemporary H.H. Richardson (1838–1886).[5] Lars Sonck's magnificent Tampere Cathedral of 1902–1907 would be illustrative (**Figure 5.2**). It is entirely built of granite of differing textures and finish,

4 Siza 1991. Aalto's remark "God made paper for drawing architecture on. Everything else – at least for me – is a misuse of paper" comes just after the one on teaching (note 2 above).
5 See Miller Lane 2000.

Figure 5.1 Alvar Aalto: Seinäjoki Town Hall on an April morning, low Finnish sun angles

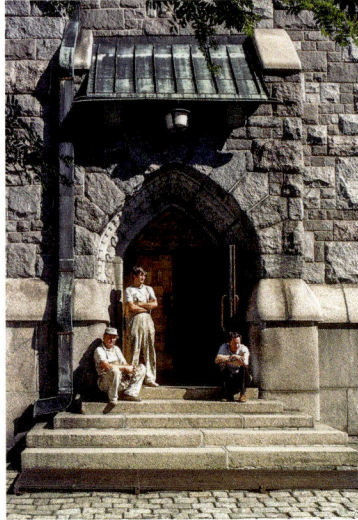

Figure 5.2 Lars Sonck: Tampere Cathedral, 1899–1907, porch

its carefully detailed thin copper porch roof and downpipes providing an effective contrast. 'National Romantic' celebrated the country's nascent nationalism, characteristically by exaggerating the solidity and scale of the buildings' mass and often incorporating iconographic elements relating to national myths.

5.2 Neo-classical beginnings

For Alvar Aalto and his generation, however, following his training in Helsinki between 1916 and 1921, the style was both too overtly nationalistic and too romantic. They sought a return to the order and calmness of the neo-classical tradition. The model for such an approach was the earlier work of the Swedish architect Gunnar Asplund (1885–1940),

Figure 5.3 Alvar Aalto: railway workers' apartment rainwater hopper and down pipe, Jyväskylä

who was himself to undertake a journey, as it were, from a refined neo-classicism towards an accommodation of the technology and social aspirations of the modern movement. A modest early building by Aalto in Jyväskylä was a block of flats for railway workers of 1923–1924, with painted brick walls and a low-pitched metal roof (**Figure 5.3**). The careful texturing of the concrete plinth, eloquent handling of the base of the chimney on the gable end, and most especially the delicate spiral decoration to the rainwater downpipes, collecting rain or melted snow from pronounced hoppers, are all evidence of a sensitivity to detail and material that Aalto was to carry on into his mature work.

Aalto moved his office to the city of Turku in 1927, possibly to be closer to the modernism that was emerging in Germany and also to Asplund in Sweden. Asplund's courthouse extension at Gothenburg offered a compelling model for Aalto and his fellow Nordic architects. It was designed over a 12-year period from 1925–1937; Asplund had begun in a classical manner and ended with a similar plan form but employing a quite different architectural vocabulary, in a version of modernism (**Figure 5.4**). Comparing the interior perspective of the central atrium space with the same volume as constructed, the stylistic difference is clear but the character is consistent: a personal interpretation of each manner, so that the first-floor paired classical columns in the earlier project are realized as paired modernist columns supporting profiled brackets. The use of veneered plywood and the general lightness of touch might remind us of Wright's houses, but it also anticipates architecture at the time of the 1951 Festival of Britain. This is no accident because in the post-war era British architects admired and learnt from Asplund's work, especially his designs for the 1930 Stockholm World Fair, which Aalto reviewed enthusiastically for a Finnish journal.

Asplund died in 1940, aged only 55. Aalto wrote an obituary in which, while Gropius and Le Corbusier were still alive, he lamented the loss

Figure 5.4 Gunnar Asplund: Gothenburg Law Courts, 1925–1937, as realized

of the greatest architect of the twentieth century. What he says about Asplund's architecture is particularly revealing:

> The motifs of a large proportion of our conventional architecture still are fragments of a bygone era. Another architecture has arrived, which builds for man and essentially regards people as a social phenomenon, while at the same time taking science and research as the point of departure.
>
> But beyond that a newer architecture has made its appearance, one that continues to employ the tools of the social sciences, but that also includes the study of psychological problems of "the unknown human" in his totality. The latter has proved that the art of architecture continues to have inexhaustible resources and means which flow directly from nature and the inexplicable reactions of human emotions.[6]

Aalto was contrasting the scientific attitude of what had by then become the orthodoxy of Bauhaus modernism with the psychological sensitivity of a 'newer' architecture practised by Asplund and (he implies) himself.

5.3 Paimio, Villa Mairea and Aalto's own house

The tuberculosis sanitorium that Aalto designed in 1929 at Paimio, near Turku, illustrates what is widely recognized as Aalto's humane functionalism. He claimed that it was partly the experience of a period in hospital that led him to a number of the details in the building. It is also clear that the various motifs he used have been skilfully culled from the

6 *Arkkitehti*, No. 11–12, 1940, reprinted in a slightly different translation in Schildt 1998, pp. 242–243.

Figure 5.5 Alvar Aalto: Paimio Sanitorium, 1929–1933, stair wrapped around chimney

emerging European style and yet fashioned into something that we can recognize as Aalto's own manner. The long horizontal window strips are recognizably 'International Modern'; the entrance porch is a fairly literal quotation from Le Corbusier; the glass enclosed lift has learnt something from Russian Constructivism and the cylindrical stair wrapped around the boiler chimney seems to be Expressionist (**Figure 5.5**). When we examine detailed decisions, however, Aalto's very careful attention to function and how functional solutions can be put to poetic use is apparent. Every room contained two patients, and they each had a basin that Aalto claimed was splashproof because of its geometry (the taps even seem to be set particularly high to demonstrate it) and a specially designed spittoon. The ceiling is painted a cool grey-blue, but a semicircular disc above the wall-light gently dramatizes the uplighting it provides (**Figure 5.6**). The door handle is returned into itself in order to prevent sleeves being caught. And in the main dog-leg staircase there is an acute sensitivity in the different treatment of the handrails: the one on the open side is substantial (as, psychologically, we might require it to be), made of laminated timber and held on chrome brackets; the one fixed to the wall is a thin metal tube with a painted grey dado rail to allow for ease of cleaning if hands touch the wall (**Figure 5.7**).

Aalto had gained a sufficient reputation by the mid-1930s to move his office to the capital city, Helsinki, though his finances were far from

Figure 5.6 Alvar Aalto: Paimio Sanitorium, 1929–1933, light fitting in the bedrooms

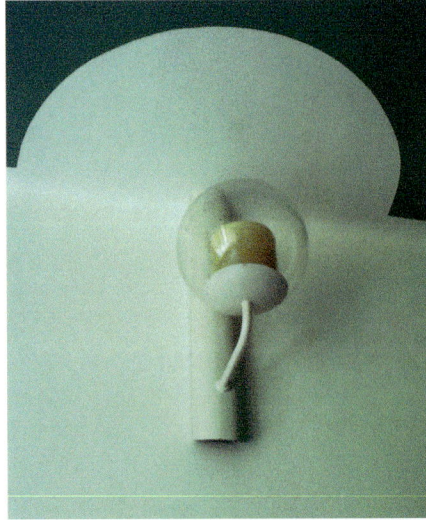

Figure 5.7 Alvar Aalto: Paimio Sanitorium, 1929–1933, main staircase

secure. Patrons particularly important to him were the sophisticated couple Harry and Maire Gullichsen: Harry owned pulp mills whose premises Aalto designed; Maire had trained as an artist in Paris. In the eighteenth and nineteenth centuries, the Gullichsens had built new houses on their estate and now they wanted a house to represent the

Figure 5.8 Alvar Aalto: Villa Mairea, entrance elevation

twentieth (**Figure 5.8**). By this time Aalto's eclecticism could embrace many different traditions not just the emerging strands of modernism we saw at Paimio. He had discovered for himself traditional Finnish farmhouses, and in fact his first scheme was too conservative for Maire (after whom the house was to be named). As constructed, Villa Mairea is a *tour de force* of sophisticated geometric adjustment and subtle appropriation of different stylistic motifs. It is also thoroughly integrated with its site – you could not imagine it in any other country or location. There is a clear contrast with the attitude of Le Corbusier, whose Villa Savoye is placed on the site rather than embedded in it: he had even envisaged a development of 17 examples of his Villa Savoye on a site in Rio de Janiero (**Figure 5.9**).

Arriving at the entrance to Villa Mairea, on the east through the trees, you are greeted by a Hans Arp sculpture and the imposing two-storey white-rendered façade with a prominent timber projection on the ground floor and a generous freely-composed porch. On entering, the main living room is to your left, up three steps, and the principal fireplace can be viewed diagonally. Compositionally, the whole ground plan can be seen as a number of squares, or near squares, which are subtly elided (**Figure 5.10**, **Figure 5.11**). Although the house proper is roughly L-shaped, across a partly enclosed area with a free-formed pool lies the traditional sauna, so the effect (as so often in Aalto's buildings) is of a courtyard – the space made by the built volumes is as important as the building itself. The large living space is itself made up of nine squares, their intersections marked by columns of many varieties: steel or concrete, clad in timber or bound with sisal, sometimes single, sometimes in pairs and sometimes in clusters of three.[7] One of the squares was occupied by Harry Gullichsen's study, but the south-west corner was a conservatory space with a straight-flight stair up to Maire's painting studio above. Illustrative of the different treatments is the plain

7 Though evocative descriptions of its atmosphere are more common, there are compelling formal analyses of this complex space, and indeed of the villa itself, one of the most thorough being Gamble 2014.

Figure 5.9 Le Corbusier: sketch of villas in Argentina

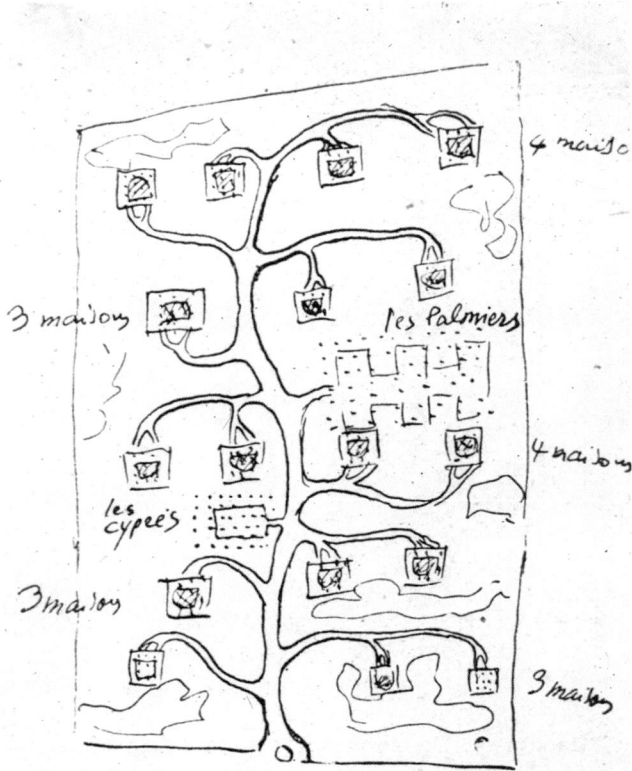

Figure 5.10 Alvar Aalto: Villa Mairea, ground floor plan

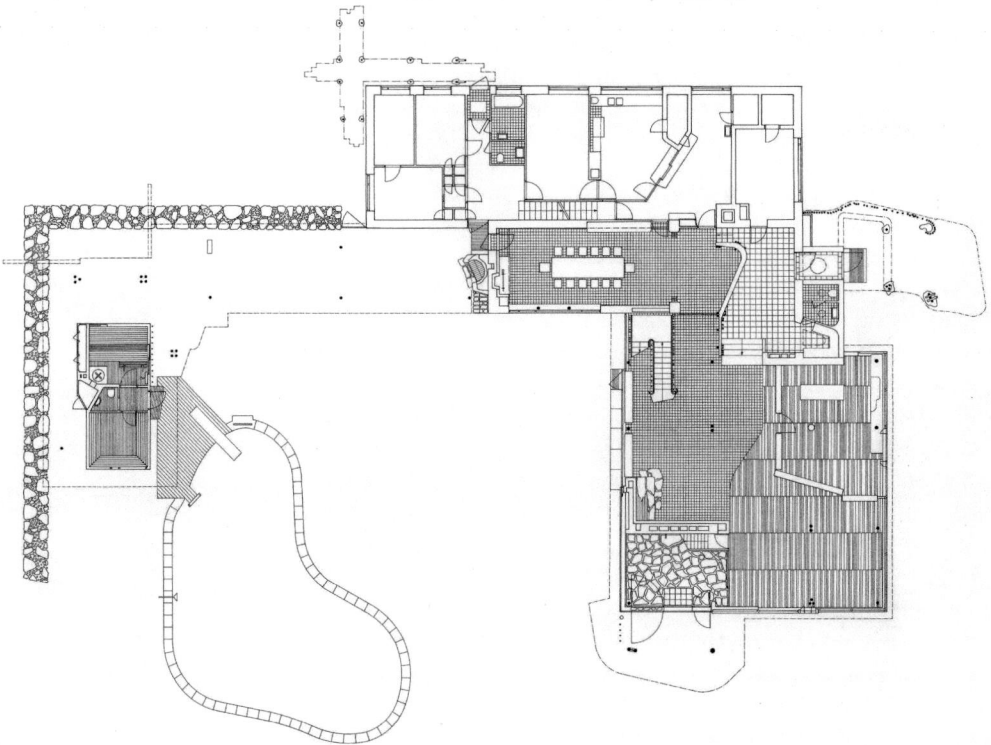

Figure 5.11 Alvar Aalto: Villa Mairea, diagonal view towards the fireplace

whitewashed brickwork of the northern façade and the main staircase, seen on entering, which has a forest of timber posts clearly relating to the trees outside. Even more unusual was the canopy, with its primitive 'Corbusian' *piloti*, linking the house to the sauna, which is built in traditional Finnish timber vernacular (**Figure 5.12**). The conservatory was clearly Japanese in style: it had subdivided windows with rush matting and irregular stone paving.

Such confident handling of many materials and manners to make a satisfactory whole is also visible in Aalto's own house of a few years earlier in Munkkiniemi, a suburb of Helsinki, which also acted as his office until he built his studio nearby. The L-shaped structure is quite pragmatic – a mixture of frame and load-bearing elements with different types of cladding. Some have compared its plan to the Bauhaus Masters' houses, but others saw it as reflecting traditional Karelian (Eastern Finnish) vernacular architecture in a modern way. The interior is furnished with pieces by Artek, the furniture company which Alvar and his wife, Aino, had founded, in which Maire Gullichsen was deeply involved, and which provided his office with valuable income when times were tight. Artek pieces use a steam technique, which the Aaltos developed with Otto Korhonen, to bend laminated wood and make elegant, mass-produced furniture, much of it still in production today.

Figure 5.12 Alvar Aalto: Villa Mairea, canopy link to sauna

Aalto's office also occupied itself with mass-produced housing comparable to the timber systems promoted by Schmitthenner (p. 106), particularly after the war.[8] Villa Mairea and his own house can be regarded as experiments that investigate formal and material properties. His buildings for the employees of various industries could also investigate less usual building forms – stepped on a hillside, for instance, so each dwelling used the roof of the one below as a terrace while being accessed at ground level.

5.4 Baker House, some of the post-war brick buildings and Finlandia Hall

Aalto's reputation grew as a result of the publication of his buildings, most importantly by Sigfried Giedion, who was bowled over by his visit to Villa Mairea and later devoted a whole chapter of the second edition of his canonical *Space, Time and Architecture* to Aalto as a glorious exception to dogmatic modernism.[9] Aalto was invited to America to teach at MIT and given the commission in 1946 to build a substantial dormitory block on the banks of the Charles River. In order to allow a river view to every room, Aalto adopted a sinuous wave-like shape with the corridor mostly single-banked. The rooms were all similar but very few were identical – an example of what Aalto described as flexible standardization, provoking rationalist critics who pointed out the inherent paradox of that phrase. The rear of the building has a pair of

8 At Rovaniemi, from 1947, for example. See Korvenmaa 2012.
9 Giedion 2008.

giant staircases, hung off the back, which provide a dramatic indication of the circulation pattern and also, by the manipulation of landings at each level, allow for a variety of social spaces for the students. Both the drama and the particular quality of these spaces arise directly out of a concern for student life. This project has often been compared with Gropius' dormitories at Harvard of the same period: efficient but dull buildings, as we have seen, relieved by the occasional decorative incident (**Figure 4.5**).

The period after the war was hugely productive. Tragically, Aalto's wife and architectural partner, Aino, who had contributed to his practice especially in managing his office and the design of the furniture, fabric and glassware, had died of cancer in 1949. He had contemplated a career in the United States, like his compatriot Eero Saarinen (1910–1961), but in Finland Aalto won a series of competitions which resulted in some of his most famous buildings, the best known of which is the Civic Centre of Säynätsalo. The young job architect, Elissa Mäkiniemi, became his second wife in 1952.

The plan of the building reveals a mixed-use south-facing courtyard with openings to the east and west, but on section the court is raised a storey above ground level, exploiting (or, rather, exaggerating) the slight change of level from north to south. Aided by the gentle monopitch roof of the library on the south of the court, south sun can penetrate the court even in the Finnish winter. The main council chamber has a prominent profile and is approached up a winding stair lit by high-level strip windows to enter it from two levels. Offices are on the north and east sides of the court and flats on the west. The character of the complex that results is simultaneously domestic and monumental: just as visitors are surprised by the scale of Villa Mairea, where the main living room has the generosity of a saloon on a steamship, they are usually astonished at the way such a small building as the Civic Centre at Säynätsalo can contain so many rich and varied incidents. Viewed from the east, Aalto's remarkable compositional freedom is evident: there is no attempt to reveal 'truthful' structure, and the texture of the masonry walls is deliberately rustic and rough (**Figure 5.13**).

A closer look at the north-east corner of the courtyard gallery will serve to illustrate Aalto's typical inventiveness in detail (**Figure 5.14**). It has a continuous bench over hot water convector heaters. Rather than being made out of metal or timber, this is made of brickwork, echoing the flooring material below and providing a comfortable thermal mass like a continuous night-storage heater. The brick is held away from the timber-framed windows so as to form a slot, up which warm air can pass to avoid condensation on the glass. But instead of being held on masonry piers, the brick beam is supported on elegantly profiled steel legs, which of course allows for maximum exposure of the convectors beneath and hence up-draught of air from below. Materials that are used in unexpected and apparently illogical ways therefore turn out to serve environmental purposes. There are innumerable enjoyable examples of a similar level of detailed

Figure 5.13 Alvar Aalto: Säynätsalo, view from east

consideration both at Säynätsalo and in Aalto's other buildings – one such being the detail of the inviting handrail for the Rautatalo building in Helsinki (1952–1955): this was one of the earliest examples of an 'atrium' office, with a central top-lit space containing a café and surrounded by marble-clad balconies, like the courtyard of a refined Italian palazzo.

The National Pensions Institute was the most substantial in this spate of competition-winning buildings of the early 1950s. Initially intended for a different location, the substantially revised design occupied a triangular site at the head of a broad landscaped boulevard and incorporated planted terraces that respond to its context. On the other (city) side, rocks that were already present were incorporated into the granite-clad lower floor, literally embedding and grounding the building. The central function – the places where members of the public met the pensions officers to discuss their arrangements, was not contained in rooms distributed along a corridor but celebrated by creating individual cubicles in the main atrium-like space, which was crowned by a remarkable double rooflight containing specially designed light fittings in the interspace. The staff restaurant and circulation spaces were all surprisingly generous, but one of the most memorable rooms, or pair of rooms, was the library: its inner portion was a top-lit intimate space containing a book-surrounded lower section with a gallery a few steps higher up, itself lined with books (**Figure 5.15**). The arrangement was one that Aalto had devised for an earlier library in Viipuri (now Viborg, ceded to

Figure 5.14 Alvar Aalto: Säynätsalo, courtyard gallery

Figure 5.15 Alvar Aalto: National Pensions Institute, Helsinki, library

Figure 5.16 Alvar Aalto: National Pensions Institute, Helsinki, light fittings in the boardroom

Russia as war reparation) and was one that he returned to many times. The board room on the top floor was modest in size and proportion but managed to indicate the hierarchy of those who occupied it by the simplest means: a 150-mm raised plinth and special light fittings to distinguish the different members of the board (**Figure 5.16**).

The last one of the red-brick buildings of the 1950s illustrated is the Otaniemi Technical College (1952–1956), which has since expanded considerably and is now known as Aalto University (**Figure 5.17**). It showed Aalto's compositional principles at a large scale: the distinctions he drew between the ordinary and the special. Most of the building complex is a simple arrangement of rooms and corridors with a calm horizontal rhythm of window strips and upstand walls. But particular moments were emphasized by their special geometries: the lecture spaces, for instance, and especially the main aula, a grand lecture room that could be subdivided unequally into two spaces. Its roof accommodated an outdoor amphitheatre, clearly referencing Greek precedents, and from the rear it appeared as a large unpunctuated drum. Internally, the roof structure was fashioned to create giant light baffles; as always, Aalto was concerned to make structure serve experience, never merely to be an expression in itself (**Figure 5.18**).

By the 1960s, Aalto enjoyed an international reputation and was asked to take on commissions all over the world, though he still entered competitions, in which he was often successful. He was commissioned in 1959 to prepare a masterplan for the Töölö Bay area of Helsinki and conceived a grandiose urban development scheme allowing for a number of public buildings for the arts to be designed by different architects, including an opera house, theatre and art gallery, to be realized by Steven Holl only in 1996. Aalto himself designed Finlandia Hall, an auditorium for music and for conference purposes, which was one of the masterpieces of the final years of his career, even if in two respects

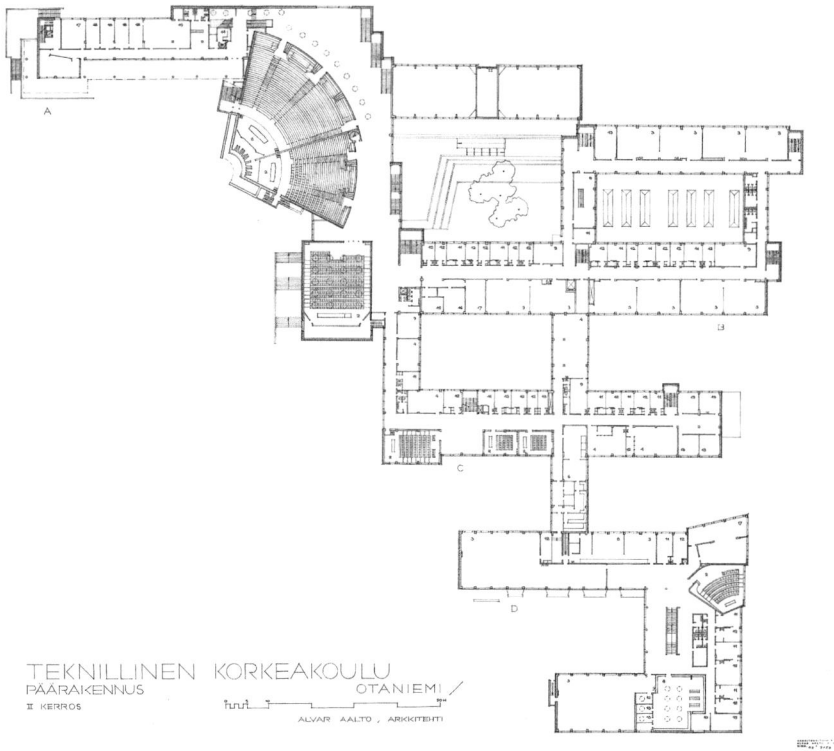

Figure 5.17   Alvar Aalto: Otaniemi Technical College (now Aalto University) plan, 1952–1956

it did not perform as well as expected. The first of these was the marble cladding, which warped after a few years in the Finnish winter and had to be replaced. The second was acoustic: Aalto had hoped to vary the acoustic invisibly (in a void above the ceiling) to accommodate both speech and music. As a result, a separate auditorium (Musiikkitalo) was constructed in 2011 just to the south, and Finlandia Hall is now used exclusively for conference purposes.[10] Aalto was working on an opera house in Essen, Germany, at the same time, which was completed post-humously by the Aalto office under his widow Elissa and benefited from their having learnt from those two issues.

The most memorable aspect of Finlandia Hall was probably the sequence of spaces, from the cavernous ground floor, with generous free-flowing cloakroom desks, up a broad flight of steps to a large, grey-blue carpeted foyer from which one was drawn to a further staircase pushed beyond the wall plane, allowing it to be invisibly lit from the side, and finally back down into an auditorium lined with diagonally profiled timber slats. It was somewhat like passing through a landscape, such is the scale of the spaces and the nature of the various forms that surround them. But there were also enjoyable details at every scale. A typically thought-ful detail was the powder-coated bent metal strip beneath bronze exter-nal lighting brackets that one might consider merely decoration but is

10 In common with many twentieth-century architects, Aalto tended to regard the behaviour of sound waves as analogous to the behaviour of light. With the advent of computer modelling techniques, the prediction of the acoustic character of auditoria has improved considerably.

Figure 5.18 Alvar Aalto: Otaniemi Technical College (now Aalto University), roof lights in the aula

essential in order to prevent the bronze staining the marble surface. As at Paimio, functional requirements stimulate detailed inventiveness.

5.5 Some underlying themes

The purpose of describing a tiny selection of the more than 200 buildings, as well as town planning studies, mass housing schemes, furniture and art works of various kinds, that Aalto's office produced has been to discover any thematic continuity that lies behind this phenomenal productivity, and hence approach the philosophical principles that might lie behind his work.

The first of the five themes I have chosen is landscape and place-making. Aalto always sought a relationship with landscape: if the building was not in a rural landscape, planting and mounding was brought to the building, as we saw at Säynätsalo and at the Pensions Institute. His buildings tend to embrace external spaces, not stand as distinct separate objects. His interiors, including his own studio space, often had integral internal planting. The second, as we saw at Paimio, is Aalto's careful accommodation of function – the way he raised the meeting of functional needs to a different, sometimes poetic, level. Even the everyday activity of descending a staircase is varied by frequently making the stairs and landings broader and more accommodating as they reach the ground. His imagination was not limited to the visual; indeed he seems to have had an intuitive sense of human comfort so that in environmental terms his buildings functioned much more effectively than those of most of his contemporaries.[11] In fact, it is only by using an Aalto building as intended that one can appreciate the way in which his forms seem naturally to look after you: things always appear to be comfortably ready-at-hand, as it were.

Next, Aalto resisted easy formal resolutions and was prepared to countenance quite unusual combinations of materials or forms. His Paimio trolley could serve as a material example. Originally designed to carry doctors' implements in its basket, it was marketed successfully by Artek as a multi-purpose trolley for domestic use and in architects' offices. If you describe its components, it seems it would be rather an ugly object: 16 ceramic tiles on a square timber-framed tray, supported on curvilinear legs attached to plywood wheels, from which is slung a vernacular wickerwork basket held on a galvanized strap. But in fact it is surprisingly elegant, as well as useful. The same could be said for his buildings as a whole. Otherwise lazy resolutions, where elements simply line up, are often disrupted. So, for instance, the rear entrance of the Aula at Otaniemi illustrates how Aalto allows (or encourages) functional considerations to thwart our formal expectations. Above the three symmetrical double doors, with carefully centred and integrated light fittings, are three fixed-light windows and a narrow casement for ventilation, and this of course ensures that the mullions are not centred on the door frames below but drift across the opening.

Then we could point to his view of the proper place of art. Aalto painted all his life, as well as producing many hundreds of sketches for all the projects in his office and for pleasure when he travelled. But he never regarded his artistic work as separate from his architecture: it was a means towards an end. The same went for his stained-glass designs and the exercises he conducted with different kinds of timber – investigations that preceded or meditated on his bentwood Artek furniture designs. When the art dealer Louis Carrée, for whom he and Elissa built a house in France, offered to hold an exhibition of his paintings, Aalto refused. We can compare his attitude to that of Le Corbusier, who famously once said to Picasso, "You and I are the two great artists of the Twentieth Century".

Finally, what can we say of his compositional method? It seems to be a careful negotiation between formal order and creative freedom. He is often compared to organic architects, such as Hans Scharoun or Hugo Häring, but his compositions are seldom entirely free-form. Demetri Porphyrios, borrowing terminology used by Michel Foucault, called his spatial ordering "heterotopic".[12] The plan of the library at Seinäjoki (an example of the library type described above) exploits a contrast between the splayed form of the bookstack and lowered reading area and the rectangular set of rooms of various kinds (**Figure 5.19**). The same building in section contrasts the stepped ground plane with a floridly fashioned concrete ceiling that acts as a reflector for natural and artificial light (**Figure 5.20**).

11 See Hawkes 2008, pp. 61–85, for a detailed study of Asplund's and Aalto's environmental understanding.
12 Porphyrios 1982.

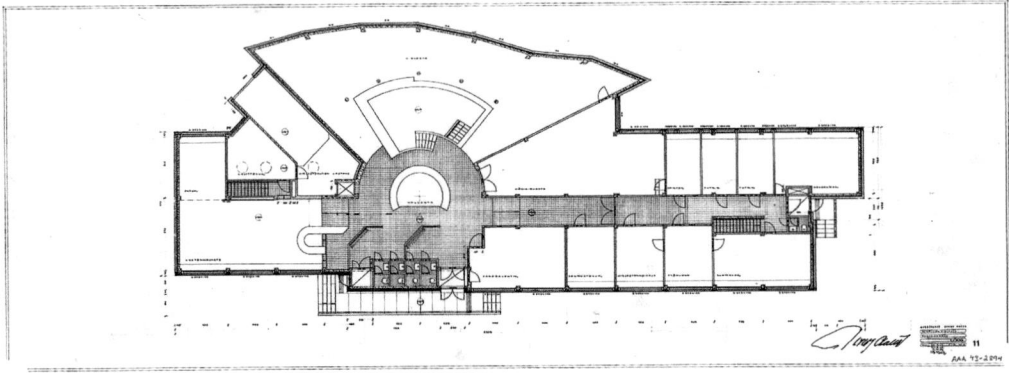

Figure 5.19 Alvar Aalto: Seinäjoki Library, plan, order and freedom

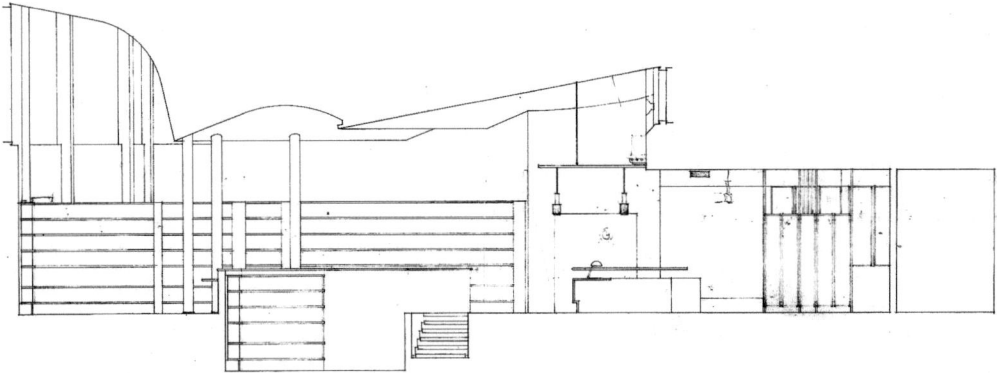

Figure 5.20 Alvar Aalto: Seinäjoki Library, section: order and freedom

Critics and admirers of Aalto's work have written eloquently about it in relation to each of these five themes, with varying emphasis.[13] A conclusion as to the philosophy that lies behind the work, however, must be more speculative. While resisting idealist positions, Aalto seems to subscribe to an optimistic version of nominalism, which holds that though aesthetic structures are not mimetic of an ideal world, they can assist in improvements: meanings which used to be supported by a symbolic language relating to a higher order can to some extent be re-established as an allegory.

5.6 The philosophical nature of Aalto's scepticism

13 See Reed 1998, for example.

Aalto outlined the position of what he called a positive sceptic in an address to his old school, the Jyväskylä Lycée, in 1958:

The much-discussed sceptical world view is in reality a necessary condition for anyone who would like to make a cultural contribution. This is of course dependent on scepticism's transformation into a positive phenomenon, an unwillingness to 'move with the stream'. On a higher level scepticism is transformed into its apparent opposite, to love with a critical sensibility. It is a love that lasts, as it rests on a critically tested foundation. It can result in such a love for the little man that it functions as a kind of guardian when our era's mechanized life style threatens to strangle the individual and the organically harmonious life.[14]

Aalto refers back to his own experience under a favourite teacher, Gabriel Ronimus, at the Lyceum, whom he recalled as first "planting a positive seed of doubt" in his mind. As well as the classics, Aalto would have read authors such as Goethe and Voltaire. Ronimus had referred him to the writings of Erasmus, the first great Renaissance Humanist scholar, whose satires on the established church were one of the instigators of the Reformation.[15] Luther had increasingly seen Erasmus as more of a threat than an ally, writing in 1517:

> My liking for Erasmus declines from day to day. . . . The human is of more value to him than the Divine.[16]

Aalto designed several churches, however, and won competitions for crematoria which remained unrealized.[17] He seems to have appreciated two aspects of the Lutheran faith: its sympathy for the sinner, which would mean the same as what he frequently referred to as the 'little man', and its respect for cultural tradition, which accounts for the relative conservatism of his church designs. In Finnish Lutheranism, doubt is also seen as an aspect of faith; Aalto's church patrons were unconcerned at commissioning a non-believer as their architect. The value of sceptical religious architecture lies not in being disengaged from religious discourse but in acknowledging the absence of posited ultimate truths; its provisionality defines its relevance. At its most fruitful, a sceptical position can foster not only an anxious uncertainty but also joy. There are other interpretations: in his article "Aalto the Thinker", Kirmo Mikkola claims that what Aalto meant by scepticism was part of the Kantian process of attaining knowledge: from dogmatism through scepticism into a critical appreciation.[18] It was thanks to Yrjö Hirn, Professor of Aesthetics and Modern Literature at the University of Helsinki from 1910–1937, that Aalto had become familiar with the thinking of Kant, Schopenhauer and Nietzsche. Other writers in Finland in the 1920s such as Eino Kaila and the physiologist Robert Tigerstedt had also sought a balance between vitalism and mechanism. Many of Aalto's speeches seem to reflect the vitalist position, which was essentially a revival of an earlier anti-materialist tradition of thinking which had been discredited in the wake of Darwinism. As medical science, aided by organic chemistry, found rational reasons for diseases, the idea of some vital force that explained the mysteries of bodily organisms had fallen into disfavour. But, largely as a result of lectures and books by the French philosopher

14 "What is culture?", keynote speech at the centenary of the Jyväskylä Lycée, 1958, reprinted in Schildt 1998, pp. 15–16.
15 Indeed, Aalto's thinking seems always to have been closer to Erasmus' than to that of Luther, who was to turn Erasmus' scepticism into a different kind of orthodoxy. When I interviewed Göran Schildt in 2004, we discussed Aalto's humanism and how Aalto was suspicious of all systems – political, social, architectural and philosophical. He followed up our conversation with a postcard on which he underlined the connection with Erasmus (whose 'humanism' was never, of course, atheistic): "The name of the inventor of Gift of Doubt: ERASMUS from Rotterdamus [sic]. Remembered this 5 minutes after your departure".
16 Aalto's reference in the same speech, echoing Goethe, to a "positive seed of doubt" calls to mind Erasmus himself: "For so great is the obscurity and variety of human affairs, that nothing can be clearly known . . .; or if it could, it would but obstruct the pleasure of life" Erasmus 1931, pp. 91–92. Literary critics are fond of recalling Keats' concept of 'negative capability' in an 1817 letter: "when a man is capable of being in uncertainties, mysteries, doubts, without any irritable reaching after fact and reason".
17 Sofia Singler has been researching Aalto's religious buildings, and I have benefited from discussions with her. Aalto's speech to the Lyceum closely echoes the thinking of Bishop Simojoki, an important influence on the design of his Church of the Three Crosses at Vuoksenniska, Imatra. Some of the following sections draw on Singler and Ray 2017.
18 Mikkola 1976.

19 Mikkola 1976.
20 Williams 1978.
21 Naturally, this is a simplification. For a historical account, see Burneat 1983, and for a concise review of contemporary scepticism, referring to a number of recent arguments and counter-arguments, see www.iep.utm.edu/skepcont/.

Henri Bergson (1859–1941), questions continued to be raised about the nature of invention, or artistic creativity, which could not be so readily explained by mechanistic models. Mikkola also suggested that Aalto inherited this thinking from his wide reading in fiction, pointing to the way in which Aalto quotes Goethe, Anatole France, Strindberg and Bernard Shaw in his lectures.[19] Aalto was profoundly influenced by Goethe's thought, in particular by his attitude to science and art and the pact with technology that man must make. Technology for Aalto was potentially benign, depending on how it was employed, whereas for many who have argued for a less positivistic architecture, from Ruskin onwards in the nineteenth century, as we saw, its influence was to be deplored, and frequently this involves an appeal to the transcendental – a religious faith. Aalto is not sure about the heavens or the gods: that is a question that can be held in abeyance while the conditions of mortals on earth are dealt with. That does not mean that there is no room for poetry, or a kind of transcendence, in which Aalto's stance agrees with that of Goethe.

At any rate, in Finland in the late 1920s, there were active and well-informed debates. It seems that in referring to 'creative scepticism' Aalto positioned himself carefully: he was prepared to acknowledge mystery but not to indulge in mysticism. All philosophical positions are problematic, and that of the sceptic is no exception. For a start, there are several types of sceptic. Descartes, for example, regularly castigated as a positivist, was famously sceptical about claims that could not be proved to be true, starting from the most basic foundations of what it is possible to know. He was suspicious, above all, of the evidence provided by the senses. As Bernard Williams put it, we need only the universal possibility of error, not the possibility of universal error, to destroy all conviction.[20] Descartes fought back from that position, however, so that eventually, for him, the belief in oneself (one's own existence) and thereafter in God can rescue us, and thence rational behaviour can proceed.

Aalto's scepticism is not Cartesian. In one reading, it is more extreme. Descartes persuaded himself that a benign deity guides our thoughts (though he acknowledged it could be an evil demon). But the sceptic would hold that truly we have no grounds whatsoever for belief in things in this world or the next. We have no alternative but to accept the world as it presents itself to us, and our senses are the only means we have of apprehending it.[21] This does not mean that rationality has no place: the purpose of reason, which, as peculiarly well-endowed sentient beings, we are bound to apply, is to correct our misplaced perceptions, although it can never prove things infallibly. If sense-impressions come first, that gives primacy to imaginative intuitions. In their imaginations, architects can therefore assemble new forms from sets of previously experienced complexes (buildings and places): they can envisage the extraordinary. Architects could not do this by the strict application of logic, however, since logic is an analytical tool that comes after sensory impressions. Hence Aalto's quarrel with a modernism that purports to proceed seamlessly from the logical analysis of building problems towards design. The claims of an architect such as Hannes Meyer (p. 8) are clearly absurd: he produced interesting and innovative buildings, despite, rather than in support of, his efforts to ridicule the notion of individual imaginative talent.

Nor does Aalto seem to subscribe to Kant's heroic attempted resolution of the subjective/objective problem. Kant suggested that the world as we apprehend it is in some way fashioned by the way we think of it, with the result that, as Paul Guyer puts it:

> Kant's transcendental idealism asserts that things other than our own representations – indeed even our own selves as contrasted to our representations of ourselves – really do lack spatial and temporal properties.[22]

In common with many of his generation who rejected such an over-intellectualized systematic construct, Aalto's acceptance of the world as we find it is rather more commonsense – hence a 'positive scepticism'.[23] There may be a mystery as to why there is a world at all, but all we can do is operate within it, in all its complex physicality. Metaphysical speculation is therefore futile: the important questions to determine are what it is right to do in the circumstances in which we find ourselves. Sceptics need not be atheists, but they are at least agnostic. David Hume, for instance, ridiculed the idea that we should "have recourse to the veracity of the Supreme Being in order to prove the veracity of our senses", while holding in abeyance his own position on the existence of a divinity – this was something that could not be determined.[24] Ludwig Wittgenstein spent his whole life deliberating on what we could say and came to believe that though we could say nothing about the most important things in life, we might be able to show them. He illustrated the implications of his beliefs not only by his forfeiting a substantial private fortune (in favour of other members of his family) but also, we might postulate, in the design of the house in Vienna for his sister and of his own retreat in Norway (see p. 61 and p. 231).

The Finnish philosopher Georg Henrik von Wright was a pupil of Wittgenstein's and later one of his literary executors. In some respects his thinking resembles Aalto's, and in August 1988, along with Alvaro Siza, he contributed to the fourth Alvar Aalto symposium in Jyväskylä on the theme of "Architecture and Cultural Values". Von Wright's paper, "The Myth of Progress", reveals he was not a straightforward sceptic. He says the most important of the ideals of the (essentially secular) French Revolution is that of *fraternité*, to "transcend all boundaries of nation, race or religion so as to become a consciousness of global responsibility". This surely chimed with Aalto's "love for the little man", as von Wright was well aware. He went on to claim, however, that this ideal was at the same time "nothing but a fulfilment of the Christian command that we should love our neighbour as we love ourselves". And von Wright, who did not reveal whether he was himself optimistic or pessimistic about

22 Guyer 2014b, p. 79.
23 This paradoxical phrase perhaps has similarities to the 'creative scepticism' advocated by the economist Piero Sraffa, who is credited by some as influencing Wittgenstein's later thinking. See Sen 2014; Monk 1991.
24 Hume 1975, p. 153.

the future, concluded: "The only answer we can give to the question whether there is hope for the future of man runs: Let us work for its fulfilment!"[25] This conclusion accords with the argument of von Wright's best-known book, *Humanism as an Approach to Life*, which in turn reflects the philosophical debates in Finland in the early years of the twentieth century and the classical humanist education that Alvar Aalto himself had received in the Jyväskylä Lyceum. But von Wright's criticism in the paper of Hume's participation in the Enlightenment split and Hume's (latent) secularism would probably have made his interpretation too mystical for Aalto. As Juhani Pallasmaa has noted, Aalto seems to have been able to position himself ambiguously in relation to dichotomies of "nature and culture, history and modernity, society and the individual, tradition and innovation, standardisation and variety, the universal and the regional, the intellectual and the emotional, the rational and the intuitive".[26] To that list we could add faith and doubt. As we shall see in Chapter 9, just as phenomenologists such as Pallasmaa, following Merleau-Ponty, could claim Aalto, so his approach can be seen as pragmatic in the way that Dewey or Rorty would define it.

To summarise: for Aalto, art was not the imitation of transcendental structures, nor their despairing rejection, but the affirmation that human constructions are none the less real for being merely human. Art is the name we give to the affirmation of aspirations that are utopian but secular. As a pragmatic architect, Aalto knew that buildings only got built by tricky political processes, at which he was adept, of charming his clients and influencing local officials. They were realized using the technologies that were available and in the face of the hard facts of climatic conditions and budgetary constraints. A building was not just the solution to a mechanical set of problems: an act of invention was required, and sometimes the practice of building could result in something that others would recognize as architecture. What the act of invention consisted of, who could tell? But Aalto recognized in himself a highly creative individual who had the ability, time and again, to produce works that transcended their particular contexts and took on wider meanings.

To use the terminology that the philosopher of science Thomas Kuhn made popular, and which a number of critics have applied fruitfully to architectural design, Aalto's work could be said to have contributed to the creation of new architectural paradigms.[27] Whereas most architects operate within a set of conventions that are inherited (a style), it is given to some to forge new sets of conventions. Aalto was one of these but did not attempt to foster imitators, believing that he should concentrate on his practice rather than preaching to others on what should be done or how they should be doing it. But, as I have suggested, that is not to say that he did not think seriously about what it was to be an architect in the twentieth century and hold strong views.

On the other hand, as members of the next generation were to point out, Aalto's forms, though sometimes inspired by those of antiquity such as

25 Von Wright, with Elizabeth Anscombe, was involved in a discussion as to whether Wittgenstein should be given a Catholic funeral; they decided that he should.
26 Reed 1998, p. 21.
27 Kuhn 2012.

Greek amphitheatres, were largely personal. In the hands of less talented and sensitive individuals, such formal licence could be disastrous.
We shall return to that discussion in Chapter 9; in the next chapter we
shall examine the thinking and buildings of Aalto's contemporary Louis
Kahn, who came to a different conclusion as to the direction twentieth-
century architecture should take.

6

IDEALS AND THEIR REPRESENTATION

Louis Kahn

Introduction

As in the previous chapter on Alvar Aalto, his near contemporary, we shall follow Louis Kahn's work chronologically. Four themes will be emphasized – the institutions of man, form and design, served and servant spaces and ornament begins with the joint. These appear repeatedly in texts recording his addresses to students from the late 1940s, when he combined teaching with practice, and their implications are visible in his built projects. We shall discuss only eight of these in detail, all in America.[1] Kahn's work can be seen as a potent critique of modernism because he came to believe that architecture was in danger of losing the essence of what it should be: solid and enduring rather than flimsy and evanescent, and redolent of history and memory rather than a response to new conditions that could afford to dispose of the lessons of the past.

6.1 Education and early work

Like Aalto, Kahn was born in the north-east of Europe, in his case on the Baltic island of Saaremaa, Estonia. In 1906, aged only 5 and together with his mother and his younger sister and brother, he joined his father, who had emigrated to Philadelphia two years earlier. Kahn was to remain there until his death in 1974, two years before Aalto's.[2] As a child he was musically talented and excelled in art: he turned down a music scholarship and had decided to attend the Pennsylvania Academy of Fine Arts when a course he took on architectural history inspired him to concentrate on architecture. Kahn studied at the University of Pennsylvania school of architecture from 1920, and he acknowledged the influence of a number of his teachers there, the most important of whom was Paul Cret (1876–1945), a French-born architect who had himself been trained at the École des Beaux-Arts in Paris. Cret directed his students' attention not only to the oversimplified procedures advocated by Durand but also to Viollet-le-Duc's concern to integrate principles of construction; the compositional discipline of Beaux-Arts planning and a deep respect for the nature of materials were to remain central to Kahn's architecture. In 1928–1929, Kahn visited Europe,

1 From 1959, when he received a commission for the United States Consulate Chancellery in Angola (which remained unbuilt), Kahn was also involved in projects in Israel, India (Ahmedabad) and in Dacca, Pakistan (which, as Dhaka, became the national capital of Bangladesh).
2 McCarter 2005 provides the most accessible recent survey of Kahn's life and work. See also Frampton 1995, pp. 209–246.

DOI: 10.4324/9781003244943-7

for the first time since childhood, making sketches that became freer as his tour progressed and subsequently worked for Cret for a couple of years. After a spell unemployed during the Depression, which he spent with other young architects honing his knowledge of emerging modernist architecture, Kahn went to work for the Philadelphia Planning Commission, mostly on social housing. From the mid-1930s he undertook individual commissions, while collaborating with others such as George Howe and Oscar Stonorov, though his reputation rests on projects begun from the middle decades of the century. He did not establish his own office until 1947, the year in which he also began teaching.

Two houses, designed with Anne Tyng, illustrate the development of Kahn's manner in this period.[3] The house for Morton Weiss and his wife (1947–1950) in East Norton Township, Pennsylvania, in which the couple lived until their deaths in 2004, is not so different from conventional modernism of the period: a timber-frame structure with some exposed stonework at the hearth, which owes something to Frank Lloyd Wright and contemporary Californian architecture. Entry was into a linking block with a bedroom wing to one side, and the main living space on the other. But when Kahn republished the plan many years later, he scribbled above it a crude diagram to illustrate a principle that was yet to emerge clearly in his architecture: served and servant spaces. He was trying to indicate how the service elements (kitchens and bathrooms) are grouped along the central circulation spine with clearly defined rooms either side. These kinds of distinctions, between bedroom wings and living spaces, circulation areas and rooms, were a characteristic of modernism; it was Kahn's ambition to find a way of re-integrating them into a coherent whole. The Adler House in Philadelphia, of 1954–1955, illustrates Kahn's later concerns (**Figure 6.1**). The project remained on paper, but in the finalized plan, five square elements, defined at their corners by monumental piers, are somewhat clumsily placed together. Between the piers, and occupying the same depth, were cupboards and storage areas and, in the case of the bedroom wing, bathrooms. Kahn by then had moved away decisively from the asymmetrical planning with slender columns characteristic of modernism.

6.2 Yale Art Gallery extension and Trenton Community Center

During a second visit to Europe in 1950–1951, Kahn admired the monumental structures in Rome, where he was attached to the American Academy and was also able to go on to Egypt. His drawings of the Great Hypostyle Hall at Karnak and of other monuments became increasingly bolder, more colourful and abstract. On his return, Yale University, where Kahn had been teaching two days a

3 Kahn had married Esther Israeli in 1930 but also fathered children by Anne Tyng and Harriet Pattison. He divided what little time he did not spend teaching or in his practice between three different households. For an affectionate portrayal of his life and work, see the film *My Architect* by his son Nathaniel, HBO/Cinemax Films 2003.

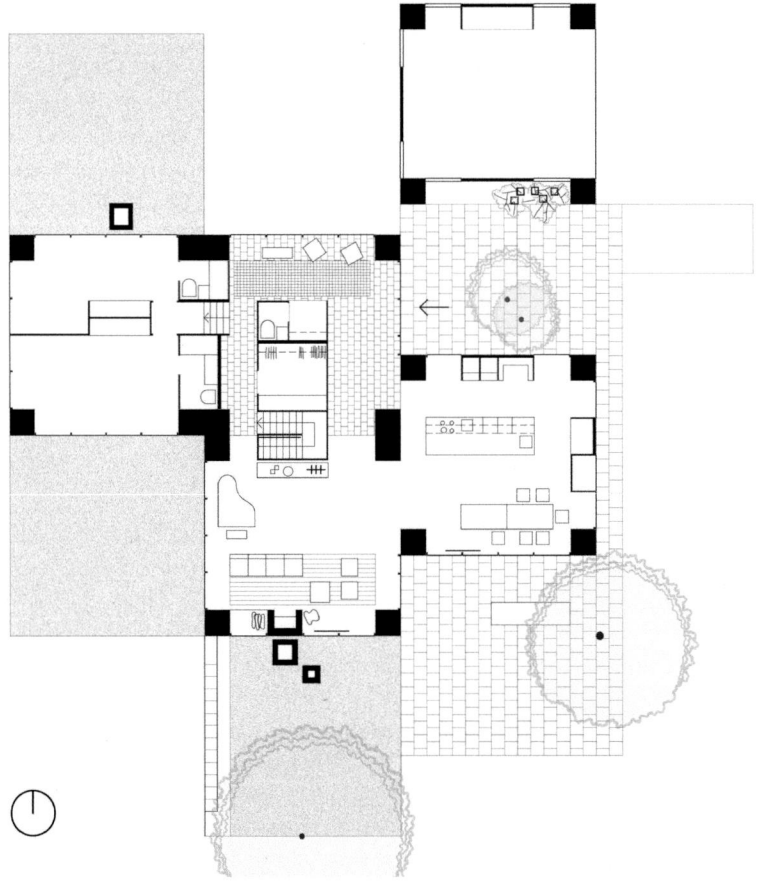

**Figure 6.1 Louis Kahn:
Adler House project,
1954–5**

week since 1947,[4] commissioned him to build the first of the projects for which he is well known – an extension to the university's Art Gallery at New Haven, Connecticut (**Figure 6.2**). Directly
opposite is his Mellon Center for British Art, completed posthumously, which will be discussed later. The 1950s gallery extension presents a blank brick façade to the street and is entered off
a recessed bay between the existing building and the extension.
The interior consists of two open-plan areas separated by a zone
containing services and a triangular staircase within a circular concrete drum (**Figure 6.3**). We see Kahn's emerging preference for
clear geometries and a separation of served and servant spaces. The
structure itself is an in situ triangulated concrete waffle slab cast
in two stages, with services running in the interspace. It is prob-
able that the charismatic engineer Buckminster Fuller influenced
this arrangement: Anne Tyng admired his work and Kahn used
to commute with Fuller from Philadelphia to Yale. Fuller became
famous for his geodesic domes and the dymaxion principle – doing
more with less. His dome structures, the largest being for Expo 67
in Montreal, depend on keeping all the triangulated members in
tension rather than compression. But it is clear that Kahn's floor

4 Teaching with him was
Josef Albers, who had been
responsible for the Vorkurs
at the Bauhaus and was then
at Black Mountain College.

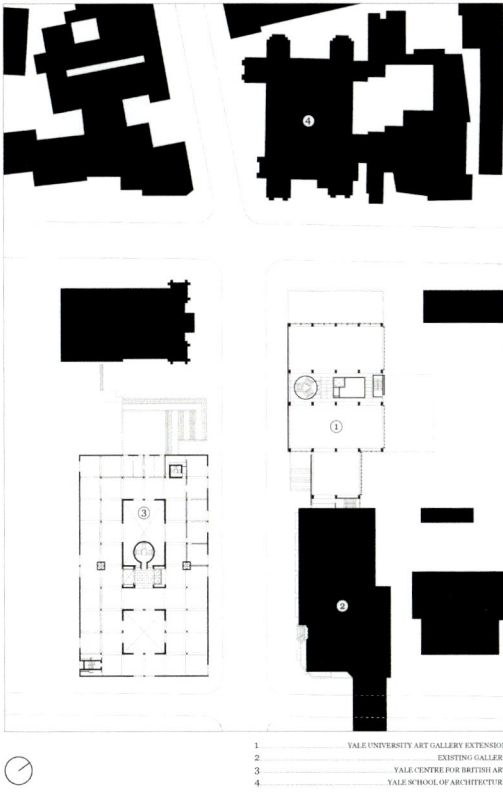

Figure 6.2 Louis Kahn:
Yale University Art
Gallery extension,
1951–53, figure-
ground block plan

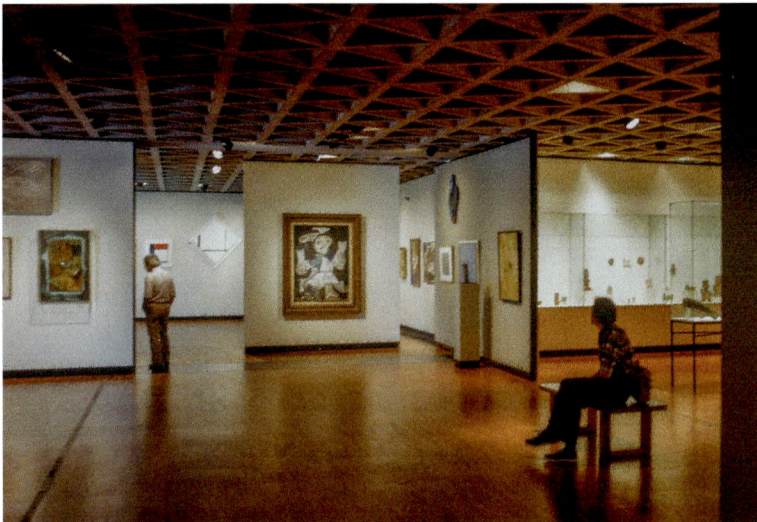

Figure 6.3 Louis Kahn:
Yale University Art
Gallery extension,
1951–53, interior

did not behave like this at all, and he was certainly not interested in keeping everything as lightweight as possible. The frame idea had initially been intended to be constructed in steel but there were shortages because of the Korean War, and Kahn was happier with concrete even though the structure was hardly efficient. He

5 See Saint 2007,
pp. 403–404.
6 McCarter 2005 empha-
sizes the important influence
of Wright on Kahn's architecture. He also notes that
in 1955, Colin Rowe gave
Kahn a copy of Wittkower's
*Architectural Principles in
the Age of Humanism*. For
Rowe's correspondence
following their meeting, see
Merrill 2021.
7 One such, the Sangraha-
laya, 1958–1963, by Charles
Correa, forms part of the
Gandhi Memorial Institute
in Ahmedabad, India.

succeeded in realizing his idea by persuading not only the engineers
and contractor charged with building the project but also his client,
Whitney Griswold, the president at Yale, apparently by means of the
sheer force of his personality.[5]

A year after the completion of the gallery, Kahn was commissioned
to design a Jewish Community Center at Trenton, New Jersey
(**Figure 6.4**). A sequence of ambitious projects illustrates geometrical characteristics we have already seen. The third scheme for
the centre, of 1956, consists of a tartan grid of squares defining the
rooms and minor bays, about one third the width of them, which
are used for corridors and service spaces. Larger rooms like gym-
nasia occupy several bays. Superficially the plan resembles a Beaux-
Arts composition because of its symmetries and consistency, but
Kahn made the entrance in one of the minor bays, and circulation
also runs along the narrow bays, unlike the centralized *marche* from
bay to bay of classical composition. The plan is in fact more like a
'carpet' without such hierarchies. The circulation pattern may also
owe something to Frank Lloyd Wright's practice both in his Chicago houses and at his 1905–1908 Unity Temple, where, to preserve
the integrity of the principal volumes, movement is peripheral and
sometimes quite tortuous.[6] Kahn's approach was in turn to influence his near contemporaries, such as Aldo van Eyck, and a younger
generation who were members of Team Ten, the subject of the next
chapter.

**Figure 6.4 Louis Kahn:
Trenton Community
Center, third project,
1956**

Funds for the ambitious centre did not emerge, however, so all that
was completed in 1955 was the less extravagant, mostly open-air,
bathhouse (**Figure 6.5**). But this building was enormously influential, and imitations shortly appeared all over the world.[7] Its four

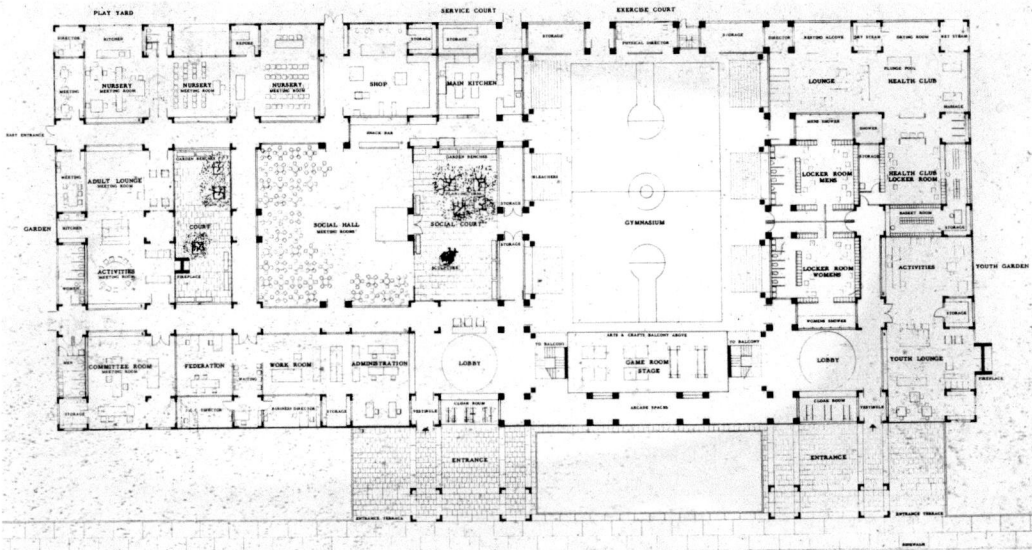

**Figure 6.5 Louis
Kahn: The Trenton
Community Center:
Bath House as realized**

covered bays and central open area are defined by pyramidical roofs resting on substantial corner blocks – hollow rather than solid – between which run the minor bays containing servant elements. In the mid-1950s modernism meant asymmetry, flat roofs and machine-like finishes. The bathhouse was recognized as both redolent of previous architecture and yet, in its abstraction, unmistakably of its time. Kahn seemed to be distilling the influence of his Beaux-Arts-trained professor by making use of the concept of *poché* space – literally pocketed space, meaning, in this case, not a drawing that would be easily portable but a volume tucked into the thickness of a wall. As he explained:

> From poché, I learnt the difference between the hollow wall and the solid wall. . . . I made the wall a container instead of a solid.[8]

This notion pre-dates the Beaux-Arts, however. When Kahn visited Europe, as we have seen, he was attracted to Roman and Egyptian architecture rather than Renaissance masterpieces or Gothic cathedrals. In the United Kingdom what he most admired were Scottish castles, where precisely this principle of *poché* can be observed: staircases and subsidiary rooms are embedded in the thickness of the walls (**Figure 6.6**). Kahn's preference for self-enclosed castle-like forms can be seen in his urban design project for Philadelphia where huge (presumably masonry) silos, some containing car parking, are grouped around the

8 Kahn 1991. This useful if highly repetitive collection contains writings, letters, talks to students and interviews. Quotations hereafter are referenced by page number rather than by the locus of the text or address.

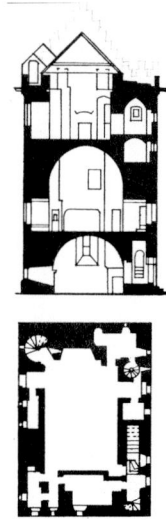

Figure 6.6 Section and plan of a Scottish castle

city core, protecting a pedestrian area. A curious exception is the tower seen in the background, with its pronounced diagonal bracing. Kahn always wanted to find ways of illustrating structure; suppressing the expression of what was necessary to deal with wind loads concerned him. He had developed the project with Anne Tyng, and it was presented in 1953.[9]

6.3 Richards Research Laboratory

Kahn's discovery, that he could use the *poché* spaces to form the ducts that modern buildings require, was clearly illustrated in the Richards Laboratory in Philadelphia for medical research, begun in 1957 (**Figure 6.7**, **Figure 6.8**). Having moved from teaching at Yale, where he had refused the offer of a chair to ensure he maintained sufficient time for practice, Kahn had resumed teaching part-time at the University of Pennsylvania in Philadelphia. The sketch elevations reflected his admiration for the clusters of brick towers he had sketched in Italian hill towns like San Gimignano, while the plan shows how he struggled to separate out the circulation and servicing to leave clearly defined square laboratories. In a second phase, for biological research, he was forced in some cases to introduce corridors through the centre of the rooms. He was clear that it was not that he *liked* services – they should just be given their appropriate place:

> I do not like ducts; I do not like pipes. I hate them really thoroughly, but because I hate them so thoroughly I feel they have to be given their place. If I just hated them and took no care, I think they would invade the building and completely destroy it. I want to correct any notion you may have that I am in love with that kind of thing.[10]

9 The presentation is reprinted in Kahn 1991, pp. 28–52.
10 Kahn 1991, p. 262.

PHASE 1   PHASE 2

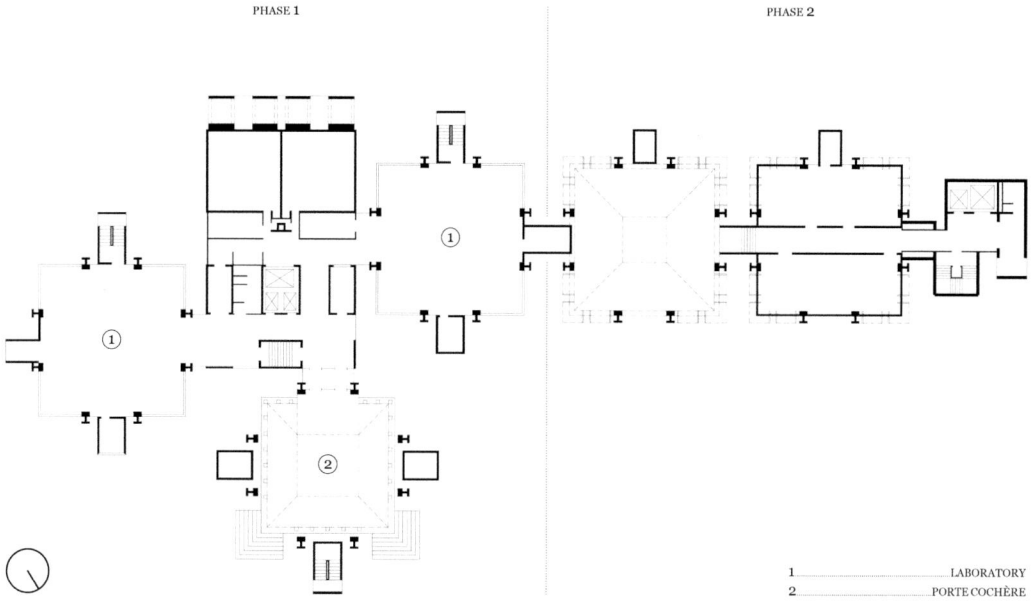

1 .... LABORATORY
2 .... PORTE COCHÈRE

Services and vertical circulation are pushed to the edges not primarily in order to express them, as the members of groups such as Archigram later sought to do, but to make each laboratory space a well-lit room, like a studio.[11] Paired columns occur in the centre of each square bay, so the beams, which are perforated to take pipes and ducts, cantilever outwards diminishing towards the corners, an intention visible in Kahn's elevation sketch and evident in the window pattern as realized.

Kahn was not the first within the modernist tradition to stress verticality in this way. Frank Lloyd Wright's Larkin office building of 1904–1906, sadly demolished seven years before Kahn began work on the Richards building, had a narrow central atrium space with open-plan offices all around on five levels. Staircases and vertical ventilation shafts stand around the perimeter as blank brick towers. What made Kahn's building so influential was that it re-validated a way of composing buildings that had been forgotten: modernism by the middle of the twentieth century was meant to be predominantly horizontal (exhibiting the ribbon windows Le Corbusier had christened *fenêtres en longueurs*) so that the verticality of Kahn's laboratory towers was in striking contrast to expectations. His insistence that "Architecture comes from the making of a Room" (**Figure 6.9**) – an aphorism frequently accompanied by a sketch, as was typical of his teaching style – is quite different from the orthodoxy of the open-plan and free-flowing space found in the plans of Mies van der Rohe and celebrated in books like Sigfried Giedion's *Space, Time and Architecture*.

6.4 Rochester Unitarian Church

The five projects for the Unitarian Church at Rochester (1959–1967) indicate Kahn's compositional technique (**Figure 6.10**). He distinguished between what he termed form and design. Form was the

Figure 6.7 Louis Kahn: Richards Research Laboratory, Philadelphia, 1957–1960, plan

11 Kahn's procedure influenced architects such as Richard Rogers, whose Lloyds Building in London (won in competition 1978 and completed in 1986) pushed circulation and services to the outside of the underwriting room, but also dramatized them in a way that Kahn deliberately eschewed.

Figure 6.8 Louis Kahn: Richards Research Laboratory, Philadelphia, 1957– 1960, view

idea of the building: very often in Kahn's compositions this would be expressed as a central room surrounded by subsidiary subservient rooms. The process of design was accommodating the architectural idea to cater for the circumstances of a particular brief, site and budget. As he explained:

> If I were to define Architecture in a word, I would say that architecture is the thoughtful making of spaces. It is not filling prescriptions as clients want them filled. It is not fitting uses into dimensional areas . . . it is a creating of spaces that evoke a feeling of use.[12]

The first iteration had subsidiary spaces surrounding a truncated polyhedron (surely derived from his interest in Buckminster Fuller), with a circular ambulatory; in a second version the central church was rectangular, and so it remained in the third version. In the fourth version, the worship space was square with roof lighting at the four corners, and that remains the pattern as constructed but with a thickened service wall between the main space and the ambulatory. The incidental pattern of the architecture might have varied, but the ideal form held. The form itself derives from a meditation on the nature of the institution – in this case a church. Kahn used the idea of a school to explain his process:

12 Kahn 1991, p. 116. The second sentence of this quotation is often printed "It is note filling prescriptions . . .", which is clearly an error.

> I am trying to find new expressions of old institutions. The institutions of learning, let us say, with which we are so concerned today,

The drawing contains Kahn's handwritten text:

Architecture comes from The Making of a Room

The Plan A society of rooms is a place good to live work learn

A great American Poet once asked The Architect 'What slice of the sun does your building have, what, light enters your Room as if to say the sun never knew how great it is until it struck the side of a building.

The Room

is The place of the mind. In a small room one does not say what one would in a large room. In a room with only one other person could be generative The vectors of each meet. A room is not a room without natural light. natural light gives the time of day and the mood of The seasons to enter.

Figure 6.9 Kahn's idea of the room

probably began with a man under a tree and around him the listeners to the words of his mind. The marvel of the first classroom never leaves me, and now I approach a problem with the desire for the sense of beginnings. I think we need in all schools reverence for the marvels of beginnings.[13]

Kahn was concerned, in other words, to celebrate what he called the institutions of man, and in philosophical terms his distinction between ideal form and circumstantial design reveals his idealism: each particular example is the reflection of a higher ideal. The compositional technique forsakes the Bauhaus orthodoxy of an exhaustive analysis of functions followed by the choice of freely-expressed forms to revert to something much closer to that of the Beaux-Arts described in Chapter 2 (pp. 38–39): an *esquisse* that encapsulates the idea of the project, by the

13 Kahn 1991, p. 229.

Figure 6.10 Louis Kahn: Rochester Unitarian Church, 1959–67, initial design and five iterations

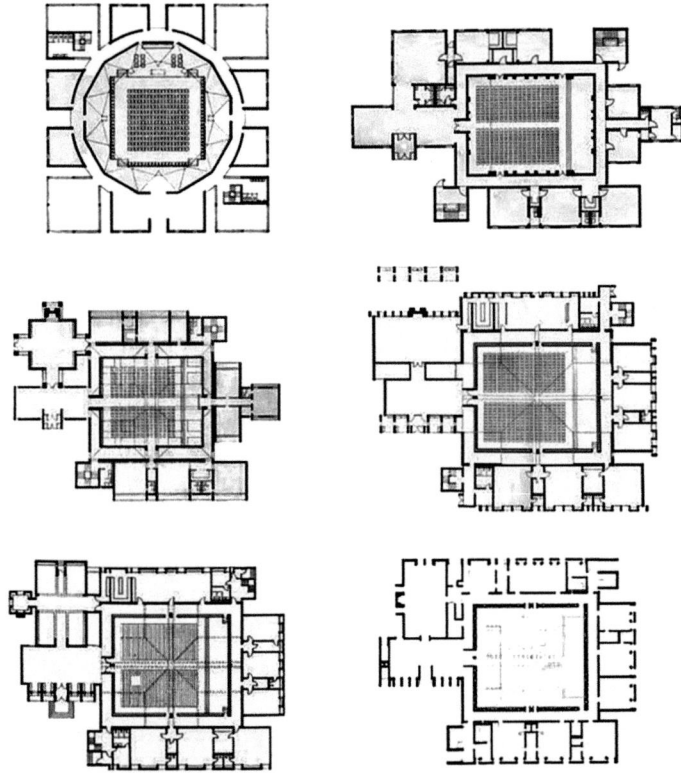

choice of a formal *parti*, which is modified and refined in subsequent design work while retaining the conceptual idea.

6.5 Salk laboratories

14 The Richards laboratories were functionally far from satisfactory. As Edward Ford noted, "Seldom has a building received simultaneously the adulation of so many critics and the condemnation of so many occupants" (Ford 2006).

15 Arthur Vierendeel was a Belgian engineer (1852–1940) who developed a truss for bridge designs employing rectangular rather than the more common triangular perforations. Kahn depended on an excellent engineer, August Komendant, for nearly all his projects: see Saint 2007, pp. 402–409.

The Rochester design process was an extended one, taking about eight years, and during this time Kahn was also engaged in the design of laboratories at La Jolla, California, for the famous biologist Jonas Salk, discoverer of the polio vaccine. The original conception was for a collection of buildings, more like a university campus, but only two parallel ranges of laboratories were constructed. Here Kahn separated services from the laboratories on section, which was a much more satisfactory solution than the separation on plan we saw at the Richards laboratories (**Figure 6.11**).[14] Large Vierendeel trusses,[15] which are nearly floor-depth, span across the open-plan laboratories, which run east-west either side of a paved plaza overlooking the Pacific Ocean. All the pipes and ducts run in between the structural supports, effectively therefore providing alternate floors of laboratories and services. Such spatial generosity is seldom affordable within the budgets of most laboratory projects, but it provides ideal flexibility allowing services to be reconfigured or replaced without affecting the work in the laboratory spaces themselves. Pulled out from the main laboratory spaces on the plaza are studies for the scientists to write up their experimental research, angled towards the west and the view of the ocean. Kahn had intended to plant trees in the central plaza between the two laboratory blocks but was persuaded by the Mexican architect Luis Barragán that it would be much better devoid of vegetation with only a central water channel (**Figure 6.12**). The result is a much admired, memorable and noble space.

The principal material is beautifully fashioned in situ concrete; it is supplemented by timber, which partly clads the small study towers and is carefully detailed to be flush with the concrete. The fastidious way materials are fashioned and connected is the only form of decoration: "ornament begins with the joint", as Kahn frequently said.

6.6 Philips Exeter Academy

Over a six-year period from 1965, Kahn designed a library building for a school at Exeter, New Hampshire (**Figure 6.13**). It's a solid, castle-like block in comparison with the neo-colonial style buildings that form the immediate context, though unlike a castle, the corners are cut away to reveal the four thick walls that turn out to contain reading carrels within their depth. Apparently, the massive block is only four or five floors high, but this is an illusion because there are mezzanines. An arcade is formed all around at ground floor level. The plan is a square with stairs and services in the corners and books arranged around a central seven storey void (**Figure 6.14**): Kahn talked of "taking a book to the light", and that is what readers do, either to the day-lit perimeter carrels or to a more informal reading shelf at the edge of the top-lit void space. Enormous circular cut-outs in the concrete structure present the library floors to the atrium void, a space not called for in the brief, which seems to embody the essence of the institution or, to use Kahn's own words, to "evoke a feeling of use". Only on closer inspection can one see that the piers that frame desks and carrels are modulated by getting a little narrower on each floor.[16] The timber carrels are detailed, on alternate floors, to engage with the window joinery (**Figure 6.15**), and the timber panels are brought flush (as at the Salk laboratories) with the masonry piers externally and internally at the upper mezzanines (**Figure 6.16**). A precedent for this material treatment, of which Kahn may have been aware, was Hendrik Berlage's Beurs, or Stock Exchange, in Amsterdam, constructed at the beginning of the twentieth century, where it seems as if a knife has sliced through the fabric to emphasize its planar surface and celebrate the articulation of mass and void. Berlage was engaged in the modernist abstraction of historic precedent; Kahn was engaged in transforming modernist abstractions to remind us of history – or of what he would have stressed was the essence that lies behind historical precedents.

6.7 The Kimbell Museum and Mellon Gallery for British Art

The two other examples briefly illustrated are art galleries completed at the end of Kahn's life. In Fort Worth, Texas, Kahn designed what appears,

16 For a detailed analysis of the construction of the Phillips Exeter Library, see Wickersham 1989.

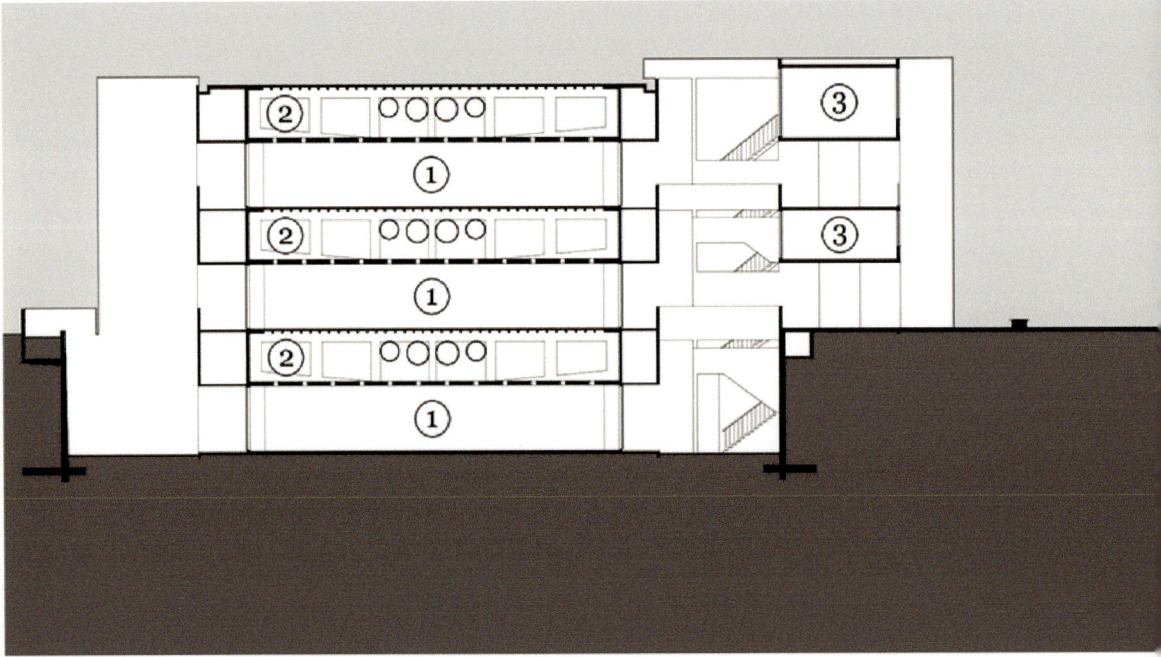

Figure 6.11 Louis Kahn: Salk Institute for Biological Studies, 1959–65, section with central plaza

Figure 6.12 Louis Kahn: Salk Institute for Biological Studies, 1959–65

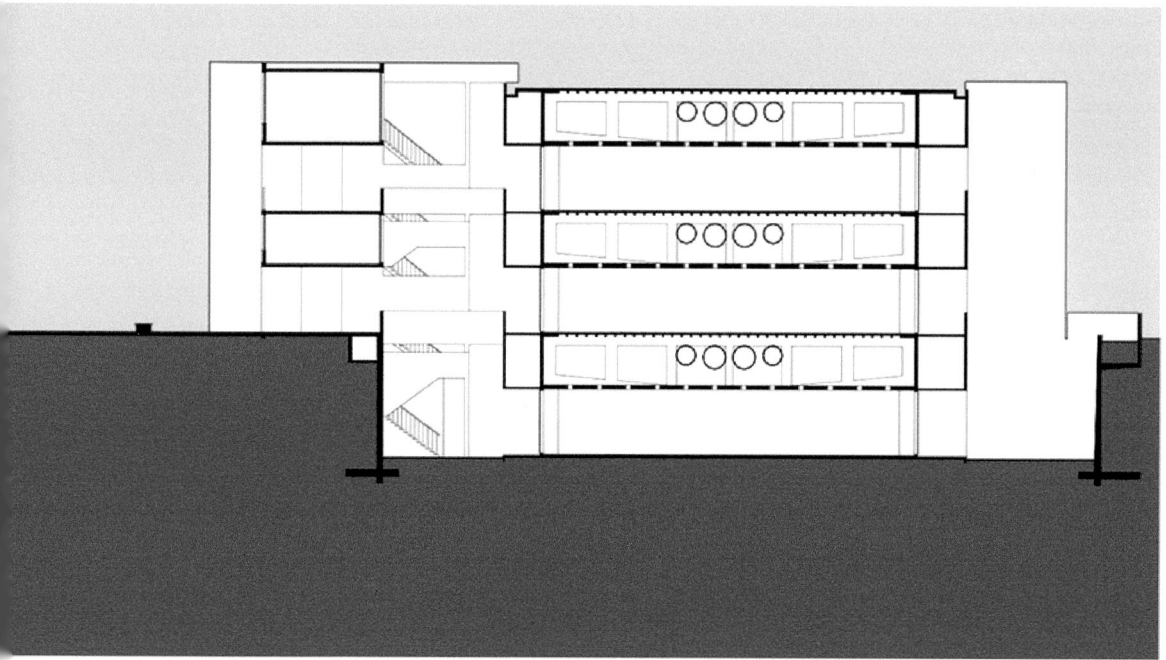

1 .... LABORATORY
2 .... SERVICES
3 .... STUDY CARREL

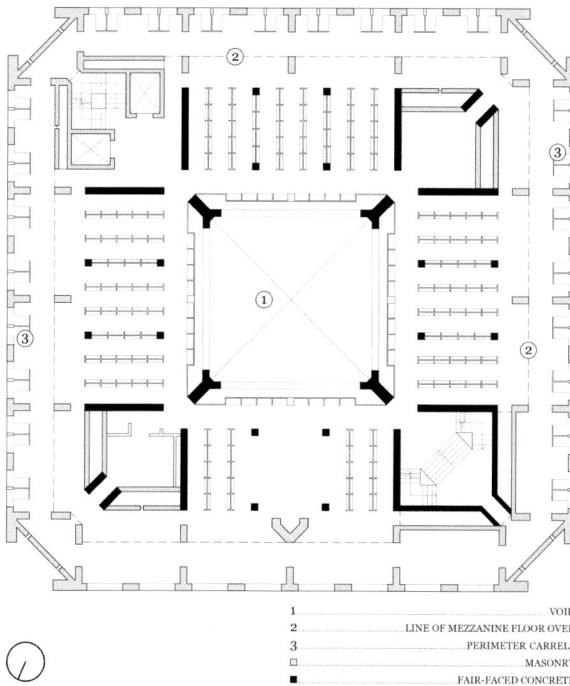

1 .... VOID
2 .... LINE OF MEZZANINE FLOOR OVER
3 .... PERIMETER CARRELS
□ .... MASONRY
■ .... FAIR-FACED CONCRETE

Figure 6.13 Louis Kahn: Phillips Exeter Library, 1965–71, plan at third floor level

Figure 6.14 Louis Kahn: Phillips Exeter Library, 1965–71, central atrium

Figure 6.15 Louis Kahn: Phillips Exeter Library, 1965–71, study carrels

Figure 6.16 Materials brought flush to the same plane: Phillips Exeter Academy

Figure 6.17 Louis Kahn: Kimbell Museum, Fort Worth, Texas, 1966–72, entrance from park

from the main entrance off the surrounding park, to be a single-storey gallery (**Figure 6.17**).[17] In fact there is a substantial lower floor containing storage and staff accommodation and a secondary entrance from a parking area on the other side[18] (**Figure 6.18**). The structure seems to consist of six rows of barrel vaults, but again this is deceptive: the vaults

17 The effective planting was the work of the landscape architect Harriet Pattison, mother of Kahn's son Nathaniel.
18 This is naturally how most visitors arrive, but

1	AUDITORIUM
2	COURTYARD
3	TEMPORARY EXHIBITS
4	VAULTED CANOPY
5	GARDEN

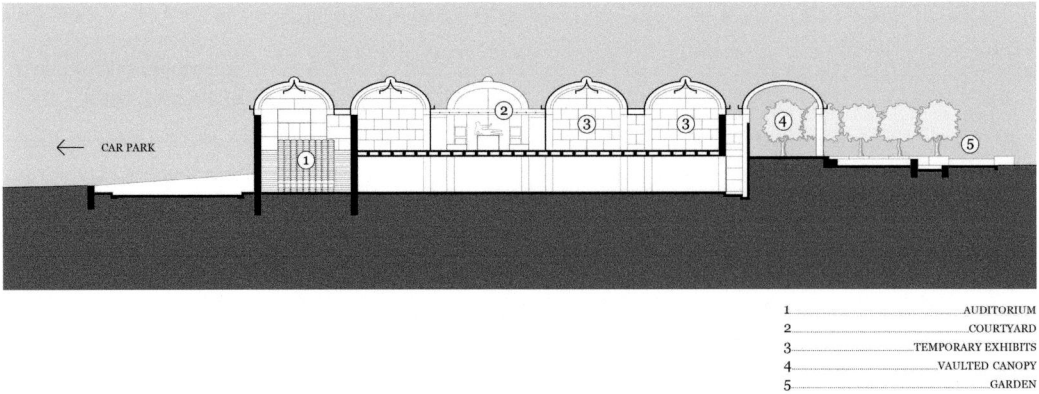

Figure 6.18 Louis Kahn: Kimbell Museum, Fort Worth, Texas, 1966–72, section

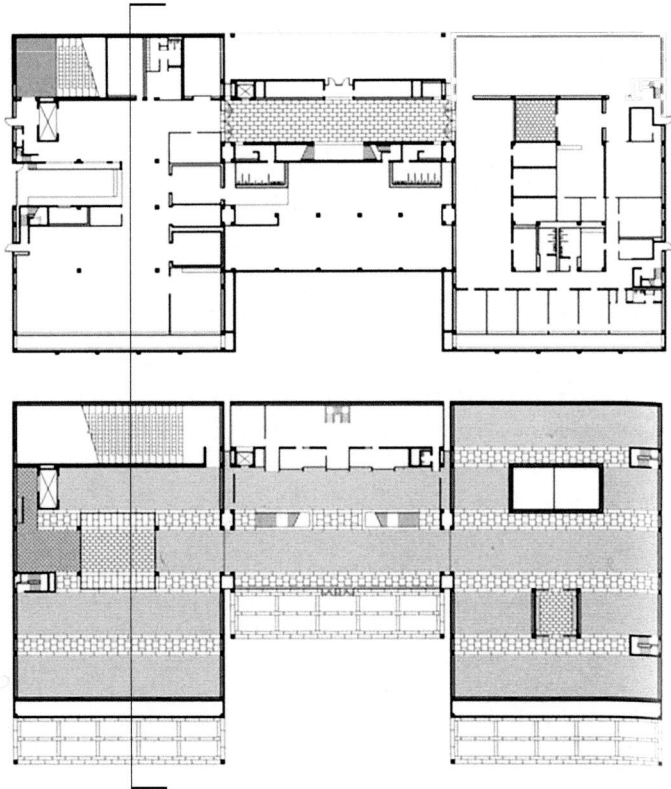

Figure 6.19 Kimbell Museum, Ground and first floor plans

Kahn characteristically privileges the idealized approach through the landscape. See Frampton 1995, pp. 243–246.

are cycloids and mostly split in two. The main gallery floor has a permanent collection to the right as you enter from the park, with two internal courts, a bookshop straight ahead and temporary exhibitions and a café to the left with a single courtyard (**Figure 6.19**). In the galleries, the walls are of travertine, and the half-cycloids are a finely finished concrete, day-lit from the central top-light, which has a suspended partly perforated aluminium baffle against the fierce Texan sun (**Figure 6.20**). Between the major bays of the vaulted ceiling are minor flat-ceilinged bays that carry tracks for artificial light (as do the baffles) and also

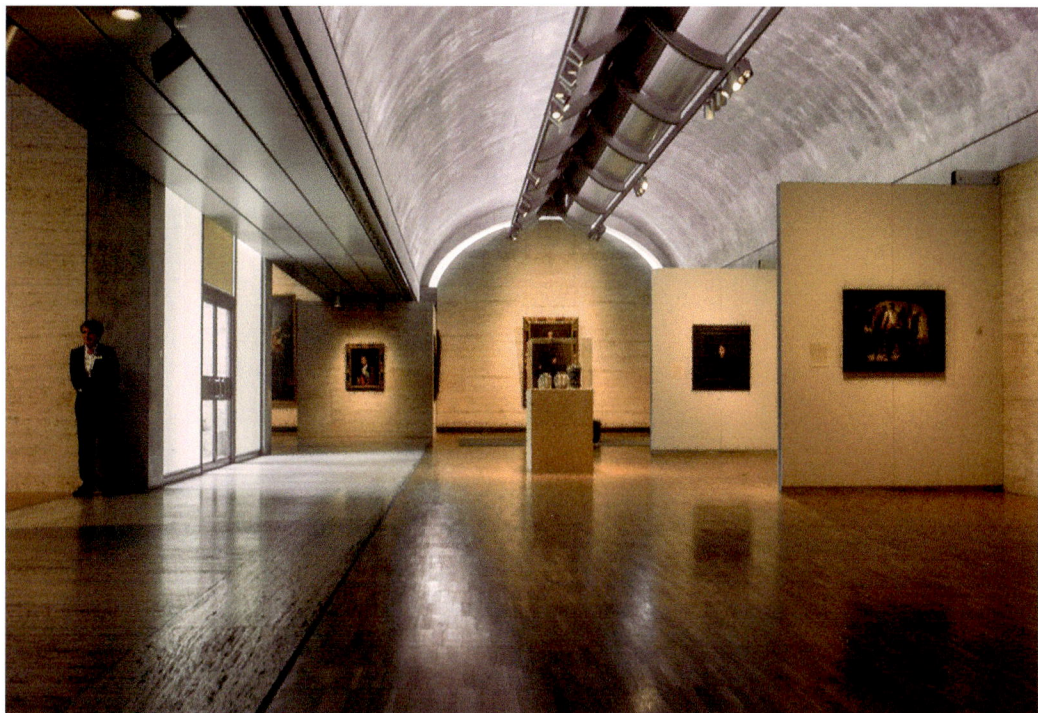

Figure 6.20 Kimbell Museum, permanent collection gallery

Figure 6.21 Kimbell Museum, light baffle and column junction

give support for subsidiary partitions, the location and orientation of which can be varied. A thin slot at the edge of the flat bays provides controlled air conditioning. At the gable to each vault, the difference between the wall geometry and the geometry of the beams supporting the half-cycloids, which vary in depth to take account of differential stresses, is revealed by a slice of light. The whole ensemble – column, beam, cycloid vault, gable light and ventilation slot – comes together in a typical detail of considerable evocative power (**Figure 6.21**). As with all Kahn's buildings, numerous formal imitations followed, but they seldom came close to the complex subtlety of their model. Indeed, as Kahn constantly stressed in his teaching, the particular forms of his buildings were beside the point: it was the spirit of the institution he was trying to capture.

The Mellon Center is in New Haven, just opposite the Yale University Art Gallery. The entrance porch on the ground floor is at the south-east corner, and the external walls are of brushed stainless steel, aligned flush with the concrete frame (**Figure 6.22**). The building is composed around two top-lit voids (**Figure 6.23**) – a four-storey high entrance atrium, square in plan, and on the first floor a magnificent three-storey high room, hung with pictures but also containing a massive concrete staircase drum. Surrounding these is a neutral square grid of spaces that

Figure 6.22 Louis Kahn: Yale Centre for British Art, façade

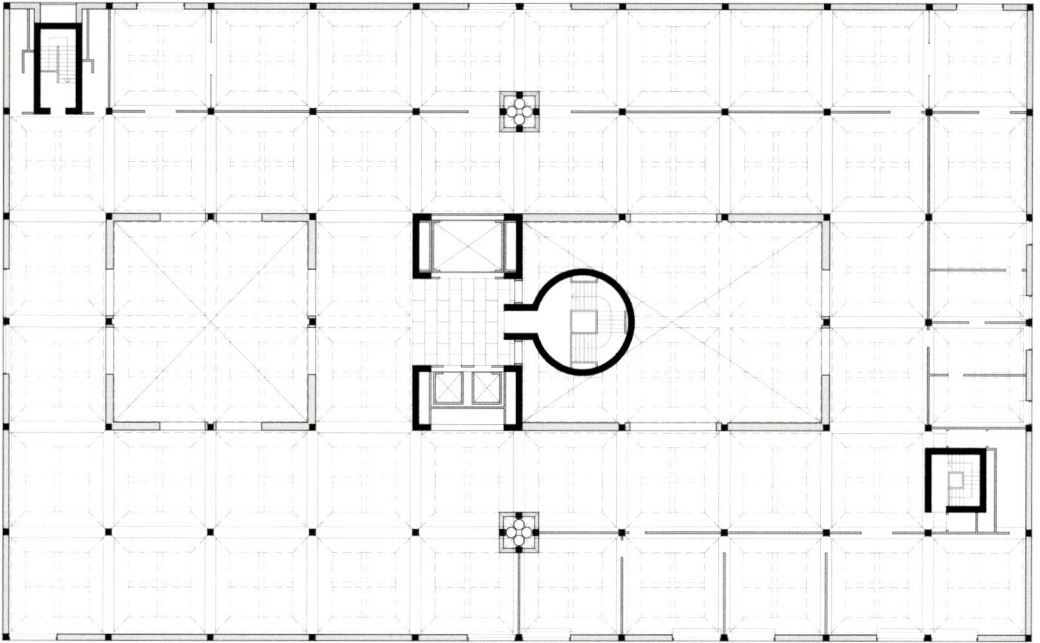

Figure 6.23 Louis Kahn: Yale Centre for British Art, fourth floor plan

Figure 6.24 Yale Centre for British Art, main room

19 The German word *mate-rialgerecht* probably captures that sense best.

can be subdivided to form smaller galleries. The main room simultaneously evokes the scale and dignity we associate with a grand English country house and is studiously abstract (**Figure 6.24**). Its top lighting and the exposed drum of the staircase also give it something of the quality of an outdoor court. In Kahn's treatment of structure in the first court – the entrance hall – where a central column is omitted the beam doubles in depth, and the columns, which do not need to be as thick as the beam, are kept back: Kahn (unlike Aalto) was not prepared to allow other considerations to obliterate the way he felt the structure wanted to manifest itself and was constantly concerned to express what was happening 'truthfully'. In the same way, Kahn wished not to conceal, but on occasion to exploit, the differences which arise from an acknowledgement of a material's intrinsic character.[19]

The top floor benefits from pyramidical concrete skylights over each of its bays. These uniform square carpeted spaces are defined by strips of travertine, and the full-height screens on which pictures are hung do not extend to the corners. Views through the gallery are therefore frequently enlivened by diagonal glimpses, and there are openings from this floor looking down into the great top-lit court, containing the monumental staircase drum and hung with the finest and grandest of the gallery's pictures. As at the Kimbell gallery, and indeed in the first project for the Trenton Community Center, the ordered apparently classical composition is experienced in a way that is particularly twentieth-century and non-hierarchical.

6.8 Kahn's primary concerns, strengths and weaknesses

The four themes mentioned at the start of this chapter (the institutions of man, form and design, served and servant spaces, and ornament begins with the joint) summarize Kahn's primary preoccupation with the starting point for design being a meditation on the nature of the institution; his distinction between ideal form and the circumstantial issues that an architect necessarily deals with; his compositional method whereby he privileged the major spaces, usually in a strongly figurative form, with subsidiary service spaces providing a thick wall to protect them; and his scrupulous treatment of detailed connections of materials as the only permissible form of decoration. He was swimming against the stream, not only of modernist aesthetics but also of the way the building industry was developing. As Edward Ford put it:

> It was clear by the early 1970s that what Kahn considered to be a good building and what the American building industry considered to be good building were diametrically opposed. It wished to separate utilities; Kahn wished to integrate them. It wanted independent building components; Kahn wanted them interdependent. It wished to conceal structure and services; Kahn wanted to expose them. It sought maximum flexibility; Kahn sought a tight fit of form

and activity . . . The building industry wanted veneers; Kahn wanted bearing walls. It wanted steel; Kahn wanted concrete. Kahn wanted all to be monolithic; it wanted it layered.[20]

A consequence of Kahn's resistance to the direction that industry was taking was the inordinate expense of his buildings: his Capital complex in Dhaka, Bangladesh, reputedly cost a significant proportion of the country's gross domestic product.[21] Just as his students were in awe of Kahn as a charismatic 'guru' teacher, so his clients were also prepared to wait, sometimes for several years, as he developed his projects through many iterations. And to achieve the apparently lucid clarity of his buildings, certain sacrifices had to be made. The lecture hall at the Kimbell Museum, running from the ground to lower ground floors, is awkwardly long and narrow; in the same building the library is uncomfortably squeezed into a mezzanine (and therefore invisible in the two plans illustrated) with particularly crude horizontal light fittings fighting the shape of the vault; and the gallery staff are consigned to the lower ground floor where they are denied a view of the park and have to look on to a concrete retaining wall. But these are sacrifices that we, as visitors, would seem to readily accept, if we are even aware of them, when encountering gallery spaces that are amongst the most serene and beautiful to have been constructed in the twentieth century. By contrast, Alvar Aalto's concern for those who worked within his buildings meant that he was more prepared to compromise their form.

A comparison between the plans of Kahn's Exeter Library (**Figure 6.13**) and Aalto's library at Seinäjoki (**Figure 5.19**) reveals the different preoccupations of these two great architects. Kahn's building is symmetrical and carefully layered from the outer skin to the inner void. Aalto would not have devoted so much of the volume to this central apparently purposeless space: his building is far more casually arranged, contrasting the 'ordinary' cellular offices and a reading space that fans out in plan and effloresces on section to capture daylight and modulate the artificial lighting. But an arrangement such as Aalto's can never achieve the static monumentality that Kahn sought. Kahn's treatment of natural light (which he regarded as sacred in its revelation of structure and architectural form) is sometimes more appropriate for the illumination of a sculptural ruin than for daily use, and the quest for monumental dignity can make for uncomfortable spaces.[22] His artificial light fittings are usually simple drums with none of the refinements of Nordic designs. Beside the library at Exeter is a much less successful building: a single-storey dining hall, of a similar footprint, where the kitchen (as service space) occupies the centre and the served space is pushed to the periphery. It was precisely the kind of brief that Aalto could respond to with fluent ease. But Kahn, as ever, sought forms to reflect ideals, even at the cost of awkwardness. This can be an aspect of his architecture that moves us, rather as the art of Giotto (a painter Kahn admired) affects us partly because it reveals the difficulty he had in achieving what he intended. Kahn told Anne Tyng that he preferred the early Greek

20 Ford 2006, p. 335.
21 In utilitarian terms, this is straightforwardly unethical behaviour. Edward Ford claims this reputation was undeserved, at least in the case of the galleries: Ford 2006.
22 The bleak common room surrounded by study bedrooms at Kahn's 1960–1965 Bryn Mawr College building would be one such example.

23 Tyng 1997, cited in
McCarter 2005.
24 Scully 1962b.
25 Benedikt 1991.

temples at Paestum to the Parthenon:[23] he had a reverence for the origins of institutions in general and a greater respect for works that reveal an authentic struggle than for more widely admired masterpieces with all their refinements.

Early advocates of Louis Kahn's work included Vincent Scully (1920–2017), a prolific architectural historian, who taught at Yale from 1947 until 2009.[24] A more complex reading of Kahn's work is well illustrated in Michael Benedikt's slender volume *Deconstructing the Kimbell, An Essay on Meaning and Architecture*.[25] Benedikt employed the deconstructionist literary techniques developed by Jacques Derrida to illustrate the considerable subtleties of Kahn's architecture. As we saw, nothing is quite as expected. The overall plan is symmetrical, as all Kahn's institutional buildings aspire to be, but the placing of the courtyards is varied. They are different sizes: the larger square court in the visiting gallery occupies the subsidiary bays, whereas the square court in the permanent collection is only within the major bay, and its rectangular court, which penetrates down to the floor below, is two squares wide but completely invisible from the gallery level. More fundamentally, once the sectional arrangement which caters so well for natural and artificial light had been determined, the apparently bounded and symmetrical composition seemed extendable either by extrusion or by additional bays. Sketches by Kahn provide evidence for this possibility, yet, when the gallery wished to extend, plans by Romaldo Giurgola to add to it in strict imitation were strenuously resisted, as had

Figure 6.25 Louis Kahn, Exeter library in context

been plans to extend Kahn's Salk laboratory, in that case unsuccessfully.[26] The composition is both open and closed. Benedikt is at pains to show that the order Kahn sought and his buildings exhibit contains its opposite: a tension and disaggregation. Derridean perceptions, with their literary origin, surely reframe qualities that we recognize in all great art. Mozart's music (of which Kahn was fond) characteristically expresses joy while simultaneously conveying a deep sadness. Benedikt also finds that aspects of the Kimbell gallery, which I suggested earlier are merely awkward, can be redolent of deeper meanings. The invisible library squeezed under the conoidal vault in a mezzanine, for example, is located centrally above the bookshop and accessed by a dog-leg staircase concealed in a range of cupboards. Kahn was Jewish and by withdrawing the book from view and elevating it beneath an ark-like vault, he can be understood as sanctifying it in accordance with his religious tradition.[27]

Undoubtedly, Kahn's best buildings, as do all great architectural masterpieces, lend themselves to such subtle and fascinating readings, and it must be a matter of debate as to when we can see the irresolutions that lie behind his apparently resolved buildings as strengths or as weaknesses. One characteristic of Kahn's refusal to make easy accommodations is the problem he had in signalling entrances. Frequently these are under-celebrated and achieved simply by omitting a structural bay, as at the Mellon Gallery (**Figure 6.22**). Adjacent to his Exeter Library is a mundane neo-colonial building (**Figure 6.25**). Kahn's library has a uniform cloister all around the ground floor, so that it is far from clear to visitors how to enter, but in the traditionally decorated building it is quite obvious where the front door is and indeed where we would find the most important room, on the first floor. These signals, of entrance and hierarchy, are achieved by conventional decoration – the application of motifs that are intended to convey an appropriate level of dignity. But Kahn could not bring himself to do this; the joint for him was the beginning of ornament but also its fulfilment. As we shall see, these issues were to be the principal focus of criticisms levelled by Kahn's pupil and sometime teaching assistant Robert Venturi, who questioned the abstraction that was characteristic of modernism as a whole and that had been inherited by Kahn.

At the same time, the absolute aesthetic probity with which Kahn behaved[28] and the struggle he had, and which we witness, to express what an institution ought to be and how the materials to realize it should be employed, give the best of his buildings an authority which it is hard to equal in any others of the twentieth century.

26 See Spector 2001, pp. 166–181. The difficulty in extending Kahn's buildings suggests that, simultaneously modern and yet traditional as they are, they share with classical architecture a quality (of beauty) which Alberti described as "that reasoned harmony of all the parts within a body, so that nothing may be added, taken away or altered but for the worse" (Alberti 1988). The solution at the Kimbell was to build a separate pavilion, for which Renzo Piano was the architect.

27 Benedikt 1991, pp. 88–91.

28 An illustration of the financial sacrifice he made in the pursuit of his career (and demanded of his loyal employees) was that on his death his office was more than $500,000 in debt (Ford 1996, p. 335). Other judgments of Kahn's behaviour are less charitable: "When Louis Kahn died of a heart attack in Pennsylvania Station in 1974, he left a legacy of a handful of great buildings, 3 neglected families (two of which were secret) and a personal debt approaching half a million dollars despite the fact that his employees often went unpaid" (Spector 2021, p. 147). See the discussion later in the same book, particularly Chapter 4, as to whether it is acceptable to regard as exemplary the careers of such architects, as opposed to admiring some of their buildings as aesthetic artefacts.

7

HUMANIZING MODERNISM – TEAM TEN AND THE DUTCH

Introduction

Chapter 4 identified a critique of orthodox modernism, as represented by CIAM and its two most vocal apologists, Gropius and Le Corbusier – its dogmatism in relation to the city, and the inadequacy or inappropriateness of its compositional principles, at least in the hands of those without some special talent. We went on to look at two architects who sought to enrich or question the inheritance of modernism while remaining broadly within modernist conventions: Alvar Aalto, an architect sceptical of overarching idealistic principles who offered an alternative, less prescriptive version, and Louis Kahn, who was concerned to recover and incorporate ideals of past architecture and even some of its compositional principles. We now turn to a group of architects who called themselves Team Ten (often written as Team X) and attempted to humanize architecture from within the modernist tradition and redirect its attention to the everyday.

The reason this loose affiliation of European architects called themselves Team X was that they came together at the ninth meeting of CIAM in 1953 (CIAM IX), at Aix-en-Provence, as the members of the younger generation who undertook to present their work three years later at the tenth meeting in Dubrovnik. What they presented at CIAM X went beyond a refinement of modernist principles and acted as a critique in many instances. As we shall see, their relationship to their predecessors was ambivalent. Their most articulate spokesman was the Dutch architect Aldo van Eyck (1918–1999), and we shall look at some of his writings as well as his buildings.[1] There were numerous other European contributors to the group, however, and some of their buildings will be considered in the light of how far they reflected the positive contributions of modernism and how far they can be seen as a critique.[2]

7.1 Say leaf, say tree

Aldo van Eyck's most pungent statements were reprinted in the *Team Ten Primer*, a book that collected the thoughts and projects of the members of Team Ten in order to promulgate their ideas.[3] In a poetic little diagram he asked architects to think of a city as they might think

1 For a compilation of van Eyck's work, see Ligtelijn 1999; for biography, see McCarter 2015.
2 The Team Ten website, www.team10online.org/, distinguishes between "the inner circle", "participants" and "incidental participants and guests". Although the group was European, the participants included Amancio Guedes from Mozambique and architects from India and Japan. Louis Kahn is not listed at all, although his work was influential and was illustrated in *The Team Ten Primer* (Smithson 1968).
3 Smithson 1968.

DOI: 10.4324/9781003244943-8

of a house and to consider making houses much as they would make a city (**Figure 7.1**). The perception is not a new one (Alberti had said something similar), but the intention is both to criticize the highly reductive 'four functions' defined in the *Charter of Athens* (see p. 91) and to suggest that buildings should not be considered as abstract sculptural objects but composed as a framework offering several possibilities for occupation and interpretation.

A small project by van Eyck illustrates his thesis very clearly. Just as the Serpentine Gallery does in London, Arnhem hosted temporary exhibition pavilions for sculpture. In 1955 it was by Gerrit Rietveld, the architect of the famous 1924 De Stijl house for Madame Schröder, executed in a characteristic modernist vein.[4] Van Eyck's Sonsbeek pavilion dates from 1966; it was demolished a few months later but a replica was constructed in 2006 in the garden of the Kröller-Müller Museum in Hoenderloo in the Netherlands. As with Kahn's Trenton bathhouse scheme, this little pavilion had an influence that transcended its modest scale and brief original lifespan. It consists of a series of parallel walls, which we can understand as streets, interrupted by larger spaces, which might be miniature squares or piazzas, within which sculptures are placed, and where, just as importantly, people meet each other as well as

4 See Curtis 1982 pp. 98–101; Frampton 1980 pp. 144–147.

Figure 7.1 Aldo van Eyck: Arnhem Pavilion plan, 1966, worm's eye view

the art works.[5] It is non-hierarchical in that there is no principal axis or entrance: a neutral network of routes and places. Van Eyck's formal vocabulary may be as abstract as Rietveld's, but the intention is to make a free-standing composition that is appreciated not as a sculptural object in itself but principally as a setting for human encounter.

This project therefore questions the compositional procedures of orthodox modernism – not only Rietveld's in his earlier pavilion, but the kind of town planning exemplified in Le Corbusier's grandiose theoretical projects and in the bleak Bauhaus-inspired parallel blocks of flats that were going up all over Europe. At the Team Ten meeting in Otterlo in 1959 van Eyck complained:

> We have only to look at one of the new towns, or a recent housing development, to recognise to what extent the spirit has gone into hiding. Architects left no cracks and crevices this time. They expelled all sense of place. Fearful as they are of the wrong occasion, the unpremeditated event, the spontaneous act, unscheduled gaiety or violence, unpredictable danger round the corner, they made a flat surface of everything so that no microbes can survive the civic vacuum cleaner.[6]

What we value about old towns and cities is the accidental as much as the planned, and an apparently democratic non-hierarchical arrangement can encourage that. The *Team Ten Primer*, which was first published as an issue of the British journal *Architectural Design* in December 1961, displayed a number of examples of what were to be called carpet or mat planning. In the same journal, in September 1974, Alison Smithson wrote an essay explaining the virtues of the form, its increasing sophistication and the way that Louis Kahn's projects had anticipated it.[7] But the members of Team Ten could not wholly disapprove of Le Corbusier because, as Colin Rowe memorably explained, Le Corbusier was a fox rather than a hedgehog, in having many ideas rather than just one big idea.[8] His first project for the student hostel that became the Pavillon Suisse (discussed in Chapter 4), which he published in *Vers une Architecture*, is an example of a mat building, conceived like a little city (**Figure 7.2**). His unbuilt 1964 project for a hospital in Venice is another example, possibly inspired not only by the city of Venice itself but by the work of Team Ten members, whom Le Corbusier had encouraged in the promulgation of their ideas[9] (**Figure 7.3**). Amongst them was the firm of Candelis Josic Woods (the principal members of which had worked in Le Corbusier's studio), and one of their most ambitious projects was for the University of Zurich. The plan is on the scale of a Hellenistic town such as Priene, in what is now Turkey. When it was published in the *Team Ten Primer*, the section ran vertically, like a slender tower block: you have to revolve the book to see how it justified its description as a groundscraper. A smaller version was built as the Free University in a Berlin suburb.

5 Van Eyck was interested in how the environment can encourage such encounters and was influenced by the writings of Martin Buber, which he had read in Zurich, in his belief that the encounter with others is existentially fundamental: Withagen and Caljouw 2017.
6 Smithson 1968.
7 Smithson 1974.
8 This parable goes back to the ancient Greek poet Archilochus: πόλλ' οἶδ' ἀλώπηξ, ἀλλ' ἐχῖνος ἓν μέγα ("a fox knows many things, but a hedgehog one important thing"). The distinction was picked up by the Oxford philosopher Isaiah Berlin in a famous essay on Tolstoy in 1953. Rowe quotes it in turn: Le Corbusier was a fox who *pretended* he was a hedgehog (Rowe and Koetter 1978).
9 For an analysis of Le Corbusier's project, which is characteristically complex, see Colquhoun 1985, pp. 31–41.

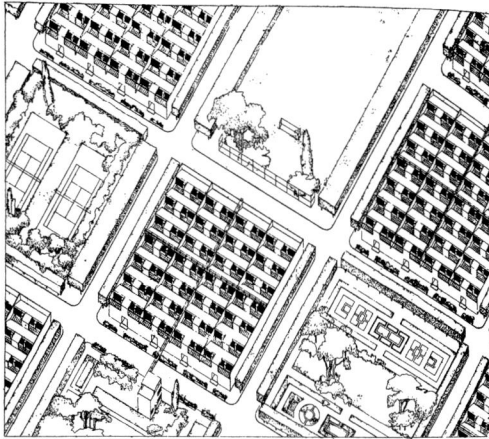

UNIVERSITY QUARTER

Attempts are made at enormous cost to build quarters for university students which may reproduce the poetry of the old buildings at Oxford. A costly poetry, disastrously so! The modern student is in any case inclined to protest against an old-world Oxford: an old-world Oxford is the dream of the modern Maecenas, the donor of such a university quarter. What the student wants is a monk's cell, well lit and heated, with a corner from which he can look at the stars. He wants to find opportunity for games with his fellow-students at a stone's throw. His cell should be self-contained, as far as possible.

PLAN AND SECTIONS

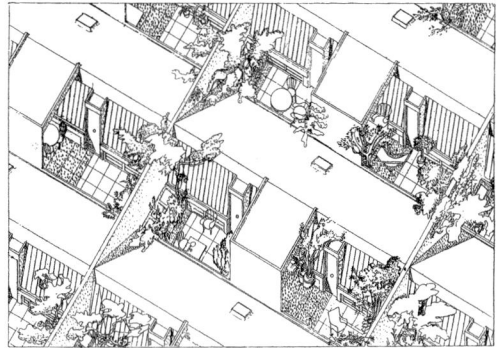

Every student has a right to exactly the same type of cell: it would be invidious that the poor student should occupy a cell different from that of the rich student. There is the problem to be solved: the university-quarter-caravansary: each "cell" has its antechamber, its kitchen, its W.C., its living-room, its sleeping-loft, its roof-garden. Each student is cut off by walls from his neighbours. All the students can forgather on their sports-grounds or in the communal halls in the large buildings destined for communal services. We have to classify, form a type and settle the form of the cell and its elements. Economy. Efficiency. And Architecture? We can always achieve this when the problem is clear.
The university quarter is here conceived in a "shed" form; a mode of construction which allows of indefinite expansion, with ideal lighting and an absence of constructional (and so costly) masses. The walls are mere fillings in light insulating materials.

260

PLAN AND SECTION

DETAIL OF THE TERRACE-GARDEN
261

7.2 Ralph Erskine – a Sweden-based member of Team Ten

Amongst the members of Team Ten was Ralph Erskine, an Englishman educated at the Quaker Friends' School, Saffron Walden, who as a pacifist had moved to Sweden in 1939. He contributed a climate diagram to the *Team Ten Primer* for a theoretical Arctic City, showing a settlement responding to the particularities of arctic conditions: low sun angles, mosquitoes and avalanches (**Figure 7.4**). His clearly modernist aesthetic nevertheless took its inspiration from climate as well as local conditions, emphasizing, for example, the avoidance of cold bridging in the detail of a block of flats in Kiruna and the somewhat tacky frontier-town character of the town of Luleå, where the aluminium cladding to the world's first indoor shopping mall referred respectfully to the adjacent timber-clad traditional buildings. His compositional method in all his projects was deliberately casual – freehand drawings of buildings that accommodate themselves to the topography and have bits hanging off them in a way that can seem quite ad hoc.

Erskine is best known in England for his large scheme for social housing in Byker, Newcastle (**Figure 7.5**), and for the Ark building on London's

Figure 7.2 Two pages from *Vers une Architecture* showing Le Corbusier's project for student housing

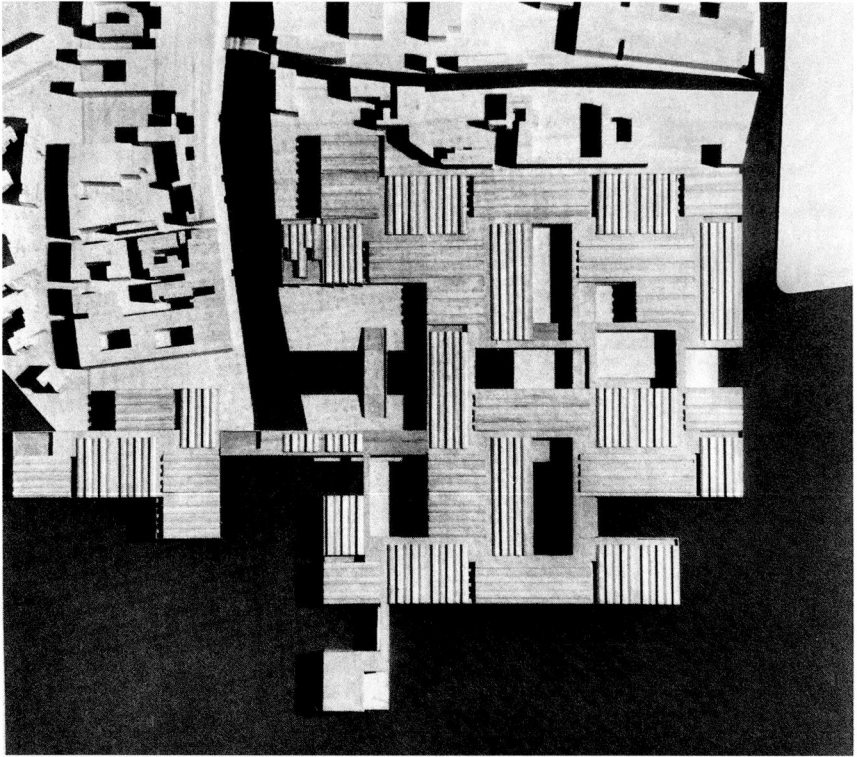

Figure 7.3 Le Corbusier, Venice Hospital project

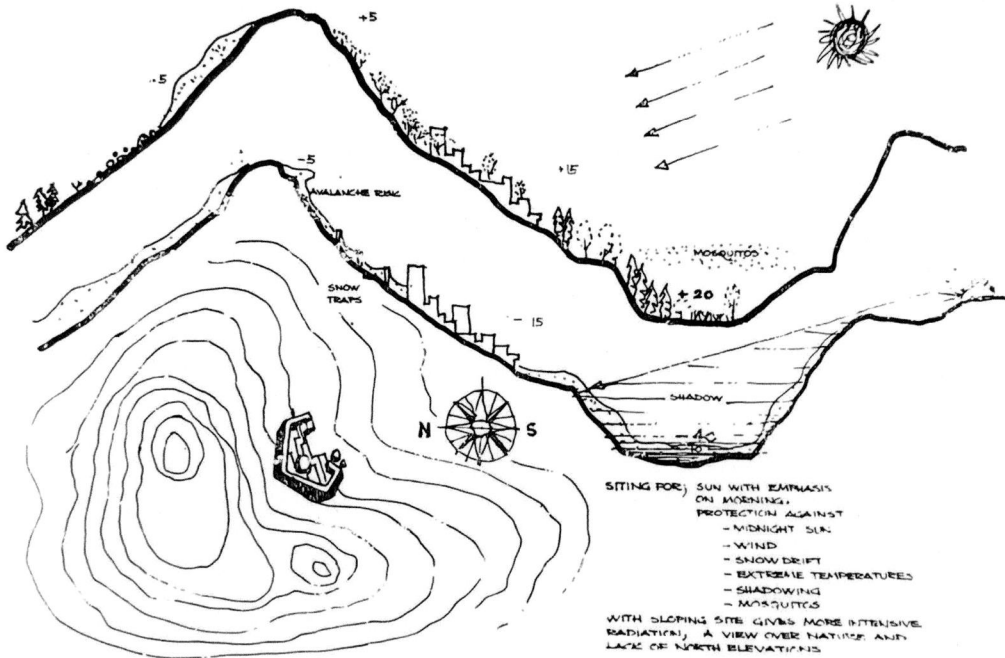

Figure 7.4 Ralph Erskine, living with the climate diagram (from *Team Ten Primer*)

Figure 7.5 Ralph Erskine: Byker Wall

Westway. Both illustrate the social agenda he pursued. At Byker, working with local architects (as was his method, in order to keep his own studio small) he established a project office on site so as to engage the local community in choosing the character and material finishes of their environment. His fluid aesthetic allowed for such freedom, within an overall framework, which resembles his theoretical Arctic City project for Team Ten – a tall embracing wall on the north side sheltering smaller dwellings to south. In the case of Byker, the wall is not primarily a defence against wind or avalanches but a barrier towards a projected motorway. As in many instances of social housing, the estate went into some decline in the years after its construction but was subsequently refurbished when a proportion of the flats and houses were purchased by owner-occupiers.

At Cambridge in 1966, Erskine was appointed to design a building for Clare Hall, a newly-founded institute for post-graduates and researchers, which subsequently became a fully-fledged graduate college (**Figure 7.6**). His plan is more like that of a village than a typical collegiate arrangement with different uses arranged around larger courts. Two pedestrian streets run from north to south through the carpet or mat-like plan. The academic walk to the east has the common room and dining room off it and a group of study and seminar rooms around a small court. To the west, off the family walk, are

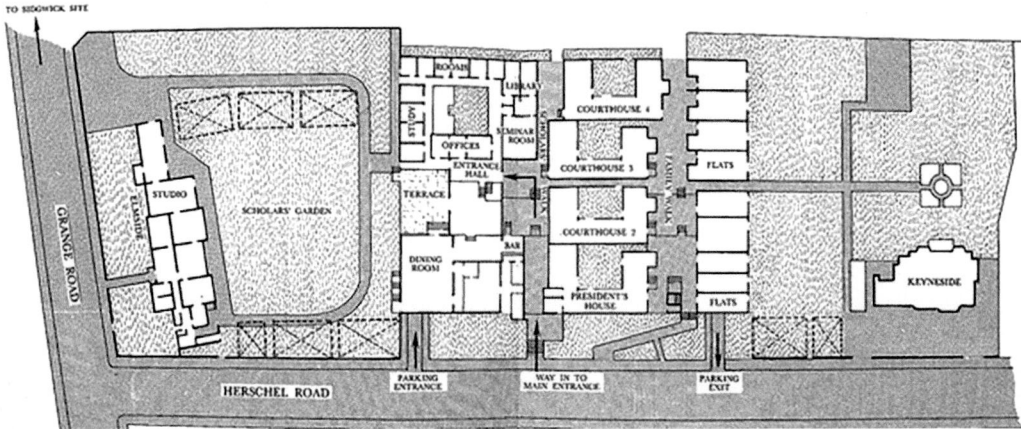

Figure 7.6 Plan of Ralph Erskine's Clare Hall, Cambridge, 1966–1969; south is to the top of the drawing

flats on several levels, under a long monopitch roof, all facing west towards a garden. Bridging between the two north-south walks are u-shaped courtyard houses with studies looking eastwards on to the scholars' walk and kitchens with bay-windowed dining spaces opening to the family walk on the west. In freehand drawings filled with notes, which gave instructions to his colleagues on how the building was to be developed, Erskine characteristically included people and flowers along with details of the construction he intended. On the rear elevation, just as Aalto had done on the north-facing elevation of his Villa Mairea, Erskine arranged his window openings quite casually, generally not aligning them with one another either horizontally or vertically: the wall was treated as a skin, rather than a tectonic element that determines how openings should be placed in it. The timber posts in his common room are reminiscent of Aalto's use of timber on the staircase at Villa Mairea. The whole complex steps down from north to south, over a partially sunken car park, and that allows the roof rather than the floor to be a datum, sheltering a number of seating areas in the common rooms.

In the early 1980s, Erskine provided designs for the first of a number of additional buildings. A Christmas card dating from that period clearly reveals his social attitude[10] (**Figure 7.7**). Over a sketch of a village in Dalmatia he had visited, he wrote:

> In old towns and villages all over the world, I observe and analise [sic] the important elements of an Humane Architecture and Planning by and for People! Can we learn to create – without nostalgic imitation – similar qualities using the construction, materials and aesthetics of today and of the future?

10 In my possession, because my practice in Cambridge worked as executive architects for the construction of an addition – the Michael Stoker Building.

The problems of modernism for Erskine, and other Team Ten members, were social rather than stylistic: it was experienced as inhumane, and architects needed to find ways of making an architecture that was more

In old towns and villages in all
parts of the world I observe and
analise the important elements of an
Humane Architecture and Planning for
People!
Can we learn to create, - without nostalgic
imitation, - similar qualities using the
constructions, materials and aesthetics
of today and of the future ?

Figure 7.7 Ralph Erskine: Christmas card, circa 1983

friendly and approachable for people. How that could be achieved, and the philosophical implications of the attempt, will be the focus of discussion to come.

7.3 British contributors to Team Ten

Alison and Peter Smithson, the husband and wife team and editors of the *Team Ten Primer*, were a self-consciously avant-garde couple adept at promoting their enthusiasms. Their first major building, for Hunstanton School, was clearly influenced by Mies van der Rohe, and they continued to revere Le Corbusier but sought to humanize his prescriptions. The Economist complex, off St James' in London, is a mixed-use block with four elements: a tall office tower, a smaller office block with a bank on the street frontage, a slender block of flats and a small bay that is an extension to the adjacent club. Together they create a raised deck that makes a short-cut between the street and St James' Square – an "area of quietude" as the Smithsons described it. People could meet there, as in van Eyck's Arnhem pavilion; children could even play cricket against the columns and, in affording these kinds of opportunities, the complex provided a contrast to the bleak and wind-swept plazas, occasionally decorated with a sculpture, that were the modernist norm.

James Stirling, later to become one of the most celebrated British architects of the second half of the twentieth century, contributed a scheme for village housing to the *Primer*, which shows a characteristically powerful formal control. The houses have lean-to roofs and are organized along a central spine wall. Stirling did not share the Team Ten preoccupations with humanizing modernism so much as enriching its vocabulary. The *Primer* also illustrated Louis Kahn's plan for downtown Philadelphia, since the ambitions of the group extended to the scale of the city, though the younger generation seldom got the opportunity to build their larger projects. It is clear that the positions of this loose group were varied; the core of their critique can nevertheless be found in the statements and projects of van Eyck and his younger protégé Herman Hertzberger.

7.4 Aldo van Eyck

Van Eyck's orphanage, or Children's Home, in Amsterdam was recognized on its completion in 1960 as the canonical Team Ten building (**Figure 7.8**). He had developed his spatial, or place-making ideas, which we have already briefly described, partly from a study of the villages of an African tribe, the Dogon of Mali (part of the French Sudanese Republic until 1959) which he visited in a series of trips from 1947 to 1952 with colleagues of the anthropologist Marcel Griaule. Van Eyck had encountered the work of Griaule and his colleagues in a 1933 special issue of *Minotaur*. Griaule himself had been studying African culture since 1928, but from 1935 until his death in 1956 he concentrated on the Dogon, interviewing a Dogon cosmologist, Ogotommêli, in 1946 and publishing the results in French in 1948 as *Dieu d'eau* (translated into English as *Conversations with Ogotommêli* in 1965). Griaule's findings have since been questioned, and some have claimed that to a large extent Griaule imposed his own Eurocentric interpretations.[11] Be that as it may, it is clear that what van Eyck took from his understanding of the Dogon culture had a profound effect on his architectural thinking and in turn influenced architects who became interested in ethology and anthropology.[12] Fundamental to what van Eyck understood was an appreciation of the importance of ambiguity: rich and memorable spaces are ambiguously interpretable. A common example from European culture (as well as others) would be an arcade. It is part of a building, and yet it can be part of the space of the street or square or courtyard that it adjoins. The spatial ambiguity that results can be distinguished from the kinds of formal ambiguities that interested Robert Venturi, an architect whose work will be considered in the next chapter.[13] Importantly, it encourages, or at least does not prevent, certain kinds of activity that van Eyck claimed are actively discouraged in the abrupt transitions characteristic of a reduced and mechanical modernism. All the threshold spaces of traditional architecture had been abandoned (or rather swept away by the 'civic vacuum cleaner') so that

11 See van Beek 1991, who claims: "The Dogon ethnography produced by Griaule after World War II cannot be taken at face value. It is the product of a complex interaction between a strong-willed researcher, a colonial situation, an intelligent and creative body of informants, and a culture with a courtesy bias and a strong tendency to incorporate foreign elements". But from the discussion that followed it's clear that several distinguished anthropologists, including Mary Douglas, disagreed.

12 Many architects in the 1960s read Claude Lévi-Strauss (1908–2009), whose idea of 'structuralism' imported ideas from linguistics to explain social patterns and behaviour.

13 At times van Eyck was prone to accuse Venturi of eavesdropping on one of his lectures and appropriating the ideas of complexity and contradiction, but this seems unlikely.

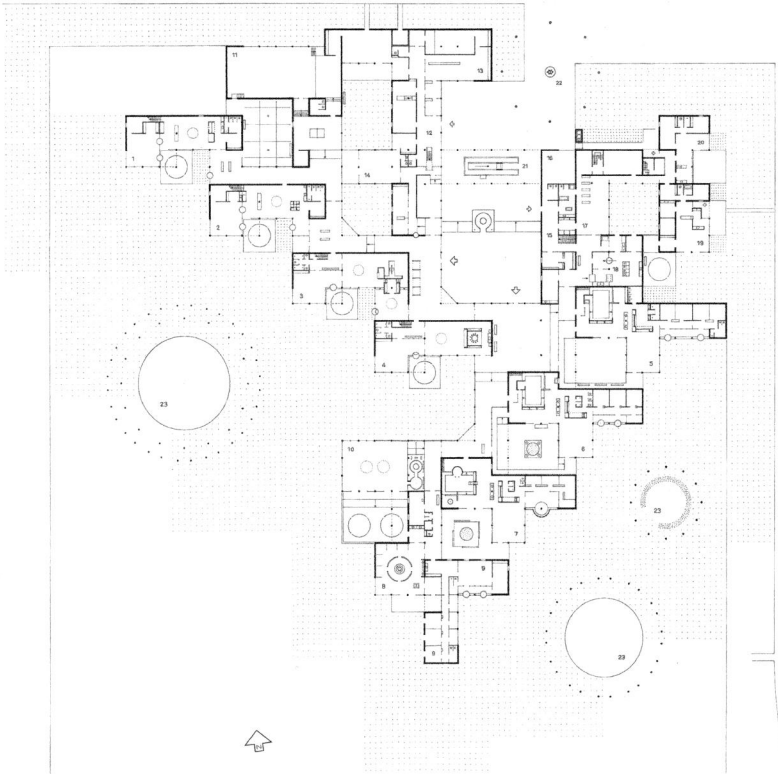

Figure 7.8 Aldo van Eyck: Children's Home, Amsterdam, 1956–1960, plan

the ambiguous and interpretable conditions he regarded as crucial had disappeared. Van Eyck therefore sought to incorporate numerous transition spaces in his buildings.

The orphanage was located on an unpromising site under the flight path to Schipol airport and was conceived of as a miniature village to both house and educate young orphans. The plan had a wandering internal street, dividing the houses on the west, appearing as series of L-shapes at ground floor level but square on the upper floor, from the classrooms, also L-shaped but single storey, on the east. The administration is a long first floor flat-roofed block, but all the other roofs are vaulted with small or large domes. A diagram that van Eyck prepared shows the elaborate sequence of thresholds from the city's street to the two front doors off the internal street: first a place is established, by a circle of trees, around a sculpture (*plastiek*); the next defined area is of the northern half of the courtyard, divided by the first-floor administration block which is held on *piloti* over a cycle store. This in turn provides a threshold to the southern half of the court, which itself is divided in two-by-two steps. Finally we reach the two entrances, one towards the houses, the other towards the classrooms.

The interiors of the orphanage, under larger or smaller domes, consist of what van Eyck referred to as "bunches of places" rather than standard rooms off a corridor; the L-shaped plans allow an ambiguous portion to each function that can either be seen as part of the internal street or as part of the classroom. In the detailed events within the building, van Eyck benefited from his experience of designing more than 200 playgrounds for the city of Amsterdam, where he had employed simple geometrical forms to stimulate play (**Figure 7.9**). The aesthetic drew from contemporary art (he was a friend of abstract painters), but the concept of play and its importance for culture in general was deeply embedded in the Netherlands.[14] As with Erskine, there is no attempt to imitate traditional styles, but in his case the aesthetic is rather more puritanical: the building is mostly clad in concrete. Van Eyck's mat plan is one that Kahn had already anticipated in his unbuilt Trenton Community Center, though van Eyck's project is much looser and more meandering, even if it is carefully organized in square bays. It has proved itself to be surprisingly adaptable. The orphanage closed down in the 1990s, and there was a danger that this important and influential building would be demolished. It was saved, however, to be used for a time by the Berlage School of Architecture, a function it served very well, and then converted in 1990–1994 by Aldo and Hannie van Eyck to become the social centre of the office development they designed that now surrounds it.[15]

It is not by accident that the term 'place' has been employed in the description above, rather than 'space'. In an article entitled "The Medicine of Reciprocity Tentatively Illustrated", van Eyck wrote:

> The time has come to think of architecture urbanistically and of urbanism architecturally . . . to arrive at the singular through plurality and vice versa. As for this home for children, the idea was to

Figure 7.9 Aldo van Eyck: Children's Home, Amsterdam, 1956–1960, interior

persuade it to become both "house" and "city": a city-like house and a house-like city. I came to the conclusion that *whatever space and time mean, place and occasion mean more, for space in the image of man is place and time in the image of man is occasion.* Split apart by the schizophrenic mechanism of deterministic thinking, time and space remain frozen abstractions.

Place and occasion constitute each other's realisation in human terms. Since man is both the subject and object of architecture, it follows that its primary job is to provide the former for the sake of the latter. Furthermore, since place and occasion imply participation in what exists, lack of place – and thus of occasion – will cause loss of identity, isolation and frustration.[16]

Clearly van Eyck is criticizing the limitations of Sigfried Giedion's influential book *Space, Time and Architecture.*[17] Van Eyck believed that how human beings experience their environment had nothing to do with Albert Einstein and was much as they had experienced places at all times: his pungent italicized statement, interpreted in philosophical terms, can be seen as an ontological pre-cursor of much later twentieth-century anti-Cartesian critique.

Van Eyck's orphanage influenced architects all over Europe. We have already seen the example of Ralph Erskine. In Italy, Giancarlo de Carlo's buildings for the University of Urbino, on a hillside outside the old city, is a further interpretation of the idea of a building that is a miniature city. Narrow pedestrian paths tumble down the hill from the central complex. The architectural expression is entirely abstract but the way that the complex is perceived and experienced contrasts significantly with the way one encounters the ensemble of independent blocks of orthodox modernism. De Carlo went on to create modest but memorable buildings for the university embedded within the old city, discreet in their external appearance but surprising and spatially inventive internally. A later project by van Eyck, The Hubertus House of 1973–1981 for single parents and their children, was similarly embedded in the city of Amsterdam (**Figure 7.10**). It is in one way a building: new construction on the street frontage, adjacent to existing buildings through which one gains access to the main raised ground floor via a series of ambiguous thresholds (**Figure 7.11**). But it also contains an internal first floor glazed street off which one enters the individual houses that the mothers and their children occupy, dropping down the two-storey space into apartments that run from top-lit bedroom space under the street to individual east-facing gardens. Van Eyck's concern for threshold and the way in which houses should be like little cities could hardly be clearer. Rather than concrete, van Eyck employed spindly metalwork here and, unlike the predominantly monochromatic Children's Home, the Hubertus House is polychrome: "the rainbow is my favourite colour", van Eyck said. There is also a clear accommodation to context: Van Eyck claimed that the reason he arched the window heads in the raised ground floor common room was that it would allow unobstructed views for people

16 Originally published in *Architects' Year Book*, no. 10, 1962 and reprinted in Ligtelijn 1999, pp. 88–89.
17 Van Eyck and his wife, Hannie, had been friends with Sigfried Giedion and Carola Giedion- Welcker since first meeting them in Switzerland.

Figure 7.10 Aldo van Eyck: Hubertus House, Amsterdam, ground floor plan

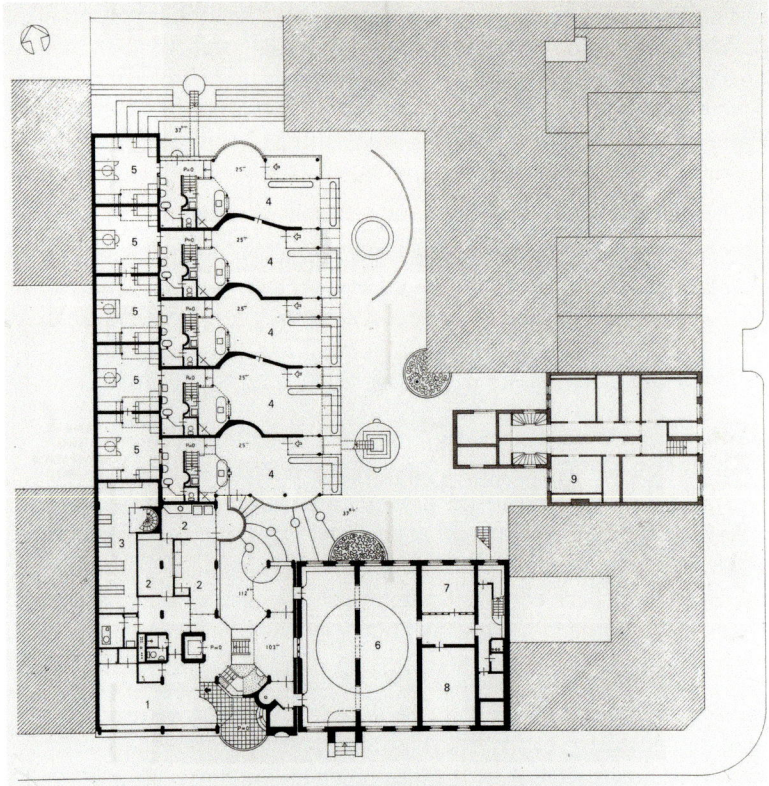

Figure 7.11 Aldo van Eyck: Hubertus House, stairs

standing as well as those who were seated, but it was surely no accident that they also chimed with the rhythms of the adjacent building, which was incorporated in the complex.

7.5 Herman Hertzberger

As a young protégé of van Eyck, Herman Hertzberger edited *Dutch Forum*, a journal that contained numerous articles on the Team Ten approach. He went on to build more extensively than his elder colleague,[18] including schools, housing and offices, as well as teaching and writing books specifically addressed to students of architecture. A relatively early building in his career, a student hostel on a busy Amsterdam street, uses multiple levels on the ground and basement floors to create pockets of space that offer different possibilities for occupation (**Figure 7.12**). It was built of the plainest materials but offered many interpretations in use. Seen from the main road, it is like a version of a Le Corbusier *Unité d'habitation*, though much smaller and with an open-air gallery on the fifth floor rather than an enclosed street. Its narrow flank elevation, however, sits politely on the canal bank. Between each bay, defined by the chunky ground floor columns, are substantial concrete benches that are actually external light fittings designed to allow people to use them as benches or tables as they pleased. The architectural vocabulary is abstract – almost like Rietveld – but the forms are intended to provoke. In the ground floor café-restaurant, students (in the 1960s) behaved in ways that would not be tolerated in today's

18 Though van Eyck did undertake larger projects between 1971 and 1982 in collaboration with van Bosch Architects.

Figure 7.12 Herman Hertzberger: Student Hostel, Amsterdam, 1966

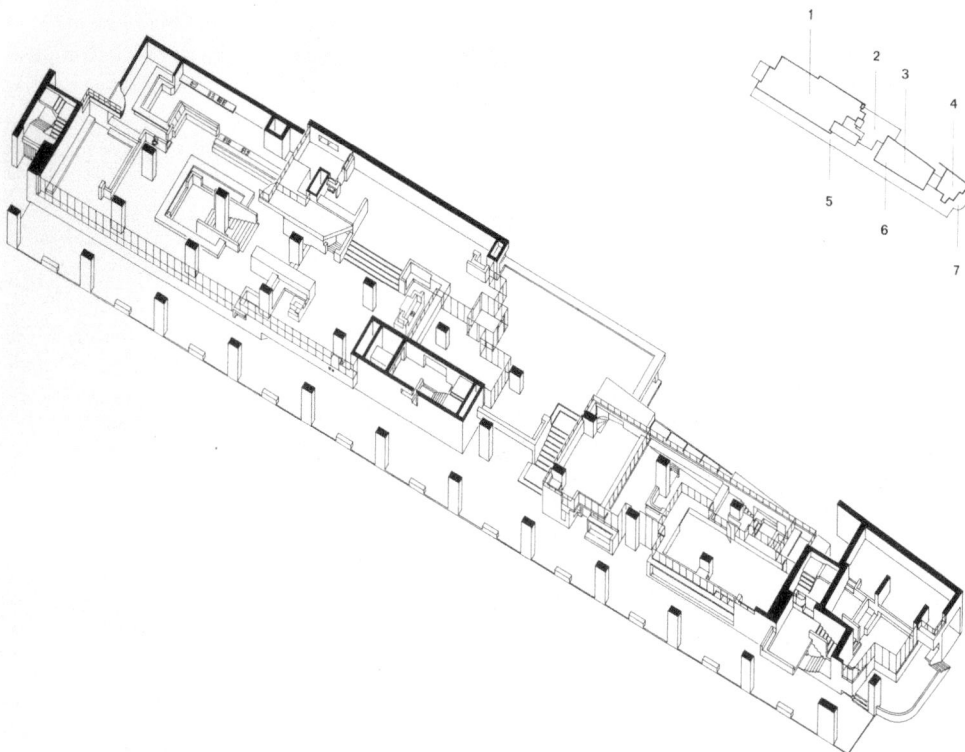

Figure 7.13 Herman Hertzberger: Student Hostel, Amsterdam, 1966, interior

accident-averse culture, perching on broad balustrades so that they could survey the scene (**Figure 7.13**). On the upper floor gallery, the light fittings occur again and can be used for informal supper parties.

Hertzberger was quite explicit about the theatrical nature of the architect's task:

> Everything we design must be a catalyst to stimulate individual people to play the variety of roles through which their own identity will be enlarged. The aim of architecture is to achieve a condition where everyone's feeling of identity is maximized . . . It is a question of right dimensions, the right placing . . . Designing is nothing more than finding out what person and object want to be; form then makes itself. There is really no need for invention – you must just listen carefully.[19]

Hertzberger's most celebrated building was the extraordinary office completed at Apeldoorn for Centraal Beheer in 1974 (**Figure 7.14**). The plan is formed of sequences of square platforms, with paired columns defining a central passage, when needed, between each platform and its neighbour: we are reminded of Louis Kahn's structure at the Richards Research building (**Figure 6.7**), but here the interruption caused by people moving through the space is quite deliberately provocative: the architecture is intended to encourage interaction and personalization (**Figure 7.15**). The square bays can be occupied by as many as eight people, as a meeting space, or by only one or two people, or as service rooms of various kinds. Frequently the platforms overlook voids, which become top-lit streets, and the intention was that a public right of way lined with shops would travel right through the building, beneath an adjacent road and on towards the nearby railway station: some of the urban precedents Hertzberger studied were the glazed arcades in Montmartre – buildings in some way but also streets.

19 Hertzberger 1967.

basisstruktuur

konstruktie/leidingen/
cirkulatie zone

door superpositie van geprefa-
briceerde struktuur op gestorte
onderbouw draait het hoofdstra-
mien 45° dit levert de parkeer-
maat 8,40 h.o.h.

interpretabele zone

invulbaar met primaire
bouwstenen

primaire bouwstenen

kantoorplek   vergaderplek   toiletgroep

zit-wacht plek   pauzeplek   restaurantplek

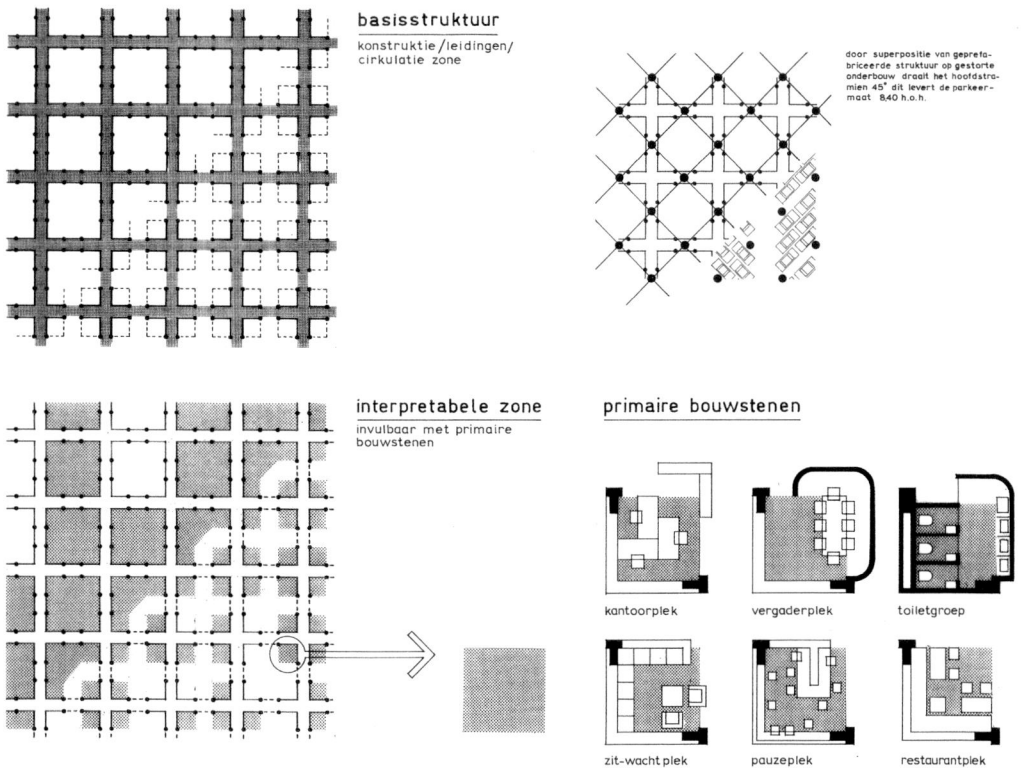

Figure 7.14 Herman Hertzberger: Centraal Beheer, plan diagram

Fruitful comparisons have been made between Hertzberger's Centraal Beheer and Norman Foster's building for Willis Faber Dumas in Ipswich, built at just the same time and also the headquarters for an insurance firm moving from a capital to a provincial city (**Figure 7.16**).[20] Both were open-plan (rather than conventionally cellular) office buildings. Foster's tidy architecture accords with, and indeed advances, the principles and the aesthetic of modernism. Whereas, internally, Hertzberger encouraged the occupants to personalize the space, sometimes with extraordinary results, the furniture in Foster's neutral and flexible building was not permitted to rise beyond 1.5 metres, and the colour throughout was consistently grey. Externally, the piled-up components of Hertzberger's building created a vernacular casbah-like character, while Foster's Ipswich building presented a compelling smooth corporate image. This is not to say that Foster's building was necessarily less 'democratic' than Hertzberger's: he had provided a café on the roof for the staff and a swimming pool on the ground and basement floors. It was just the social expression that differed, quite radically. Hertzberger offered individuals a potentially anarchic freedom, which proved popular for the office staff but too radical for his patrons: later alterations normalized his adventurous experimentation and the future of the building, even though it is now a UNESCO monument, is in doubt.[21]

20 See Frampton 1980, pp. 293–295, for example.
21 A video describing Hertzberger's philosophy in relation to this building and containing interviews with its inhabitants can be found at www.ahh.nl/index.php/en/projects2/12-utiliteits bouw/85-centraal-beheer-offices-apeldoorn.

Figure 7.15 Herman Hertzberger: Centraal Beheer interior

Hertzberger's civic projects exhibit the same difficulty he had with Centraal Beheer – an incoherent public face. As an architect he was more comfortable with the interconnections that buildings can make to form parts of a city. His Music Centre in Utrecht, for instance, was sliced through by an internal street, like a glazed arcade, part of the city yet engaged with the activity in the foyer. But it was in a number of housing schemes that Hertzberger provided the most vivid illustrations of the ambiguous spatial character that he and van Eyck valued so highly (**Figure 7.17**). He was careful, as was Erskine, to include people and the clutter of daily life in drawings of the projects and photographs of them as realized. Staircases were not simply the means of rising from ground to upper floors but considered in relation to the opportunities they might offer for interaction and interpretation. Balconies tended to be part covered and part open, encouraging people to define their preferred relationship with their neighbours by screens and planting. The housing research at the time of John Habraken (1928–) argued that architects should provide only the supporting framework, within which people could arrange their own dwellings – an idea that Le Corbusier (characteristically) had anticipated in his 1933 Orbus plan for Algiers, which involved a perforated megastructure underneath

Figure 7.16 Norman Foster: Willis Faber Dumas, interior

a sinuous motorway. Hertzberger believed people could be provoked to alter their interior space and redetermine their relations to their neighbours, as illustrated in his deliberately incomplete 'Diagoon' housing in Delft (1967–1971). This experimental scheme drew on the way Le Corbusier's 1926 housing for Henry Frugès, at Pessac near Bordeaux, had been altered by its inhabitants; it also anticipated the work of architects such as Alejandro Aravena (1967–) who seek to provide housing forms that can grow incrementally.[22] Between 1984 and 1987 the city of Berlin undertook a substantial housing programme, discussed in more detail in Chapter 9, and Hertzberger's Lindenstraße housing block was one of the most highly articulate projects precisely because of his concern to offer many different combinations of relationship between inside and out.

7.6 The architectural contribution of Team Ten

The membership of Team Ten was heterogeneous and included some whose ideals remained broadly modernist. Jacob Bakema's practice, for example, prepared the plans for Amsterdam East mentioned in Chapter 4 (**Figure 4.13**). In fact, Team Ten acknowledged the problems that modernist architects had set out to solve and admired aspects of their achievement. The car had arrived and had to be catered for and that would involve new urban patterns and an architecture for which

22 For Le Corbusier's Pessac, see Boudon 1979. The most successful housing schemes in developing countries build on this approach, not only Aravena's Elemental group in Chile, but in India housing at Indore (1983–1986) by Balkrishna Doshi or the remarkable Sector 22, Ghandinagar, Gujarat.

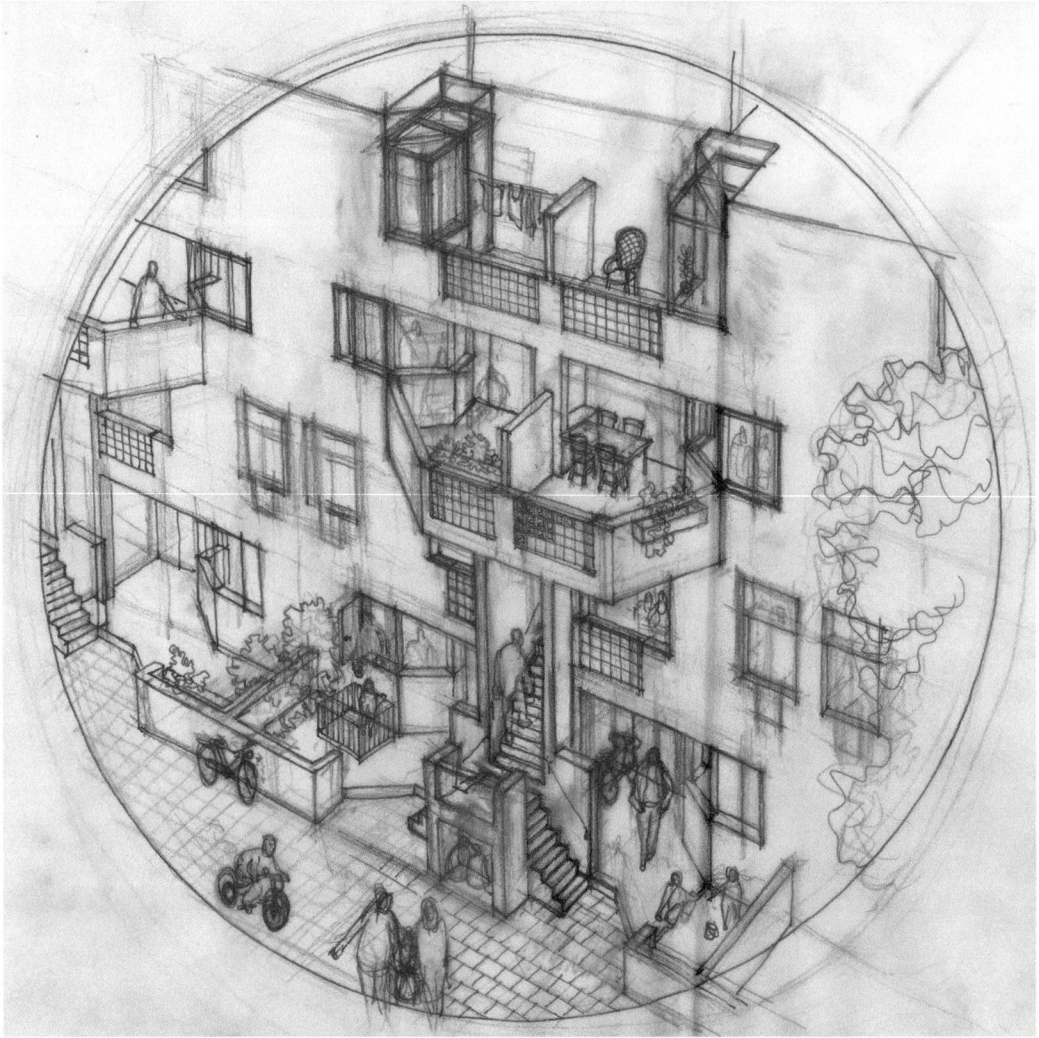

Figure 7.17 Herman Hertzberger: sketch of Haarlemmer Houttuinen housing, Amsterdam

traditional forms were no longer suitable. This did not mean that Team Ten members were unsympathetic to past architecture and urbanism. Alison and Peter Smithson eulogized the city of Bath,[23] but also investigated, in their 1958 Berlin Haupstadt competition undertaken with Peter Sigmond, the dramatic new urban configurations that would emerge if architects took their task seriously: in the case of Berlin a new upper-level pattern overlaid on the previous morphology of the city preserved below. Team Ten's most vocal and articulate members, while acknowledging the genius of an architect like Le Corbusier (one of the twentieth-century's "great gang", in van Eyck's words, along with Joyce, Schoenberg and Picasso) were critical of the urban prescriptions they had inherited. In their enthusiasm to counter cholera and tuberculosis, architects had forgotten that the city was the place of human interaction and that people's needs could not be reduced to CIAM's four functions. At a detailed scale, a close attention to how people reacted to buildings, old

23 Smithson 1971.

and new – clustering in doorways, especially the in-between thresholds half in and half out – could inform designers how forms could be made friendly rather than alienating: Hertzberger sought 'adhesive' form which provoked a reaction rather than sanitized space that purported to offer flexibility. He promoted his ideas not only by what he built but also in his three books aimed at students.[24]

For Team Ten members, any association with traditional stylistic motifs could be abandoned. So the aesthetic of their buildings is clearly 'modern', within the tradition of Rietveld in the case of the Dutch. Hertzberger built on that formal vocabulary and combined it with a systematic and repetitive discipline that was indebted to the work of his Dutch contemporary Piet Blom (1934–1999) and became known as Dutch Structuralism. Behind the notion in the 1960s described earlier, that people should also take the fashioning of their environment into their own hands, there were philosophical and political ideals. The period saw a flowering of social critique evident in books such as Robert Ardrey's *Territorial Imperative*,[25] which emphasized the common instinctive origins of human understandings of space and would justify van Eyck's claim that the behaviour of people from distant climates and cultures, such as the Dogon villagers, had pertinent lessons for twentieth-century European architects. In the political sphere, for a brief moment it seemed that the Kantian Enlightenment consensus on the limits to individual freedoms, already dissected as a version of repression by Freud in his *Civilization and its Discontents*, would collapse. The philosopher Herbert Marcuse (1898–1979) saw the prevailing twentieth-century consumerist culture as a sinister form of tolerance, masking the alienating effects of capitalism. It would be part of architects' task to assist people in their refusal to conform to bourgeois ideals, as those associated with the Situationist International group argued.[26]

Architects who seek to build, however, and not just to theorize, need patronage and have to accommodate themselves according to the societies in which they practice. The concept of play, already mentioned, is probably more relevant as a means of understanding the approach of Team Ten architects. It was already evident in the way that Alvar Aalto talked about his design process – Aalto being an architect whom van Eyck admired even though formally their buildings are quite different.[27] Johan Huizinga (1872–1945), a Dutch historian and most famous as the author of *The Waning of the Middle Ages*, was a friend of van Eyck's father.[28] His influential book of 1938, *Homo Ludens*, claimed that the concept of play lay behind the law, 'agonistic' activity such as war, poetry and myth, knowledge, philosophy and indeed the whole of civilization: people become who they are in relation to others in society by a creative reaction that originates in imaginative play. It was especially evident in rituals.[29] Van Eyck's playground equipment may have been formally quite disciplined and abstract, like the sculptures of Brancusi which he admired, but it was intended to provoke multiple interpretations because of the many ways of playing on it or with it.[30]

24 Hertzberger 1991, 2000, 2009.

25 I remember discussing this book with Herman Hertzberger in 1969, a contribution to the discussion of ethology instituted by Konrad Lorenz.

26 Marcuse was a member of the influential Frankfurt School, arising between the wars, which evolved a generally pessimistic view of twentieth-century society derived from the work of Marx and Freud. Publications from 1957 onwards by Guy Debord described the evolving Situationist philosophy. The events in Paris in May 1968, when people reclaimed the streets to discover *Sous les pavés la plage!*, represented the heyday of the movement.

27 Charrington 2011.

28 I am indebted to Robert McCarter for confirming that Herman Hertzberger also acknowledged that he was directly inspired by Huizinga (correspondence, January 2016).

29 "Primitive society performs its sacred rites, its sacrifices, consecrations and mysteries, all of which serve to guarantee the well-being of the world, in a spirit of pure play truly understood. Now in myth and ritual the great instinctive forces of civilized life have their origin: law and order, commerce and profit, craft and art, poetry, wisdom and science. All are rooted in the primeval soil of play" (Huizinga 1949, p. 9). Play had also been an important component in the aesthetics of the German Idealist philosopher Friedrich Schiller (1759–1805).

30 Van Eyck's playgrounds have attracted the attention of cognitive psychologists interested in discovering how different objects afford different interpretations in use: see Withagen and

When Hertzberger or van Eyck visited buildings, old or new, what they observed and recorded were the reactions of people to the building forms – how they sat on the grand flights of steps up to the portico of the museum to eat their sandwiches – rather than the meanings that might be inferred from their architectural motifs. If architects could only forsake their fixation on form for its own sake and became more attuned to everyday behaviour, they would be able to make a better world.

In 2015, Robert McCarter summed up van Eyck's critique as follows:

> Van Eyck criticized the betrayal by midcentury modernism of its own legacy in all the arts; the now widely recognized failings of modern urban design; the destruction of historic centers so as to make them accessible by automobile; the failure to make new buildings that were appropriately accommodating to their contexts; the incapacity of the contemporary profession to engage the history of building culture; the failure of architects to take into consideration the social and domestic habits of those for whom they built; the escalating destruction of the natural environment; and the abandonment of the architecture profession's fundamental ethical responsibility "to avoid the mean and meaningless", working "in a way that achieves something useful for people, just as the doctor or the baker on the corner does".[31]

7.7 The philosophical context of the Team Ten critique

If the work of the disparate group of architects that went under the name of Team Ten can be shown to have some consistency in the forms they thought it was proper for architects to create, it remains to speculate how far their thinking is characteristic at a more theoretical level of a younger group – the children of modernism, who inherited the powerful polemics of their elders.

Psychologically, we could observe that inventive individuals faced with dominant members of an older generation need to assert their own authority.[32] Each of the architects mentioned earlier had a powerful personality and wanted in some way to make their mark in the world. Even as they sought to humanize the design criteria they inherited, they refused to subscribe to Gropius' notion of anonymous teamwork as the ideal way to contribute to their discipline.

Philosophically, we might see the response of Team Ten as moving towards an Aristotelian, or more empirical position, in the face of a Platonic idealist inheritance of sweeping statements about the future state of cities, the compelling requirements of twentieth century technology and the necessity to forsake anything that spoke of tradition. In this, they anticipated concerns that were to be articulated later in the century within several disciplines. Team Ten members did not concern themselves so much with projects for new cities on an idealized *tabula rasa* as with what was to be done with the nineteenth century (or older) urban context they inherited. Anticipating later more widespread sociological

Caljouw 2017. For the concept of 'affordance', see Chapter 11, p. 228.
31 McCarter 2015.
32 For Freud this was encapsulated in the myth of Oedipus: see p. 61.

critiques, they studied the 'practice of everyday life' rather than assuming that people would refashion their behaviour to accommodate themselves to radically new conditions.[33] Their concern for how differences of climate would stimulate differing design solutions contrasts with the universal prescriptions of their predecessors.[34] This does not mean that they forsook ideals but that they worked from particular circumstances towards those ideals rather than seeing individual projects as reflections of an overarching principle that needed to be obeyed. Where they drew the line in most cases was in direct stylistic quotation: their architecture was to be "without nostalgic imitation" in the words of Erskine's Christmas card, and in that sense can also be seen as a continuation of the modern tradition.[35]

A defence of these modified ideals of modernism was advanced in a book edited by the British architect Denys Lasdun, appearing 16 years after the *Team Ten Primer* and entitled, significantly enough, *Architecture in an Age of Scepticism*.[36] It was subtitled "A Practitioner's Anthology" and five of the 12 presentations of their projects, accompanied by descriptions that vary from the prosaic to the poetic, are by Team Ten members: De Carlo, Erskine, Stirling, van Eyck and the Smithsons. Lasdun explained in his Preface that those he had invited to contribute were "Europeans who work in the tradition of the modern movement" – finding a way of retaining its ideals rather than retreating into scepticism. They had each "kept faith with and continued the essential living tradition and are daily concerned with the practice of architecture". By the 1980s, however, they needed to distance themselves not only from the reductive functionalism associated with CIAM's view of the city but also from a reaction, by then in full swing and usually described as postmodernism, which had challenged the taboo of stylistic imitation, albeit that in many instances quotations were filtered through an ironic lens.

33 The title of an influential book by a philosopher historian, originally published in French in 1980, was *The Practice of Everyday Life* (de Certeau 2011).

34 Kenneth Frampton's concept of Critical Regionalism (building on a 1981 article by Alex Tzonis and Liliane Lefaivre) was later to reinforce an argument that the most authentic expressions of the modernist project would arise out of the work of talented individuals working within their local cultural and climatic context. It would resist both the concept of an 'international style' and the seductions of a lazy post-modernism: Frampton 1983.

35 A prominent exception was the Torre Velasca in Milan, by Ernesto Rogers of BBPR, which provoked furious debate within Team Ten. In an article at the time in the *Architectural Review*, Reyner Banham described what he saw as a general Italian retreat from orthodox modernist principles as an "infantile regression": Banham 1959.

36 Lasdun 1984.

8
POSTMODERNISM

Irony and inclusiveness

Introduction

When architects talk of the reactions to architectural modernism, they usually refer to postmodernism and particularly to the figure of Robert Venturi (1930–2018). Although he did not approve of being called a postmodernist,[1] there was a good reason for it, because his publications and practice provided the most articulate and influential advocacy for the position. Its origin, as we shall see, was at least partly literary. He and his colleagues spearheaded what became a widespread critique of orthodox modernist architecture, not only publishing two influential books but also designing buildings that illustrated their ideas. In this chapter we shall also consider a second figure, Michael Graves (1934–2015), probably not as well regarded today, but representative of other aspects of the critique.

Postmodernism is the term generally used to describe a sceptical reaction to the utopian idealism associated with modernism, in philosophy and all the arts. Its origins are disputed but it is clearly a response to the certainties that seemed to be promoted in the first half of the twentieth century. Because of its recovery of decoration and playful use of motifs from the past, architectural postmodernism can be seen as a somewhat trivial reaction to modernist taste, with its Calvinistic rejection of such trivialities. But it is also a reflection of a wider phenomenon and potentially therefore a much more profound rejection of modernist tenets than the reactions of the members of Team Ten. In 1993 the critic Robert Maxwell, looking back on a long career, described its continuing force:

> In the wider area of cultural studies, postmodernism is not an aberration of fancy architects, but a pervasive condition of life that follows from the recognition that modernity has not removed us from history or conferred the certainty of logic on the choices of life; an inescapable condition that follows more specifically from the evolution of cultural consciousness, the collapse of the Enlightenment belief in progress and perfectibility, the discovery of the subconscious and its dependence on symbols, and in a more general sense, a perspective that accepts the process of secularization and the Nietzschean proclamation of the death of God.[2]

In just the same period, Jacques Derrida was working on the books for which he became most well known (*Of Grammatology* and

1 In his obituary, F.A. Bernstein recorded that in 2001, in an effort to set the record straight, he appeared on the cover of *Architecture* magazine proclaiming, "I am not now and never have been a postmodernist". In an interview with Bernstein at his house in Philadelphia in 2009, he had told him "It is one's fate to be misunderstood". See Bernstein 2018.

2 Maxwell 1991, pp. 312–313.

DOI: 10.4324/9781003244943-9

Writing and Difference, both published in 1967), which argue that the very structure of our writings, so far from eliciting truths, determines our thought much more than we acknowledge. In popular media more generally, Marshall McLuhan's *The Medium is the Message* of 1964 had made analogous arguments. Derrida's work, which apparently questions the foundations of ideology, was treated with respect by some philosophers, such as Richard Rorty, and ridiculed by others from within the analytical tradition, but it undoubtedly had a profound effect on literary criticism and, as we saw in Chapter 6, can be fruitfully applied in discussing works of architecture.[3] There are alternative ways of understanding reality to those that are amenable to scientific analysis. It can be open to us as to how we manipulate and play with meanings, if indeed we are in control of the meanings in the first place.

We could question, however, how far such perceptions were new. Defenders of the Enlightenment would point out that in any case post-Kantian thinking contained within itself the seeds of doubt and, as follows from earlier chapters, doubting in itself has a long history.[4] Most postmodern literary experiments were anticipated by James Joyce in his *Ulysses* (1922) and *Finnegan's Wake* (1939); musical eclecticism was already flourishing when the apparently ultra-modernist Stravinsky adopted neo-classical techniques in the 1920s; and after the First World War, Pablo Picasso was as likely to be influenced by the paintings of Ingres as he was to be pursuing the implications of cubism. In architecture, modernism was by no means the only manner evident, especially in the United Kingdom, where the influence of the Arts and Crafts gave way in general to a dilute neo-Georgian. There was little intellectual justification, however, for alternatives to modernism in the face of the compelling polemics of Gropius and Le Corbusier, and that is why Venturi's arguments had such an effect.

8.1 Venturi's critique

Robert Venturi was born in Philadelphia in 1925 and educated at Princeton, where his studio teacher Jean Labatut had a Beaux-Arts background and instilled in him a respect for historical architecture, just as Paul Cret had done for Louis Kahn. He briefly worked for Kahn before winning a prize fellowship to study in Rome from 1954–1956. A few years after returning to America, Venturi began to practise independently and simultaneously worked as Louis Kahn's teaching assistant for eight years at the University of Pennsylvania. He was well aware of literary sources,[5] but his formal ideas came from questioning Kahn's work and from his observation of the rich tradition of European architecture in comparison with what was being built at the time in America. His interests were wide and embraced designers of many periods whose work challenged conventional tastes, in particular Mannerists, late Baroque architects, the Edwardian British architect Edwin Lutyens, contemporary Italians working in a free manner and the emerging pop culture on both sides of the Atlantic.

3 When Derrida was proposed (successfully) in 1992 by members of the English department for an honorary degree at the University of Cambridge, many members of the philosophy department and a number of distinguished philosophers wrote letters of objection. (The present author voted in favour.) For a useful set of essays on the limits of epistemological relativism, which paradoxically itself can be understood as a grand theory, see Skinner 1985, especially pp. 3–20.
4 For a passionate defence of Enlightenment political and social ideals, see Neiman 2009.
5 In his *Complexity and Contradiction in Architecture*, discussed later, Venturi referred to T.S. Eliot's influential essay "Tradition and the Individual Talent" of 1919 and William Empson's *Seven Types of Ambiguity*, first published in 1930 but not widely read in the United States until the 1950s.

One of the problems Venturi set out to address was the signification externally of entrance and hierarchy. In Chapter 6, we saw how Kahn's Exeter Library appears more or less impenetrable and mute, in comparison with an undistinguished adjacent building that clearly indicates on its façade the location of the front door and the most important room on the first floor (**Figure 6.26**). Venturi believed making such things clear represented some of architecture's most important tasks. Modernism kept silent where it ought to be articulate. In contrast, Mannerist and Baroque architects had no compunction in treating church façades as expressive decorated screens to a less ornate building behind. Venturi's teaching from 1968 onwards investigated these ideas, using the apparently unlikely case study of Las Vegas. In 1972 the results of joint research were published in an influential book, *Learning from Las Vegas*, effectively written and inspired by Denise Scott Brown, the British-trained architect-planner.[6] They worked together from 1960 and from around 1967 she took the initiative for the early design concepts of their architecture projects, based primarily on the natural settings and activity patterns of the cities and neighbourhoods they were in.[7]

Venturi's first book, *Complexity and Contradiction in Architecture*, first published in 1966 and establishing his reputation, had attacked the compositional principles of orthodox modernism, arguing that, despite claiming to be functional, a major fault was the way in which it compromised functions by over-simplification. A clear example of what Venturi objected to, albeit still on the drawing board in 1966 and not completed until 1968, is Mies van der Rohe's Berlin Neue Nationalgalerie, where the permanent collection is in an artificially lit undercroft beneath a totally glazed pavilion for temporary exhibits, neither proving very satisfactory as display spaces. A more obvious target was Philip Johnson, a much less refined and principled architect than Mies (for whom Johnson had worked on the famous Seagram Building, New York). In 1947 Johnson had designed a glazed pavilion for his own summer residence in New Canaan (**Figure 8.1**). For his guests he provided what appears from the entrance side to be a windowless brick box of similar proportions, though it had porthole windows at the rear (**Figure 8.2**). Inhabiting either house was peculiar. In *Complexity and Contradiction in Architecture*, Venturi criticized another house by Johnson directly: the 1952 Wiley house, where the living spaces occupy a glass box and the bedrooms a masonry block below. Venturi advocated an inclusive rather than an exclusive architecture, writing:

> I am for richness of meaning rather than clarity of meaning; for the implicit function as well as the explicit function. I prefer "both-and" to "either-or", black and white, and sometimes gray, to black or white.[8]

We cannot fail to be persuaded by Venturi that the oversimplified aesthetic contrast between solid and transparent in these three examples serves in

6 It was at the invitation of Denise Scott Brown that Venturi attended a jury in UCLA, Los Angeles, where she had prepared a studio programme based on Las Vegas. They married in 1967, and she became a partner in the practice in 1969.

7 "Excluding houses which were his preserve, I frequently produced a first design concept, working from outside inward based on surrounding city patterns. This outset distributed activities and circulation and showed the block and the outlines of structures. Then Bob produced a second design concept based on this one, but starting from site entrances and working inward to develop main public spaces. We then went on to what architects define as functionalism i.e. relationships on the inside" (Personal communication with Denise Scott Brown, March 2022).

8 Venturi 1984.

Figure 8.1 Philip Johnson: Glass House, 1947

each case to compromise their function and create a vacuous architecture. On the other hand, it is worth pausing a moment to consider whether the search for 'clarity' is not essential, if one is to pursue meaning, even if we admit that deep meanings carry ambiguities within them. Aldo van Eyck had a more nuanced expression: his search for what he called twin phenomena – spaces that could be both public and private, partly inside and partly outside – did aspire to clarity, but a "labyrinthine clarity".[9]

8.2 Mother's House and a Lutyens precedent

Venturi's first building, the house for his widowed mother, described in some detail later in this section, was intended to convey a vivid picture of the kinds of qualities he found lacking in modernism. Homewood is an interesting precedent from some 60 years earlier that makes a convenient illustration of Venturi's principal preoccupation – the richness of expression that architecture had forgotten. It is a house at Knebworth in Hertfordshire designed by an architect whom Venturi much admired, Edwin Lutyens, for his mother-in-law, the Dowager Lady Lytton. In the 1960s Lutyens was seen by his admirers, as well as his critics, as representing the end of a long tradition – the very tradition which Venturi was attempting to revive in some respects. The modernist historian Nikolaus Pevsner even suggested that Lutyens would somehow have been a better architect if he had

9 This was a phrase he employed in van Eyck 1963 and many times thereafter.

Figure 8.2 Philip Johnson: Brick House

been born 50 years earlier.[10] Pevsner appreciated Lutyens' skill, however; he just did not think it accorded with the spirit of the twentieth century, where rational Bauhaus forms were most appropriate. Significantly, an article on Lutyens he wrote is entitled "Building with Wit", a characteristic to which we shall return.[11] Like those of Baillie Scott, Lutyens' house designs were always conceived at one with their gardens – indeed, his first patron, the landscape gardener Gertrude Jeckyll, continued to work closely with him.

At first glance, approaching from the north, Homewood is an Arts and Crafts cottage. Lawrence Weaver described it as such in 1921:

> The building owes its beauty largely to the skill with which it has been gabled. There is a welcoming charm to the entrance front.[12]

He went on to remark:

> The south-east front with its loggias is a conception of unusual grace . . . an experiment that few would have dared to make, and fewer brought to satisfactory achievement.

In fact, this building, which is small compared to most of Lutyens' houses, is a sophisticated example of the formal games at which Lutyens was particularly adept. First, we can note the complex geometry that

10 Not surprisingly, he was ridiculed for this suggestion: see Watkin 1977.
11 Pevsner 1951. Pevsner's appreciative, if somewhat bemused, article appeared at the time of the publication of three magnificent memorial volumes on Lutyens' work (reprinted as Butler 1999).
12 Weaver 1921, p. 57.

underlies an apparently simple house. The diagonal approach passes a small lodge on the same alignment as the house, then suddenly reveals the symmetrical three-gabled cottage-like elevation before sliding onwards to the garage. The rear of the house is symmetrical as well, but the symmetry is slipped towards the south-west (**Figure 8.3**). This is only the start of a formal game that goes on to involve a series of interior volumes usually entered at corners or edges.[13] On closer inspection, there is another level of game – a number of references to classical precedents that serve to dignify this dower house. The axial entrance has a flying keystone and leads to a porch where the main front door is to the right: the door straight ahead leads to servants' quarters. The rusticated reveals here, and at the corners of the house, hint that something more substantial is embedded within the vernacular shell. Around the west flank, all is calmly rustic, but on the south-east front the loggias Weaver admired have been pulled aside (or, you could say, the hipped roof has drawn back its skirts) to reveal a miniature classical temple, sporting an Ionic order that has lost its full entablature: the experiment to which Weaver alluded (**Figure 8.4**, **Figure 8.5**). Though he was famous for his wit and light-hearted manner socially, Lutyens was perfectly aware of what he was about in a house such as this. In a much-quoted letter of 1903 to his friend Herbert Baker, about Heathcote, a house in Ilkley, Yorkshire, of a few years later, Lutyens wrote: "That time-worn Doric

13 Inskip 1979 has a careful formal analysis of this house, as well as several others.

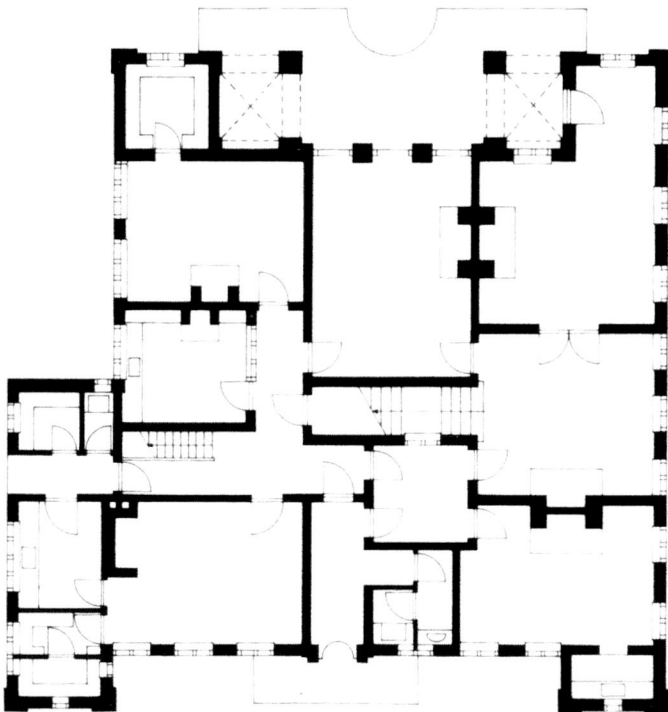

Figure 8.3 Edwin Lutyens: Homewood, 1901, plan

Figure 8.4 Edwin Lutyens: Homewood, 1901, garden front

Figure 8.5 Edwin Lutyens: Homewood, garden front, detail

order – a lovely thing – I have the cheek to adopt it". Describing the formal discipline it imposes, he continued:

> It means hard labour, hard thinking, over every line in all three dimensions and in every joint; and no stone can be allowed to slide . . . You alter one feature (which you have to, always), then every other feature has to sympathise and undergo some care and

invention. Therefore it is no mean game, nor is it a game you can play lightheartedly.[14]

As we saw, in the quotation from Sigfried Giedion in the Introduction (p. 2), it was part of the mythology of modernism that it was not a style at all: form would emerge merely as the result of the rational analysis of functional and technical considerations. But Lutyens was clear that style was a choice, and part of the pleasure that architecture could give depended on how well the architect could play 'the game'. A consequence of his formal sophistication, however, is that though Homewood springs surprises – the central staircase arrives at a well-lit landing, achieved by means of Lutyens' favourite device of steep roofs concealing valleys and roof lights – it is not very comfortable. To achieve the proportions he desired, window sills are high, the dining room windows come right to the edge of the internal walls, and there are few cozy recesses or alcoves to be enjoyed. Adopting the game has led to a certain stringency compared with the more informal and homely work of an architect such as Baillie Scott. But, with Venturi, we can admire the skill with which Lutyens played the game of form (abstractly, by the manipulation of axes) and style (associationally, by the way in which he used classical quotation) and how he can achieve extraordinary moments when the vernacular, classical and abstract appear in tense conjunction.[15]

Robert Venturi played some of the same games in what became an internationally famous house for his widowed mother, Vanna, built in a Philadelphia suburb in 1962–1964 (**Figure 8.6**). First, the axiality of the plan is denied by the way in which one moves around it, negotiating the staircase, which in turn is impacted on to the rear of the centrally placed fireplace. On elevation, the economical timber-frame plywood-faced building is decorated with motifs that refer to classicism (**Figure 8.7**): the split pediment of the entrance façade, the simplified arch and horizontal mouldings and an overscaled thermal window at the rear.[16] Internally, the spaces jostle for position, indicating how they have been pressed together so that the geometry of every room on the ground floor is compromised by diagonals. We know why this is so, as it happens, because Frederick Schwarz and Venturi himself have illustrated a number of his preliminary designs (**Figure 8.8**).[17] The earliest project was highly influenced by Kahn: a single-storey building with a clear definition of served and servant spaces and each room defined by its cupboards and closets. There is an under-stressed entrance since circulation occurs in a minor bay. Cardboard models of preliminary projects show prominent central chimneys. There are several similar iterations, but Venturi had to acknowledge that his mother simply could not afford the cost of his more grandiose ideas. The building needed to occupy about half the original footprint, so as constructed it is a half-house with all the constraints that this imposes – awkwardnesses that Venturi does not seek to suppress but to actively exploit.

It is clear that Venturi could have smoothed out the difficulties had he been prepared to abandon some of his formal aspirations, such as the

14 Quoted in Summerson 1980.

15 Adrian Forty neatly summarised the subversion of hierarchical order that Lutyens engaged in with his "small houses for bourgeois clients . . . built with the mannerisms of aristocratic mansions", although in this case, as it happens, his mother-in-law was a minor aristocrat. See Forty 2000, p. 242.

16 A round-arched window with three subdivisions is so called because it was used in the monumental public bath buildings (*thermae*) of Imperial Rome.

17 Schwarz and Venturi 1992.

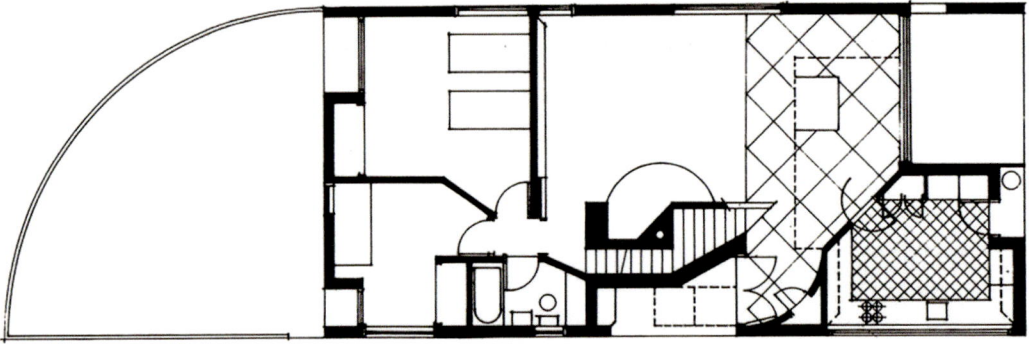

Figure 8.6 Robert Venturi: Vanna Venturi House, 1962–1964, ground floor plan

Figure 8.7 Robert Venturi: Vanna Venturi House, entrance façade

powerful central chimney and the concern for symmetry that enabled him to place his mother under a split-pediment aedicule (much as Lutyens gave his mother-in-law a little temple nestling inside her vernacular cottage). From 1934 until the late 1950s, Frank Lloyd Wright had designed a number of what he called Usonian Houses – low-budget, single-storey dwellings built on a standard timber-frame module. They were informally arranged, usually L-shaped, under broad spreading roofs with living spaces connected to outdoor terraces. Venturi's approach is more like that of Louis Kahn in his unbuilt Goldenberg house, where he had established an ideal atrium plan that he manipulated to cater for

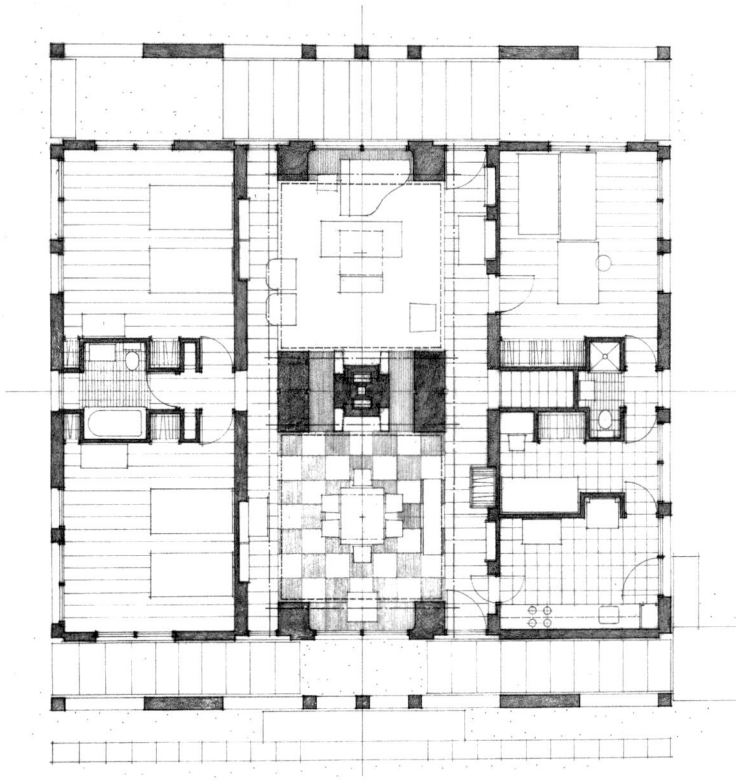

Figure 8.8 Robert Venturi: Vanna Venturi House, 1962–1964, first scheme, July 1959

circumstantial requirements, resulting in four diagonal walls. In Venturi's case the distortion was much more radical. He wished to place his mother in a little palace, not just a casual arrangement of rooms that wandered over the site, but budgetary circumstances required him to undertake a radical compression where the tensions between ideal and circumstantial are visible at every instance and indeed characterize the architecture.

8.3 Ducks and decorated sheds

The theory embedded in *Complexity and Contradiction in Architecture* had been illustrated by buildings in Rome, especially Mannerist and Baroque buildings, and some by Lutyens. In *Learning from Las Vegas*, Venturi and Scott Brown described the buildings that line the strip – hot dog or hamburger stalls – as "decorated sheds", just like the Baroque churches in Italy, they pointed out, displaying decorative façades that mask relatively plain buildings behind. In most instances, designing a decorated shed is a more appropriate way to proceed than contorting the form of the whole building to evoke its function – creating a 'duck'. An example briefly described and illustrated in Chapter 4, Pei's gallery at Cornell (**Figure 4.21**), would be a typically heroic duck in Venturi's and Scott Brown's terms, as would the dining hall at Churchill College, Cambridge (**Figure 4.26**).

18 Spector 2001. See
Vitruvius 1960, 1999 for
alternative translations.
19 The most popular early
translation into English was
by Henry Wotton in 1624,
which renders the assertion:
"Well building hath three
conditions: firmness, commodity, and delight". Guyer
2021 is a recent book built
entirely around Vitruvius'
influential 'aside'.

They also pointed to what they believed was a prevalent misreading of
the influential Roman author Vitruvius (see p. 1). Tom Spector explained
the influence of a pungent statement by Vitruvius as follows:

> In his *Ten Books on Architecture*, Vitruvius creates a portrait of the
> architect as a person of broad learning and various talents. Most of
> the philosophical advice presented by the author, however, is either
> too antiquated or prosaic to be of much service to contemporary
> designers. No one can be expected, for example, to examine the livers
> of a few slaughtered cattle to determine the propitiousness of a
> proposed site. One Vitruvian assertion, however, has exercised a
> tenacious hold on architectural imagination. This is the statement,
> delivered almost as an afterthought in a discussion of building types,
> that all architecture "must be built with due reference to durability,
> convenience and beauty", in Latin *firmitas, utilitas* and *venustas*. All
> subsequent theories of architecture's basic values have been obliged
> to grapple with the simple wisdom of Vitruvius' statement.[18]

Later in this book (pp. 245, 270), the "simple wisdom" of Vitruvius'
remark will be revisited because other criteria such as 'propriety'
were very important to him. It is certainly the case, however, that the
statement has always received widespread acceptance as a convenient
definition of the scope of architecture.[19] Venturi claimed that a critical
problem with the polemics promulgated by Gropius and his followers
was that they had misunderstood the message of Vitruvius by assuming
that beauty (by which we might understand the artistic expression of a
building) would arise naturally once you had solved the technical and
functional issues. That was never the case in any architecture of the past
and certainly not in the architecture that Venturi and Scott Brown particularly admired, which met functional needs as closely as the budget
would allow and then added the appropriate signs as decoration.

One of Venturi's early buildings illustrates this principle: a fire station
in Columbus, Indiana, completed in 1967 (**Figure 8.9**). An abstract
screen of brickwork and white painted render presents itself to the
street, but round the back it is apparent that much of it is a mask to two
different kinds of volumes: a larger shed to accommodate fire engines
and a smaller set of rooms for the fire fighters (**Figure 8.10**). The fire
engines need the extra height, but it would be absurd and extravagant
to give the offices such high ceilings. An expression on the main road
of the difference would not suffice to give the building the presence it
deserved, however, and that is the task the screen wall is designed to
fulfil. The hose tower was placed centrally, and the façade composed as
a consciously proportioned abstract pattern made of two contrastingly
coloured materials; the oversized window to the staff common room
was deliberately placed so that it seems to slide between the two.

A strength of Venturi's approach is that it can be appreciated on several
levels. A pair of timber holiday houses on Nantucket can appear to be
perfectly in accordance with the vernacular, while only cognoscenti may
be able to appreciate the tensions generated by the overscaled windows

Figure 8.9 Venturi, Rauch & Scott Brown: Fire Station 4, Columbus, Indiana, street view

that barely fit within the façades, thus subverting the convention. At the same time, the awkward compressions of the smaller of the two houses make for the kinds of idiosyncratic and characterful spaces that would be enjoyed by its occupants but proscribed by modernism.

Venturi provided this justification for adopting conventional local symbols:

> An essential reason for using symbolism today is that it can provide a diversity of architectural vocabularies appropriate for a plurality of tastes and sensitive to qualities of heritage and place. This use suits the need to respond in our time to both mass culture and pluralist expression. Today the world is at once smaller and more diverse,

Figure 8.10 Venturi, Rauch & Scott Brown: Fire Station 4, Columbus, Indiana, rear view

more interdependent yet more nationalistic; even small communities seriously maintain ethnic identities and carefully record local history. People are now more aware of the differences among themselves yet more tolerant of these differences.[20]

In a similar way his 1974–1977 shingle-roofed Faculty Club for Penn State is at one level a simple and uncontroversial vernacular shed – but sophisticated architectural historians have suggested a deliberate (and somewhat shocking) reference to Claude Nicolas Ledoux's "House of Pleasure", which was to have been constructed in his proposal for an ideal city that he worked on from 1775 to 1799.[21] The building is one of the most extreme examples of the twin readings that Venturi's buildings invite – perhaps only a small proportion of faculty might be aware of the architectural reference.

8.4 Irony as the only truthful response to twentieth-century conditions

Robert Venturi's philosophy is premised on the necessity of ironic expression as a fundamental component of an authentic contemporary architecture. One of the most significant passages in his *Complexity and Contradiction in Architecture* explains why:

> Ironic convention is relevant both for the individual building and the townscape. It recognizes the real condition of our architecture and its status in our culture. Industry promotes expensive industrial and electronic research but not architectural experiments, and the Federal government diverts subsidies toward air transportation, communication, and the vast enterprises of war or, as they call it, national security, rather than toward the forces for the direct enhancement of life. The practising architect must admit this. In simple terms the budgets, techniques, and programs for his buildings must relate more to 1866 than 1966. Architects should accept their modest role rather than disguise it and risk what might be called an electronic expressionism, which might parallel the industrial expressionism of early Modern architecture. The architect who would accept his role as combiner of significant old clichés – valid banalities – in new contexts as his condition within a society that directs its best efforts, its big money and its elegant technologies elsewhere, can ironically express in this indirect way a true concern for society's inverted scale of values.[22]

Not only is an ironic expression necessary and truthful to the financial context, it also fits the prevailing spirit of the age. In a radio interview in 1983, Venturi said:

> At the beginning of this century you could be Bernard "Sure" – you could be a very strong artist and take unambiguous stands. The good guys and the bad guys – it was obvious who they were. Now, I think, intelligent people are no longer that sure of simple answers and

20 Robert Venturi in Sanmartin 1986.
21 Published in Ledoux 1804. For a more general essay on phallocentrism, see Alessandra Ponte, "Architecture and Phallocentrism in Richard Payne Knight's Theory", in Colomina 1992.
22 Venturi 1984.

drastic actions, and this is reflected in the fact that there are inevitable contradictions and ambiguities in the work.[23]

A clear illustration of what is meant by an ironic and ambiguous response is the extension to an art gallery in Oberlin College, Ohio. The original 1917 Allen Memorial Gallery had been designed in a dignified Italian Renaissance style by Cass Gilbert (1859–1934), who was a skilful eclectic architect most famous for his 1913 Woolworth Building in New York, employing Gothic decoration.[24] A dull modernist extension lay behind the gallery, and Venturi's practice was employed to extend it again in 1976–1977. They could not afford the sober classicism of the original, even if they had wanted to, because the budget was more appropriate for a mundane shed than an art gallery. So we are shown the shed, rather like a school gymnasium and, with a nod to Cass Gilbert's delicate patterning on his façade, it is decorated with a bold chequerboard pattern derived from some social housing in London by Edwin Lutyens.[25] The rear corner was cut on a diagonal to reveal a deliberately clumsy parody of a classical column – 'ironic ionic' (**Figure 8.11**). The humour is all the more appropriate in that the overblown timber column can be seen in conjunction with the pop art paintings and sculptures that the new extension was designed to display. Behind the joke, however, lies a melancholic irony: perhaps Venturi would have preferred to have designed a gallery with the dignity

23 The pun is characteristic. It may be relevant that Venturi's mother, Vanna, taught English, including the plays of George Bernard Shaw. The interview appears in Games 1985.
24 For the 17 years thereafter the tallest building in the world.
25 These were his blocks of flats in Page Street, Pimlico.

Figure 8.11 Venturi, Rauch & Scott Brown: Allen Memorial Gallery extension, Oberlin, 1976 interior

and fine materials of the original building, but to be truthful to the context in which he found himself, in common with all architects in the last quarter of the twentieth century, all that he could afford was a parody of what he could not have. There is a parallel here with the wit that Pevsner discerned in Lutyens' work: the surprising appearance of an Ionic temple concealed inside the cottage for Lutyens' mother-in-law is a joke at one level, but also suggests a wistful lament for the more dignified architectural manner which the family had decided was unaffordable.

At Gordon Wu Hall, in Princeton, a game is played with motifs from seventeenth-century English architecture that some of the older buildings reflected. The brick façade has a thermal window placed on a major axis through the campus, and the main staircase sits within an enormous bay window. The entrance is symbolized by marble and slate motifs; on the landing upstairs the decorative panel over the fireplace is painted, but as you proceed towards the library, any decoration is omitted. The thermal window does not indicate a major space, but just a simple room with computer stations on a gallery. Apparently, the only kind of decoration that is affordable is graphic and even that disappears, again reminding the occupants of what they once might have enjoyed had their institution been able to pay for it.

At London's National Gallery, a double irony is evident. Following an abortive and controversial first competition, where the brief required the extension to be partly funded by including commercial development, the gallery had received a major donation from the Sainsbury family.[26] A second competition was held, after a thorough search by the trustees and donors to make up a suitable shortlist, and Venturi's practice was appointed in 1986.[27] The scheme for the top-lit upper floor gallery spaces was derived from John Soane's 1817 Dulwich Picture Gallery, and its spaces were arranged around an effective false perspective axis from the old gallery, ending at a particular painting. Venturi had some fun in the interior where walls collide with windows, and externally he unpeeled the classical decorations so that columns become pilasters and eventually disappear entirely as the building turns the corner to leave something like a 1930s cinema. The most revealing detail, however, is the treatment of the columns that frame the interior false perspective (**Figure 8.12**): their bases have been crudely chopped and their entasis is caricatured so they look like bulbous MDF tubes that have been fashioned to imitate the *pietra serena* columns of an Italian church. In fact, they *are* made of *pietra serena*: ironically, the generous budget did in this case allow for fine materials, the absence of which was a foundation for Venturi's philosophy of ironic caricature.

26 The proposals by the winners of the first competition, meeting the commercial brief and designed by the practice of Ahrends, Burton and Koralek, had been described by Charles, Prince of Wales, in a speech at the RIBA in 1984, as like a "monstrous carbuncle on the face of a much-loved friend". 27 According to the late Colin Amery (personal communication), the trustees initially wished to invite Louis Kahn, not realizing he had died a few years earlier. See Amery 1991, particularly pp. 50–65 for the shortlisting process. It was germane to Venturi's inclusion on the short-list that he had worked with Louis Kahn.

8.5 Michael Graves and a referential architecture

The work of Michael Graves, who was four years younger than Venturi and a prolific architect, who taught all his career at Princeton, serves to illustrate the development of postmodern sensibilities. Initially he

Figure 8.12 Venturi, Rauch & Scott Brown: National Gallery extension, London, 1987–1992 detail

Figure 8.13 Michael Graves: Hanselmann House, Fort Wayne, 1967

was seen as a 'white' architect – an admirer of early modernism along-side Richard Meier and others – in comparison to Venturi and the 'gray' postmodernists.[28] His Hanselmann House of 1967 in Fort Wayne, Indiana, certainly looks Corbusian, though at a miniature scale and of timber-frame construction (**Figure 8.13**). But his Benacerraf House

28 He appears in Eisenman 1975, alongside Gwathmey, Meier, Hejduk and Eisenman himself.

29 Graves admired the sculptures of Anthony Caro, among others. The early houses were published in Graves 1979.

30 Alan Colquhoun points this out in his essay "From Bricolage to Myth, or How to Put Humpty-Dumpty Together Again", reprinted in Colquhoun 1985, pp. 169–189.

31 Major renovations were necessary later to improve the technical performance of the Public Services Building. Since its construction, aesthetic opinions as to its worth have varied widely, while its historical importance as the first substantial postmodern building seems assured: it predated Philip Johnson's own AT&T building (the so-called Chippendale skyscraper) in New York.

extension, a year later, shows that he was already manipulating the language quite playfully and, seen in context with the existing house, it resembles a piece of sculpture.[29] By 1974, at the Claghorn House, Graves was employing classical allusions, such as inscribed pediments, and the 1976 Schulman House had a quasi-Egyptian fireplace and a game of scale on the frontage achieved by varying the proportion of the horizontal claddings, motifs that are only skin deep. The timber balloon frame technology of small houses allows the architect to make any kind of shape reasonably economically, and Graves certainly exploited that opportunity (**Figure 8.14**).[30] His own house, however, was a converted masonry building, and here he indulged in painterly illusions, as Mannerist architects like Giulio Romano had done in the years after the High Renaissance (**Figure 8.15**).

The 1982 Public Services Building in Portland, Oregon, won in competition, was Graves' first opportunity to explore a referential architecture at an urban scale (**Figure 8.16**). Philip Johnson, by then a vocal advocate of architectural postmodernism, was one of the competition judges. Graves' building acts as a criticism of the banal modernist slabs that had been going up nearby and harks back to a more traditional language. But all the motifs, such as giant keystones, are caricatured, and, as in the houses, the motifs are skin deep, so that windows to identical office spaces slide behind the false pilasters or are expressed as stripes or appear as square holes in walls, however it pleases the architect. This kind of thin surface treatment was undoubtedly all that could be afforded in the budget available; unlike Venturi, however, Graves seemed prepared to play the game without irony.[31]

For the Humana Corporation, a private health company, in Louisville, Kentucky, Graves had a more substantial budget. The context was important: the riverfront site already had a Miesian tower (by

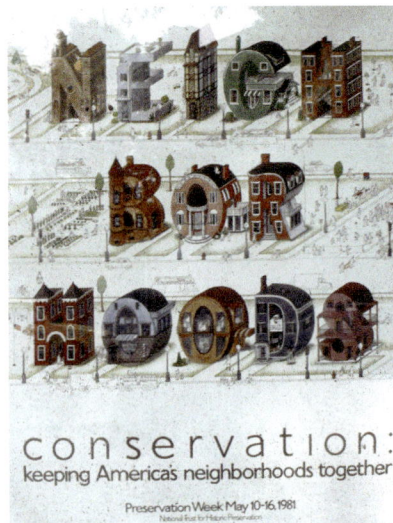

Figure 8.14 1981 poster

Figure 8.15 Michael Graves: Warehouse, Princeton, 1976

Figure 8.16 Michael Graves: Public Services Building, Portland, Oregon

Harrison and Abramovitz) that had replaced nineteenth-century row houses. The entries by the other short-listed architects reveal the difference of a postmodernist approach from that of those of a more orthodox modernist persuasion.[32] Cesar Pelli's neat octagonal tower anticipated his later work at London's Canary Wharf: a glass column emerging from a more substantial base. Helmut Jahn's spiral version was more thrusting and dynamic (**Figure 8.17**). Jahn, a Chicago-based architect, appeared to have been particularly fond of towers, as photographs reveal (**Figure 8.18**). A Freudian reading of the phallic symbolism involved is unavoidable in the light of images of his youthful naked body displayed in a monograph of his work.[33] Ulrich Franzen's was the weakest of the five proposals, built around a concave response to the corner and topped by oculi. The most convincing of the modernist solutions was that by Norman Foster, who proposed a circular drum with a helicopter landing pad on top (**Figure 8.19**). His seductive explanatory sketches attempted to relate the building to its immediate context, but like each of the other three entries, his building could really be placed on a corner site in a city anywhere in the world.

In contrast, Graves self-consciously attempted to distance himself from international modernism in the way he related his building to

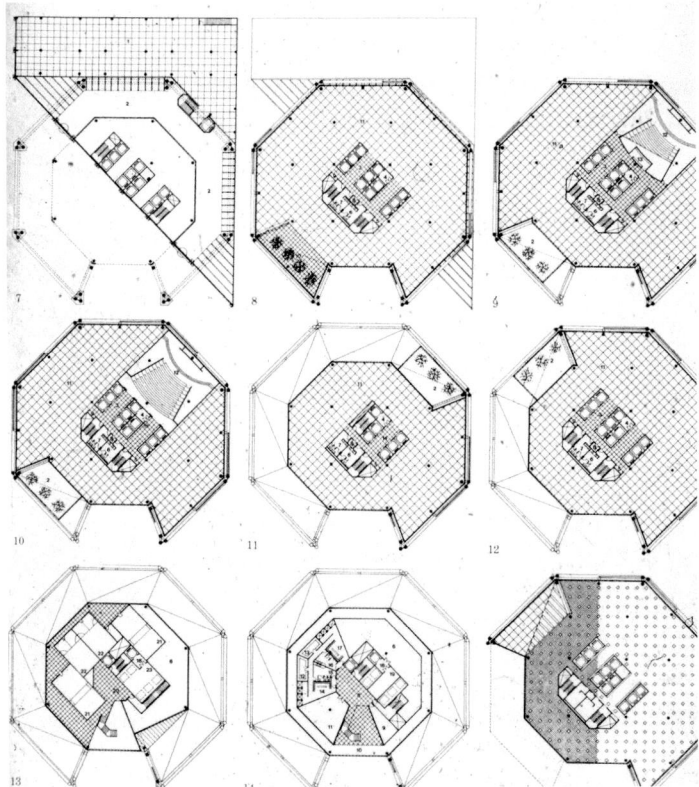

Figure 8.17 Humana Building competition, floor plans by Helmut Jahn

Figure 8.18 Helmut Jahn and a colleague amongst models and drawings of towers

Figure 8.19 Humana Building competition, model by Foster + Partners

Louisville (**Figure 8.20**, **Figure 8.21**). As he explained to Stephen Games:

> The Humana building . . . would be very awkwardly placed in any other location in that city. There are five or six storey Victorian

**Figure 8.20 Michael
Graves: Humana
Building competition
sketches and model**

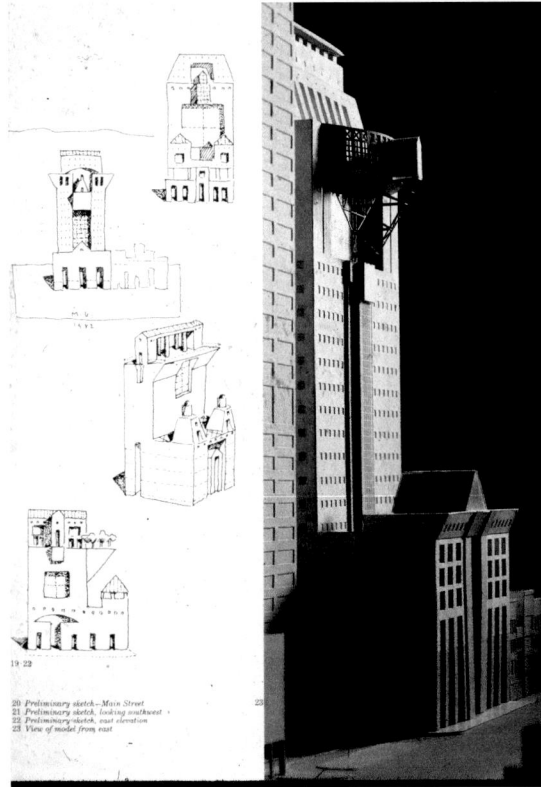

storefronts adjacent to the building and because of that I've employed
a reference to a loggia or colonnade in the building, and on the face
of the building, and hoped that the point would be caught that there
is a similarity. However, our building is much taller and therefore
there is a gradual build-up of scale from the neighbouring buildings
to the final height of our building. There is also an enormous water-
fall within the loggia of our building which looks back to the Ohio
river. Louisville was founded on the Falls of the Ohio . . . So that's
where my 'take' on architecture – general and specific – becomes
localised to the site.[34]

The loggia of the Humana Building is the same height as the adjacent
four and five-storey nineteenth-century buildings, and the street frontage is some four storeys higher. Behind that frontage, partially masked
by it when viewed from the street, rises the tower. Its flank elevation
enters into direct dialogue with the adjacent Miesian block: an inclusive and referential architecture speaks to an exclusive modernist tower,
dependent for its expression entirely on materials, proportion and a celebration of technology.

In the interview, Graves went on to explain his attitude to decoration in
his buildings:

34 "Digging Graves", in
Games 1985. See also
Macrae-Gibson 1988.

Figure 8.21 Michael Graves: Humana Building, Louisville, in context

> In their figurative and thematic aspect they attempt to reaffirm and re-establish humanist aspirations which have been too long neglected by modern architecture. . . . The idea of decoration on a wall – it's pure invention; we don't have to have it in a pragmatic sense. But it might be said that our lives would not be terribly rich without it in a symbolic sense.

Graves did not define "humanist aspirations" very clearly, though presumably he meant that those buildings people can recognize as reflecting the place where they live and, by means of conventional motifs, as signifying a relationship between themselves as individuals to the composition as a whole, are likely to be more approachable. As Venturi had found, recovering the iconographic power of traditional symbols as decorative motifs, such as a pediment to signify an entrance, allowed architects to enlarge the ways in which architecture could be appreciated by people in their everyday lives and discussed by those who wished to debate questions of meaning and symbolism. Abstract good taste, at a time when all the arts were pushing at the boundaries of popular culture, was no longer enough and could even lead to a vacant *anomie* when cities were formed of nothing more than random collections of cubic boxes or more complicated parallelopipeds.

The reputation of those postmodernist architects whose work has been described, and that of others of their persuasion, fluctuates with different generations. Graves went on to build for numerous organizations all over the world, including the Disney Company, for whom he designed its corporate headquarters at Burbank, California, the Dolphin and Swan hotels at the Walt Disney World Resort in Florida and the Hotel New York at Disneyland Paris. He also busied himself with product designs for Alessi and others: kettles, salt and pepper mills, butter dishes and cafetières. Many postmodern products can seem facile at any scale, whether the designers heroically attempted to recapture the richness of the architecture of a past era, contented themselves with an ironic expression of lament, or merely contributed to consumerist taste in the last decades of the twentieth century. The problems of modernist expression that they identified have not gone away, however; neither have the mostly inadequate construction budgets; nor the problem architects faced in being asked to build very large buildings in contexts that could hardly accept them. The next chapter turns to a critique of modernism that retains, and in some respects reinforces, an idealist perspective: in addressing contemporary issues at a more profound level than visually communicated symbolism, it attempted to recover the importance of a fundamental typology of architectural form.

9

THE TYPOLOGICAL CRITIQUE

Introduction

This chapter discusses a group of architects whose criticism was as much philosophical as architectural. As with the members of Team Ten, they had a range of views and produced different kinds of buildings, sometimes approaching a postmodernist aesthetic and sometimes an apparently accurate revivalism. I use the powerful critique of modernism mounted by Léon Krier (1946–), which he usefully summarized in a special issue of the journal *Architectural Design* in 1984,[1] as an introduction to the principal themes of a typological critique, before describing the origins of the notion of typology.

Krier's attack was described by Colin Rowe therein as "the most complete and consistent rejection of Modern Architecture which is yet available". Krier built little himself but his polemic was highly influential. The critique is indeed compelling, though his solutions, to which we shall turn later in the chapter, are less persuasive. Krier's campaign against the orthodoxies of modernism adopted the technique of Le Corbusier, its most visible practitioner and theorist, of encapsulating ideas in equally powerful simplified freehand diagrams. The sketches referred to in this chapter lamented what he saw as three consequences of modernism: "no describable public space", "un-nameable objects" and "absence of hierarchy"; they illustrate both the strengths and limitations of his position. There follows a discussion of the idea of typology and its eighteenth-century origins and an analysis of the work of one of its foremost exponents, the Italian architect Aldo Rossi.

9.1 No describable public space

Léon Krier's criticism of modern architecture under the heading of "no describable public space" is that modernist buildings tended to be entirely self-referential objects dropped onto their sites without treating the space they made as a positive phenomenon: it was unfigurative and merely the ground against which the buildings appeared (**Figure 9.1**). An aerial view of Place de la Libération in front of the Ducal Palace in Dijon provides a good example of what Krier pointed out was lacking in modernist urban composition. Clearly here the space is figurative: the curved architectural façade addressing the palace masks a variety of older structures to create a perfect semicircle. Robert Venturi would have enjoyed the way that at some points the screen-like nature of the

1 Porphyrios 1984.

DOI: 10.4324/9781003244943-10

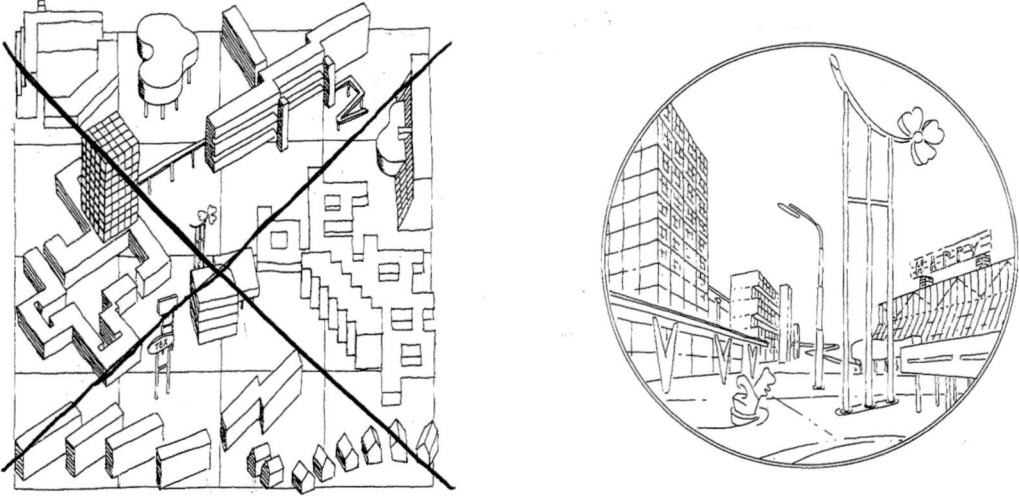

Figure 9.1 Diagrams by Léon Krier: "no describable public space"

façade is evident, but at this stage in his argument Krier was not stressing ambiguities of reading, nor the iconographical significance of the new screen, simply the primacy of space over object.

It was no accident that Colin Rowe admired Krier for his critique of modernist space, because however fond Rowe was of Le Corbusier's skills as an architect (as we saw in Chapter 4), he recognized the way in which Le Corbusier had inverted traditional procedures at the architectural and urban scale and worried all his career about the effects. Rowe influenced generations of students in England and America, especially at Cornell University where he taught from 1962 to 1980. His book *Collage City*, with Fred Koetter, examined the phenomenon of public space at the urban scale.[2] Rowe and Koetter contrasted Le Corbusier's unrealized project for the city of St Dié, which had been severely damaged in the Second World War, with the plan of the Italian city of Parma (**Figure 9.2**, **Figure 9.3**). In Le Corbusier's plan, the buildings are generally free-standing against a background, or on a field, of undifferentiated space, like objects arranged on a table in a still life. In Chandigarh, India, Le Corbusier finally had the opportunity to compose an urban complex, against the dramatic backdrop of the Himalayan foothills, and the effect is similar – sculpturally magnificent but quite different from any traditional city. The separation of the buildings as discrete objects, even if they enjoy a relationship with each other as monumentally scaled sculptures, is even more extreme than that which Camillo Sitte criticized on Vienna's Ringstrasse (p. 57) when he had complained that "a free-standing building remains forever a cake on a platter". It is therefore very difficult to give names to the spaces that are left around modernist buildings, compared to the figurative spaces (streets, squares, passages, alleys, courtyards) in a traditional town like Parma. A drawing much studied and admired by critics and students at the time was Giambattista Nolli's evocative 1748 map of Rome, which showed the

2 Rowe and Koetter 1978. Rowe advocated a process of 'collage' rather than 'tabula rasa' in urban design, arguing that memorable cities such as Rome, built over time, could be seen as a collision of unrealized utopias.

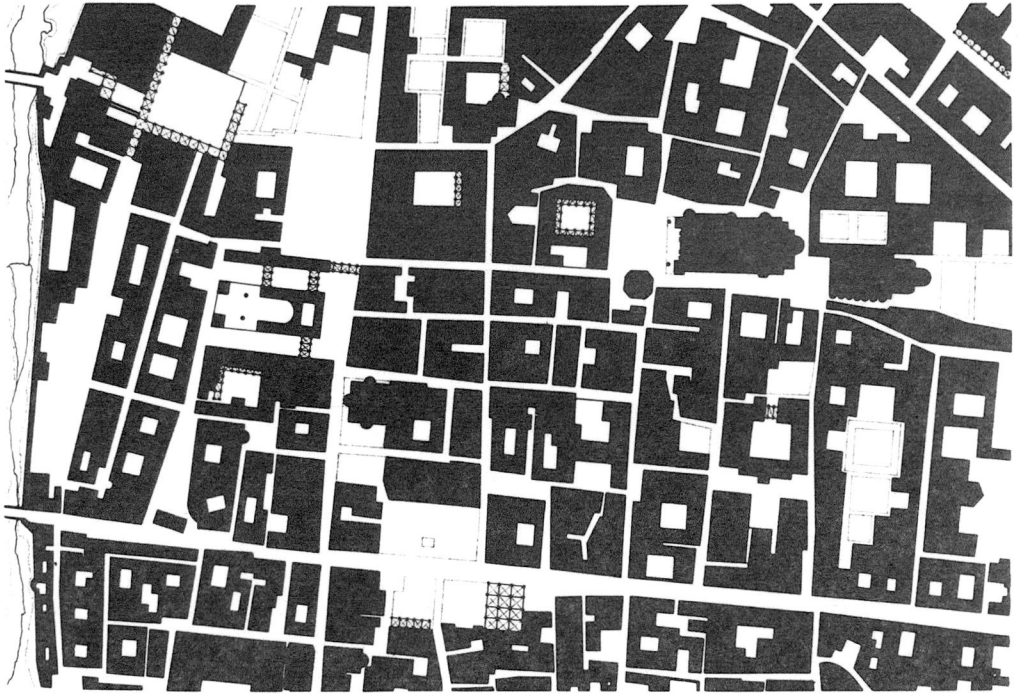

Figure 9.2 Le Corbusier: proposal for St Dié, after Rowe and Koetter

city building fabric in black and open spaces white. It also indicated the ground floor plans of public buildings, including churches, distinguishing them from the solid background of ordinary housing.

One of Rowe's many pupils was Michael Dennis, author of *Court and Garden, from the French Hôtel to the City of Modern Architecture*.[3] Amongst the French examples that he uses, perhaps the clearest and most compelling is that of the Place des Vosges in Paris, where the phenomenon of figurative space can be seen at many scales (**Figure 9.4**). First, the Place itself is a clearly defined square, with chamfered corners, surrounded by grand private urban houses – the hôtels of Dennis' title. An interconnecting pair of these was owned by a single extended family. In more detailed explanatory plan diagrams, Dennis continued to tone in the 'ground' in each case, leaving the figurative space white. So the Place is white and all the hôtels are grey; then the courtyards of the two hôtels are white, while the surrounding hôtel buildings are grey; at the next scale down, the principal rooms are white, while the circulation and service spaces are grey. Thereby Dennis emphasizes the distinction Louis Kahn had described (see Chapter 6) between 'served' and 'serving' spaces. Finally, at the smallest scale that his diagrams illustrate, we see the vestibule and the balcony (where one part of the family can overlook the courtyard of another) remaining as figurative white space, leaving only the embedded servants' staircase and storerooms as grey *poché*.

3 Dennis 1986.

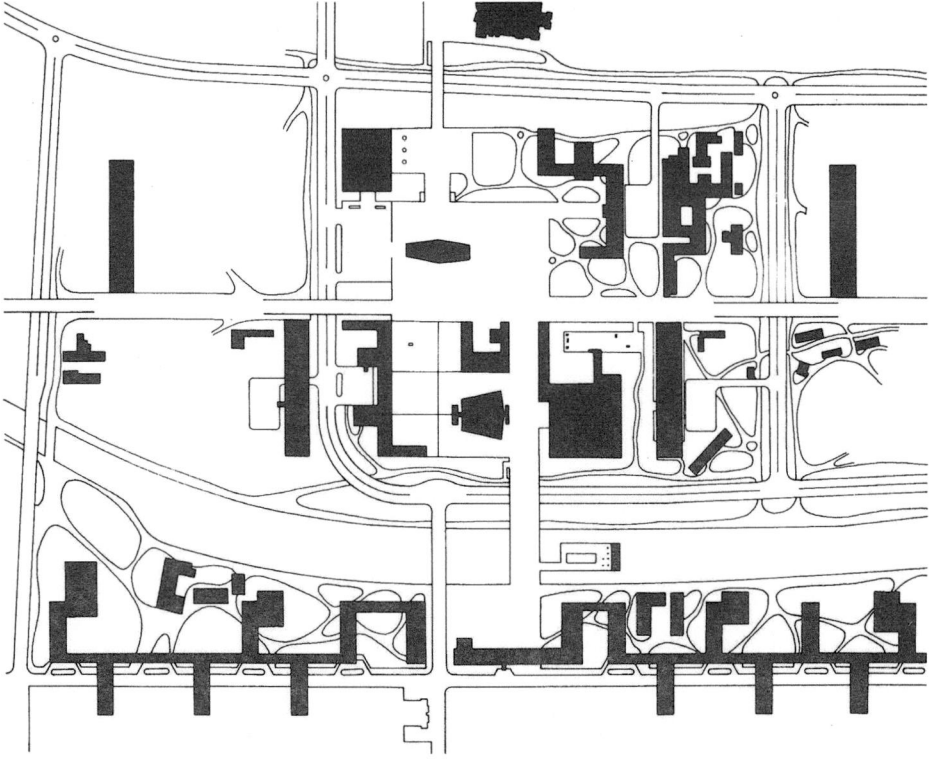

Figure 9.3 Map of Parma, after Rowe and Koetter

Dennis went on to illustrate the interiors of two villas, one by Palladio and the other by Le Corbusier, which was the kind of comparison that Rowe had been intrigued by ever since his 1947 *Mathematics of the Ideal Villa*. Both have columns and walls, straight and curved. In the case of Palladio, the walls are curved to define the space, and the columns are attached to reinforce and dignify the effect. In the plans of Le Corbusier's Villa Savoye, there is no *poché*, so curvature on one side of a wall in the entrance hall would mirror that on the other. The larger curve of the glazed wall responds to the turning circle of the car; the column is free standing in the space, clasped by a table supported on a spindly post and the sculptural spiral stair retains a figurative quality as an object in space.

9.2 Un-nameable objects

Just as Krier had pointed out that it was difficult to name the spaces that remained once buildings had been positioned in a modernist city, he used the diagram in **Figure 9.5** to focus on the buildings themselves and asked whether we could readily identify them. In the left-hand column are three examples of a similar freely-shaped form, which might have emerged from the architectural studio of an adherent to the organic strand of modernism – perhaps by Alvar Aalto, or an imitator for whom the same form could make a vase or a theatre or a museum. In each case the description is preceded by the words "so-called". We already

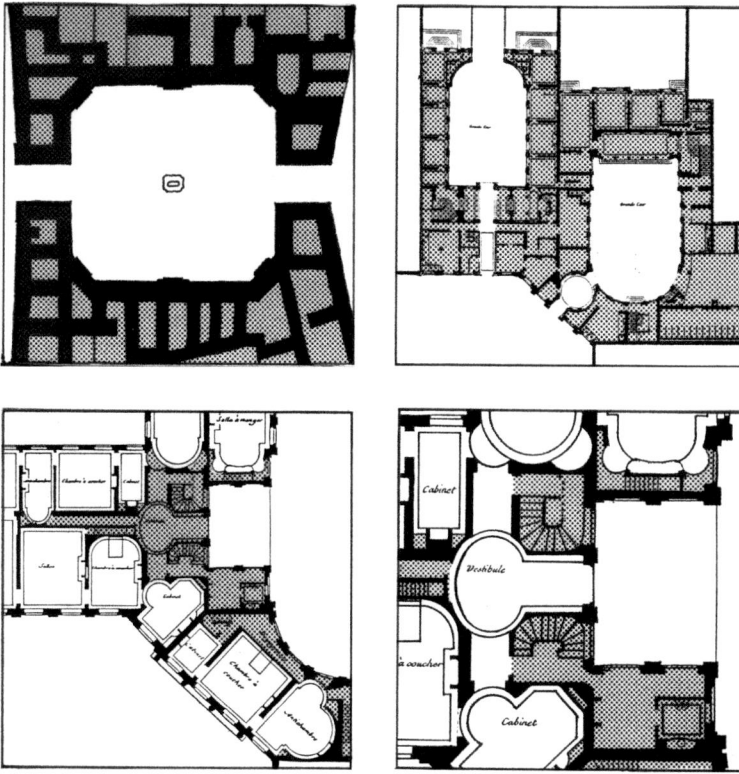

Figure 9.4 Diagrams of figurative space at all scales, in the Place des Vosges, Paris, after Michael Dennis

saw (**Figure 4.23** and p. 103) how a vocabulary of free sculptural forms might be justified in the hands of a master like Le Corbusier, but was not as compelling in those of an architect less skilled. The column on the right of Krier's diagram is formed of boxes roofed by a lightweight metal space-frame and labelled house, garage and church. Mies van der Rohe's tasteful chapel at the Illinois Institute of Technology would be an adequate illustration of his point: only when it was lit up at night would one realize what its purpose was. Or we could consider projects by Norman Foster's office that used 'generative components' to create a concert hall, a youth centre and a school. Krier suggests, by analogy with everyday utensils, that such freedom to employ a sculpturally seductive form, a tidy prismatic shape or an efficient technology and simply give it a label such as church, theatre or school is simply inadequate. Robert Venturi's compensatory proposal that a façade should act as an obvious sign would seem to be equally insufficient: it is the overall form that is Krier's concern. There is an authority, he argues, to the conventions we have inherited which should determine limits to which forms should be employed. Of course it is possible to pour wine from a coffee pot, or serve coffee from a wine bottle, but the reason we do not do so is that it contravenes deeply embedded traditions within our culture.[4]

Krier argued it should be so with buildings: freely formed compositions lead to a collapse of the order that traditional architecture and urban

4 In non-Western cultures, conventions might differ. Krier was born in Luxembourg and his first urban design projects were based there. While his detailed examples may relate to European conventions, that should not affect the strength of his general argument.

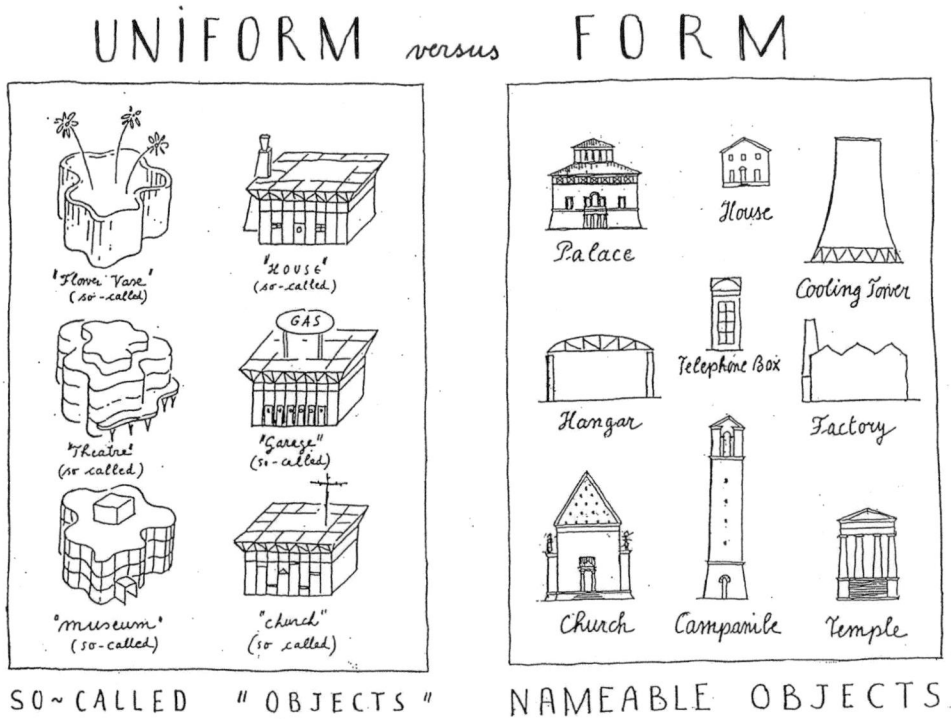

Figure 9.5 Diagrams by Léon Krier: "un-nameable objects"

design used to ensure. Looking again at the illustration of his first point (**Figure 9.1**), we can see that the shapes of the buildings he drew, which failed to describe a public space, are cartoons of well-known examples of modernist practice. There is an Aaltoesque free-form cultural complex, a gridded tower tenuously joined to a gallery-access slab by a raised walkway and, in the top left-hand corner, an L-shaped building with a lower wing cut at 45°, reminiscent of the shape of the History Faculty library in Cambridge by James Stirling, where the space between the two wings is covered by a glazed conservatory-like structure.[5] Léon Krier had worked for this talented British architect for a brief period, just when Stirling was moving from an apparently modernist position to one that has been described, rightly or wrongly, as postmodernist. There is some argument as to how far Krier may have assisted in this process, but there is no doubt that he played an important role at a critical moment in Stirling's career, and Stirling's later projects were usually carefully embedded in their urban contexts rather than appearing as objects in space.[6]

9.3 Absence of hierarchy

Krier's third area of criticism is more concerned with the disordered symbolism of modern, and indeed postmodern, architecture (**Figure 9.6**). Using the example of a school, he illustrates two typical

5 For an essay examining some of the complex issues surrounding this building, see Chapter 8 of Ray 2005b.
6 In particular, three competition projects in Germany, one of which, at Stuttgart, was realized. Arguably Stirling was always an eclectic architect, like Norman Shaw or Edwin Lutyens. See Ray 2015.

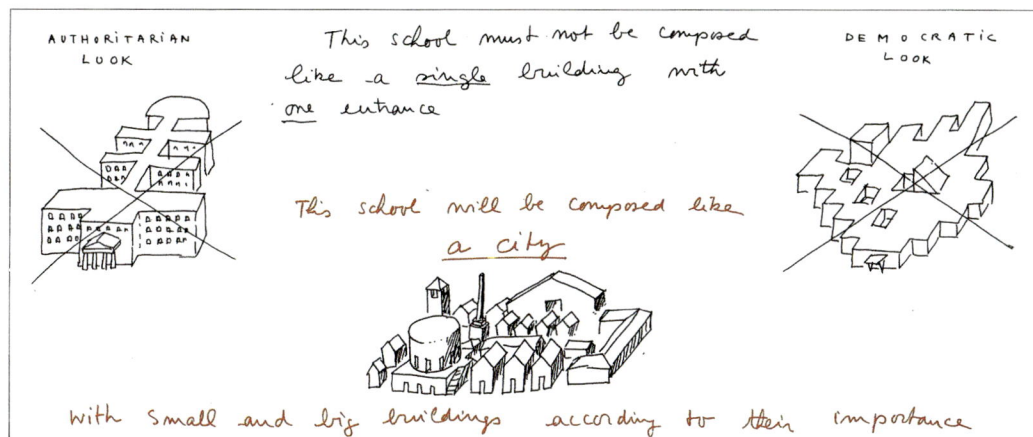

AUTHORITARIAN
LOOK

This school must not be composed like a single building with one entrance

This school will be composed like *a city*

DEMOCRATIC
LOOK

with small and big buildings according to their importance

Figure 9.6 Diagrams by Léon Krier: "absence of hierarchy"

solutions, the first of which he calls the authoritarian look: a plain monumental block, which happens to have a token pediment on the front. The style is not the principal issue at stake, however; it is the scale. In the case of housing, all over the Soviet Union bleak undecorated blocks were being erected at minimal cost, often using pre-fabricated concrete components. Yet we can find a similar problem with schemes by an architect like Ricardo Bofill (1939–2022), who condemned the inhabitants of his housing at Marne-la-Vallée to live up among the triglyphs of a grotesque postmodern fantasy (**Figure 9.7**). Krier rejects the monumental solution but is equally critical of the so-called democratic model. Here his sketch might remind us of a building such as Aldo van Eyck's Amsterdam orphanage (**Figure 7.12**). This, for Krier, is a muddle: you could not easily discover which part of the school was the accommodation or which were the classrooms, or where the main entrance was. Krier had entered a competition for a school building, and his diagram shows that his proposal tried to avoid monumental bureaucratic composition by breaking the components into smaller units and to clarify the meanings of the parts by distinguishing their forms. Even in the diagrammatic drawing of his proposal, which he says has to be composed like a city, you can distinguish an aedicular structure in the background framing a gateway, a library drum like a miniature version of Asplund's 1922–1932 City Library in Stockholm, and more ordinary spaces (classrooms) in separate aedicular units. What Krier craved at an urban scale was a city in its traditional size and form – small buildings with their own gardens arranged in coherent streets and squares, contrasted with articulate public structures that demonstrate their place in the cultural and physical context by employing an appropriately dignified architectural language.

Like Aldo van Eyck, Krier thought a building could be like a miniature city but with a crucial difference: that clear hierarchies should be established. If the first two critiques can be seen as a straightforward attack on modernist compositional technique (particularly evident in Le Corbusier's work), the third suggests a deeper philosophical theme.

Figure 9.7 Ricardo Bofill: Abraxas Development, Marne-la-Vallée, 1982

'Hierarchy' was a term originally applied to religious distinctions, as its Greek etymology suggests (ἱερός, or 'hieros' meaning sacred; αρχή or 'arche', meaning rule). The assumption that all hierarchies could be eliminated implied that the sacred was no different from the everyday – we recall Adolf Loos' definition of what would constitute genuine architecture and Kraus' distinction between two receptacles: the chamber pot and the urn (p. 61). Though Krier himself did not indulge in philosophical explanations, a way of encapsulating this critique is to say that modernism had adopted, or misunderstood, a Hegelian teleology by discounting its metaphysical foundations.

We shall withhold a discussion of how Krier believed his ideals could be achieved until we have examined the origins of the concept of typology and the theories and practice of one of its foremost advocates, Aldo Rossi.

9.4 Architectural typology

Especially in the second of his diagrams, Krier made an explicit appeal to the notion of architectural typology, said to have first appeared in the *Dictionnaire d'Architecture* by Quatremère de Quincy (1755–1849). De Quincy has also been credited with the invention of that useful if sometimes misleading linguistic analogy, to which we saw John Summerson refer in his 1956 RIBA lecture and thereafter in his book *The Classical Language of Architecture*. De Quincy invoked forms that he said

accorded to the history of the discipline and acknowledged the authority of precedents, but, as ideals, transcend any particular example or
model: they are a distillation of the past. De Quincy's intention was not
to point architects towards imitating a particular architect, such as Palladio, but towards the long-standing tradition of certain forms: domed
or vaulted spaces, for instance, being more important and dignified than
flat-roofed spaces. Krier was careful to ensure his advice was similarly
generalized and not necessarily tied to the classical tradition. Typology
therefore has two characteristics: it can reflect an ideal, but it is also a
response to inherited conventions within a given culture.

De Quincy's balanced notion could become diluted and formulaic in
French academic architectural teaching. Jean-Nicolas-Louis Durand's
Précis des Leçons d'Architecture, delivered at the École Polytechnique in
1813, produced a catalogue or lexicon of elements derived from classical precedents that could be combined to solve the functional problems
that were emerging for larger institutions (like hospitals) or even for
smaller villas (**Figure 9.8**). The rigorous character of Durand's uniformly
gridded elements has an entirely instrumental character, for which he
has been criticized and seen as representative of all that architecture
should not be – namely, devoid of transcendental aims. Joseph Rykwert,
for example, explained that Durand, as the most influential teacher of the
discipline in his day, achieved his aim of making architecture a rational
science at the expense of "sacrificing most of the matters which were the
meat of architectural theory before his time".[7] Rykwert continued:

7 Rykwert 1984. For an
alternative view, interpret-
ing Durand and French
neo-classicism as a harbinger of modernist abstraction
and general force for good,
see Kaufmann 1968, first
published in 1955.

**Figure 9.8 Part of
Durand's lexicon of
types at the École
Polytechnique**

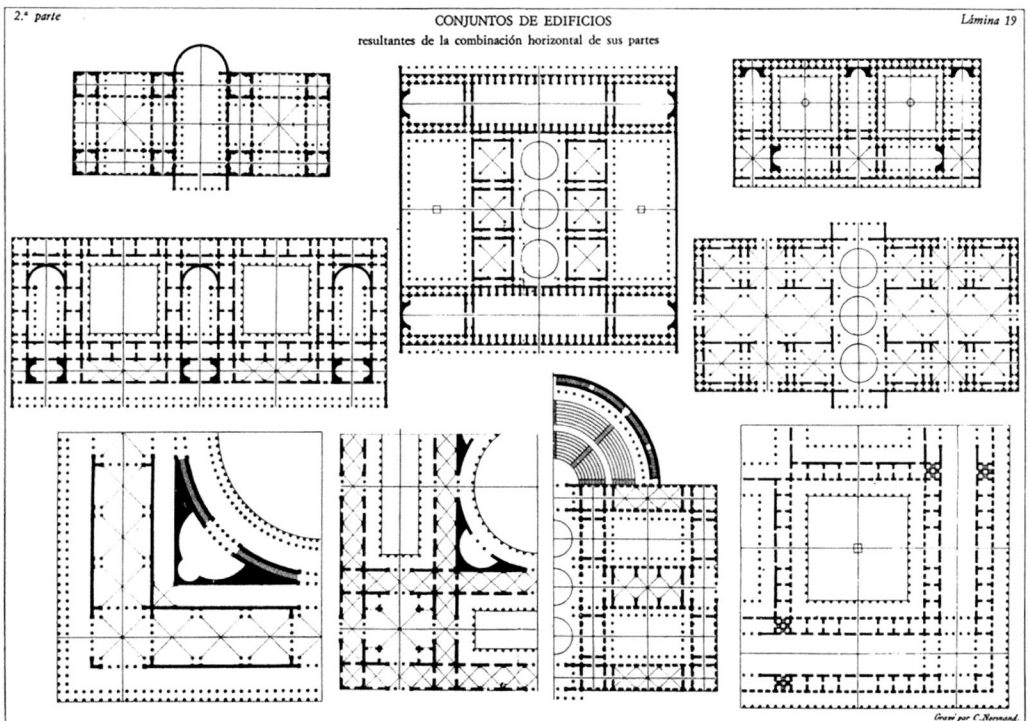

8 Pérez-Gómez 1983, p. 311.
9 For a useful description of
Durand's educational task,
see Saint 2007, pp. 442–443.
On p. 492 Saint takes
particular issue with Pérez-
Gómez's reading of Durand,
though in the process he also
questions the notion of the
'Enlightenment split'.
10 Vidler 2014.

For his part, he was able to formulate, once and for all time, the permanent principles of architecture framed in terms of both structural
analysis and geometrical composition. His formulae were widely
applied, and his pragmatic teaching methods are the source of many
of our troubles today.

Alberto Pérez-Gómez, discussing in particular Durand's use of geometry, is even more explicit in blaming him for a reduced vision of what
architecture involves:

> In Durand's theory, number and geometry finally discarded their sym-
> bolic connotations. From now on, proportional systems would have the
> character of technical instruments, and the geometry applied to design
> would act merely as a vehicle for ensuring its efficiency. Geometrical
> forms lost their cosmological reverberations; they were uprooted from
> the *Lebenswelt* and their traditional symbolic horizon, and they became
> instead signs of technological values. This in turn led to the geometry
> of the Bauhaus, the International Style, and the Modern Movement,
> which was essentially the undifferentiated product of a technological
> world view. As part of a theory that cast off metaphysical speculation,
> the simple and anonymous geometry of most contemporary architec-
> ture speaks only to a technological process, not to the world of man.[8]

A milder view would hold that Durand's methodology was useful, but
of course not in itself sufficient. Many other factors are involved in creating architecture, so it was a quite inadequate answer. Faced with the
problem of teaching a two-year course to young men, many of whom
were destined to be engineers, Durand had embraced an instrumental
notion of an architecture made by an assembly of parts in order that it
could respond to new programmatic requirements.[9] An abstract theory
of composition allowed architecture to be freed from the necessity of
being conceived as a whole, so that in turn it could become a tool to
enable the construction of emerging institutions such as the hospitals,
prisons, schools, arsenals, warehouses and ports that were needed in
post-revolutionary France. Liberated from closed traditional types, the
combination of parts could deal with any particular need. Durand's
pragmatism, his ambition to respond to current social and economic
conditions rather than submit to conventional ideals and traditions,
stimulated his most important contribution to architecture – the organization of parts and elements of a building as an ordering system that
supersedes a global or unitary conception.

In a useful article originally published in 1976, Anthony Vidler suggested that, after the arrival of modernism, three kinds of typology
might be relevant.[10] The first derived from the idea of the origins
of architecture, which Vitruvius had first discussed and the Abbé
Marc-Antoine Laugier had reiterated in his 1753 *Essai sur l'Architecture*
(see pp. 35–36 and **Figure 2.8**). Laugier advocated a return to architectural first principles in order that design could be rescued from
the disorder of the Baroque and Rococo styles, and six years later the
British architect William Chambers made a similar point. So the first

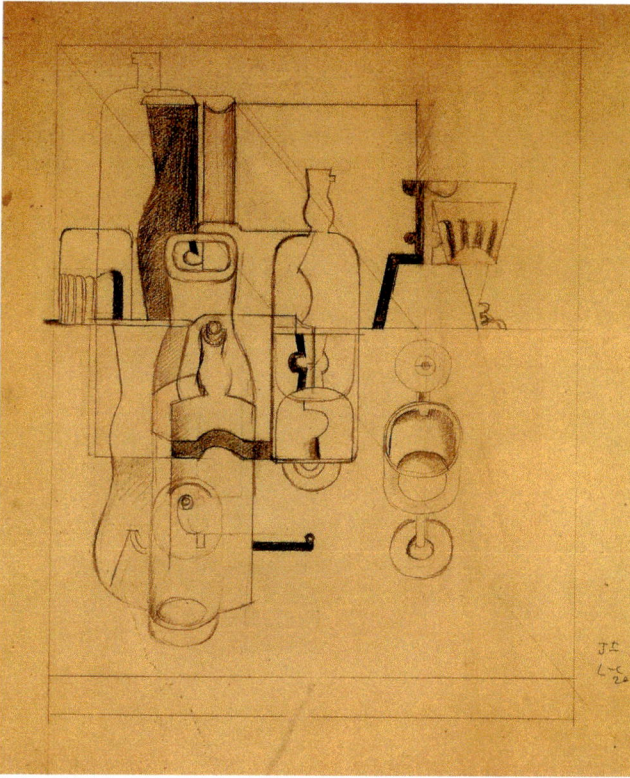

**Figure 9.9 Le
Corbusier: drawing
showing examples of
the *objet-type***

typology is natural, or organic. A second typology is man-made. This
is what Le Corbusier called the *objet-type* (**Figure 9.9**). His Purist
paintings used the forms of mass-produced objects as their subject
matter, and his *Vers une Architecture* ends with a picture of a briar
pipe – a functional type-form that had been distilled to reveal its very
essence. The third typology, according to Vidler, is provided by the
rich tradition of architecture itself, summarized in paintings such as
Thomas Cole's *The Architect's Dream* of 1840, which shows a pyramid,
a Gothic cathedral and a number of classical buildings and fragments
(**Figure 9.10**).

9.5 The argument for typology in the twentieth century

The most coherent answer to the question of why typology should
become such a subject of interest in the later twentieth century was
provided in an essay entitled "Typology and Design Method" by the
British architect Alan Colquhoun, who lectured at Princeton where
Michael Graves was also teaching. He recalled a statement by the
Argentinean architect Tomás Maldonado, who had been trained at
the Bauhaus and taught and was later rector at the Hochschule für
Gestaltung at Ulm. The faculty members at Ulm were dedicated to discovering rational design methodologies, but Maldonado had to admit
that in their absence architects needed some kind of starting point:

Figure 9.10 Thomas Cole: *The Architect's Dream*, 1840

ideas could not simply arrive out of the rational analysis of problems – or up till now they could not, although eventually they somehow might be able to. Colquhoun did not believe a rational design procedure would ever be forthcoming for a cultural phenomenon such as a work of architecture. The problem with modernism was precisely that it had depended on the 'scientistic' myth of a rational design process as a starting point, leaving architects to choose freely how to express the result in form. Modernism, as he memorably put it in the quotation already cited (p. 23), "consists of a tension between two apparently contradictory ideas – biotechnical determinism on the one hand and free expression on the other".

Colquhoun is careful not to ascribe a quasi-divine authority to the concept of typology, however. It could just be that past forms collectivley formed a precedent that had become a cultural convention. He borrowed from Ernst Gombrich the example of traffic lights.[11] All over the world, red means 'stop'. But why should that be the case? One could make an argument for red symbolizing dynamic activity and therefore encouraging movement, while green, as a relaxed, peaceful colour, should suggest staying put (like resting on the grass under a tree). But at some stage the convention was established that red meant danger, and therefore 'stop', and green was appropriate for 'go'[12] Conventions can therefore be arbitrary in their origin, but over time they gather an authority: the classical orders might have exactly that kind of origin.[13]

11 See "Expression and Communication" in Gombrich 1994.

12 Another interpretation, justifying the near-universal convention, might be that bloodshed is red and signifies danger and even death; wounds could be staunched by the application of (green) leaves.

13 An essay of 2005 by Rafael Moneo, "Sul concetto di Arbitrarietà in Architettura", made this point with reference to the invention of the Corinthian order. Reprinted in English as "On the concept of the Arbitrary in Architecture" in Moneo 2009. See also González de Canales and Ray 2015, p. 196.

Colquhoun concluded his essay by comparing what had happened in architecture to the revolution in other arts. In abandoning the diatonic system of harmony, Arnold Schönberg did not entirely forsake traditional formal devices, but substituted his own language, in the same way that Le Corbusier proposed his own rules. There was a difference, however, between conventions that had grown over a significant period of time and those that were twentieth-century inventions. Some architects can therefore regard typological precedent as absolute, and one who did was Aldo Rossi (1931–1997).

9.6 Aldo Rossi

As one of the earliest and most influential architects arguing for a typological position, Aldo Rossi claimed it was a duty for architects to acknowledge typological authority. In his 1966 book *Architecture and the City*, he wrote:

> We understand that there is no possibility of typological invention if we realise that typology is shaped only through a long process of time and possesses highly complex links with the city and society.[14]

In the Introduction to the 1973 German edition, he continued:

> Topography, typology and history come to be the measure of the mutations of reality, together defining a system of architecture wherein gratuitous invention is impossible. Thus they are opposed theoretically to the disorder of contemporary architecture.

Invention – that is to say arbitrary new forms, arising out of individual architects' imaginations – is impossible, since architecture, for Rossi, necessarily needs to conform to a type that is historically sanctioned. Rossi taught in Venice, intersecting with the Team Ten member Giancarlo de Carlo (who taught there from 1955 to 1983 and had very different priorities) with stints in Milan, Zurich, New York and Cornell. He also built, engaging in a practice that eventually became international. His teaching, writings and buildings were influential and widely discussed. Part of the reason for his widespread influence was his ability to encapsulate his ideas in powerful drawings and black and white etchings.

In *Architecture and the City*, Rossi argued that it was not primarily as a result of the Industrial Revolution and the advent of motor vehicles that cities had changed for the worse. Such sociological or economic determinism was altogether too simplistic. In a similar way, it was a modernist myth that buildings were ever functionally determined in the past: historic structures, such as the medieval Palazzo della Ragione in Vicenza, which had been remodelled by Palladio in the mid-sixteenth century, had accommodated many different functions but retained its presence in the city because of its iconic and typological character, symbolizing the continuity that is so important in such monuments.[15] Twentieth-century cities were not only in danger of forgetting their own histories but were

14 Rossi 1984.
15 Even mundane buildings with a coherent form and presence can become important artefacts within a city: an example in Camden Town, London, would be the so-called Round House, a building completed in 1847 to hold the turntable for steam locomotives that was converted very satisfactorily in the 1960s to create a space for theatrical performances.

losing their coherence precisely because of a prevailing architectural dis-order. Buildings had been designed and erected without any kind of the-oretical foundation – they were directionless, without any 'tendency' (or *tendenza* in Italian) – with the result that they were either efficient but banal shapes in response to technical demands or, fashioned by irrespons-ibly artistic architects, gratuitously picturesque.

Rossi saw returning a coherent order to the city as the principal task for architects. He divided buildings in the city into two broad categories, rather as Nolli's map of Rome had suggested: housing, which consti-tutes the normal background, and what he called urban artefacts, which were significant interventions into its fabric, of which individual monu-ments formed a sub-group. In his etchings, housing is represented by simple aedicular structures – forms which he found in vernacular build-ings and even in bathing huts (**Figure 9.11**). An enlarged aedicule can become a forum or social space. Much as Louis Kahn had rediscovered and, as it were, re-validated formal characteristics that had been pro-scribed by orthodox modernism (such as symmetrical composition at the Trenton bath houses or a predominantly vertical emphasis at the Richards research laboratories), Rossi reintroduced forms that archi-tects had consciously avoided for many years. In each case he sought out the most powerful and memorable motifs: houses should be little aedi-cules; windows, unless they were oculi in a triangular pediment, should

Figure 9.11 Aldo Rossi: etching of bathing huts

always be square and, if subdivided, formed of four smaller squares; towers should terminate in octagonal roofs with wind vanes, and so on. These are archetypal 'ur-motifs', elements reduced to their most primitive form. His typical window, for instance, would be such as usually appears in children's drawings of windows.

Sometimes, Rossi pointed out, there was historical justification for housing to be fashioned into a larger complex that itself became an urban artefact: he referred to the example of Robert Adam's eighteenth-century Adelphi development in London, between the Strand and the Thames – unfortunately almost entirely demolished in the 1930s. Rossi was teaching with Carlo Aymonino, who was responsible for the masterplan of the Monte Amiata housing, a development in the Gallaratese district of Milan, and he invited Rossi to design part of it, which was his first substantial commission (**Figure 9.12**). Although the components of Rossi's housing block were entirely domestic, unlike the Adelphi complex, its scale ensured it would be seen as an artefact in the city. His building contrasts with Aymonino's, which were more conventionally modern: predominantly horizontal, richly coloured and sculpturally embellished by projecting and receding balconies. Rossi's building was much less expressive and had an undeniable presence, as if it had survived from some previous era. The hugely enlarged columns and sombre, overscaled arcade gave it a surreal quality, like the paintings

Figure 9.12 Aldo Rossi: Gallaratese housing, Milan

16 Rossi 1982.
17 The article was published in *Oppositions* 13, Summer 1978, and was reprinted in the so-called "Imperative Anthology", Moneo 2014, pp. 585–607.

of Giorgio de Chirico. Perhaps Rossi's most seductively beautiful project was designed in 1979, the Teatro del Mondo, a temporary floating theatre in Venice. Its cupola is one of Rossi's motifs distilled from the many domes and cupolas in the city of Venice itself, and this pavilion seemed to summon up the qualities of that most evocative of cities. The poetic sources for his work are evident in his book *Scientific Autobiography*, in which Rossi described how forms with the resonance and authority of history are mediated by personal experience.[16]

Amongst those who took Rossi's theoretical position very seriously was the Spanish architect Rafael Moneo. In an article in 1978 he rehearsed the history of the typological idea, describing how De Quincy's notion of type had degenerated into functional prototypes as a result of the influence of the Bauhaus and commending the efforts by Giulio Carlo Argan and Aldo Rossi to re-establish it.[17] He distinguished Platonic notions of type, such as those held by Rossi, from the more cautious Aristotelian approach of Colquhoun, and this distinction was to reappear in his statement of 2010 (quoted on pp. 21–22) describing one of his own projects. Moneo believed that although the notion of type had historical authority as a convention, twentieth-century conditions meant that it was wrong to proscribe architectural invention. Some of Moneo's own buildings, such as his Logroño Town Hall (**Figure 9.13**), reflect his interest in the work of Rossi and his pupils, who came to be known collectively as La Tendenza – architects with a clear theoretical position. One

Figure 9.13 Rafael Moneo: Town Hall at Logroño

wing of the Logroño building has extended spindly columns (rather in the manner of Giorgio Grassi), but other parts show many different treatments of the column, depending on their context. In his teaching, at Barcelona, Madrid and later Harvard, Moneo became increasingly critical of the limitations of a typological approach, which could either become so dogmatic as to create positively uncomfortable spaces or degenerate into picturesque sentimentality.[18]

In Rossi's later work, his typological motifs reappear at all scales – Alessi commissioned him, as it did Michael Graves, to design cafetières and other items of tableware. Rossi also contributed a number of buildings to the 1987 IBA redevelopment project in Berlin.[19] The first IBA had been held in Berlin 30 years earlier and included free-standing buildings by first-generation modernists, including Le Corbusier, Hans Scharoun and Alvar Aalto. In contrast, the principle adopted in the 1984–1987 IBA, under the general direction of Josef Paul Kleihues, was one of respecting the morphology of the traditional Berlin block. Rossi's building on the corner of Rauchstraße and Drakestraße is L-shaped, forming part of an urban block master-planned by Rob Krier, brother of Léon. Together with students in Stuttgart, where he was teaching, Krier had examined many variations that could be wrought within the basic typological discipline and published them in a book, *Architectural Composition* (**Figure 9.14**).[20] Krier invited several architects to contribute. He himself provided a gateway building at the apex, and most of the other buildings were cubic blocks that reflected the historic forms of grand Berlin villas. It was unfortunate for Rossi that he was given one of the two L-shaped corner blocks. Although Rossi employed his favourite motifs, such as square windows and an octagonal cupola, the result is rather more ordinary than it would have been if he had been given one of the square pavilions (**Figure 9.15**). And it certainly denies the kind of spatial appropriation and interpretation that occurs in Hertzberger's contemporary Berlin block.

Rafael Moneo, admirer though he might have been in some respects, also brought Rossi's limitations out in his remarks on his 1979–1981 Broni School, a symmetrical imposition on its context (**Figure 9.16**):

> The photographs of the Broni school show a cruel scenography, one provocatively divorced from everything that has to do with a sense of comfort or with indulgence in the perception of space. Life is a court of tears, so the courtyard of the Broni school is precisely that. The fountain offers nothing but pain and misery.[21]

Powerful typological motifs can make for a bleak environment, somewhat more suitable for a cemetery than for a school – indeed, Rossi's largest and one of his most admired projects was for the San Cataldo Cemetery in Modena.

9.7 The slide into historical pastiche

Rossi's work may have become somewhat ordinary, uncomfortable or even miserable, but it did not approach a literal pastiche. Having effectively analyzed the defects of modernism, Léon Krier needed to

18 For Moneo's practice and theoretical position generally, see González de Canales and Ray 2015. Moneo's critical understanding of his contemporaries is contained in Moneo 2005. For an appreciative essay on the Legroño Town Hall, see https://eardleydesign.com/halls/logrono/.
19 His Friedrichstadt block, for example, which has a trademark massive column on the corner. IBA stands for *Internationale Bauausstellungen* – International Building Exhibitions.
20 Krier 1988. Many of the examples Krier uses at all scales are drawn from the work of Otto Wagner.
21 Moneo 2005.

say what principles should take its place. We have already seen how he
advocated the establishment of a hierarchy of forms in his proposed
design for a school. The diagram criticizing modernist formalism also
gives us an idea of the nameable building types that he hoped would
allow for clarity of urban forms: house, palace, temple, campanile and
church (**Figure 9.5**). There was scant demand in the later twentieth century, however, for palaces, temples or campaniles, and fewer churches
were required for an increasingly secular society.

In the late 1980s, Krier found a sympathetic patron in the Prince of
Wales, though for Poundbury, an extension of the town of Dorchester
on Duchy of Cornwall land, rather than for a palace (**Figure 9.17**).
Its first phase successfully recovers the scale and something of the
character of traditional settlements partly because of royal patronage:
the gas, electricity and water authorities were persuaded to coord-
inate their service runs and route them through private gardens
instead of occupying swathes of roadside verge; visibility splays for
road vehicles were severely restricted. The prescriptions following
Buchanan's *Traffic in Towns*, which had been enshrined in a docu-
ment used all over the United Kingdom called *Roads in Urban Areas*,
were successfully overthrown.[22] The garages, distribution centres and
out-of-town shopping malls that were essential supports were kept
a suitable distance away. The architects employed to realize Krier's

22 The engineer who negoti-
ated these crucial relaxations
was Alan Baxter.

Figure 9.15 Aldo Rossi: housing at Rauchstraße, Berlin

Figure 9.16 Aldo Rossi: Broni Middle School, 1979–1981

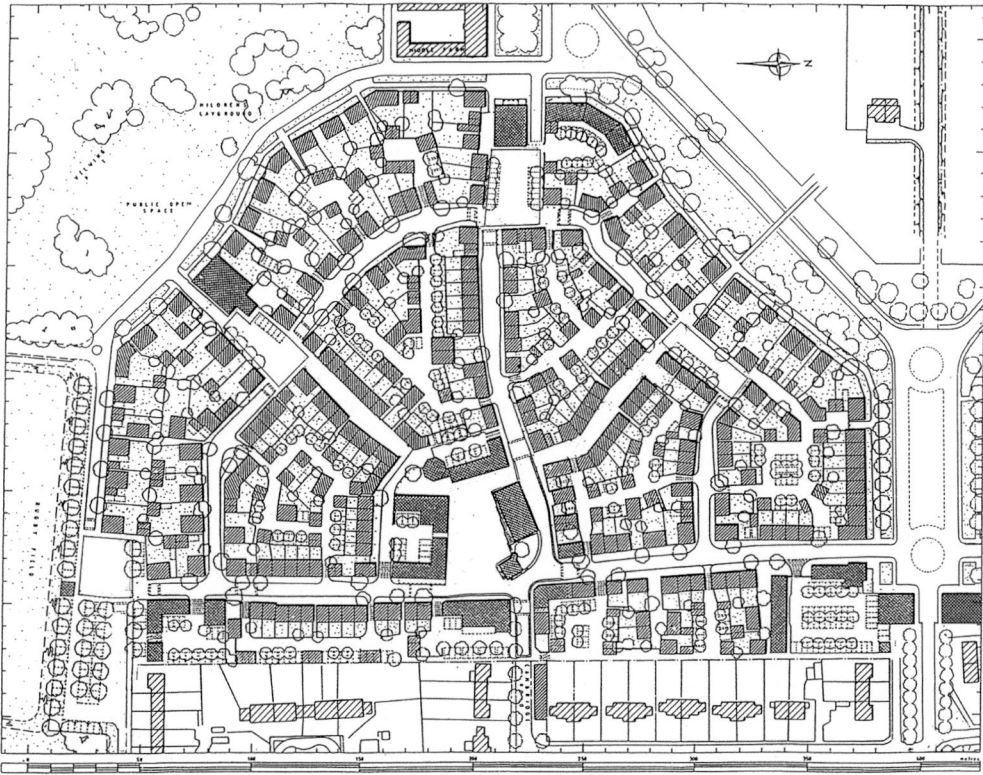

Figure 9.17 Léon Krier: Poundbury Phase 1

masterplan were required to work in period style, sometimes with awkward results (**Figure 9.18**), and unsurprisingly the architectural profession regarded the result as little more than a sentimental costume show. Martin Richardson, in a letter to the *Architects' Journal*, put the matter succinctly.[23] Most architects shared Krier's "intentions to urbanise, to civilize and to restore continuity with history", but the normal budgets in the late twentieth century simply did not allow this, even in Poundbury:

> If the Prince of Wales would, from his own pocket, subsidise the proposal by a factor of two or three, yes, perhaps the vision could – almost – be convincingly realized. The walls could be thick, the detail might delight us, privileged residents could enjoy their elevated storey heights, lucky tenants could afford the rents of their workshops and bakeries, and the churches would be full of those singing His Royal Highness's praises. The costume drama could be staged.

While the urban design at Poundbury is broadly successful, the buildings themselves have the appearance of a stage set. Léon Krier's

23 Richardson 1989. Martin Richardson was an experienced housing architect, having begun working with large-scale pre-fabricated components for the Yorkshire Development Group, but subsequently designing housing for sale in the new city of Milton Keynes.

dream, as depicted in the paintings of his colleague Carl Lubin, is of a world that is irrecoverable, if it ever existed, closely analogous to that of Thomas Cole (**Figure 9.10**). After the First World War, as architects and artists at the Bauhaus realized, handiwork on site by skilled craftsmen on minimal wages had been superseded by factory employment at rather more reasonable rates. The imagery of the past could be reproduced in temporary structures, as at the 1899 Chicago World's Fair (**Figure 2.3**) or in holiday villages, such as Portmeirion in North Wales (**Figure 9.19**) – designed and then extended on and off between 1925 and 1975 by the eccentric aristocrat Clough Williams-Ellis – but clients were seldom prepared to pay for permanence. Ivy League universities might be an exception. Demetri Porphyrios, who earlier in his career had written a sensitive analysis of the architecture of Nordic countries, especially that of Aalto,[24] had become an admirer of Léon Krier and edited a special issue of *Architectural Design* on his work.[25] In his own practice he revealed his conviction that quite explicit historical references were required for university buildings in Princeton, Oxford and Cambridge (**Figure 9.20**). Even here, however, the elements, which were intended to recall an architecture that had grown over time, seem clumsily put together, like a series of disconnected quotations. Such buildings tended to use twentieth-century technologies – steel, concrete, double-glazed factory-made windows and suspended ceilings that conceal ducts and wiring. But architects who advocate a return to pre-twentieth-century forms usually acknowledge that one of the factors that give them resonance and

Figure 9.18 Building in Poundbury village centre

24 Porphyrios 1982.
25 Porphyrios 1984.

Figure 9.19 Clough Williams-Ellis: Portmeirion

authenticity is that the direct way in which traditional materials are used – stone columns supporting masonry vaults, for instance – both ensures a human scale, in that large column-free spaces cannot be constructed, and carries conviction because the 'pattern language' and 'form language' are consonant.[26] As we saw (pp. 143–144, 147), these were problems with which Kahn wrestled: how would you make a flexible laboratory that still retained the character of a 'room'?

9.8 A Kantian apologist for the continuing relevance of the classical language and pragmatic responses

Roger Scruton's 1979 *Aesthetics of Architecture* was one of the most accessible books that argued for the validity of the classical tradition. Because of his pronounced right-wing views, most architects did not take his arguments very seriously, but much of his book seems innocuous enough. He explained that architecture is a public art, in the way that music and painting are not, and that is why architecture cannot become 'modern' in the way those arts can: this would parallel the practice of Otto Wagner, for instance (pp. 64–72). Positivistic functionalism involves a 'doctrine' of space and devalues the importance of detail, while abstracted theories of proportion cannot explain how buildings

26 The terms are those used by Christopher Alexander (Alexander *et al* 1977; Alexander 1979). Salingaros 2013 concurs with Alexander's position and relates the argument to neuroscientific discoveries.

Figure 9.20 Demetri Porphyrios: Whitman College, Princeton

are actually experienced, reducing their effect to one of mathematical correctness. Proportion can only be described in the framework of a complete aesthetics.[27] Kant was correct, wrote Scruton, in pointing out that the pleasures of architecture cannot exist in the absence of an act of attention. While imagination is central, it cannot be merely private and poetic for only what is publicly communicable is important. A full experience thrives on ambiguity as does all great art, not just Mannerism, and is quintessentially active, not passive – aural, tactile, as well as visual. The aesthetic aim must be to bring individual experiences into a single conception.

But then he claimed:

> It seems to follow, therefore, that there can be no experience of architecture that is not also an exercise of taste . . . Perhaps there are established principles of taste; if this is so, then we shall also know how to build.[28]

A correct understanding of taste, for Scruton, would mean eschewing merely psychoanalytical and Marxist judgments because they tell us only about its primitive aspects. Taste is fundamentally a matter of articulate expression, and in that sense the 'language' of architecture – its style – is critical and this cannot be just a matter of personal

27 Scruton 1979, p. 69
28 Scruton 1979, p. 103.

self-expression. Scruton goes on to claim that "the ground plan and elevation of a building are usually affected (if not dictated) by factors beyond the architect's control – by the shape of a site or by the needs of a client – while details remain within his jurisdiction".[29] This is an extraordinary statement in relation to most buildings, whose plan and section, conceived by architects, have a very significant effect and may indeed dictate their formal possibilities and character, which could be difficult to squeeze into a conventional framework. But more importantly for our purposes, by following the German philosopher of mathematics Gottlob Frege (1848–1925) in seeking to show that architecture speaks a language, Scruton claimed that just as the meaning of a sentence is determined by the meaning of the words that compose it, so the accumulation of details on a façade together make the meaning of the whole.[30] But if architecture is like language, it is surely not like a mathematical language, and this is not at all how we gather the meaning of a sentence, as common sense would tell us, as Wittgenstein showed in his later work and as even Frege himself would have hesitated to claim. And it's certainly not how we are principally affected by encountering a work of architecture, which must be closer to how Walter Benjamin described it (p. 233), however much we may then proceed to analyze its material properties, details and so on. In fact, the sequential process of architectural experience would seem to be critical, and a formal architectural analysis sometimes misunderstands both sequence and scale.

In 1979, the year of his death, the psychologist J.J. Gibson published *The Ecological Approach to Visual Perception*.[31] He examined how humans perceive their environment, by which he meant their immediate surroundings from the scale of a mountain to that of a leaf – not galaxies or atoms.[32] The different scales 'nest' within each other. Similarly, with timescale, his book deals with years, minutes and seconds, not millenia or microseconds. He is doubtful that humans or mammals perceive 'objects in space'; in fact, with Aldo van Eyck (p. 172), he is sceptical of the concept of space being of much value to humans in terms of their everyday experience. Thus, Gibson thinks Kepler's theory to be completely misleading in relation to human perception. It was an extraordinary intellectual invention – that light entered the eye in a 'limitless set of pencils' – and has proved hugely useful in the design of cameras and projectors. But it was thoroughly mistaken of Gropius to claim the eye was like a camera (p. 101).

Gibson is most famous for the notion of "affordance", a word he invented:

> a glass wall affords seeing through but not walking through, whereas a cloth curtain affords going through but not seeing through. Architects and designers know such facts, but they lack a theory of affordances to encompass them in a system.[33]

What Gibson suggested was that the qualities of a room with a 'cozy' atmosphere, such as Baillie Scott or Parker and Unwin sought to provide (**Figure 2.7** and p. 33), can be directly communicated: it is a

29 Scruton 1979, p. 211.
30 Scruton 1979, pp. 164–165. Frege was admired by Bertrand Russell and Ludwig Wittgenstein, who nevertheless contributed to undermining the foundations of his mathematical theory.
31 Gibson 2015. I owe my introduction to this book to Simone Schnall, of Jesus College, Cambridge.
32 Gibson's commonsense attitude to scale reminded me of a conversation with a former student. She was entranced by cosmologists' conviction that there were 14 dimensions, not just three, and showed me a 'deconstructed' project that was designed to illustrate that. I asked Lord Rees, the Astronomer Royal, whether there were in fact 14 dimensions: he said there probably were, but 11 of them were at a sub-atomic level. The important thing for architects was to design staircases you could ascend and descend without bumping your head. And you probably had to take time into account as well.
33 Gibson 2015, p. 128.

room that affords comfortable inhabiting and hence coziness. And he claimed that this 'affordance' is neither something embedded in the object nor dependant on subjective interpretation: it's transmitted to us, just as it might be to domestic animals, like cats, which we know are adept at finding the most congenial places to settle themselves.

While appearing to promise a down-to-earth theory, however, Gibson inevitably found he had to invoke philosophy. In relation to the Greeks, Gibson claimed that, at the ecological level – the level of *surface* which is how we perceive the world, and which is what concerns him – Aristotle was right that there is a genesis of things and a passing away, even if Democritus and Parmenides were more correct at the atomic level. He saw little usefulness in the realm of ideas that Plato posited. Since substantial media, such as the earth, are experienced as stable, though they may differ in hardness, viscosity, density, elasticity, plasticity and so on, they exhibit primary qualities afforded to perception, so Gibson could dismiss Locke's distinction between primary and secondary qualities as "quite unnecessary". He believed Descartes to be quite mistaken and is critical of the Kantian a priori. Although Gibson claimed his theory short-circuited the "endless debate among philosophers and psychologists as to whether values are physical or phenomenal, in the world of matter or only in the world of mind" at best he could only defer them, and mostly his position is clear. Gibson set out his anti-Kantian position in his final paragraph:

> . . . explanations of perception based on sensory inputs fail because they all come down to this: In order to perceive the world one must already have ideas about it. Knowledge of the world is explained by assuming that knowledge of the world exists. Whether the ideas are learned or innate makes no difference: the fallacy lies in the circular reasoning.

You might expect Gibson to be more sympathetic to Hume, who after all believed that the characteristics of human behaviour and intelligence were comparable to those of animals, which certainly have brains and can make rational decisions and are subject to emotions and conventions in the same way. So Hume saw no need to postulate that humans, unlike animals, have souls, and argued reason would not be God-given but would arise naturally. Perhaps Gibson would have concurred with his radical scepticism that there can be any provable grounds for believing that our perception reveals the 'truth', so that we are condemned to suffer from "a malady that can never be cured", but that for all practical purposes this is irrelevant. What he would have quarrelled with, however, is both Hume's claim that we cannot perceive causation, only succession, and his atomistic theory that our complex impressions are composed of a cluster of perceptions – going from a simple perception (golden) towards the more complex impression (golden mountain).[34] Gibson believed that from the very start we apprehend a complex whole.

34 Hume 1975, II:13.

35 Rorty 1980, p. 5.
36 Seaside was a privately funded initiative and hence able to bypass normal planning laws; Celebration, also in Florida, which was planned along similar lines, was originally developed by the Walt Disney Company.

Gibson was an American, and his argument could be described as exhibiting a characteristic anti-metaphysical pragmatism associated with William James and John Dewey. The earlier work of Richard Rorty (1931–2007), an American philosopher rather than a perception psychologist, has been similarly interpreted. For him, the three most important philosophers of the twentieth century were Wittgenstein, Heidegger and Dewey, each of whom broke away from, or at least 'set aside', fundamental Kantian conceptions.[35] They did not attempt to erect a system with a set of arguments so much as to question the possibility of such a system – they are 'edifying' philosophers, and their principal achievement would be to contribute to a conversation. For a Kantian such as Scruton, this is simply a feeble relativism.

9.9 Legacy

We can conclude that at an architectural scale it was much easier to be critical of the formal legacy that architects inherited from heroic modernism than it was to construct a convincing alternative. But Krier's critique of modernist urbanism retained its force, and by the final decade of the twentieth century had become mainstream for urban designers. In America, the Congress for New Urbanism was established in 1993 and resulted not only in such well-known examples as Seaside, Florida, but influenced design teaching internationally.[36] Especially as technologies to make buildings of many different geometries became affordable, there was every incentive for architects and urban designers to conceive parts of cities as a collection of 'un-nameable' objects placed in somewhat amorphous space (**Figure 9.21**). Urban designers turned to typological perceptions to try and resist this pattern. Notably, Jan Gehl (1936–) re-

Figure 9.21 Zaha Hadid Architects: Aljada Central Hub, Sharjah

MAKING PEOPLE-FRIENDLY TOWNS
Improving the public environment in towns and cities

Francis Tibbalds

Figure 9.22 Francis Tibbalds: *Making People-Friendly Towns* **book cover**

directed attention in several influential publications to privileging the space between buildings rather than celebrating buildings themselves as admirable objects. A book like Francis Tibbalds' *Making People-Friendly Towns* reflected Krier's arguments for the continuity of urban forms but suggested this might be a quality that transcends questions of style.[37] The front cover shows characteristics urban designers regarded as most important: dynamic skylines, a rich variety of incident and detail and – illustrated by a figure-ground plan of part of Cambridge, a city of courts – positive nameable external spaces (**Figure 9.22**).

Such an emphasis on how people experience and inhabit space, rather than a concentration on how much authority for architects inherited conventions may possess, had been an undercurrent of modernist thinking for some time. The term 'townscape' had been coined in the 1950s to describe the creation of towns as people experienced them, and regular articles in *The Architectural Review* throughout the second half of the twentieth century criticized the effect of rapacious commercial development and inflexible road engineering prescriptions on urban development.[38] The critique was largely ineffectual at the time, however, partly because architects had little influence on planning policies and partly because the profession in any case was somewhat divided. Townscape could be seen as a sentimental remnant of eighteenth-century ideas of the picturesque; it had little theoretical coherence. Megastructures and the aesthetic of the New Brutalism were more convincing.[39]

37 Tibbalds 2000.
38 See Cullen 1961. For a perceptive and sympathetic study of the origins of the notion in the eighteenth century, see MacArthur 2007.
39 Banham 1980, 1981.

Both Townscape and the pragmatic view of perception by J.J. Gibson could be seen as superficial, however. Rorty cited Heidegger as one of his three most important philosophical predecessors, and with good reason. It was his thinking that underpinned fundamental challenges to the post-Kantian tradition which were to have the most profound influence, directly and indirectly, on the way architects thought about their design. The next chapter examines two strands of an existential critique that had a metaphysical, not merely epistemological, purpose, and illustrates some of its implications.

10

CONFLICTING EXISTENTIAL IDEALS

Introduction

How we experience the environment as individuals – our 'being in the world' – and what effect that might have at a profound level on architectural theory and design came to the forefront of architects' minds in the last decades of the twentieth century. We might characterize this concern as a belated response to many fundamental existential changes: the effect of two World Wars erupting in Europe and then, as the century drew towards a close, the way people could no longer expect to have jobs for life or to occupy their own dwellings for significant periods of time, while new media had begun to alter their whole manner of experiencing the world.[1] Should architects embrace these changes, with all the excitement and danger which that might entail? We might enjoy being nomads rather than being constrained to settle in a single place, and celebrate global connectivity with people from entirely different cultural backgrounds. Or should we strive to retain or enhance a sense of belonging to particular locations, in the face of alienating modern conditions, harbouring and conserving the planet's resources, and reaffirming an embodied understanding of the individual in a threatening world?[2] In either case, one might be optimistic or pessimistic about the likely outcome.

The pre-war work of a number of important thinkers illustrates alternative responses to changing conditions that were to emerge in the second half of the twentieth century. Ludwig Wittgenstein has already been mentioned (p. 61) as a philosopher who also engaged in design. The most obvious alteration to the conventional timber type that Wittgenstein adopted in the house he erected for himself in Norway was filing down its decorative window hinges, though he also designed an ingenious pulley that brought food up from the lake. In Vienna, his sister Margarete (also called Gretl) had already employed Paul Engelmann, a family friend and pupil of Adolf Loos, to design her house, when she suggested in 1926 that Ludwig assist him as a way of recovering from his traumatic experience as a primary school teacher. Wittgenstein seems to have taken control, and, with some difficulty,[3] created a building that, unlike those by Loos, is as austere inside as out and was obsessively detailed down to the bespoke ironmongery.[4] His philosophy was dedicated to showing the limits of what could be properly said, so that just as

1 Mobile phones began to become widely available in the 1990s. Of course, there has been a proliferation of alternative media for instantaneous communication since then.

2 Amongst literature in the post-war period that predicted issues that were to become ever more evident, we might instance Rachel Carson's 1962 *Silent Spring* (on the effect of pesticides on nature), Paul Ehrlich's neo-Malthusian *The Population Bomb* of 1968 and the Club of Rome's *Limits to Growth*, published in 1972. See Blewitt 2018 for a broad overview.

3 See Turnovsky 2009 for a fascinating examination of some of the formal problems with which Wittgenstein wrestled. I am grateful to Margit van Schaik for drawing this book to my attention.

4 Wittgenstein himself felt it lacked passion: "the house I built for Gretl is the product of a decidedly sensitive ear and *good* manners, an expression of great *understanding* (of a culture etc.). But primordial life, wild life, striving to erupt into the open – that is lacking" (Wittgenstein 1980, p. 38). Gretl was happy with it, but their sister Hermine found it acutely uncomfortable. For a more extended and nuanced discussion, see Sarnitz 2017.

DOI: 10.4324/9781003244943-11

5 At least according to Steve Hoenisch, *The Myth of Psychoanalysis: Wittgenstein Contra Freud*, www.criticism.com/md/tech.html (accessed 11.10.2021).

6 For a lively account of the parallel lives and thought of Wittgenstein, Heidegger, Benjamin and Cassirer during the inter-war years, see Eilenberger 2020.

7 There are numerous interpretations and critiques of Benjamin's provocative thinking. See Elliot 2010 for an introduction and Smith 1988 for a fascinating set of essays.

8 First published as *Das Kunstwerk im Zeitalter seiner technischen Reproduzierbarkeit* in 1935. Reprinted in Benjamin 2009. Television, video and mobile devices in recent decades of the twenty-first century reinforce Benjamin's perception.

9 Kantians would argue that because being enveloped in a film is rather like experiencing architecture, it does not follow that experiencing architecture is entirely like being enveloped in a film: much else might be involved.

10 Benjamin committed suicide rather than being forced to return to France, whence he had fled and where he believed he would have been handed over to the Nazis. For Heidegger's relationship to the Nazi party, see the discussion following.

he was distressed to discover that his *Tractatus* was misread as advocating a form of positivism, it is unlikely that he would have seen his architecture as a general prescription so much as a personal investigation that inevitably reflects the loss of political, scientific and metaphysical certainties. There was a "tension for Wittgenstein between his own loyalty to science and his intuition that it is our mythologies, our inventing new manners of speaking, that dissolve problems lying beyond the reach of scientific analysis".[5]

Two other important figures were Walter Benjamin (1892–1940) and Martin Heidegger (1889–1976).[6] Benjamin's family was Jewish, but he was influenced by Marxism, became friends with Theodor Adorno and was on the fringes of the Frankfurt School of social theorists.[7] Heidegger's background was Catholic, and he initially read theology at university before falling under the influence of the phenomenology of Edmund Husserl (1859–1938). Benjamin's "Work of Art in the Age of Mechanical Reproduction" was to become one of the most influential critical essays of the twentieth century.[8] It is at least as much about politics as it is about the problem of the 'aura' – the authenticity of a work of art and our experience in the face of it, and whether photography or film can be called art. As the essay circles around these issues, however, Benjamin suggests that when we watch a film we are absorbed and enveloped by it, much as we have always been enveloped by architecture. If that is right, architects should concentrate on the choreography of the experience rather than the manipulation of form.[9] The way we experience a work of architecture is not, as Kantian aesthetics would assume, by a process of cognition and the analysis of the parts and their conjunction to assess its aesthetic worth.

Before his untimely death in 1940, Benjamin had contemplated a book on Heidegger's work, the importance of which he understood although he was critical of its implications, particularly its potential political consequences.[10] Both he and Heidegger were concerned with the existential question of how it was 'to be' in the twentieth century. For Benjamin, the changed conditions of modernism required a fundamental reconsideration and re-evaluation of traditional practice; in Heidegger's metaphysical thinking, breaking with a 2,000-year philosophical tradition as we briefly described in Chapter 1, the essential question was one of recovering the authenticity of 'Being', which had been forgotten ever since Plato and Aristotle forsook pre-Socratic understandings. The architects considered later in this chapter can be seen as responding to these fundamental existential questions by a process of either embracing their implications or resisting them.

10.1 Some consequences of the destruction of a post-Kantian world-view

Because of its widespread post-war influence, it is worth describing in more detail the fundamental questions that Heidegger's thinking raised. In Chapter 4, we saw the philosophical differences that emerged between those who emphasized Kant's orientation towards scientific objectivity (associated with Marburg) and those who studied the way in which his thinking contributed to the interpretation of cultural history, anthropology and aesthetics. Martin Heidegger had been appointed a professor at Marburg in 1923 and contributed with others to a shift in its orientation towards wider metaphysical issues. Then, in October 1927, he succeeded Edmund Husserl, whose phenomenological enquiries were aimed at broadening the definition of objective understanding, to the chair at Freiburg. Husserl was anxious because his successor had already revealed startlingly unorthodox interpretations of the nature of philosophical enquiry, and this trait became clearer in what turned out to be a famous debate with Ernst Cassirer in Davos two years later.[11]

Cassirer was an establishment figure, elected to his chair at Hamburg in 1919, author of the monumental three-volume *Philosophy of Symbolic Forms*, and by all accounts a mild and decent person, extraordinarily knowledgeable, scholarly but a little dull. Heidegger was the reverse – a charismatic outsider, welcoming the cultural inter-war crisis as an opportunity to refashion the very foundations of thinking. In a lecture at Davos prior to the debate, Heidegger claimed that Kant was wrong, in his second 1787 edition of his *Critique of Pure Reason*, to downplay the originary nature of human imagination, compared to his view in the earlier 1781 edition: in fact, Heidegger went so far as to state that he had discovered what Kant intended to say but had felt bound to suppress, because it threatened to undermine the whole structure of his belief in the final authority of rationality. In the debate itself, Cassirer tried to accommodate Heidegger's criticism: he had over-emphasized Kant's scientific side, whereas what Kantianism provided was a methodology for precisely the kind of debate in which they were engaged. But he did question how Heidegger would square his position – the view of 'truth' as dependent on the temporality of Being – with a demand for a common morality. It was not enough to say 'what sort of philosophy one chooses depends on what sort of man one is' because once different viewpoints are established debate should be possible. And debate is possible only because, in intersubjective understanding through language, there is 'a common objective human world'.

It is impossible to determine who 'won' the fascinating Davos debate (which is a good deal more complex than the description here), but there is no doubt that Heidegger's views had considerably more influence than Cassirer's for much of the twentieth century and beyond. Reviewing a book on the Davos debate in 2013, one philosopher wrote:

> Gordon's Cassirer character elegantly holds his own (though he was not feeling well on the day) against the crudely charismatic Heidegger, and yet I felt entranced by the power of Heidegger's quest for the primordial night from which man emerges aware of his own existence.[12]

11 See Gordon 2012 for a thorough description of the positions of the two participants and a transcription of the debate itself. In a remarkable way, as many have observed, Thomas Mann's 1924 novel *The Magic Mountain* anticipated precisely the terms of the debate that was to happen at Davos five years later.

12 Isaacs 2013, reviewing Gordon 2012.

And he went on to say that he was persuaded that "what Cassirer exhibited at Davos was the type of anemically liberal rationalism that led Weimar Jewry to its catastrophic end". That statement echoes the position of Adorno and Horkheimer in their 1947 *Dialectic of Enlightenment* – a gloomy analysis of the failure of the Enlightenment to provide any kind of liberation, resulting in both the totalitarian regimes of fascism and communism and, under advanced capitalism, the rampant commodification of culture.[13] As a Jew who encountered pronounced anti-Semitic behaviour from 1922 onwards, Ernst Cassirer was forced to leave Germany in 1933, having resigned his chair at Hamburg. Heidegger, in contrast, was appointed rector of Freiburg University in April 1933, joining the Nazi party the following month, and did not resist the removal of the academic privileges of his predecessor, the Jewish Edmund Husserl, who had been the most important influence on *Sein und Zeit* and, indeed, its dedicatee.

How far the politics of these two inheritors of the Kantian tradition can be associated with their respective philosophical positions has been and no doubt will remain a matter for debate. What is important for architects is the way in which Heidegger's influential thought affected both architectural practice and critical understandings of architecture. (Eventually, the issues concerning Heidegger's phenomenological viewpoint are metaphysical, and I shall hold over a discussion of those until the next chapter.) When the prevailing neo-Kantian orthodoxy, already undermined in the nineteenth century by Nietzsche, is thoroughly discredited, another understanding of existence is required. Whereas Heidegger's own orientation was towards an existential idealism that tends to an acknowledgement of the divine, another strand can be seen in the numerous writings of Simone de Beauvoir (1908–1986) and her lifelong companion and lover Jean-Paul Sartre (1905–1980). They read the work of Edmund Husserl and Emmanuel Levinas, one of Husserl's most brilliant pupils, and developed an Existentialism that was less didactic than Heidegger's and stridently anti-religious.[14] Sartre's *Being and Nothingness* of 1943 was clearly indebted in many respects to Heidegger's 1927 *Being and Time* (which Sartre read with difficulty because there was no French translation at the time[15]), but by the end of the Second World War their differences were clear, and when they met in 1953 it was an awkward conversation. The Existentialism that Sartre and de Beauvoir forged emphasized the choices that individuals have to make – freely, though necessarily within the constraints imposed by an imperfect society. This ambiguity is the cause of the anxiety we all feel. Because we acknowledge our own freedom to act, we must also acknowledge that others should be free to act. Politically, we might espouse a Marxist politics (as Benjamin and Sartre and de Beauvoir did), but that should not mean there were constraints on the shapes that we might want to make our high-rise buildings, and this is even truer in the conditions of rampant late capitalism. As with a Heideggerian phenomenology, there is no clear indication as to the forms that architecture should adopt, which is of course what architects are seeking and, as we shall see, that sometimes leads to somewhat literal transcriptions of philosophical

13 Adorno was also critical of Heidegger, as he makes clear in *The Jargon of Authenticity*.

14 Over their careers, de Beauvoir and Sartre modified their positions. For a transcript of a lively rhetorical lecture delivered by Sartre in 1945, describing his ideas at the time in simplified form, see Sartre 2007.

15 He had attempted to read *Sein und Zeit* while a prisoner of war in Stalag 12D between 1940–1941, assisted by a Catholic priest.

notions.[16] But first, we shall consider two architects who embraced changed conditions and critics and architects who claimed to resist them.

10.2 Embracing the conditions of a changed world: Rem Koolhaas

The theory and practice of Rem Koolhaas (1944–), founder in 1978 of OMA (the Office of Metropolitan Architecture) and its research wing, AMO (established in 1999 and directed by his partner Reinier de Graaf), illustrates the position of those architects who have accepted the challenge of forging their careers in a world that seems fundamentally hostile to the creation of architecture as it has been traditionally understood. Rem Koolhaas initially intended a career in journalism and film-making and has said that he sees similarities between script writing and architectural design.[17]

Koolhaas has consistently advocated the necessity of understanding the world as it actually is, rather than seeing it through some idealization of the past. His first book, *Delirious New York*, showed that the way the city of Manhattan was occupied differed radically from the tidy conceptions that architects had imagined, such as the Cartesian visions of Le Corbusier.[18] The skyscrapers contained numerous uses jammed together in unlikely combinations and, much as Venturi and Scott Brown had asked fellow professionals to take Las Vegas seriously, Koolhaas believed architects should embrace this apparent confusion rather than seek to deny it or call it to order. In 1995, Koolhaas' twentieth-century work, through OMA, was recorded in a volume entitled *S, M, L, XL*, which is typographically and visually witty and inventive.[19] One of the theses of the book is that sheer scale (rather than architectural meanings, or formal ordering devices traditionally used in architectural design) determines the conditions for architecture today. Amongst the small projects illustrated, Villa Dall'Ava is a house in a suburb of Paris, completed in 1991 (**Figure 10.1**). Readers of *S, M, L, XL* are introduced to the brief for the house by means of an apparent film-script. Koolhaas had received a letter from the client requesting a meeting:

> He would pick me up at Charles de Gaulle Airport. When I came out, there was an enormous scandal: someone was trying to kill a policeman. It turned out to be him. The policeman had asked him to move, but since he was waiting for his architect he had tried to run over the policeman.

Like many of Koolhaas' buildings, Villa Dall'Ava is a commentary on the heroic optimism of the twentieth century but seen from a melancholic perspective. The house is close to two of Le Corbusier's famous villas. Its ribbon-windowed elevation clearly refers to the *fenêtres en longeur*, which constitutes one of Le Corbusier's 'five points' of the new architecture. But the walls, instead of being formed of a machine-like white render, are made of rust-coloured corrugated metal, and the columns,

16 There have been similar attempts to translate provocative, poetic and highly metaphorical concepts into architectural form – such as the rhizome in *A Thousand Plateaus* (Deleuze and Guattari 1987).
17 Parts of the description that follows appear in Illies and Ray 2018. There are several recordings of interviews and talks given by Koolhaas on the web – one that reveals his position most clearly is an address to the Lee Kuan Yew School of Public Policy in 2009: www.youtube.com/watch?v=UViIVN6pCJo, "What Architecture Can Do".
18 Koolhaas 1978.
19 Koolhaas and Mau 2002.

Figure 10.1 Rem Koolhaas, Villa Dall'Ava, Paris

or *piloti*, are angled, not vertical. The house celebrates the Corbusian 'essential joys' and has a swimming pool on the roof, but white protective pipe railings originally proposed have been removed in favour of orange fencing, which is apparently temporary. Le Corbusier had promoted the analogy between steamships and buildings: ships with their decks and promenades, repetitive cabin structures and a general air of purposiveness represented the paradigm of an architecture which would speak its function. In *S, M, L, XL*, Koolhaas reproduces draft drawings of Villa Dall'Ava on which he has scribbled in red biro: "I hate the ship metaphor. Railings are very hard to do without resurrecting the ocean liner from the 20s".[20] The completed house is illustrated by photographs presented as if they were stills from a surrealist movie (the quintessential artistic medium of the twentieth century), many taken at night. People appear as shadows or reflections; there is a giraffe in the garden.

A 1983 essay reproduced in *M*, the second section of *S, M, L, XL*, is entitled "Typical Plan". It celebrates "zero-degree architecture, architecture stripped of all traces of uniqueness and specificity" (**Figure 10.2**). The product of the "new world", Typical Plan answers the programmatic needs of business – neutral, artificial, repetitive, an example of utilitarianism "refined as a sensuous science of co-ordination" so that the architecture "transcends the practical to emerge in a rarified existential domain of *pure objectivity*". The Typical Plan "is to the office population what graph paper is to the mathematical curve", but of course it has attracted criticism, especially in Europe: "Suddenly the graph blamed

20 Koolhaas and Mau 2002, p. 180.

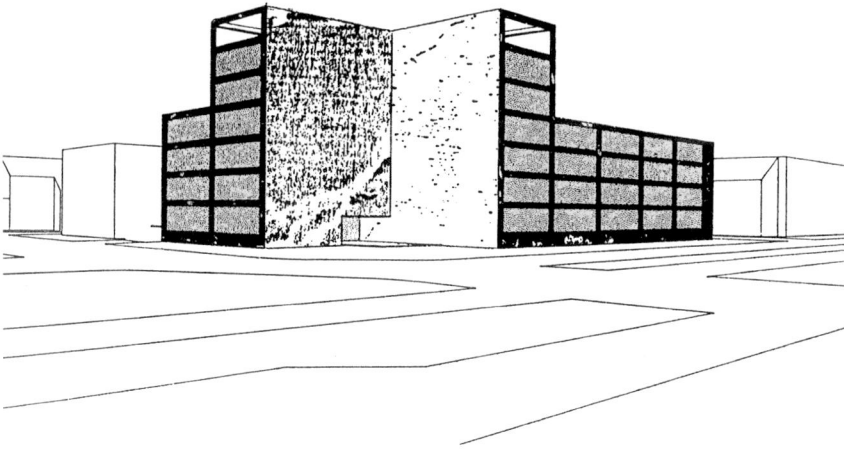

Figure 10.2 Rem Koolhaas, Morgan Bank, the result of "Typical Plan"

the graph paper for its lack of character . . . Nietzsche lost out to Sociology 101". The sociology class is shown the alienating effect of modern office life, compared to the 'cottage industries' of old, for which the grids of the office plan provide graphic evidence. Should architects soften and humanize the environment in some way? Koolhaas has no time for such sentimentality: the typical office plan represents *par excellence* the conditions of twentieth-century capitalism, and there is nothing that architects can do about that – attempting to conceal it by 'humane' design is both futile and fundamentally dishonest. Koolhaas illustrated a version of Typical Plan with his competition entry for the Morgan Bank in Amsterdam, which ruthlessly imports the benefits as well as the disadvantages of the model: "abstract office space, its dimensions chosen to enable a maximum number of permutations, introducing, in Holland, unusual (and ultimately unwelcome) depth".

The Congrexpo (Grand Palais) at Lille is one of Koolhaas' 'Large' buildings, completed in 1994, and sitting within an 'Extra-large' masterplan for Euralille, for which OMA had been selected as planners in 1989 (**Figure 10.3**). The scale of the total proposals, as a new city ("the centre of gravity for a virtual community of 50 million Western Europeans") on the periphery of the old city, means that any attempt to relate to the former urban context is doomed. The real context in fact is travel at the scale of the continent, not the city on the perimeter of which Euralille happens to sit. Koolhaas acknowledges that his proposal to build over the TGV tracks is an investment in symbolism, at an additional cost of between 8 and 10 per cent, but judged by his clients to be worth it. The Congrexpo itself has three components: a 5,000-seat concert hall, a conference centre with three auditoria and a 20,000-square-metre exposition hall. His assembly of the parts is 'scandalously simple': they are jammed together on an enormous sloping plane of concrete and under a single unifying roof. The client, Jean-Paul Baietto, director of

Figure 10.3　Rem Koolhaas, Congrexpo diagrams

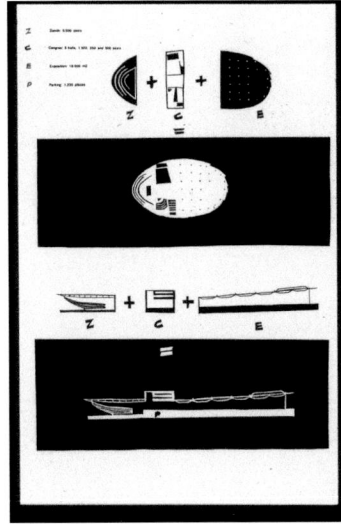

Euralille, particularly appreciated the skills and approach of Koolhaas and his team. In such a context, the audacity to provide complexity of programme within extreme simplicity (or arbitrariness) of form was precisely what was required: Koolhaas had established "a *dynamique d'enfer*, a dynamic from hell".[21]

Koolhaas goes some way towards explaining his attitude in the following passage from *S, M, L, XL*. All the certainties of architecture no longer prevail in the conditions of the late twentieth and early twenty-first century city. The previous generation was "making sandcastles. Now we swim in the sea that swept them away". To survive, he writes:

> urbanism will have to imagine a new newness. Liberated from its atavistic duties, urbanism redefined as a way of operating on the inevitable will attack architecture, invade its trenches, drive it from its bastions, undermine its certainties, explode its limits, ridicule its preoccupations with matter and substance, destroy its traditions, smoke out its practitioners. The seeming failure of the urban offers an exceptional opportunity, a pretext for Nietzschean frivolity. We have to imagine 1,001 other concepts of city; we have to take insane risks; we have to dare to be utterly uncritical; we have to swallow deeply and bestow forgiveness left and right. The certainty of failure has to be our laughing gas/oxygen; modernization our most potent drug. Since we are not responsible, we have to become irresponsible.[22]

One of Koolhaas' examples of scale indicates the force of his thesis: the huge sheds built in Tahoe Reno in California. In the face of such giantism, which will be entirely necessary in the twenty-first century, sentimental attempts by Léon Krier and the New Urbanists to revert to former settlement patterns made no sense at all. Architects have to address the world as they find it and acknowledge both that Eurocentric aesthetic notions

21　Koolhaas and Mau 2002, p. 1208.
22　Koolhaas and Mau 2002, p. 971.

Figure 10.4 Montage of global iconic buildings

had no justification and that the baton had been passed to developing nations such as China, which will determine the patterns of the future. Koolhaas acknowledged the results may well be problematic. In several lectures, Koolhaas illustrated the building for which he is perhaps most famous, the CCTV headquarters in Beijing, which has an unprecedented form, but then went on to show a collage of similarly iconic and innovative shapes: a desperate striving for original forms by architects internationally. While OMA competed to be the most innovative, Koolhaas and his colleagues at AMO enjoyed "deflating a bubble we were partly responsible for inflating", so that OMA could subvert expectations by proceeding to create the plainest box in Dubai (**Figure 10.4**). For Koolhaas, neither rational interrogation of formal principles on the basis of precedent, nor the superstructure of ethical responsibilities (both products of the post-Socratic philosophical tradition) come into the equation in the changed world in which we find ourselves.[23]

10.3 Embracing the conditions of a changed world: Bernard Tschumi

A second architect whose work questioned the traditional concern for form is Bernard Tschumi (1944–). Since the aura of an original art work had been rendered illusory by technology, architecture should concentrate on event rather than form. In fact, all prevailing certainties in the discipline had been superseded. In the 1990s a series of conferences was arranged, each beginning with the word 'any': architecture was liberated from its conventional associations with place – it could be *anywhere*; style was no longer an issue since with modern technology buildings could be made *anyhow*; function was certainly no determinant.[24] Tschumi collected essays he had written between 1975 and 1991 into a book entitled *The Architecture of Disjunction*.[25] Citing Benjamin's essay, he said its lesson was that the twentieth century had become the age of the image and that the task of the artist was to exploit the de-familiarization, the *Unheimlichkeit*, that is its characteristic, not to provide comfort or solace by reference to conventional forms. Tschumi was able to illustrate his own projects,

23 For a critical review of the design process within OMA from an ethical standpoint, see Owen 2017.
24 The conferences were held in different cities worldwide and were organized by Peter Eisenman and his wife Cynthia Davidson, with 32 papers published in ten issues of *Any* magazine (MIT Press): *Anyone, Anywhere, Anyway, Anyplace, Anywise, Anybody, Anyhow, Anytime, Anymore* and *Anything*.
25 Tschumi 1996. Tschumi's vocabulary is indebted to Deleuze and Guattari 1987. For a general introduction to their thought, see Bogue 1989.

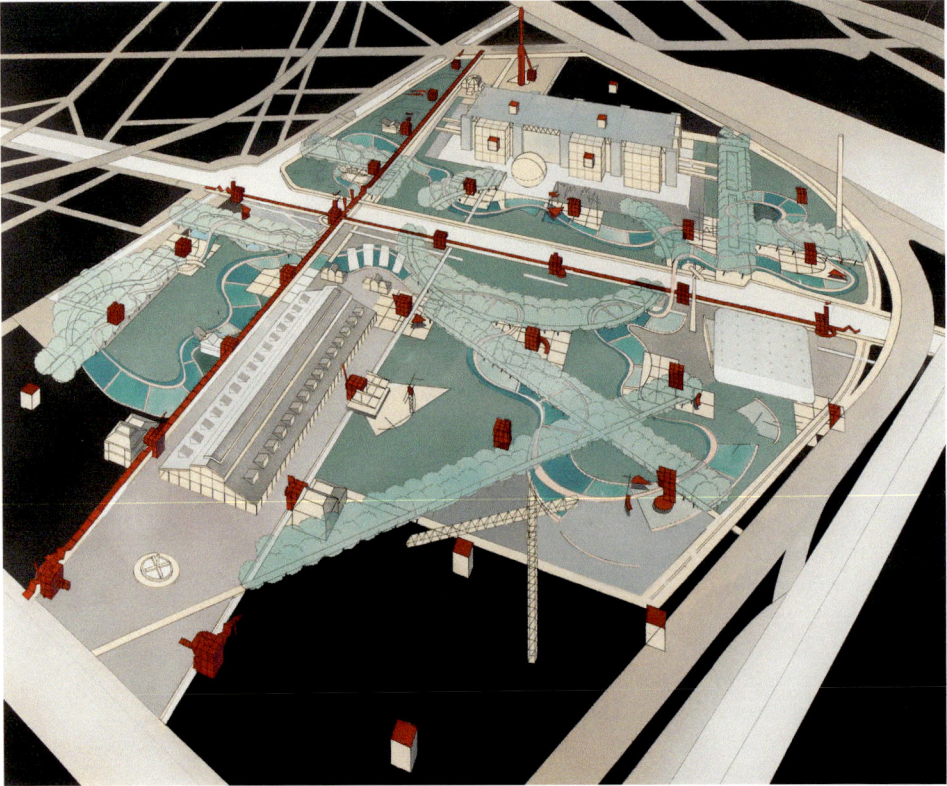

Figure 10.5 Bernard Tschumi: Parc La Villette, Paris, aerial overall plan

including his prize-winning design for Parc La Villette, Paris (where the runner-up was Rem Koolhaas), which was immediately recognized as an illustration of a deconstructive approach to architecture (**Figure 10.5**).[26]

The deconstructionist accepts the contradictions inherent in designing in the late twentieth century and claims that a resolution of the meanings that buildings might convey is neither desirable nor achievable. What would be deconstructed, in other words, is not truth (for it is doubtful what a truthful architecture would be) so much as meaning. At Parc La Villette, an abattoir about four times the size of the Pompidou Centre had been converted by Adrien Fainsilber (1932–) into a Museum of Science.[27] The language was that of high technology: glossy stainless steel and glass but with a dash of postmodernism in the form of granite cladding at low level and the hint of a keystone here or there. It may be said to represent the orthodoxy of the early 1980s. Bernard Tschumi's project for the park itself, however, set out deliberately to subvert what remaining authority such a language might possess. It was ruthlessly abstract, at one level, being conceived as a regular series of points and lines across the space of the park. But each of the points is a *folie*, effectively enamelled bright red against the green foliage, and fashioned as a knowing architectural quotation. The most striking was a miniature version of Tatlin's proposed 1,000-ft Monument to the Third International, a project of 1919 that was one of the most potent symbols

26 Architectural Deconstruction had been the subject of an exhibition in the New York Museum of Modern Art in 1988. 'Deconstruction' was a term intended, in architecture, to describe the questioning of 'structuralist' readings of space and form, such as van Eyck and Hertzberger engaged in; again, it echoed literary and anthropological discourse.

27 Rice, Francis and Ritchie were responsible for developing the façade design.

Figure 10.6 Bernard Tschumi: Parc La Villette, Paris, *folie café*

of Russian Constructivism. Tschumi rendered it as part of an ice-cream pavilion, albeit revolutionary red (along with all the other *folies*) rather than Neapolitan (**Figure 10.6**). The work is obviously deconstructivist as well as deconstructionist. Other *folies* were inhabited by children as small rooms for pottery and art. The platforms and bridges were delicate, even flimsy. The philosopher Jacques Derrida was consulted by Tschumi on the project and wrote about it appreciatively.

The irony displayed here was subtler and more knowing than Venturi's and also appropriately located since it was in a pleasure park and, what is more, in a park in a city which has a tradition of urban parks with highly charged iconographic programmes. But critics at the time wondered whether such sophisticated gamesmanship would be capable of dealing with the more intractable problems of architectural representation (or its absence) that are involved in building institutions within the city proper.[28] We saw in Chapter 6 (p. 156) how Michael Benedikt employed the deconstructionist literary techniques developed by Derrida to illustrate the considerable subtleties of Kahn's architecture at the Kimbell Museum, arguing that deconstructionist procedures were a valuable critical technique but not necessarily a firm basis for fashioning architecture.

Tschumi won another high-profile international competition in 2001 for the Acropolis Museum in Athens to house reproductions of the marbles from the Parthenon (or the marbles themselves, should they ever be returned by the British Museum). As at Venturi's National Gallery extension, there was a certain irony in appointing an architect whose

28 Including the present author: see Ray 1989.

Figure 10.7 Bernard Tschumi: Acropolis Museum, Athens, external view 1

practice was dedicated to expressing uncertainty to house and assist in the interpretation of artefacts that have been acknowledged for many centuries as paradigmatic of European culture.[29] Tschumi achieves this by concentrating on the route up through the building (a *promenade architecturale*, in Le Corbusier's terms), which culminates in the space where the sculptures are placed. Points along the route itself and (just as importantly) different views externally of the glazed façade are choreographed to present cinematic reflections and partial glimpses up to the Acropolis itself (**Figure 10.7**). The building, as a form in itself, is hardly his concern – indeed it is rather lumpen and overscaled in its context on the edge of a nineteenth-century quarter of the city (**Figure 10.8**). Benjamin had correctly stated that we are enveloped by films in a cinema, rather as we have always been in our experience of architecture. That is not to say, however, that composing a building as a sequence of moments or experiences is sufficient: architects need to pay attention to form even if that should not be their exclusive concern. Tschumi effectively acknowledged this in the analytical drawing he provided to indicate the organizational idea of the building (**Figure 10.9**).

10.4 Resisting the conditions of a changed world: a phenomenological critique

Martin Heidegger was moved by a Greek temple in a way that Tschumi would claim was thoroughly anachronistic and pre-twentieth century. He did not visit Greece until he was in his seventies, when he encountered

29 As Tschumi wrote (Tschumi 1996, p. 210): "my own pleasure has never surfaced in looking at buildings, at the great works of the history or the present of architecture, but, rather, in dismantling them".

Figure 10.8 Bernard Tschumi: Acropolis Museum, Athens, external view 2

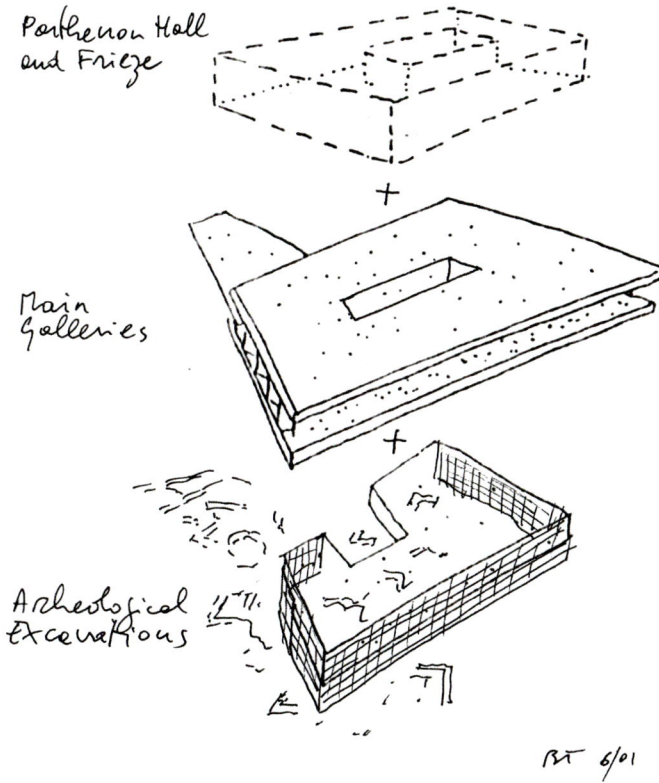

Parthenon Hall and Frieze

Main Galleries

Archeological Excavations

BT 6/01

Figure 10.9 Bernard Tschumi: Acropolis Museum, diagram

the Temple of Poseidon on Cape Sounion and noted that the way it sat on its promontory open to the sky "suggests the invisible nearness of the divine".[30] His experience confirmed the view he had expressed in his essay "The Origin of the Work of Art", originally drafted in the 1930s but first published in 1950, where he had rhapsodized on a Greek temple:

> Standing there, the building rests on the rocky ground. This resting of the work draws up out of the rock the mystery of that rock's clumsy yet spontaneous support. Standing there, the building holds its ground against the storm raging above it and so first makes the storm manifest in its violence. The luster and gleam of the stone, though itself apparently glowing only by the grace of the sun, yet first brings to light the light of the day, the breadth of the sky, the darkness of the night. The temple's firm towering makes visible the invisible space of air.[31]

The poetic character of the language in this essay and in Heidegger's other post-war writings is characteristic. Indeed, Heidegger drew many of his insights from the poetry of Friedrich Hölderlin (1770–1843) and liked to quote his dictum: "poetically, man dwells on this earth". As Paul Guyer has pointed out, in his pre-war magnum opus *Being and Time*, Heidegger had set out to analyze *Dasein* and then *Sein*, but he only undertook *Dasein* (being there, in the world). Intrinsic to *Dasein* is the idea of disclosure: the world presents itself to us as a complex which we have to accept.[32] So, aesthetically, an exercise of the imagination for the reception of a work of art does not seem to be required: we just have to be receptive to the truth. Unlike his pupil Hans-Georg Gadamer (1900–2002), Heidegger saw little role for play, which, as we noted in Chapter 7 (p. 177), was so important to the thinking of the Dutch Team Ten architects.[33]

Despite these limitations, Heidegger's post-war meditations have had a profound effect on architectural criticism, on how students of architecture approach their designs and on certain strands of practice. The Norwegian architect, teacher and writer Christian Norberg-Schulz (1926–2000) wrote a PhD thesis that became his first book, entitled *Intentions in Architecture*. In it he translated Vitruvius' three summary terms ("Firmness, Commodity and Delight") into twentieth-century language as Technics, Function and Form, and advocated a modern version of Alberti's ordering principles, but with perceptions derived from Gestalt psychology, so that, for instance, the purest Platonic forms should be reserved for buildings of importance. Later, he needed to absorb the postmodern argument that formal disorder or contradiction might also be valid, particularly in the conflicted twentieth century. He became a firm adherent to an existential/phenomenological approach, two of his many subsequent books being entitled *Existence, Space and Architecture* and *Genius Loci*.[34] In a number of publications, Juhani Pallasmaa, whom we have already recognized for his perceptive appreciation of Alvar Aalto's work, drew extensively on the phenomenological tradition,[35] particularly the work of Maurice Merleau-Ponty (1908–1961). Most relevant for architects are Merleau-Ponty's 1945 *Phenomenology of Perception* and his incomplete and posthumously

30 Heidegger 2005, pp. 43–44, cited in Bakewell 2016.

31 Heidegger 1993, pp. 167–168.

32 Thereby, suggests Guyer, accounting for Heidegger's "embrace, or at least acceptance, of Nazism": Guyer 2014a, p. 33.

33 Gadamer's magnum opus was Hans-Georg Gadamer, Truth and Method, Second Revised Edition, tr. Joel Weinsheiner and Donald G. Marshall, Continuum 1998, which established his hermeneutical technique. In his later work, *The Relevance of the Beautiful* (Gadamer 1987), he relates his ideas to architecture, and stresses the architect's "decorative task". As Paul Guyer notes: "One might well think that Gadamer's hermeneutical approach emphasizes the conditions for understanding existing forms of art and existing forms of culture more than it does the possibility of creating genuinely novel works within existing forms or whole new forms of art" (Guyer 2014a).

34 Norberg-Schulz 1971, 1980. In a conversation with the author, Norberg Schulz denied that he had changed his position, claiming that *Intentions in Architecture* had established the foundations on which his subsequent work was built.

35 Pallasmaa 2009, 2011, 2012.

published *The Visible and the Invisible*,[36] the latter emphasizing a concept that had already been introduced by Edmund Husserl, the idea of the 'chiasm' or intertwining of objectivity and subjectivity:

> We have to reject the age-old assumptions that put the body in the world and the seer in the body, or, conversely, the world and the body in the seer as in a box. Where in the body are we to put the seer ...? ...There is There is reciprocal and intertwining of one within the other.[37]

Humans are not just 'moist robots', but necessarily embodied beings who are deeply affected by their environment, natural and constructed.[38] The duty of architects is therefore to respect and enhance our embodied dwelling in the world. They necessarily employ techniques to do so, but a concentration on the technical which loses sight of primary existential conditions is disastrous. In examining the history of architecture, we can follow the progressive influence of a view of the world that privileges scientific objectivity – from the formulation of logic in Athens to the Enlightenment and ideas of positivism – and see that reflected in a progressively instrumental attitude on behalf of designers to the treatment of the natural environment and the culture they have inherited.[39] Indeed, the work of architects such as Koolhaas would seem to illustrate that phenomenon.

10.5 Architectural interpretations of a phenomenological position

An American architect who has practised extensively, taught since 1981, and explicitly acknowledged the influence of phenomenology on his work is Steven Holl (1947–). We have already mentioned his Kiasma gallery in Helsinki, forming part of Aalto's masterplan for Töölö Bay. Amongst his many other buildings is the Simmons dormitory block for MIT, close to Aalto's Baker House. It is curiously scaled, with four small windows to each room, so that from the outside it can appear much larger than it is. The larger windows on the façade indicate interruptions to the plan where common areas are lit from above through several storeys ('driven voids'). A similar motif appears in his later building for the Glasgow School of Art opposite Macintosh's masterpiece. Holl's interiors are characterized by a careful control of natural light, which is also evident in the Helsinki gallery.

Kiasma is the Finnish translation of 'chiasm', the intertwining of which Merleau-Ponty wrote, and Holl's play with the name is perhaps symbolic of a worryingly superficial interpretation of what Merleau-Ponty was describing. Holl tended to begin his designs (and instruct his staff) by means of simplified watercolour drawings that evoked imaginative spaces and the quality of the light in which they would be bathed (**Figure 10.10**). Holl designs fabrics, art works and ironmongery, as did Alvar and Aino Aalto (**Figure 10.11**). But the overall forms of his buildings can approach an arbitrariness that far exceeds the licence that Aalto

36 Merleau-Ponty 1962, 1968.

37 Merleau-Ponty 1968, p. 138.

38 The phrase "moist robot" was used by the philosopher Douglas Dennett, encapsulating his argument that human consciousness is merely the result of Darwinian evolution. See Dennett 1993. At a 2013 workshop entitled "Moving Naturalism Forward", Francis Crick similarly claimed: "Who you are is nothing but a bunch of neurons".

39 See Vesely 2006 for an extended treatment and Pérez-Gómez 1983 for a particular focus on the eighteenth and nineteenth centuries. Vesely set out to explain (p. 8) "why it is important to return to poetics and why a new poetics of architecture, together with contemporary hermeneutics, can provide the most appropriate framework for restoring the humanistic nature of architecture".

Figure 10.10 Steven Holl: interior watercolour sketch

allowed himself, in the careful distinctions he drew between what was ordinary and what was special; as we have seen, Aalto had nevertheless been criticized by Krier from a typological perspective (**Figure 10.12**). Clearly, in seeking to recover the poetic origins of architecture, dependence on the aesthetic whims of an individual architect is unwise. A truly phenomenological approach would be as critical of the architect as an individual apparently endowed with artistic gifts as it would be of the architect as a rigorous technician, both being products of the catastrophic disjunction between subjective and objective views of the world.

If the issue is much deeper, it becomes difficult to find twentieth century examples that illustrate the phenomenological position adequately. Though there are articulate advocates, who (echoing van Eyck's plea at Otterlo in 1959) seek to emphasize the sense of place that needs to be the foundation for an embodied experience of our being in the world, and hence of the way we should fashion our architecture,[40] much of the theoretical writing is steeped in a nostalgia for a lost era that appears irrecoverable and is inevitably deeply pessimistic. We might look at settlements in Ancient Mesopotamia and find in them the authentic representation of a mythically embodied society where every portion of the fabric of the city, not just its temples, carried symbolic significance.[41] But few would now be prepared to accept the hierarchical structure of

40 See, for example, Malpas 2018.
41 See, for example, Carl 1983. The notion that the everyday world continues to carry symbolic significance, which is important for a strand of phenomenological critique, was explored in Eliade 1959.

Figure 10.11 Steven Holl: carpet design

such societies, to say nothing of the consequences in human terms of some of their rituals. It appeared to be easier to employ a phenomenological understanding as a form of critique or appreciation (as Pallasmaa did in his treatment of Aalto) than as a prescription for the composition of buildings in the final decades of the twentieth century.[42] Yet Heidegger's poetic understandings can act as a stimulus to a sensitive designer, much as literature or film may. Peter Zumthor (1943–), an architect acutely aware of the specific qualities of material and location, quotes from Heidegger's "Building Dwelling Thinking" and describes his approach as follows:

> Our times of change and transition do not permit big gestures. There are only a few remaining common values left upon which we can build and which we all share. I thus appeal for a kind of architecture of common sense based on the fundamentals that we still know, understand and feel. I carefully observe the concrete appearance of the world and in my buildings I try to enhance what seems to be valuable, to correct what is disturbing and to create anew what we feel is missing.[43]

Zumthor is careful in the commissions that he undertakes and has only built for those clients he knows can realize his work without compromise. It is a far cry from the social vision that underpinned the ambitions

42 See Harries 1997 for sensitive analyses of historic buildings, particularly Baroque and Rococo examples, but inadequate attempts to illustrate a contemporary interpretation. Vesely 2006 mostly instances student work in drawings and models, though he does endorse a carefully designed office building at Stockley Park, London.

43 Originally delivered as a lecture in 1988 at SCI-ARC, California, reprinted in Zumthor 1998, pp. 9–26.

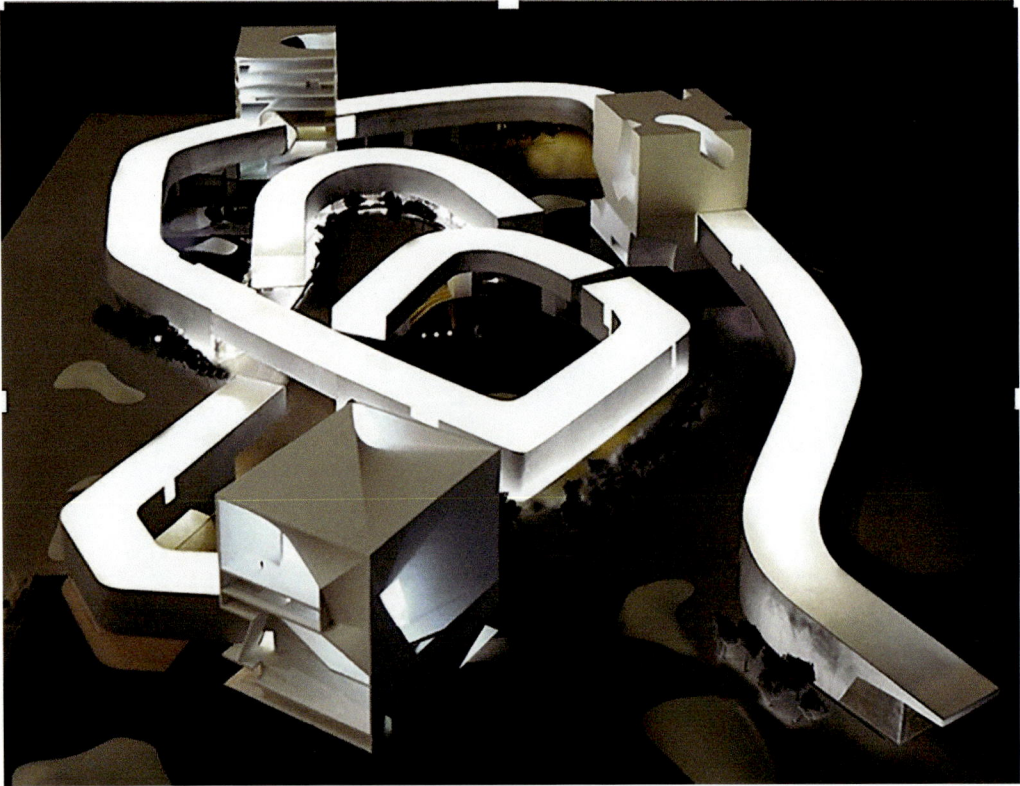

Figure 10.12 Steven Holl: Qingdao Culture and Art Center proposal

of modernists in the earlier years of the twentieth century, to reflect a new spirit in building for society as a whole.

Zumthor trained initially as a cabinet maker and later worked in Switzerland on the repair of historic buildings. Because of a suspicion of over-riding formal 'solutions' and a concentration on the fragment, it was probably in the treatment of pre-existing fabric that the phenomenological approach bore most fruit. A sensitive new intervention in a complicated multi-layered context can both serve to celebrate and to preserve the work of the past, which Ruskin and Morris had argued we have no right to tamper with unnecessarily, and at the same time to add a further layer to its history. Architects who have contributed to this tradition have generally been less celebrated in the histories of architecture since they tended not to engage in polemic. Those who are increasingly admired, at least by an architectural subculture, include the Italian Carlo Scarpa (1906–1978). As Richard Murphy summarized Scarpa's achievement from 1958–1974 at the Museo di Castelvecchio in Verona (**Figure 10.13**):

> Castelvecchio is an intervention in an historic structure, and is the most complex and didactic [of all his buildings] particularly considering the way in which Scarpa set about to display the many different layers of history pre-existing his own intervention. Until

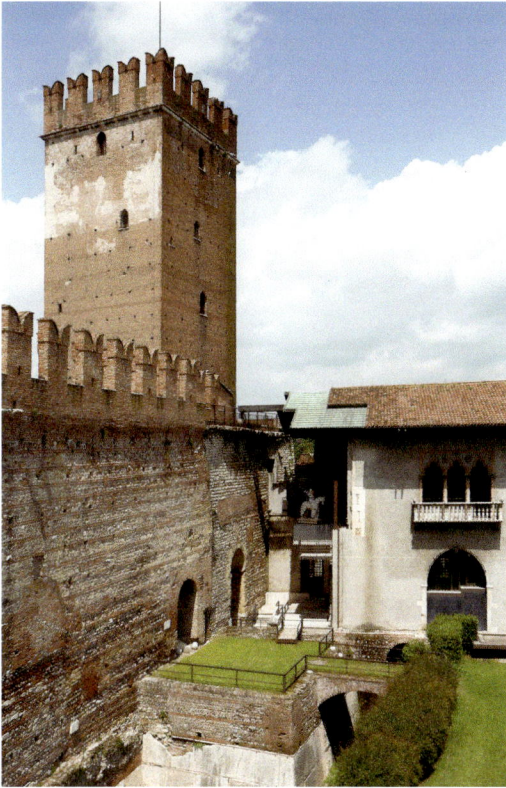

Figure 10.13 Carlo Scarpa: Castelvecchio, Verona

Scarpa, architectural energy expended on working within existing buildings was not considered mainstream. Indeed one struggles to cite a single building or project from any of the "greats" of modern architecture of this type of work. Since Scarpa, and Castelvecchio in particular, it is considered just as valid as new constructions.[44]

Scarpa's Quirina Stampalia in Venice is equally inventive and provocative, if sometimes over-obsessive: every junction detail is articulated to celebrate the nature of the materials as they come together and exploit the conjunction of new and pre-existing fabric (**Figure 10.14**).

Scarpa's work, like Zumthor's, was mostly at a small scale. Another Italian, Giancarlo de Carlo, already mentioned as a contributor to Team Ten, worked on a larger canvas, almost continuously from the early 1950s until his death, on the repair and reinvigoration of the city of Urbino and for its university (**Figure 10.15**). He uncovered previously forgotten portions of the city, including the extraordinary Ducal staircase, a helical ramp designed by Francesco di Giorgio Martini, now used with its adjacent lift as a principal means of access to the old city. His new buildings outside the historic context were clearly of their time, such as Ca' Romanino, a house for the philosopher Livio Sichirollo (who in his role as deputy mayor of the city worked with de Carlo on its development plan[45]), but those within the city are hardly identifiable.

44 This is part of the introduction to an exemplary study of the building: Murphy 2017.
45 See McKean 2019.

Figure 10.14 Carlo Scarpa: Quirini Stampalia, Venice, detail

Figure 10.15 Giancarlo de Carlo: interventions in Urbino, 1951–2005

De Carlo taught at a number of schools of architecture and founded his own research and teaching group, ILAUD (International Laboratory of Architecture and Urban Design). Politically, he was inclined to anarchism, and his work in general shows a complex mixture of respect for tradition, ensuring the closest analysis and understanding of the context of the work to be undertaken (which is fully in accord with the principles of Husserl) together with a passionate and optimistic advocacy of the continual role of architectural invention.

10.6 Understanding history from a phenomenological perspective

When we look at a city such as Urbino, it is possible to identify clearly different ways in which we can understand and describe it. We can gather facts about its history as a matter of information: its foundation as a Roman settlement, the reigns of Federico de Montefeltro and the Borgias and its subsequent development. In many cases, these would be verifiable. Inevitably, an element of interpretation is involved as soon as we try to relay to others the history and its effect on the fabric we see. But architects might visit the city primarily for inspiration and then the experience of this remarkable and memorable city would be fundamental.[46] What architects need is an interpretative capacity: how to understand historical material as useful. After all, misunderstandings of history can be peculiarly creative – even inspirational. Palladio believed that the orders and classical pediments were used on Roman private houses, for which there was no evidence, and by confusing temple fronts with the honorific entrance motifs of grand family dwellings thereby initiated an extraordinarily influential architectural tradition, examples of which can be found all over the world. Does it then matter if the facts are misinterpreted?

We saw how Heidegger was moved by his experience of a Greek temple. In 1962 the American historian Vincent Scully (whom we encountered as an early champion of Louis Kahn) published his first and one of his best-known books, *The Earth, the Temple and the Gods*.[47] He reinterpreted Greek temples, which had formerly mostly been treated as sophisticated aesthetic objects, obeying complex formal and linguistic rules, as artefacts in dynamic dialogue with the landscape: they were oriented towards sacred mountains or towards the valleys between mountains. Classical scholars pointed out that he misinterpreted the evidence in at least three ways.[48] First, Scully apparently forgot the presence of walls around the *temenos*: many of the views that he showed in his book simply could not have been obtained from within the sacred precincts. Second, he had cast back into history a post-Enlightenment picturesque theory to support his observations of how ancient Greeks thought about landscape: there is no textual evidence to support that they did so in the way that Scully's book suggested. Third, and most embarrassingly, some of the detailed manipulations of the site that Scully enthusiastically recorded and illustrated were not original at all – they were the result of interventions in the early twentieth century by American archaeologists. Scully's interpretation tells us more about his own sensibility than

46 Architects and architectural writers who were inspired in the twentieth century by Italian hill towns would include Gunnar Asplund and Alvar Aalto, Edmund Bacon, Vincent Scully, Kevin Lynch, Jan Gehl and many others. Their writings and drawings would in turn inspire students at summer schools, including those at ILAUD. For the reciprocal influence, particularly on Nordic architects, see Alici 2016, 2018.
47 Scully 1962a.
48 John Boardman made the three points that follow in lectures in the 1970s. His published review of Scully's book is a little gentler, though not complimentary: Boardman 1964.

49 In a somewhat similar way, classical scholars have cast doubt on some of Heidegger's etymological derivations of various words that he used to illustrate the points he was making about the loss of 'Being' in the twentieth century. But that is not the point, defenders would argue: his poetics seeks to 'open up' the meanings of words.

50 Norberg-Schultz 1975, pp. 44–50.

51 Nietzsche 1997, p. 59. His principal target was Hegel's view of historical progress.

52 Nietzsche 1997, p. 62.

53 Nietzsche 1997, p. 63 (Nietzsche's italics).

54 Dana Villa has very neatly summarized the implications of this dichotomy at the scale of urban design: "It is the choice between a politics of mourning and a politics of parody, a politics that remembers the *res publica* and a politics engaged in the endless subversion of codes" (Villa 1992). I am grateful to Tom Spector for drawing this remark to my attention.

about how the Greeks themselves might have conceived their temples.[49] General histories, such as Christian Norberg-Schulz's *Meaning in Western Architecture*, confidently built on Scully's interpretation as a means to discovering the meaning of Greek architecture.[50] There is no doubt that Scully's perceptions, inaccurate though they may have been historically, inspired a generation of architects to put foremost the notion of a building's setting in the landscape when they set about designing.

Perhaps, therefore, the creative architect needs to forget history. In his 1874 essay "On the Uses and Disadvantages of History for Life", published as one of his *Untimely Meditations*, Friederich Nietzsche set out to show "why instruction without invigoration, why knowledge not attended by action, why history as a costly superfluity and luxury, must, to use Goethe's words, be seriously hated by us".[51] For humans, "forgetting is essential to action of any kind, just as not only light but darkness too is essential to the life of everything organic".[52] In fact, a balance must be struck: "*the unhistorical and the historical are necessary in equal measure for the health of an individual, of a people and of a culture*".[53] Anticipating the themes of his later writing, Nietzsche goes on to advocate a disregard for the opinions of the masses and praise the artist who can rise above the pedantry of Hegelian historicism. His rather more sympathetic appeal for a balance also draws on the distinction he had already made in *The Birth of Tragedy* between the Apollonian and Dionysian in Greek art.

If a renewed concern for how the environment would be perceived and a rejection of stylistic or formal obsessions (whether postmodern or typologically driven) is common to the very different architects mentioned in this chapter, it is clear that distinctions can be drawn as to how sanguine they are about reconstructing past conditions. For Koolhaas and Tschumi, that is an irrelevant impossibility in the face of changed conditions – we might try to rejoice in new opportunities that are open to us, though it is more likely that we would be subverting any tendency to idealize them; in either case, they certainly cannot be ignored. For others, there is an ethical responsibility to attempt such a recovery, difficult or even impossible though that could be.[54] This may be informed by a nostalgia for an embodied understanding embracing the divine, or from a much more 'realistic' concern for the fabric architects have inherited and belief that individual acts of invention are not incompatible with that concern.

The final chapter summarizes the philosophical standpoints of the various architects and theorists discussed in this book and suggests how hindsight inevitably plays a part in how we now read the period.

11
CONCLUSIONS – TWENTY-FIRST CENTURY HINDSIGHT

In summarizing the lessons this survey of twentieth-century architecture and what its thinking might hold for us today, I will inevitably need to make generalizations of an even more extreme nature that reveal the prejudices of my *Weltanschauung* (in Dilthey's terms) or the limitations of my horizon (as Gadamer might have said).[1] By choosing architects such as Le Corbusier, Aalto and Kahn for more detailed treatment, I already imply that for me their practice provides the clearest representation of philosophical positions during the period. An alternative narrative could be constructed with quite different principal players: Nervi, Candela, Prouvé and Calatrava, for instance, when design is seen as primarily driven by the refinement of technique. I naturally hope readers will find their own examples to subject to interrogation from a theoretical viewpoint.

11.1 Twentieth-century post-Enlightenment thinking

In the Introduction, I referred to the linguistic analogy that John Summerson used in his 1956 RIBA lecture. In Kantian terms, he was finding a way to translate the *sense* that we have of works of architecture into words that describe our *understanding*: that way not only would his audience follow what he was saying, but his speech could be published and disseminated as a contribution to knowledge. One way of describing (or perceiving) the epistemological thinking of those philosophers who were increasingly influential for architects in the second half of the century is that they suggested, in different ways, that this enterprise was fundamentally inadequate. Words could never describe the complex phenomena of the world or the place of architecture within that world. Wittgenstein's *Tractatus* had examined the limits of what could be said, admitting that words could never reveal what was really important. Either you should therefore keep silent (since metaphysics was nonsense) or admit that it was a matter of showing, not saying – "now I see what you mean" – which was the thrust of his later work. Heidegger also claimed that metaphysical enquiry in a traditional sense (and hence the epistemology that went with it) had no justifiable foundation. As we saw, the inadequacy of words to express 'Being' enabled Heidegger to claim that he understood what Kant intended to say, but had suppressed (or, in Freudian terms, 'repressed') as too dangerous to think. Derrida's deconstructive procedures also question the authority

1 Michael Heinrich usefully identifies three levels that condition our aesthetic experiences: biology, culture and biography (Heinrich 2019).

DOI: 10.4324/9781003244943-12

of the author: what is suppressed is often more revealing than what the authors think they are expressing in their texts.

Many of the other thinkers relevant to architecture that have been touched on so far could be called to witness a general scepticism about the success of the 'Enlightenment Project', of which Kant is usually agreed to be the most articulate representative, and I had to be highly selective in those I have chosen to concentrate on. By the mid-1980s it was possible to describe the 'grand theories' promulgated by Gadamer, Derrida, Foucault, Kuhn, Rawles, Habermas, Althusser, Lévi-Strauss and a host of others who have explored the framework of post-Enlightenment thinking in the light, principally, of the profound questions raised by earlier thinkers – Nietzsche, Darwin, Freud and Marx.[2] It would be a mistake, however, to presume that this framework has been demolished – far from it, and for good reason. Kant's extraordinarily detailed construction of a solution to the epistemological (and eventually metaphysical) problems of understanding that he identified remains the most thoroughgoing attempt ever made and continues to be the benchmark against which subsequent attempts are measured. Writings on architectural theory by the end of the century generally tended to reflect a melancholic scepticism: earlier twentieth-century modernism was seen as universally positivistic and teaching in schools of architecture had reinforced that reduced sense of the discipline with consequences from which we all suffer daily.[3] But there was an element of caricature in that analysis. As this book has described, the best architects in the latter part of the century, and a host of others there has been no space to mention, actively resisted a positivism that was evident in the briefs that architects were commonly handed: "please deliver a measurably optimized solution to our problem, on time and within the budget we have already determined". They knew that an act of imagination was required that would redefine the 'problem', even if they sometimes struggled to describe what was involved. Meanwhile, teachers at schools of architecture tried their best to reintroduce to students the sense of play they had possessed as children; unfortunately, in the process they sometimes encouraged them to devalue or ignore issues of technology, because to take them into account might dilute the poetry of their proposals. Clearly, architecture as a discipline needs to embrace the measurable as well as the unmeasurable, and the fundamental issue is to find the appropriate balance.

The truism encapsulated in that last sentence could, however, simply reflect a post-Enlightenment Eurocentric view of the world. Is such a division between objective and subjective culturally determined, or is it a general condition of what it is to be human? Perhaps there are other cultures, historically misunderstood and dismissed, that suggest completely different ways of thinking. In 1980, Attipate Ramanujan (1929–1993) contributed a perceptive essay to a workshop in Chicago, later published as "Is There an Indian Way of Thinking – An Informal Essay".[4] He drew equally on anglophone and Indian traditions, citing Kant, Walter Benjamin and Ludwig Wittgenstein, amongst others, but also referring to Hindu, Buddhist and Jain philosophy and his own

2 See essays in Skinner 1985 for the way that "the destructive work of the sceptics has served to clear the ground on which the grandest theoretical structures have since been raised" (p. 13).

3 Though thoroughgoing Logical Positivists (the most prominent figure being A.J. Ayer) tended to regard existential and phenomenological thinking as unworthy of serious consideration, that remains a minority position. For the Vienna Circle see Edmonds 2020 and for an intelligent (but somewhat unbalanced) survey of alternative positions, see Ábalos 2001: the Arpel's ludicrous house, encountered by M. Hulot in Jacques Tati's film *Playtime* represents modernist positivism and is compared with Heidegger's hut, Picasso's houses, Warhol's 'Factory' and other visions of domesticity.

4 Ramanujan 1999, pp. 35–51.

poems. Pupils and associates of the Indian architect Balkrishna Doshi have written appreciatively of his "poetic seeing, where myth and story, dream and imagination, integrate seeming opposites into a continuous and unbroken flow", praising his "total dedication to the art of making architecture, to its techniques and to its utterly uncompromising demands", and concluding that he "has attempted to bring these two forms of knowledge together in making works of architecture".[5] They rightly criticize the way that European historians tended to see the histories and theories of their own cultures as primary, thereby relegating foreign examples to a secondary position and only valuable insofar as they reflect their own models. Yet the dichotomy they describe Doshi engaging with would seem to be universal, which is why it has preoccupied human thought in every culture for so long.

If that is the case, we still need to address the strongest criticism of Kant and his followers – that they were irredeemably anthropocentric in believing that the world and all its resources are ripe for human exploitation. Here are five brief responses:

- Trivially, as humans, we cannot be anything other than anthropocentric: we have no means of enjoying a 'view from nowhere', even if for rationality to survive we must pretend that there is.

- Pragmatically, we ought to deal with the world as we find it and manipulate it in such a way as not to make unnecessary damage – even from an entirely anthropocentric position – because it makes it less useful to us. It is possible to create snow in Dubai, for instance, to enable a minority to engage in winter sports, but it is rational, ethically, to disapprove of doing so once we understand its environmental cost.

- Normatively, such a position implies a hierarchy of values: it is more important in that example to limit the environmental damage than it is to give pleasure to people who would enjoy such an experience.

- Metaphysically, a hierarchy of values can suggest a super-human imperative – a deity, for instance. To argue for a scale of values in entirely secular terms is as least as difficult as to argue for the existence of a deity, though many have done so, and it was Enlightenment thinking that clarified the means.

- Finally, in the face of machines that are increasingly capable of making more accurate decisions than humans (in driverless vehicles or diagnosing diseases), we may be approaching the time, anticipated in numerous science fiction novels, when we surrender control of our destiny. Maintaining the supremacy of human judgment, however fallible, that attempts to reconcile objective knowledge and subjective feelings needs to become an over-riding concern.

How does the effect of Enlightenment thinking appear in an everyday sense when we judge a work of architecture? We necessarily employ a degree of rationality whenever we try to balance different values. The Villa Savoye by Le Corbusier (**Figure 11.1** and the final diagram in

5 Chhaya 2014. Doshi himself was trained in Europe, worked for Le Corbusier realising his buildings in Ahmedabad, and also worked closely with Louis Kahn. As the founder of the Centre for Environment Planning and Technology in Ahmedabad, he had a formative influence on a generation of Indian architects.

Figure 11.1 Le Corbusier Villa Savoye, 1929–31

Figure 4.15) is usually acknowledged to be a canonical masterpiece of twentieth-century modernism. We might make the following observations, amongst many others:

- As a holiday house for privileged Parisians, the building was a suitable model for aesthetic experimentation but could hardly serve as a universal prototype, whatever the claims of its architect.

- Socially it is conventional – the chauffeur and servant (except when cleaning or cooking) occupy spaces on the ground floor next to the garage, while the clients live in the *piano nobile* and roof terrace – but formally it initiates a new and surprising typology.

- The building occupies its site as a self-contained object, rather than being embedded in it or adapting itself in other ways, displaying the associated advantages as well as disadvantages.

- Its expression as a 'machine' was compromised by the limited technology available at the time and by Le Corbusier's formal preoccupations. It has proved difficult to waterproof and does not weather well.

- Environmentally, the building was adequately tuned to the climate of Northern Europe and would be inappropriate in other locations such as Argentina. It gives excellent cross-ventilation, for instance, and is orientated to allow solar penetration to private roof terraces, even if, in the light of twenty-first century criteria, standards of insulation and air-tightness should be massively improved.

- Stylistically, the villa is a sophisticated exercise in a newly-forged vocabulary of modernism, deployed with unequalled skill and authority, and displaying subtleties that are amenable to detailed analysis of many kinds.

- To an unprejudiced visitor, prepared to absorb and enjoy the building, it offers an emotionally moving experience, cinematic in its assured handling of sequence and photogenic in its sculptural forms. In an extraordinary way, it combines the dynamic of movement with the aesthetic of stasis.

- As a construction that aspires to maximum clarity as well as possessing obsessive hygienic characteristics, in contrast to some other dwellings by Le Corbusier, it cannot provide for secret spaces, cozy ingle nooks or cool dark cellars – it is a 'nest' rather than a 'cave'.

- The formal language and the secular nature of its iconography take no account of conventional historical forms or memories and seemingly do not allow for the imprinting of individual taste. On the other hand, its spatial richness and extravagance make it ambiguous enough to enable multiple aesthetic interpretations by its occupants and those who visit it.

- However much we might admire it as a work of architecture, we should not accept it as a great work in view of its author's views on city planning (insofar as it represents or reflects them), which he promulgated widely and which had disastrous results, directly or indirectly.

A reasoned judgment of the building as a whole would need to take all such factors and others into account. Whether the building emerges as a masterpiece that can be discussed in the same breath as a villa by Palladio must be up for a debate that would entail giving due weight to many different criteria. Does the fact that some may be moved to tears by experiencing this building as visitors outweigh its manifold deficiencies? We subject the masterpieces of other ages to a similar analysis and face similar problems of judgment. Consider, for instance, bored schoolchildren being instructed as to how they can appreciate a Gothic cathedral in the unfamiliar gloom of its interior: a few may be captivated by the experience and then they might seek to understand more about how it was built, what its forms symbolized to those who designed it and used it, and even the multiple re-readings that have followed over time. As Hume explained, the 'passions' come first, and then we can move on to analyze and understand the full depth of our experience. How else would we proceed to discuss Chartres or the Villa Savoye, except by such a process?

11.2 Critical perspectives from the twenty-first century: racial inclusivity

If we accept the fundamental dichotomy between subjective sense and objective understanding, with hindsight we cannot fail to be critical of several underlying assumptions that also seem to have been inherited from the eighteenth century, even if subject to debate.[6] One such assumption, noted in passing at various points and mentioned just earlier, was that modernists felt entitled to export their ideas to other countries as universal prescriptions. But it was not only abroad that this attitude prevailed. During the twentieth century, in Western countries, architects had become professionals, usually protected by title if not universally by activity. Did this make them exclusively 'entitled', however, to decide on how buildings should be fashioned – or how people should dwell in them – a question that is particularly relevant in housing? We saw how Gropius still felt in 1956 that people needed to be educated so that they understood the benefits of living in parallel high-rise blocks of flats rather than in the inadequately lit buildings that turned corners (p. 84). Asking people how they themselves preferred to live did not immediately come to mind: such questions could be left to retrospective surveys by sociologists. Though the popular "type 1" Frankfurt kitchen, designed in the 1920s by Margarete Schütte-Lihotzky working for Ernst May, may have been efficient, it did not allow for more than one person to work in it (the 'housewife') and certainly not for families to eat together where the cooking was done. As with Aalto's criticism of the Bauhaus light fitting, what was efficient for mass-production might not be effective in use. As the century progressed, and as cooking technology improved, less rigid solutions would be required to allow for different lifestyles: perhaps people could do this for themselves rather than relying on professionals. The Swiss-born architect Walter Segal (1907–1985), who had studied housing carefully and knew Bauhaus architects well, concluded that it would be more sensible to offer people the chance to make their own dwellings, if they could be provided with a modular kit of parts that was made of readily available cheap materials.[7] His experiments in self-built structures started with a temporary garden pavilion but developed into single-family houses and, with his partner Jon Broome, groups of houses.

In the economics of the developed world, the site is the most expensive component, so that minimizing building cost and material waste, though laudable, would fail to make a substantial contribution to housing provision on any scale. In developing nations, on the other hand, on the fringes of ever-enlarging cities, informal settlements provide an increasing proportion of homes: barriadas of South and Central America and similar in Africa and India provide examples of self-built dwellings that are often subtler and more attuned to the culture, and even the climate, than government-sponsored housing, which is frequently rigidly laid out and designed by engineering firms with minimal architectural input. When architects and students visit and record informal housing, they may find they have more to learn than to contribute.

The assumption that white Europeans and Americans were innately superior was less openly acknowledged in the twentieth century than it had been in the nineteenth, but it continued to be manifested in practice and in some historical accounts, which suggest that the story of European and American practice and theoretical debate can stand for a global discourse; this will surely be impossible in discussing any later period. As in many other spheres, the influence that European cultural

6 Kant and Hume, in common with nearly all in their time, were responsible for statements on racial superiority that we now find repugnant. As ever, the situation is complex. For an argument that Kant modified his views during the 1790s, see Kleingeld 2007 (downloaded 21.12.2021).
7 McKean 1989.

traditions have maintained throughout the world is unlikely to survive, and many predict China will be the dominant force as the twenty-first century unfolds. During the period discussed, monumental buildings in South Africa, South America, India and parts of China were the witness of imperial ambitions – French, Portuguese, Spanish, Dutch. The British left their mark throughout the most expansive but also the briefest empire in history, ending with Edwin Lutyens' capital at New Delhi, completed in 1929 only 18 years before Indian independence.[8] Early twentieth-century Americans were trained in Paris; a later generation imported émigré European figures and pilgrimaged to Rome. When African or Indian states required institutional or commercial buildings, they tended to commission those who had been trained in the Western tradition – the pupils of Gropius or former assistants of Le Corbusier (such as Doshi) replaced those who had been trained in the Beaux-Arts academies or articled in a classical tradition (such as Lutyens). Only when nations routinely train their own students by means of teachers who have been able to evolve their own approaches will that legacy be shaken off. It should be clear that the purpose of this book has not been to promote the values of twentieth-century European and American architecture, under the influence of its inherited philosophical foundations, but to explain it and describe some sense of its influence. Former imperial nations now export education, maintaining a powerful influence on developing nations, so that even indigenous architecture has continued to be interpreted in Eurocentric or American terms. Nor have I tried to cover non-Western architecture, which would necessarily be superficial. The story is certainly not one of unmitigated triumphant success, but on the other hand, I have tried not to demonize architects who were working in challenging times and attempting to grapple with rapidly changing conditions.

11.3 Critical perspectives from the twenty-first century: gender inclusivity

Equally blinkered, and only beginning to be sufficiently acknowledged in the later twentieth century, were assumptions as to gender roles: why were Margarete Schütte-Lihotzky or Lily Reich (responsible for the furniture and exhibition pavilions credited to Mies van der Rohe, just as Charlotte Perriand was largely responsible for the furniture designs credited to Le Corbusier) or Aino Aalto, Anne Tyng, Jane Drew or Denise Scott Brown always secondary figures?[9] Le Corbusier himself seemed to have been so threatened by the talented Eileen Gray that he painted a mural on the wall of her house for Jean Badovici, an action she unsurprisingly found thoroughly distasteful.[10] The attitude to women in architecture unsurprisingly reflected a wider prevalence of sexism in societies as a whole: homosexuality had been accepted in Ancient Greece, but accompanied by a subservient role for women. It took until the early years of the twentieth century for women to be given the right to vote in Western democracies and until 1967 for homosexuality to cease to be a criminal offence in England (1982 in Northern Ireland). Not until the twenty-first century was it acknowledged that gender could be fluid: people are now

8 British architectural influence was briefly reasserted in the New Towns, and the best of the post-war housing and buildings for schools and universities.
9 See Kingsley 1988. More than 20 years ago, Adrian Forty suggested that the abstract characteristics of modernist critical vocabulary (form, space and order) suppressed 'otherness' and are endemically gendered: Forty 2000, pp. 60–61. From the end of the century, there was a growing literature aiming to discover the names of those who should more properly have been credited. See, for instance, Rendell, Penner and Borden 1999.
10 See Wilson 1995, pp. 120–121.

asked how they identify, in a way that would have been regarded as bizarre a century ago. How a non-binary attitude to gender will affect future architectural practice is yet to be seen. This book has recorded the work of the most prominent and discussed figures who were granted the opportunities to build and accorded the broadest publicity: the fact is they were mostly anglophone, white-skinned and male. It certainly has not sought to endorse such a situation, which will surely not persist.

11.4 Critical perspectives from the twenty-first century: sustainability

A third way in which the twentieth century looks deeply problematic from a twenty-first century perspective is its attitude to technology and particularly to energy. What modernists celebrated was structural and material innovation, while the energy required to manufacture components or to maintain comfort was taken for granted. So the Chicago frame, improvements in reinforced concrete design or the prefabrication of components in factories were the principal technical factors that would determine new forms. Reyner Banham's *Theory and Design in the First Machine Age* had recorded that enthusiasm, though he believed modernist architects were still inhibited with formalist aesthetic notions they had inherited from the past, rather than embracing the full implications as Buckminster Fuller had.[11] But three years later, in *The Architecture of the Well-Tempered Environment*, he shifted his attention to the behaviour of buildings environmentally even though, with Giedion, he thought the future would be technology-driven.[12] Reviewing James Stirling's History Faculty building in Cambridge, he predicted that the university wouldn't be brave enough to pull it down and replace it in a quarter of a century or so when it had outgrown its useful life. Indeed not, because by then attitudes had changed: despite its problematic environmental performance, it was judged more sensible to try and repair and improve the building. From the 1950s, Victor Olgyay had been publishing articles advocating an architecture that took climatic conditions seriously as a starting point, but his voice and those of others with a similar message remained minority concerns with architects, even after the 1970s oil crisis drew architects' attention to their dependence on fossil fuels.[13] Legislation has been slow to react to the realization that high levels of insulation should be insisted on, so as to reduce energy consumption, and only with the belated acknowledgement in the twenty-first century that what most scientists had been saying for some years – that the climate and ecology of the world was undergoing a potentially catastrophic alteration as a direct result of human energy use, and was a measurable phenomenon – has there been a noticeable shift in public opinion.[14]

Needless to say, there is extensive literature available that seeks to remedy what now seem three almost inexplicable deficiencies in twentieth-century practice and thinking about architecture. This book has not dealt with them at length, since its primary purpose has been to explore how architects at the time practised and reflected on their discipline,

11 See Banham 1980. The first edition was in 1966.
12 See Banham 1984. The first edition was in 1969.
13 See Olgyay 2015, the most widely read of his books, even if the lessons were largely ignored. The original edition was in 1963, with contributions from his brother, Aladar.
14 For calculations of the relative carbon footprint, embodied and in use, of buildings throughout history, see Calder 2021.

and what philosophical thinking might have brought to the subject. In the next section I summarize its contents, in relation to the forms that emerged, the ideas that underpin them and how they appeared in architectural education. There follows a brief description of three twenty-first century responses to the changed nature of what architecture might aspire to, and I conclude by mentioning a possible position but not elaborating on it.

11.5 Implications in the search for a language of form

This book has recorded how during the seventeenth and eighteenth centuries, Europeans and Americans became more willing and able to abstract and calculate natural phenomena, from the circulation of blood to the expected behaviour of man-made materials, like cast iron and steel. Scientific discovery, however, was accompanied by an increased interest in romance, in poetry and all the other arts, exacerbating a split between subjective experience and the apparently objective world. Philosophically, we observed, this distinction (which I have argued earlier is inevitable) was most clearly articulated by Descartes and modified by Kant's ingenious construction, which was to have such an abiding influence on his successors. Nineteenth-century architecture illustrated the result: mechanization to deal with the new needs of growing populations and various forms of romantic expression to symbolize feelings, sometimes colliding in memorable architectural ensembles, such as Barlow's St Pancras station and Scott's Midland hotel in London (pp. 41–42, **Figure 2.13**). At the beginning of the twentieth century, Art Nouveau attempted to resolve the dilemma by inventing a new style: engineering techniques softened by 'nature', which would be symbolized by sinuous curved forms and the representations of foliage. But the forces of rationalism could not be resisted so easily, either in city planning, when it became clear that the motor vehicle was going to transform western cities, or in architectural design. After a brief flirtation with romantic expression, a significant number of architects absorbed the effects of mechanization into a manner that we recognize as 'modern': abstract and purportedly rational solutions to the problem set by the brief. I used the influential German Bauhaus to illustrate this phenomenon. Le Corbusier was one of the very few who saw a requirement to formulate an aesthetic discipline or set of principles to bring some kind of order to the many possible forms which resulted, but he failed to create universally accepted conventions.

We traced reactions to what would become an orthodoxy: those of Häring, who believed forms would arise naturally if only they were allowed to, and Aalto, who thought it was possible to absorb the benefits of technology and exercise a personal formal freedom by embracing a version of scepticism in opposition to what he saw as a simplistic one-sided positivism. Then there were architects who believed that ideals of the past could be reaffirmed or recaptured in contemporary work – Louis Kahn being the architect whose work was used to illustrate the consequences. Few have succeeded in matching the achievements of his

best work, partly because it clearly ran counter to prevailing technological and economic forces. His pupil Venturi's postmodern position
turned out to be more influential and affordable: architects could indeed
refer to the architectural ideals of the past, but, given the circumstances
of the second half of the twentieth century, usually through a melancholic lens, so that quotations would be either playful or ironic – often
both. Team Ten architects, while accepting contemporary conditions,
clearly saw deficiencies in orthodox modernist procedures, particularly
at an urban scale, but were more successful at the immediate and local
scale of human activity than at creating buildings, or city plans, with
the representational authority of the past. An intellectually attractive
appeal to the apparently deep traditions of city patterns and architecture, namely its typological authority, ran into the twin dangers of an
alienating abstraction (in the case of Rossi and his pupils) or a nostalgic
revivalism that was unlikely to provide solutions except in very privileged circumstances. In the final decades of the twentieth century, the
stability of form in itself was questioned in favour of the celebration of
event and experience, but in the face of human needs that require buildings form was hardly a problem that could be avoided.

The reactions that have been outlined were a response to a movement
that in hindsight does indeed appear to have been naïvely optimistic,
but it may be too early to decide how far any of those 'postmodern'
responses (if they can all be bracketed under that term) have themselves established a coherent alternative. In many instances, they
can be seen as dependent on the very idealism to which they purported to offer a critique, in that without the model they sought to
demolish, their theoretical position appears feeble. Meanwhile, in
the twenty-first century, the conditions that led to modernism have
not disappeared but intensified. The global population grew and has
continued to grow; the proportion of people living in conurbations
enlarged; an insatiable demand for travel did not diminish; new
techniques were developed for construction; and the production of
architectural information became almost completely dependent on
computer draughting and more capable of being undertaken using
parametric methods. It seems that the resistance by many architects
to an enthusiastic acceptance of changed conditions as the basis for
new ways of fashioning our buildings and cities, which this book has
followed, remains as strong as ever. But in the face of forces that were
latent in the twentieth century but not taken seriously enough – global
pandemics, severe climatic and environmental change – a pessimistic
outlook has become more prevalent.

Architecture will inevitably reflect the attitudes that societies take to the
issues they face, but so long as individuals are involved, charged with
imagining designs, they will not only continue to wrestle with circumstances presented to them but will also need to find ways of accommodating personal beliefs, aspirations or ideals. One of the reasons that
some philosophers have become intrigued by architecture and architects have dabbled in philosophy is that the practice of architectural

design necessarily involves and illustrates the subjective/objective dilemma rather clearly. Architects are asked to perform against measurable criteria: it is expected that their buildings are structurally stable, comfortable to inhabit, suitable for their immediate purpose and built within an established budget and timetable. Yet they are also asked, and ask of themselves, that their buildings and the places they make will lift the spirits or, in a less optimistic mode, represent to the societies they serve something of the human condition, transcending mechanistic solutions to measurable criteria. We saw how Le Corbusier, often cited as an architect fixated by technology (because of his statements such as "The house is a machine for living in"), believed that architecture was an art distinguished from buildings or other engineering artefacts by the fact that it moves us emotionally (p. 84). Louis Kahn was prone to say to students: "the only things that are important are the un-measurable ones".[15] In one sense that is true, and Kahn's more sympathetic clients, such as Jonas Salk, while still seeking an efficient laboratory for his research, would have agreed with him. Yet, like all architects, Kahn and his loyal assistants spent much of their time trying to reconcile ideals they hoped to realize with everyday actualities (in his terms, adjusting the 'form' by 'design'). Had he not been able to do this, his proposals would never have been realized and, valuable though they may have been as ideas, would not have become 'architecture' in the full sense of the word, as I argued in the Introduction (pp. 4–5).

11.6 Some architects and writers on architecture who accept its contingent nature

We saw how Venturi can be understood as an idealist, but essentially melancholic, in believing that in the circumstances of the twentieth-century architectural ideals could not be realized and only an ironic stance made sense. A consequence of the apparent failure of idealist prescriptions, visible in the history of European and American modernism and its aftermath, has led authors at the end of the twentieth and beginning of the twenty-first century to propose an attitude that is more cautious and acknowledges the contingencies of practice. I shall refer to three, as representing that point of view from varying perspectives.

The Dutch architect Reinier de Graaf, who is a Director of OMA and AMO and works with Rem Koolhaas, has summarized the problem for architects as he sees it as follows:

> As a profession architecture presents a paradox. In economic terms, it is mainly a reactive discipline, a response to pre-formulated needs; in intellectual terms, it is the opposite: a visionary domain that claims the future, aspiring to set the agenda and precede needs. Architecture is a form of omniscience practised in a context of utter dependency.[16]

What architects are particularly dependent on is the economic system prevailing at any given time. De Graaf pointed out that modernist

15 As someone old enough to have met several of the protagonists featured in this book, I recall witnessing Kahn make precisely this claim.
16 De Graaf 2017, p. 3 ff.

idealism exactly paralleled the moment in economics when differentials were reducing:

> If Piketty is right . . . the twentieth century will have been no more than an anomaly, a brief interruption in the systemic logic of capitalism, in which the inherent accretion of capital through capital remains an unbreakable cycle. . . . [The] many blessings of a life in the later twentieth century, particularly in Western Europe, were not the natural outcome of a progressive evolutionary process but the result of a short-lived and unsustainable suspension of the real fate dictated by its contemporary economic system. . . . Nearly twenty years into the new millennium, it is as though the previous century never happened. The same architecture that once embodied social mobility now helps prevent it. Despite ever-higher rates of poverty and homelessness, large social housing estates are being demolished with ever-greater resolve.[17]

As de Graaf himself acknowledges, there is a degree of nostalgia in his lament.[18] Those who tried to practise in the period that he eulogizes remember the difficulties of dealing with the bureaucracies that were then in charge of the housing grants and subsidies. Architects are mostly concerned to make the world a better place, as well as to fulfil their own artistic ambitions, and are continually frustrated by the societies they serve. When they designed public housing, they sought to give the tenants some of the benefits that owner-occupiers enjoyed, such as the opportunity to personalize their homes. When building for profit-driven developers, they connived with planning officers to try and increase the public benefit of the private investment by providing more generous open spaces and children's play areas and building with better materials and to higher environmental standards than the developer required. So it has always been, and in every age architects have lamented the conditions within which they have had to work. Especially when being honest to students about the profession they wish to join, as de Graaf seeks to be, it is essential not to be naïve about the world, but it also seems desirable to preserve some element of idealism.

A less immediate precedent for admirable practice is celebrated by the architectural historian Andrew Saint. In *The Image of the Architect*, he contrasts the bombast of those architects who saw themselves as great artists, destined to construct their personal visions though frequently frustrated by unfavourable conditions, with the modesty of the salaried architects working for local authorities, particularly the London County Council, in the years before the First World War.[19] Admirers of the honest, builderly character of Philip Webb's work, they did not regard themselves as artists so much as craftsmen whose duty it was to serve society, respect the materials they handled and make only an essential impact on the rural or urban context. Saint predicts that in changed contemporary conditions, architects will need to harness technology, while acknowledging that they are prey to economic forces which they cannot significantly influence. He hopes for:

17 De Graaf 2017, pp. 415–425. He refers to the French economist Thomas Piketty (Piketty 2014).

18 In an interview with Mark Minkjan, de Graaf remarked: "I never realised how nostalgic I am, until I started writing. An architect is not supposed to be nostalgic but forward-looking. But I'm nostalgic for a time when mankind was a lot more forward-looking than it is today; for a gradual optimism about the future. That's the paradox" (https://failedarchitecture.com/reinier-de-graaf-architecture-is-in-a-state-of-denial/).

19 Saint 1983. Charles Canning Winmill is cited as "the most impressive designer in the radical London County Council's Architects' Department of the period 1893–1914. Because of his official position as a salaried architect, his talents were virtually unknown to a wider world" (p. 69). Saint's first chapter, "The Architect as Hero and Genius", as an extreme contrast, discusses the heroic image of an architect presented in Ayn Rand's *The Fountainhead*, made into a Warner Bros. film starring Gregory Peck in 1949.

a smaller architectural profession, in which imagination and artistic ability are more evenly balanced with technical and managerial experience, in which collaboration with other specialists takes on a realistic less high-handed meaning, and in which 'sound building' is valued over 'high art'.[20]

In his book *Architecture Depends*, Jeremy Till argues similarly: architecture has always been shaped by its contingent conditions, but architects deny this by appealing to ideals of perfection.[21] Dependency should not be a threat, however, but an opportunity to reformulate practice, to resist its marginalization and offer hope. He ends by quoting Carol Gilligan – that an ethics of responsibility emerges from "the experience of connectedness, compassion and sensitivity to context" – and Roberto Mangabeira Unger, who advocates "establishing small-scale fragmentary versions of the future": practical and imaginative, critical and visionary. De Graaf would disagree with the caution advocated by both Saint and Till, however, because he believes that architects should fight to re-establish the ideals that have been lost even though the sphere of action is in the end political rather than architectural: they should certainly not retreat because of a timid fear of failure as lead members of design teams that engage with the largest and most complex projects.

11.7 Further implications for architectural education

Students of architecture in universities, where most are now taught, are urged to liberate their creative imaginations as designers but also to be scholarly and properly academic in their essays. When it comes to studio reviews, their projects are criticized using objective criteria ('you cannot fit a car in the garage you have designed') and in subjective terms ('I find your interpretation of what a social forum means to be quite inadequate').[22] As I mentioned in Chapter 1 (pp. 24–25), anyone who has taught architecture at a university will have observed that the discipline sits uneasily between the sciences and arts – representative of that split between an apparently objective world of facts and the subjective world of experience. A subject like architecture with professional allegiances has suspiciously practical applications. If the professions are essentially nineteenth-century inventions, in the twentieth century there was an escalation of professionalization, but then, from the mid-1960s through to the early 1980s, a crisis in confidence arose in all professions. Part of the problem was that professionals could not explain what their special skills were, maybe because they had been trained in an inappropriate philosophy, which argued that professional activity consists in instrumental problem-solving made rigorous by the application of scientific theory and technique.[23] University education in the sciences had favoured a model that suggests real knowledge lay in the theories and techniques of basic and applied science and hence these disciplines should come first. More practical skills, employing those theories and techniques that had been studied should come later on: analysis first, then synthesis, as if it would logically follow. Teaching and research departments had to accept this positivistic epistemology and agree to

20 Saint 1983, p. 166.
21 Till 2013.
22 For some, the best approach to the problem would draw on the post-Heideggerian tradition, though my own view is somewhat different as will have become clear. My late colleague Dalibor Vesely used to complain that some teachers were eager and well-qualified to talk about *lighting* – whether the luminance was sufficient to enable safe working – but avoided discussing *light*, in all its complex phenomenology. The transcendental meanings of light throughout history were what were truly important for architects to understand. By concentrating on its quantitatively measurable aspect, teachers subscribed to a suspect Cartesian dualism, which swiftly opened up the way to the dangers of a thoroughly reductive positivism. See Vesely 2006 for an extended lament that traces the problem in some detail.
23 The philosopher Donald Schön made these points in his Reith lectures, subsequently printed as *The Reflective Practitioner* (Schön 1983), where he used architectural practice and education as a paradigm for responsible professional behaviour.

24 Whitehead 1929. For a description of a teaching methodology derived from his analysis, see Ray 2008.

25 There are multiple ways of describing this tripartite learning process more generally: "experience engendering the thirst for knowledge, resulting in wisdom" would be one such. It's a conventionally Hegelian, or at least post-Enlightenment framework, and could be attacked from a Nietzschean perspective, whereby "knowledge" is essentially a power-relation and dependent on context. See, for example, Foucault 2000. Nietzsche 1997 suggests a more balanced view.

26 For an argument in favour of the transcendent sense of wonder as a necessary starting point, see Holst 2018.

27 See Popper 2002a. As a thoroughgoing sceptic, Popper did not believe anything could be proved: something was true only insofar as it had not yet been falsified. Falsifiability is the criterion for science, so that the theories of Sigmund Freud, for instance, however scientific he claimed them to be, were metaphysical, as indeed was Darwinism, although it was very useful and effective as a hypothesis. Popper's ideas were refined by a number of other figures, including Thomas Kuhn, who emphasizes the 'paradigm' within which science works until it comes under intolerable stress (Kuhn 2012). Some have argued for an analogy between scientific paradigms and architectural conventions or styles – see Brawne 1992.

28 This useful phrase can act as a summary of Gombrich's anti-Platonic theory of representation (Gombrich 1997, p. 99). On pp. 271–273 he returns to and emphasizes the parallel with Karl Popper's view of science.

the transmission to their students of generalized and systematic knowledge as the basis of professional performance.

But in design education this is a most misleading model, as it perhaps is in learning more generally. In 1929, A.N. Whitehead proposed three stages to any learning experience, which he termed the stage of Romance, the stage of Precision and the stage of Appreciation.[24] Students are naturally attracted to the study of architecture by its inherent excitement and interest. To bypass the stage of Romance, by concentrating exclusively on the digestion of information, would be to risk indulging in what Karl Popper described as the "bucket theory of the mind". It would be foolish to be engaged in romantic speculation to the exclusion of the measurable, but only when the imagination is engaged can the facts and figures that are so necessary for responsible design be absorbed. The stage of Appreciation allows for the evaluation of creative ideas against established normative criteria. True knowledge (or wisdom) therefore encompasses first the experience of actualities, and then the ability to command objective data and professional techniques, so that there can be a proper engagement in debate.[25]

This may seem nothing more than common sense, and indeed it reflects the everyday experience of most within the design professions, yet it challenges the normal frameworks of much teaching at university level. As every architect knows (although sometimes it is politic to deny it), design cannot proceed according to a process of analysis preceding synthesis, which is superficially such an attractive principle. In fact it often starts in a sense of 'wonder'.[26] Karl Popper held that the scientific notion associated with Francis Bacon (1561–1626) was erroneous: it is impossible simply to gather together particular observations and thereby produce a theory, as Bacon had suggested. Scientific discoveries proceed by an imaginative leap or conjecture, which can then be subjected to analysis. If evidence is found to falsify the hypothesis (and much of scientific research consists of such a search) then an alternative hypothesis is required.[27] As Ernst Gombrich (Popper's friend and Viennese fellow-émigré) argued, this is also how painters behave: they must first invent, then match their invention with the 'reality' they seek to portray: "Making still comes before matching".[28] Gombrich emphasized that the original mark the painter makes is nevertheless conditioned very strongly by their knowledge of those artistic conventions they inherit. And so it surely is for architects.

Intrinsic to Cartesian dualism and Kantian idealism was a faith in the divine, although both accepted the ground for that faith was not something that could ever be proved by logical procedures. That led to a question for the following generations: how could the implications of Darwin's theory of natural selection, which in its most extreme interpretation sees the human race as merely the result of a process of development from primeval organic matter, be absorbed?[29] In the nineteenth century, we saw that Nietzsche provided one response: God was dead, or at least had absented Himself, and the task for individual humans was to transcend their mortal limitations by an effort of will in the time allotted to them. The alternative was to reaffirm a faith of some kind, evident in nineteenth-century Europe and America in the significant amount of church building for established denominations. Many of those who had analyzed the anxieties of the twentieth century and celebrated its aesthetic freedoms, such as the poets T.S. Eliot and W.H. Auden and the composer Igor Stravinsky, had reaffirmed a traditional faith by the time they died.[30] The early twentieth century saw the growth of beliefs such as Theosophy, which incorporated wider sets of ideas from Buddhism and Hinduism.[31] In the twentieth century, a further anxiety appeared: it became increasingly clear that the belief that humans were uniquely endowed with a soul had entitled them to treat the world – its ecology and other mammals – as a resource to be exploited.[32]

Architects can hardly be expected to provide answers to such questions, but their thinking and their work might well reflect different responses to these existential issues, some of them articulated by twentieth-century philosophers. Architecture might even anticipate emerging philosophical and political issues. Emil Kaufmann made this claim:

> Here I wish to point out a particularity of the architectural process which might be called the precocity of the architectural phenomenon. This means that the architectural transformation goes ahead of the corresponding and related changes in general thought and in social structure. In the late eighteenth century there was a revolution in architectural thinking long before the revolution proper broke out. Similarly in the seventeenth century the endeavors of Italian and French architects to set up a new architectural system came before Louis XIV established the new order in the state, and before the great metaphysical systems of the Baroque, Spinoza's theory of the all-embracing whole and Leibniz' doctrine of the pre-established harmony, originated. The Renaissance in the arts was prior to the movement of the Reformation; and the architectural upheaval about 1900 preceded the political crises of the twentieth century.[33]

Here, Kaufmann suggests that architecture can anticipate and articulate philosophical problems. We need not go that far, however, to acknowledge the intersections of architecture and philosophical thinking. Along with everyone else, consciously or subconsciously, architects necessarily find a philosophical position that acknowledges their dilemmas; the artefacts they leave behind them illustrate how they did so. What makes an architect's theoretical position philosophical is that, just as metaphysical arguments are never resolved (or if they are, they cease to be philosophical), so there can be no right answer or aesthetic position that it's reasonable to claim should be universally held. But it is reasonable to point to the risks of positions that tend to result in unsatisfactory environments and much of architectural polemic is directed towards that end: the dangers of a simplistic positivism or of an excessive dependence on the poetic perceptions of a single individual.

29 A contemporary philosopher who has ventured to approach this subject head-on is Thomas Nagel (1937–). See Nagel 2012, quoted in Chapter 1 (p. 24). Philosophical critics included, at an interdisciplinary workshop entitled "Moving Naturalism Forward" in 2013, Douglas Dennett, author of *Consciousness Explained*, who argued that it was now clear that everything about human beings, including consciousness, was the result of evolutionary adaptation.
30 Others, such as James Joyce, the author of *Ulysses*, perhaps the foremost twentieth-century literary masterpiece, did not. His autobiographical *Portrait of the Artist* records his lapse from the Catholic faith.
31 The abstract painters Piet Mondrian and Wassily Kandinsky, who taught at the Bauhaus, were both Theosophists. Theosophy influenced the educational theory of Montessori, while the Steiner schools reflect the ideas of Rudolf Steiner, whose more secular Anthroposophy has its origins in theosophical ideas.
32 For a readable and provocative book summarizing these concerns, see Harari 2016. The 1974 essay by Thomas Nagel, "What is it Like to be a Bat?", reopened the Pandora's box in which the problems of animal consciousness had been largely dormant (reprinted in Nagel 1979).
33 Kaufmann 1968, pp. 126–127.

In the debates described in this book, those with a coherent idealist position have tended to win the day. Muthesius' rational approach was more persuasive than that of the Art Nouveau architect Henry van der Velde. Otto Wagner's efficient plans for the expansion of Vienna were preferred to the appeal by Camillo Sitte for a more romantic approach, inspired by the picturesque urban compositions he had studied. Le Corbusier's polemic anticipated, if it did not entirely frame, what was to become the mainstream modernist approach, and Häring was effectively marginalized. Louis Kahn was an influential teacher – his views may have been poetic, but he did describe in somewhat gnomic terms what he believed architecture should consist of – whereas the sceptical Alvar Aalto doubted whether he could explain what architecture comprised. Aldo Rossi gathered many admirers in comparison with his Italian compatriot Giancarlo de Carlo, whose sensitive contextual architecture is less widely known.

Yet, because of the circumstances within which they are compelled to work, the vast majority of architects probably never achieve the ideals to which they aspired when they trained. They might end up as employees in those practices which had been fortunate enough to attract commissions, either because they had proved to be successful in meeting commercial briefs or because the principals in the practice happened to have sufficient personal connections. Or they might start their own small practice and find it difficult to attract commissions which would allow them to fulfil the ideals to which they aspired with the skills they knew themselves to possess.[34] Of course, this is the case in many other occupations. In his last novel, Wallace Stegner put it like this:

> Talent lies around in us like kindling waiting for a match, but some people, just as gifted as others, are less lucky. Fate never drops a match on them. The times are wrong, or their health is poor, or their energy low, or their obligations too many. Something.[35]

We could add that prejudices of various kinds, described earlier, may also have contributed to the fact that many highly talented architects in the twentieth century never had the opportunities they deserved. They nevertheless felt compelled to pursue a profession which offered the possibility of immense personal fulfilment. Perhaps that compulsion had psychological reasons. Sigmund Freud, whose views on the sublimating nature of art we have already mentioned (p. 61), recognized that for those practising a profession which had an aesthetic end there could be an effective "displacement of libido . . . an artist's joy in creating, in giving their phantasies body, or a scientist's in solving problems or discovering truths", which seem to us in some way "finer and higher". Nevertheless, he suggested:

> . . . it is not applicable generally: it is accessible to only a few people. It presupposes the possession of special dispositions and gifts that are far from being common to any practical degree. And even to the few that possess them, the method cannot give complete protection from suffering.[36]

34 Small architectural practices usually have to show they are 'resilient' enough, in terms of their turnover, to tackle large commissions, but it is difficult for them to do this unless they are already involved in substantial projects. The opportunities offered by open competition in most nations are very few.

35 Stegner 2013. Stegner was describing the frustrated careers of American authors and academics.

36 Freud 1989, p. 30.

11.8 A Humean position

The purpose of this book has not been to advance any particular position, which would take another volume of at least comparable size. But a couple of paragraphs may be appropriate. It is reasonable to be suspicious of those who are prepared to surrender rationality in favour of understandings that are fundamentally poetic yet be more attracted by Humean scepticism than by a thoroughgoing Kantian idealism. Hume preceded Kant chronologically so, unlike other philosophers since the mid-eighteenth century, such as Dewey or Rorty, he did not have to wrestle with his legacy. He understood, and disagreed with, Cartesian dualism, but dealt with the dichotomy Descartes had identified in a different way. He did not seek to erect a system that privileged rationality while allowing space for the divine, since that invited the twin extremes of positivism or of a faith that transcends the rational. He believed that humans were animal in their nature – indeed could well remain slaves to their passions and on occasion succumb to them – but that intersubjective communication could ensure an ethic that was progressive: placing constraints on cannibalism, for instance, or the wilful exploitation of other people and their resources and (perhaps in the future) the consumption of other sensate mammals.[37] That is because we can observe what follows, even if we can never prove the inevitability of a consequence, since the results of our observations must remain provisional. We can and should have *aspirations* for a better future, indeed be passionate about them, but they are not *ideals* in the sense in which I have used that word – sanctioned by an a priori set of rules or divine fiat.[38] Just as in Whitehead's description of the process of learning, in relation to architecture our aspirational ideas must come first, because the practice of architecture as a mechanical process of problem solving is clearly deficient, but there should be a proper respect for rational critique. Eventually judgment of a work of architecture is called for, and that might not be conclusive for many decades. Perhaps it is never conclusive, as different criteria become privileged in society.

In the twentieth-century history which has been the subject of this book, one of the most intriguing positions seems to be that of Alvar Aalto. His concept of 'positive scepticism' can be seen as a weak idealism – a mild, as opposed to a Pyrrhonian, version of scepticism. Although characteristically Aalto offered no clarification beyond his brief speech to his old school (p. 129), that his work did not turn out to be a merely pragmatic response to circumstances must be due to a steely determination as well as to his exceptional talent. He certainly possessed remarkable skills and was afforded enviable patronage. His humanistic aspirations meant that he took the physical and social context of his work seriously as a starting point and in every project strove for standards that he would seldom succeed in achieving in all respects. His continual stress on the concerns of the 'little man' can be seen as an empathetic ability to put himself in the position of others which is such a critical issue for architects.[39] His philosophical position – or we might say psychological orientation – in relation to the most profound metaphysical issues would appear similar

37 Hume was certainly a man of his time, apparently condoning slavery.
38 Defenders of the continuing relevance of Kant's idealism rightly point out that Humeans must acknowledge they have no systematic response to the question of where rationality, applied to ethical questions, 'comes from': it remains an intriguing mystery, perhaps endemic to the human condition, and ensures the endlessness of philosophical debate.
39 It was one of the complaints of Emmanuel Levinas, and others who took much from Heidegger, that his thinking tended to devalue the importance of intersubjective relations with others, with the ethical responsibilities that implies.

40 Vitruvius 1999, p. 21, my
emphasis.

to Hume's: persuaded neither by quasi-divine mystery (as both Heidegger and Jung were) nor a strident atheism (as Freud was, for instance, or
de Beauvoir and Sartre), but prepared to leave such matters in abeyance.
It is a position that is difficult to maintain and hardly amenable to being
taught, but can be discovered and worked towards by those individuals
prepared to do so. It will hardly guarantee fulfilment, however: Aalto,
in common with most architects, felt at the end of his life that he had
scarcely begun to achieve what he was capable of.

Aalto himself, however, would hardly have approved of a book such as
this, believing as we saw that paper was for drawing on, not for writing.
But he had been educated at a time and in a society where an understanding of European classical culture and the philosophical thinking
that underlies it was part of a young person's secondary education. That
is no longer the case, and the purpose of this book has been to try to
make good that deficiency in a small way, to assist in the interpretation
of architectural modernism and its aftermath. "All theory, dear friend,
is grey, but the golden tree of life springs ever green", runs one of the
most frequently quoted lines from Goethe's *Faust*. In the very first paragraphs of his *De Architectura*, Vitruvius, no doubt echoing an idea that
was already platitudinous more than 2,000 years ago, claimed that
"those who placed their trust *entirely* in theory and in writings seem to
have chased after a shadow, not something real".[40] In maintaining that
philosophical reflection can assist in the improvement of the world we
inhabit, this book participates in a continuing project to counter the
prevailing tendency to separate theoretical discourse from its practical
consequences – a project I remain optimistic enough to believe will
be taken on, in times that will certainly be as difficult as any, by later
generations.

Acknowledgements

This book grew out of a set of lectures and seminars to second and third-year students at the University of Liverpool. I had lectured at Cambridge on similar themes for some years, gradually postulating more philosophical connections as a way of understanding the different approaches of architects to their task. I owe the origins of this approach to a set of inspiring lectures at Cambridge, usually given in five 1-hour sessions during a one-week period to first-year students by Julian Roberts, and I have benefited over many years from intermittent conversations with him. The chapter on Alvar Aalto draws on material I used in my eponymous 2005 book for Yale University Press, the last section of which elaborates on his position of 'positive scepticism'; Sofia Singler has recently found fascinating evidence to corroborate my assumptions, and I have had the privilege of numerous discussions with her and the occasional collaboration.

In 2004 I organized a conference in Cambridge that addressed problems of professional ethics in relation to architecture. Amongst its contributors were the late Giles Oliver (an inspiration since we met as undergraduates); he had originally drawn my attention to *The Ethical Architect* by Tom Spector, with whom I have had many subsequent encounters and correspondence. Following the publication of the proceedings of that conference, as *Architecture and its Ethical Dilemmas*,[1] I was invited to lecture in Eindhoven and met Christian Illies. He asked if I would work with him on a chapter for an Elsevier Handbook, *Philosophy of Technology and Engineering Sciences*, and, on the suggestion of my Liverpool colleague Marco Iuliano and Kenneth Frampton and with the help of Ranald Lawrence, this became a small print-on-demand book, *Philosophy of Architecture*.[2] It was later expanded and issued under the same title with a Chinese parallel translation by University of Liverpool Press. In a sense, the present book represents a major expansion of the hypothesis in the last section of that book, and reuses some of the examples quoted. Maxime Turner gave invaluable help with sourcing illustrations and making new drawings, and David Webb in scanning original slides. Darren Stewart Capel, in addition to providing his drawing of the plan of Villa Mairea, made valuable comments on Chapter 3. To all those mentioned here, I owe an especial debt, but I have also benefited from conversations over the years with numerous others:

Gerry Adler, Antonello Alici, John Allan, Tom Baldwin, Alan Berman, Nick Bullock, Peter Carolin, Harry Charrington, Neelkanth

1 Ray 2005b.
2 Illies and Ray 2018.

Chhaya, Chen-yu Chiu, Michael Collins, Donal Cooper, John Cornwell, William Curtis, Martin Düchs, the late Max Fordham, Jim Friedman, Francisco Gonzáles de Canales, Miguel González-Torres, Jane Heal, Michael Heinrich, Mary Jacobus, David King, Vlatko Korobar, Melissa Lane, Mary Laven, Ron Lewcock, John MacArthur, Derek Matravers, John Meunier, Juliet Mitchell, Renaud Morieux, Richard Murphy, Johanna Muszbek, Aino Niskanen, Fernando Perez, Jim Roseblade, Jaime Royo-Olid, Andrew Saint, Montu Saxena, Simone Schnall, Celia Scott, Quentin Skinner, Sjoerd Soeters, Max Sternberg, Adam Twycross, Paul Vonberg and Ben Zucchi.

Needless to state, I am responsible for any errors in this book. I have been helped throughout by the generosity of the University of Liverpool, the privileges of my Emeritus Fellowship at Jesus College and the infinite patience of my wife, Sarah.

Select bibliography

Books have generally been listed in the most recent editions, as most likely to be available and affordable, which can make for some curious dates. Increasingly in recent years, oral history can supplement written material: for interviews of British architects who can recall twentieth-century practice, see https://sounds.bl.uk/Oral-history/Architects-Lives.

This book does not treat in any depth figures who are discussed in the useful series "Thinkers for Architects" (Routledge 2007), of which there are 15 to date, only some of which are referenced by author. Since most of those covered in the Routledge series drew on the work of figures who appear at various points in the present text (Nietzsche, Marx, Freud, Benjamin or Heidegger, for example), the more modest aim has been to prepare the ground for understanding the complexity of the many twentieth-century theorists, who certainly deserve extended study.

Iñaki Ábalos, *The Good Life: A Guided Visit to the Houses of Modernity*, Editorial Gustavo Gili SA, 2001

Leon Battista Alberti, *De Re Aedificatoria/On the Art of Building in Ten Books*, tr. Joseph Rykwert, Robert Tavernor and Neil Leach, MIT Press, 1988

Christopher Alexander, *The Timeless Way of Building*, Oxford University Press, 1979.

Christopher Alexander, S. Ishikawa, M. Silverstein, I. Fiksdahl-King and S. Angel, *A Pattern Language*, Oxford University Press, 1977

Antonello Alici, "Architects' Travel: Routes, Connections and Resonances between the Mediterranean and the Nordic Countries in the 20th Century", in *Essempe di Architettura* 3, No. 1, 2016

Antonello Alici, *Aino e Alvar Aalto. Risonanze italiane*, Caracol, 2018

Colin Amery, *A Celebration of Art and Architecture: National Gallery Sainsbury Wing*, National Gallery Company Ltd, 1991

Aristotle, *Nicomachean Ethics*, 2nd ed., Hackett Publishing Co., 1999

Peter Arnell and Ted Bickford, *A Tower for Louisville*, Rizzoli, 1982

M.H. Baillie Scott, *Houses and Gardens*, George Newnes, 1906

M.H. Baillie Scott and A.E. Beresford, *Houses and Gardens*, Architecture Illustrated, 1933

Geoffrey Baker, *Design Strategies in Architecture: An Approach to the Analysis of Form*, Taylor & Francis, 1996

Sarah Bakewell, *At the Existentialist Café: Freedom, Being, and Apricot Cocktails*, Chatto and Windus, 2016

Reyner Banham, "Neo-Liberty", in *Architectural Review*, April 1959, pp. 231–235

Reyner Banham, *The New Brutalism*, Architectural Press, 1966

Reyner Banham, *Theory and Design in the First Machine Age*, 2nd ed., MIT Press, 1980

Reyner Banham, *Megastructure: Urban Futures of the Recent Past*, Thames & Hudson, 1981

Reyner Banham, *The Architecture of the Well-Tempered Environment*, 2nd ed., Architectural Press, 1984

Daniel Barber, "Heating the Bauhaus", in *Perspecta 53*, MIT Press, 2020

Leopold Bauer, "Otto Wagner", in *The Architect* XXII, 1919, pp. 9–21

Michael Benedikt, *Deconstructing the Kimbell, an Essay on Meaning and Architecture*, Sites/Lumen Books, 1991

Leonardo Benevolo, *The Origins of Modern Town Planning*, MIT Press, 1971

Walter Benjamin, *One Way Street and Other Writings*, tr. J.A. Underwood, Penguin, 2009

F.A. Bernstein, "Robert Venturi", obituary, in *New York Times*, September 19, 2018

Bruno Bettelheim, *Freud and Man's Soul*, Pimlico, 2001

John Blewitt, *Understanding Sustainable Development*, 3rd ed., Routledge, 2018

Peter Blundell Jones, *Hugo Häring, the Organic versus the Geometric*, Edition Axel Menges, 2002

John Boardman, "Review of Scully 1962a", in *The Burlington Magazine* 106, No. 739, October 1964, p. 469

Ronald Bogue, *Deleuze and Guattari*, Routledge, 1989 (1987)

Thorsten Botz-Bornstein, "Review of Wang 2017", in *Architecture Philosophy* 4, No. 1, 2017, pp. 105–110

Philippe Boudon, *Lived-in Architecture: Le Corbusier's Pessac Revisited*, MIT Press, 1979

Michael Brawne, *From Idea to Building, Issues in Architecture*, Architectural Press, 1992

Karla Britton, *Auguste Perret*, Phaidon, 2010

C.D. Broad, *Five Types of Ethical Theory*, Kegan Paul, 1930

Colin Buchanan, *Traffic in Towns*, HMSO, 1961

Edmund Burke, *A Philosophical Enquiry into the Origin of Our Ideas of the Sublime and the Beautiful*, Oxford paperbacks, 2008

Myles Burneat, ed., *The Skeptical Tradition*, University of California Press, 1983

Colin Burrow "Ti tum ti tum ti tum", in *London Review of Books* 43, No. 19, October 2021, p. 10

A.S.G. Butler, *Lutyens Memorial: The Architecture of Sir Edwin Lutyens*, 3 vols., new ed., ACC Art Books, 1999

Barnabas Calder, *Architecture from Pre-history to Climate Emergency*, Pelican, 2021

Remei Capdevila-Werning, *Goodman for Architects*, Routledge, 2014

Peter Carl, "Ancient Mesopotamia and the Foundation of Architectural Representation", in *Princeton Journal* 1, 1983, pp. 170–186

Chamberlin, Powell and Bon, *University of Leeds Development Plan*, University of Leeds, 1960

Sophie-Grace Chappell and Nicholas Smyth, "Bernard Williams", in *The Stanford Encyclopedia of Philosophy* (Fall 2018 edition), ed. Edward N. Zalta, 2018, https://plato.stanford.edu/archives/fall2018/entries/williams-bernard/

Harry Charrington, "Alvar Aalto at Play", in *Architectural History* 59, 2011

Irene Cheng, Charles L. Davis II and Mabel O. Wilson, eds., *Race and Modern Architecture: A Critical History from the Enlightenment to the Present*, University of Pittsburgh Press, 2020

Neelkanth Chhaya, ed., *Harnessing the Intangible, Collected Essays on the Work of Balkrishna Doshi*, Council of Architecture New Delhi, 2015 (2014)

Francis D.K. Ching, *Architecture: Form, Space & Order*, 4th ed., John Wiley, 2015

Peter Collymore, *The Architecture of Ralph Erskine*, 2nd ed., John Wiley, 1995

Beatriz Colomina, ed., *Sexuality and Space*, Princeton, 1992

Alan Colquhoun, *Essays in Architectural Criticism, Modern Architecture and Historical Change*, MIT Press, 1985

Alan Colquhoun, *Typology and Design Method, Theorizing a New Agenda for Architecture*, Princeton Architectural Press, 1996 (1998)

Alan Colquhoun, *Modern Architecture*, Oxford University Press, 2002

Gordon Cullen, *Townscape*, Reinhold Pub. Corp., 1961

William Curtis, *Modern Architecture since 1900*, Phaidon, 1982

William Curtis, *Le Corbusier, Ideas and Forms*, paperback ed., Phaidon, 1992

Alain de Botton, *The Architecture of Happiness*, Penguin, 2007

Michel de Certeau, *The Practice of Everyday Life*, 3rd ed., University of California Press, 2011

Reinier de Graaf, *Four Walls and a Roof, the Complex Nature of a Simple Profession*, Harvard University Press, 2017

Gilles Deleuze and Felix Guattari, *A Thousand Plateaus: Capitalism and Schizophrenia*, University of Minnesota Press, 1987

Douglas Dennett, *Consciousness Explained*, Penguin, 1993

Michael Dennis, *Court and Garden, from the French Hôtel to the City of Modern Architecture*, MIT Press, 1986

René Descartes, *Discourse on Method*, tr. Donald Cress, 3rd ed., Hackett, 1998

Wilhelm Dilthey, "The Types of World-View and Their Development in Metaphysical Systems", tr. *Rudolf A. Makkreek and Frithjof Rodi,* vol. VI, pp. 249–294, Princeton, 2019

Gustave Doré, *London, a Pilgrimage*, Dover Publications, 1970

Martin Düchs, *Menschliche Architektur. Eine philosophische Annäherung*, Springer Nature, 2021

David Edmonds, *The Murder of Professor Schlick: The Rise and Fall of the Vienna Circle*, Princeton University Press, 2020

Wolfram Eilenberger, *Time of the Magicians: The Invention of Modern Thought 1919–1929*, tr. Shaun Whiteside, Allen Lane, 2020

Peter Eisenman, ed., *Five Architects*, Oxford University Press, 1975

Peter Eisenman, *The Formal Basis of Modern Architecture*, Lars Müller, 2018

Mircea Eliade, *The Sacred and The Profane*, Harcourt Brace Jovanovich, 1959

Brian Elliott, *Benjamin for Architects*, Routledge, 2010

Frederick Engels, *The Condition of the Working Class in England*, Reprint ed., Oxford University Press, 2009

Erasmus of Rotterdam, *The Praise of Folly (1509)*, tr. John Wilson, ed. P. Allen, Clarendon Press, 1931

Norma Evenson, *Chandigarh*, University of California Press, 1966

Karl Fleig, *Alvar Aalto 1922–1962*, tr. William Gleckmann, Verlag für Architetektur, Artemis, 1963

Karl Fleig, *Alvar Aalto 1963–1970*, Praeger Publishers, 1971

Edward Ford, *The Details of Modern Architecture*, vol. 1, MIT Press, 1990 (paperback 2003)

Edward Ford, *The Details of Modern Architecture*, vol. 2, MIT Press, 1996 (paperback 2006)

Adrian Forty, *Words and Buildings, a Vocabulary of Modern Architecture*, Thames & Hudson, 2000

Michel Foucault, "Truth and Juridical Forms", in *Power: Essential Works of Michel Foucault*, ed. J.D. Faubion, The New Press, 2000

Kenneth Frampton, *Modern Architecture, a Critical History*, Thames and Hudson, 1980

Kenneth Frampton, *Modern Architecture, a Critical History*, revised and enlarged ed., Thames and Hudson, 1985

Kenneth Frampton, "Towards a Critical Regionalism: Six Points for an Architecture of Resistance", in *The Anti-Aesthetic, Essays in Postmodern Culture*, ed. Hal Foster, Bay Press, 1983, pp. 16–30

Kenneth Frampton, *Studies in Tectonic Culture, The Poetics of Construction in Nineteenth and Twentieth Century Architecture*, MIT Press, 1995

Murray Fraser and Catherine Gregg, eds., *Sir Banister Fletcher's Global History of Architecture*, RIBA & University of London, 2019

Michael Frayn, *The Human Touch*, Faber and Faber, 2007

Michael Frede, "Stoics and Sceptics on Clear and Distinct Impressions", in *The Skeptical Tradition*, ed. Myles Burneat, University of California Press, 1983

Sigmund Freud, *Civilization and Its Discontents*, tr. James Strachey, W. W. Norton, 1989

Sigmund Freud, *A General Introduction to Psychoanalysis*, Wordsworth, 2012

Tom Furniss, *Edmund Burke's Aesthetic Ideology*, Cambridge University Press, 1993

Hans-Georg Gadamer, *The Relevance of the Beautiful and Other Essays*, Cambridge University Press, 1987

John Gamble, *Alvar Aalto: Formal Structure and a Methodical Development of an Inclusive Architecture*, unpublished PhD, UNSW Faculty of the Built Environment, 2014

Stephen Games, *Behind the Façade*, BBC Books, 1985

Alison Garnham and Susi Woodhouse, *Hans Keller 1919–1985: A Musician in Dialogue with His Times*, Routledge, 2019

Heinz Geretsegger and Max Peintner, *Otto Wagner 1814–1918: The Expanding City, the Beginning of Modern Architecture*, Academy Editions, 1979

James J. Gibson, *The Ecological Approach to Visual Perception*, Psychology Press, 2015

Ante Glibota, *Helmut Jahn*, Paris Art Center, 1987

Sigfried Giedion, *Space, Time and Architecture*, 5th revised and enlarged ed., Harvard University Press, 2008

Johann Goethe, *Italian Journey*, tr. W.H. Auden and Elizabeth Mayer, Penguin, 1970

Johann Goethe, *Essays on Art and Literature,* Goethe Collected Works, vol. 3, Princeton University Press, 1994

Ernst Gombrich, *Reflections on the History of Art: Views and Reviews*, ed. Richard Woodfield, University of California Press, 1987

Ernst Gombrich, *Meditations on a Hobby Horse*, rev. ed, Phaidon, 1994

Ernst Gombrich, *Art and Illusion*, 5th ed., Phaidon, 1997

Ernst Gombrich, *The Story of Art*, 16th ed., Phaidon, 2007

Francisco González de Canales and Nicholas Ray, *Rafael Moneo: Building, Teaching, Writing*, Yale University Press, 2015

Nelson Goodman, *Languages of Art: An Approach to a Theory of Symbols*, new ed., Hackett, 1976

Peter Gordon, *Continental Divide: Heidegger, Cassirer, Davos*, Harvard University Press, 2012

Benedetto Gravagnuolo, *Adolf Loos Theory and Works*, tr. C.H. Evans, Idea Books, 1982

Michael Graves, *Architectural Monographs 5*, Michael Graves, Academy Editions, 1979

Walter Gropius, *The New Architecture and the Bauhaus*, tr. P. Morton Shand, Faber, 1935

Walter Gropius, *The Scope of Total Architecture*, George Allen & Unwin, 1956

Paul Guyer, *A History of Modern Aesthetics*, Cambridge University Press, 2014a

Paul Guyer, *Kant*, 2nd ed., Routledge, 2014b

Paul Guyer, *A Philosopher Looks at Architecture*, Cambridge University Press, 2021

Jonathan Hale, *Building Ideas, an Introduction to Architectural Theory*, John Wiley, 2000

Yuval Noah Harari, *Homo Deus: A Brief History of Tomorrow*, Harvill Secker, 2016

Karsten Harries, *The Ethical Function of Architecture*, MIT Press, 1997

Dean Hawkes, *The Environmental Imagination: Technics and Poetics of the Architectural Environment*, Taylor and Francis, 2018

Simon Heffer, *High Minds, The Victorians and the Birth of Modern Britain*, Random House, 2013

Martin Heidegger, *Basic Writings*, ed. David Farrell Krell, Routledge, 1993

Martin Heidegger, *Sojourns: The Journey to Greece*, tr. J.P. Manoussakis, SUNY Press, 2005

Martin Heidegger, *Being and Time*, tr. John Stambaugh, SUNY Press, 2010

Michael Heinrich, *Metadisziplinäre Ästhetik*, Transcript Verlag, 2019

Klaus Herdeg, *The Decorated Diagram - Harvard Architecture and the Failure of the Bauhaus Legacy*, MIT Press, 1983

Herman Hertzberger, "Place, Choice and Identity", in *World Architecture 4*, ed. John Donat, Studio Vista, 1967

Herman Hertzberger, *Lessons for Students in Architecture 1*, Uitgeverij, 1991

Herman Hertzberger, *Space and the Architect: Lessons for Students in Architecture 2*, 010 Publishers, 2000

Herman Hertzberger, *Space and the Architect: Lessons for Students in Architecture 3*, 010 Publishers, 2009

Richard Hill, *Designs and Their Consequences: Architecture and Aesthetics*, Yale University Press, 1999

Jonas Holst, "Opening Reason to Transcendence – a Philosophical Grounding of Architecture", 2018, https://premiosrazonabierta.org/deposito-digital/

Hugh Honour, *Neo-classicism*, Penguin Books, 1968

Ebenezer Howard, *Garden Cities of Tomorrow*, CreateSpace, 2015

Johan Huizinga, *Homo Ludens; a Study of the Play-Element in Culture*, Routledge, 1949

David Hume, *An Enquiry Concerning Human Understanding*, eds. A. Selby-Bigge and P.H. Nidditch, 3rd ed., Clarendon Press, 1975

David Hume, *An Enquiry Concerning the Principles of Morals*, ed. Tom L. Beauchamp, Oxford University Press, 1998

Edmund Husserl, *Ideas: A General Introduction to Pure Phenomenology*, (known as Ideas I) tr. Fred Kersten, Kluwer Academic Publishers, 1983

Robert Iliffe, *Newton's Religious Life and Work*, Newton Project, www.newtonproject.ox.ac 2013

Christian Illies and Nicholas Ray, *Philosophy of Architecture*/建筑哲学 University of Liverpool Press, 2018

Tim Ingold, *The Perception of the Environment*, Routledge, 2011 (1986)

Peter Inskip, "Edwin Lutyens", in *Architectural Monographs 6*, ed. David Dunster, Academy Editions, 1979

Alick Isaacs, "Review of Gordon 2012", in *Common Knowledge* 19, No. 2, 2013, pp. 393–394

Charles Jencks, *Le Corbusier and the Tragic View of Architecture*, Penguin, 1987

Louis Kahn, *Louis I Kahn, The Complete Works 1935–1974*, eds. Heinz Ronner and Sharad Jhaveri, 2nd ed., Birkhäuser, 1987

Louis Kahn, *Writings, Lectures, Interviews*, ed. Alessandra Latour, Rizzoli 1991

Eric R. Kandel, *The Age of Insight: The Quest to Understand the Unconscious in Art, Mind and Brain from Vienna 1900 to the Present*, Random House, 2012

Emil Kaufmann, *Von Ledoux bis Le Corbusier, Ursprung und Entwicklung der Autonomen Architektur*, Rolf Passer, 1933

Emil Kaufmann, *Architecture in the Age of Reason*, Dover Publications, 1968

Karen Kingsley, "Gender Issues in Architectural Education", in *Journal of Architectural Education* 41, No. 2, 1988, pp. 22–25

Paul Klee, *Notebooks Volume 1: The Thinking Eye*, Wittenborn and Lund Humphries, 1961

Pauline Kleingeld, "Kant's Second Thoughts on Race", in *The Philosophical Quarterly* 57, No. 229, October 2007, pp. 573–592

Rem Koolhaas, *Delirious New York, a Retrospective Manifesto for Manhattan*, Oxford University Press, 1978

J.D. Kornwolf, *M. H. Baillie Scott and the Arts and Crafts Movement*, Johns Hopkins University Press, 1972

Pekka Korvenmaa, "A Bridge of Wood: Aalto, American House Production, and Finland", in *Aalto and America*, eds. Stanford Anderson, Gail Fenske and David Fixler, Yale University Press, 2012

Rob Krier, *Architectural Composition*, Academy Editions, 1988

Thomas Kuhn, *The Structure of Scientific Revolutions*, 50th Anniversary ed., University of Chicago Press, 2012

George Lakoff and Mark Johnson, *Metaphors we Live By, with Afterword*, University of Chicago Press, 2003

Denys Lasdun, *Architecture in an Age of Scepticism*, Oxford University Press, 1984

Ranald Lawrence, *The Victorian Art School, Architecture, History, Environment*, Routledge, 2020

Le Corbusier, *Vers Une Architecture*, Editions Crès, 1923

Le Corbusier, *Towards a New Architecture*, tr. Frederick Etchells, The Architectural Press, 1946

Le Corbusier, *The Athens Charter*, tr. Anthony Eardley, Grossman, 1973

Le Corbusier, *The City of Tomorrow*, tr. Frederick Etchells, 3rd ed. enlarged, The Architectural Press, 1987

Le Corbusier and Pierre Jeanneret, *The Complete Architectural Works Vol. 1*, Thames & Hudson, 1964

Claude Nicolas Ledoux, *L'architecture considérée sous le rapport de l'art, des moeurs et de la legislation*, Tome 1, Uhl, 1804

William Lethaby, *Architecture, Nature and Magic*, George Braziller, 1956

Neil Levine, "The Book and the Building: Hugo's Theory of Architecture and Labrouste's Bibliothèque Ste-Geneviève", in *The Beaux Artes and Nineteenth Century French Architecture*, ed. Robin Middleton, MIT Press, 1982, pp. 139–173

Vincent Ligtelijn, *Aldo van Eyck Works*, Birkhäuser, 1999

Benjamin J. B. Lipscomb, *The Women Are up to Something: How Elizabeth Anscombe, Phillipa Foot, Mary Midgley and Iris Murdoch Revolutionised Ethics*, Oxford University Press, 2021

Adolf Loos, *Principle of Cladding, reprinted in Max Risselada*, ed. Raumplan versus Plan Libre, Rizzoli, 1988, pp. 135–137

Adolf Loos, *Ornament and Crime*, Penguin, 2019

Jacques Lucan, *Composition Non-composition*, Routledge, 2012

Frank Lyons, *The Architecture of Nothingness*, Routledge, 2018

John Macarthur, *The Picturesque: Architecture, Disgust, and Other Irregularities*, Routledge, 2007

Clare Mac Cumhaill and Rachel Wiseman, *Metaphysical Animals: How Four Women Brought Philosophy Back to Life*, Chatto, 2022

Gavin Macrae-Gibson, *The Secret Life of Buildings*, MIT Press, 1988

Janet Malcolm, *In the Freud Archives*, Jonathan Cape, 1984

Harry F. Mallgrave, *Modern Architectural Theory: A Historical Survey 1673–1968*, Cambridge University Press, 2009

Harry F. Mallgrave, *Architecture and Embodiment: The Implications of the New Sciences and Humanities for Design*, Routledge, 2013

Harry F. Mallgrave, *From Object to Experience: The New Culture of Architectural Design*, Bloomsbury, 2018

Harry F. Mallgrave and David Goodman, *An Introduction to Architectural Theory, 1968 to the Present*, Wiley-Blackwell, 2011

Jeff Malpas, *Place and Experience, a Philosophical Topography*, 2nd ed., Routledge, 2018

Robert Maxwell, *Sweet Disorder and the Carefully Careless*, Princeton Architectural Press, 1993 (1991)

Robert McCarter, *Louis I Kahn*, Phaidon, 2005

Robert McCarter, *Aldo van Eyck*, Yale University Press, 2015

Norman McFadyan, *Health and Garden Cities*, Garden Cities and Town Planning Association, 1938

Iain McGilchrist, *The Master and his Emissary – The Divided Brain and the Making of the Modern World*, Yale University Press, 2009

John McKean, *Learning from Segal: Walter Segal's Life, Work and Influence*, Birkhauser, 1989

John McKean, "Domestic Architecture: Living in a House for Jumpers", in *Histories of Postwar Architecture* 2, No. 5, 2019

Maurice Merleau-Ponty, *Phenomenology of Perception*, tr. Colin Smith, Routledge, 1962

Maurice Merleau-Ponty, *The Visible and the Invisible*, followed by Working Notes, tr. Alfonso Lingris, Northwest University Press, 1968

Michael Merrill, ed., *Louis Kahn: The Importance of a Drawing*, Lars Müller, 2021

Robin Middleton, ed., *The Beaux Arts and Nineteenth Century French Architecture*, MIT Press, 1982

Kirmo Mikkola, "Aalto the Thinker", tr. Jonathan and Leena Moorhouse, in *Arkkitehti*, No. 7–8, 1976

Nory Miller, *Helmut Jahn*, Rizzoli, 1986

Barbara Miller Lane, *National Romanticism and Modern Architecture in Germany and the Scandinavian Countries*, Cambridge University Press, 2000

Rafael Moneo, "The Solitude of Buildings", in *A + U*, 1989, pp. 32–40

Rafael Moneo, *Theoretical Anxiety and Design Strategies in the Work of Eight Contemporary Architects*, MIT Press, 2005

Rafael Moneo, *Rafael Moneo: Writings and Conversations in Peru*, Oficina de Publicaciones de la Universidad Católica del Perú, 2009

Rafael Moneo, *Remarks on 21 Works*, Thames & Hudson, 2010

Rafael Moneo, *Rafael Moneo 1967–2004*, El Croquis, 2014

Ray Monk, *Ludwig Wittgenstein: The Duty of Genius*, Vintage, 1991

Ray Monk, "Ludwig Wittgenstein; a Mind on Fire", in *New Statesman*, 15 September 2021

Lewis Mumford, *The City in History, its Origins, its Transformations and its Prospects*, Harcourt Brace, 1961

Richard Murphy, *Carlo Scarpa and Castelvecchio Revisited*, Breakfast Mission Publishing, 2017

Hermann Muthesius, *The English House*, ed. Dennis Sharp, tr. Janet Seligman and Stewart Spencer, Frances Lincoln Press, 2007

Thomas Nagel, *Mortal Questions*, Canto, 1979

Thomas Nagel, *The View from Nowhere*, Oxford University Press, 1986

Thomas Nagel, *Mind and Cosmos: Why the Materialist Neo-Darwinian Conception of Nature Is Almost Certainly False*, Oxford University Press, 2012

Thomas Nagel, "Types of Intuition – Human Rights and Moral Courage", in *London Review of Books* 43, No. 11, 3 June 2021

Susan Neiman, *Moral Clarity*, Bodley Head, 2009

Friederich Nietzsche, *Untimely Meditations*, ed. Daniel Breazeale, Cambridge University Press, 1997

Christian Norberg-Schulz, *Intentions in Architecture*, MIT Press, 1965

Christian Norberg-Schulz, *Existence, Space and Architecture*, Praeger, 1971

Christian Norberg-Schulz, *Meaning in Western Architecture*, Cassell and Company, 1975

Christian Norberg-Schulz, *Genius Loci, Towards a Phenomenology of Architecture*, Rizzoli, 1980

Victor Olgyay, *Design with Climate*, rev. ed., Princeton University Press, 2015

OMA, Rem Koolhaas and Bruce Mau, *S, M, L, XL*, 2nd ed., Monacelli Press, 2002

Graham Owen, "The Anthropology of a Smoke-filled Room: Ethnography and the Human at OMA", in *The Journal of the International Society for the Philosophy of Architecture* 3, No. 2, 2017, pp. 160–188

Juhani Pallasmaa, *The Thinking Hand: Existential and Embodied Wisdom in Architecture*, John Wiley, 2009

Juhani Pallasmaa, *The Embodied Image: Imagination and Imagery in Architecture*, John Wiley, 2011

Juhani Pallasmaa, *The Eyes of the Skin: Architecture and the Senses*, John Wiley, 2012

Martin Pawley, *Theory and Design in the Second Machine Age*, Blackwell, 1990

Alberto Pérez-Gómez, *Architecture and the Crisis of Modern Science*, MIT Press, 1983

Nikolaus Pevsner, *Pioneers of the Modern Movement*, Faber, 1936

Nikolaus Pevsner, "Building with Wit", in *Architectural Review*, 5 April 1951

Nikolaus Pevsner, *Pioneers of Modern Design*, rev. ed., Penguin, 1960

Nikolaus Pevsner, *An Outline of European Architecture*, new ed., Penguin, 1990

Thomas Piketty, *Capital in the Twenty-First Century*, Belknap Press, 2014

Karl Popper, *Conjectures and Refutations, The Growth of Scientific Knowledge*, Routledge Classics, 2002a

Karl Popper, *The Open Society and its Enemies*, 7th ed., with Foreword by E.H. Gombrich, Routledge, 2002b

Demetri Porphyrios, *Sources of Modern Eclecticism*, St Martin's Press, 1982

Demetri Porphyrios, ed., *Léon Krier, Houses, Palaces and Cities*, Architectural Design 54 7/8, 1984

Jules David Prown, *The Architecture of the Yale Center for British Art*, Yale University, 1977

A. K. Ramanujan, *The Collected Essays of A. K. Ramanujan*, ed. Vinay Dharwadker, Oxford University Press, 1990 (1999)

Steen Eiler Rasmussen, *Experiencing Architecture*, MIT Press, 1964

Nicholas Ray, "Postmodernism in Architecture", in *Cambridge Review* 110, No. 2305, 1989, pp. 53–60

Nicholas Ray, *Alvar Aalto*, Yale University Press, 2005a

Nicholas Ray, ed., *Architecture and its Ethical Dilemmas*, Taylor & Francis, 2005b

Nicholas Ray, "Studio Teaching for a Social Purpose", in *Open House International* 33, No. 2, June 2008

Nicholas Ray, "An English Eclectic Abroad: Stirling in America", in *Stirling + Wilford American Buildings*, ed. Alan Berman, Artifice, 2015

Jonathan Rée, *Witcraft, the Invention of Philosophy in English*, Allen Lane, 2019

Peter Reed, ed., *Alvar Aalto: Between Humanism and Materialism*, Museum of Modern Art, 1998

Jane Rendell, Barbara Penner and Iain Borden, eds., *Gender, Space, Architecture: An Interdisciplinary Introduction*, Routledge, 1999

Martin Richardson, "Krier Street", in *Architects' Journal* 12 July 1969 (1989), p. 19

Bill Riseboro, *Modern Architecture and Design - an Alternative History*, Herbert Press, 1982

Max Risselada, ed., *Raumplan versus Plan Libre*, Rizzoli, 1988

Julian Roberts, "Architecture, Morality and Taste", in *Architecture and its Ethical Dilemmas*, ed. Nicholas Ray, Taylor & Francis, 2005, pp. 143–154

Richard Rorty, *Philosophy and the Mirror of Nature*, Methuen, 1980

Aldo Rossi, *Scientific Autobiography*, MIT Press, 1982

Aldo Rossi, *The Architecture of the City*, rev. ed., MIT Press, 1984

Colin Rowe, "The Blenheim of the Welfare State", in *Cambridge Review*, 1959, reprinted in Colin Rowe, *As I Was Saying*, MIT Press, 1999 (1959), pp. 143–158

Colin Rowe, "The Mathematics of the Ideal Villa", in *The Mathematics of the Ideal Villa and Other Essays*, new ed., MIT Press, 1982

Colin Rowe, *The Letters of Colin Rowe – Five Decades of Correspondence*, ed. Daniel Naegele, Artifice, 2016

Colin Rowe and Fred Koetter, *Collage City*, MIT Press, 1978

Colin Rowe and Robert Slutsky, "Transparency, Literal and Phenomenal", in *The Mathematics of the Ideal Villa and Other Essays*, new ed., MIT Press, 1982 (1963 & 1971)

John Ruskin, *Seven Lamps of Architecture*, Smith, Elder & Co., 1849, and Cambridge University Press, 2010

Joseph Rykwert, *On Adam's House in Paradise*, 2nd ed., MIT Press, 1981

Joseph Rykwert, *The Necessity of Artifice*, Rizzoli, 1982

Joseph Rykwert, *The First Moderns – the Architects of the Eighteenth Century*, rev. ed., MIT Press, 1984

Joseph Rykwert, *The Seduction of Place: The City in the Twenty-first Century*, Weidenfeld and Nicolson, 2000

Andrew Saint, *The Image of the Architect*, Yale University Press, 1983

Andrew Saint, *Architect and Engineer, a Study in Sibling Rivalry*, Yale University Press, 2007

Nikos Salingaros, *A Theory of Architecture*, Vajra Books, 2013

Antonio Sanmartin, *Venturi, Rauch & Scott Brown*, Academy Editions, 1986

August Sarnitz, "Wittgenstein's Architectural Idiosyncrasy", in *Architecture Philosophy, Journal of the International Society for the Philosophy of Architecture* 2, No. 2, 2017

Jean-Paul Sartre, *Existentialism Is a Humanism*, Yale University Press, 2007

Göran Schildt, *Alvar Aalto Sketches*, MIT Press, 1985

Göran Schildt, *Alvar Aalto the Decisive Years*, Rizzoli, 1986

Göran Schildt, *Alvar Aalto In his Own Words*, Rizzoli, 1998

Donal Schön, *The Reflective Practitioner: How Professionals Think in Action*, Basic Books, 1983

Carl E. Schorske, *Fin-de-Siècle Vienna, Politics and Culture*, Alfred A Knopf, 1980

Frederick Schwartz and Robert Venturi, *Mother's House*, Rizzoli, 1992

Geoffrey Scott, *The Architecture of Humanism*, new ed., Norton, 1999

George Gilbert Scott, *Personal and Professional Recollections*, Facsimile ed., ed. Gavin Stamp, Paul Watkins, 1995

Roger Scruton, *The Aesthetics of Architecture*, Methuen, 1979

Vincent Scully, *The Earth, the Temple and the Gods: Greek Sacred Architecture*, Yale University Press, 1962a

Vincent Scully, *Louis I Kahn*, George Braziller Inc., 1962b

Gottfried Semper, *The Four Elements of Architecture and Other Writings*, tr. Harry F. Mallgrave and Wolfgang Herrmann, Cambridge University Press, 1989

Gottfried Semper, *Style in the Technical and Tectonic Arts or Practical Aesthetics*, tr. Harry F. Mallgrave and Michael Robinson, Getty Publications, 2004

Amartya Sen, "Sraffa's Constructive Scepticism", in *the Trinity Annual Record 2013–2014*, Trinity College Cambridge, 2014, pp. 114–124

Victor Shea and William Whitla, *Victorian Literature: An Anthology*, Wiley Blackwell, 2014

Sofia Singler and Nicholas Ray, "Why Aalto? The Sceptic Builds for Religion", paper at the 3rd Alvar Aalto Researchers' Network Seminar, Jyväskylä, Finland, 2017

Camillo Sitte, *Der Städtebau nach seinen künstlerischen Grundsätzen*, 5th ed., Vienna, 1922

Camillo Sitte, *The Art of Buildings Cities: City Building According to its Artistic Fundamentals*, tr. Charles Stewart, Martino Fine Books, 2013

Álvaro Siza, "Views", in *Architecture and Cultural Values, Proceedings of the 4th International Alvar Aalto Symposium*, p. 15, ed. Maija Kärkkäinen, Alvar Aalto Museum, 1991

Quentin Skinner, ed., *The Return of Grand Theory in the Human Sciences*, Cambridge University Press, 1985

Gary Smith, ed., *On Walter Benjamin, Critical Essays and Recollections*, MIT Press, 1968 (1988)

Alison Smithson, ed., *Team X Primer*, MIT Press, 1968

Alison Smithson, "Mat Building", in *Architectural Design* XLIV, September 1974, pp. 573–590

Peter Smithson, *Bath Walks within the Walls*, Adams & Dart, 1971

Mark Solms, *The Brain and the Inner World*, Routledge, 2002

Tom Spector, *The Ethical Architect, the Dilemma of Contemporary Practice*, Princeton Architectural Press, 2001

Tom Spector, *The Architecture Profession and the Public Good*, The Anthem Press, 2021

Albert Speer, *Spandau, the Secret Diaries*, tr. Richard & Clare Winston, Collins, 1976

Hilde Spiel, *Vienna's Golden Autumn 1866–1938*, Weidenfeld and Nicolson, 1987

Wallace Stegner, *Crossing to Safety*, Penguin Classics, 2013

Adrian Stokes, *The Image in Form: Selected Writings of Adrian Stokes*, ed. Richard Wollheim, Harper and Rowe, 1972

Tom Stoppard, *Leopoldstadt*, Faber and Faber, 2020

Louis Sullivan, "The Tall Office Building Artistically Considered", in *Lippincott's Monthly Magazine*, March 1896

Louis Sullivan, *The Autobiography of an Idea*, AIA Press, 1924

John Summerson, "The Case for a Theory of Modern Architecture", in *RIBA Journal*, June 1957, pp. 307–313

John Summerson, *The Classical Language of Architecture*, Thames & Hudson, 1980

John Summerson, *The Unromantic Castle and other Essays*, Thames and Hudson, 1990

John Summerson, *Heavenly Mansions*, new ed., Norton, 2013

Manfredo Tafuri, *The Sphere and the Labyrinth*, MIT Press, paperback ed., 1990

Manfredo Tafuri, Alfredo Manfredo, Alfredo Passeri and Paolo Piva, *Vienna Rossa: La Politica Residenziale Nella Vienna Socialista*, Electa, 1995

Francis Tibbalds, *Making People-Friendly Towns: Improving the Public Environment in Towns and Cities*, Taylor & Francis, 2000

Jeremy Till, *Architecture Depends*, MIT Press, 2013

Bernard Tschumi, *Architecture and Disjunction*, MIT Press, 1996

Jan Turnovsky, *The Poetics of a Wall Projection*, tr. Kent Kleinman, AA Publications, 2009

Robert C. Twombly, *Frank Lloyd Wright, His Life and His Architecture*, John Wiley & Sons, 1979

Anne Griswold Tyng, *Louis Kahn to Anne Tyng: The Rome Letters 1953–1954*, Rizzoli, 1991 (1997)

David Valinsky, *An Architect Speaks: The Writings and Buildings of Edward Shröder Prior*, Exeter, Short Run Press, 2014

Walter van Beek, "A Field Evaluation of the Work of Marcel Griaule", in *Current Anthropology* 32, No. 2, April 1991, pp. 139–166

Aldo van Eyck, "The Medicine of Reciprocity Tentatively Illustrated", in *Forum* 15, Nos. 6–7, 1961, pp. 237–238

Aldo van Eyck, "Beyond Visibility", in *The Situationist Times*, No. 4, 1963, pp. 79–81

Robert Venturi, *Complexity and Contradiction in Architecture*, 2nd rev. ed., Museum of Modern Art, 1984

Robert Venturi, Denise Scott Brown and Steven Izenour, *Learning from Las Vegas: The Forgotten Symbolism of Architectural Form*, rev. ed., MIT Press, 1977

Dalibor Vesely, *Architecture in the Age of Divided Representation*, MIT Press, 2006

Anthony Vidler, *The Architectural Uncanny, Essays in the Modern Unhomely*, MIT Press, 1992

Anthony Vidler, *The Third Typology and Other Essays*, Artifice, 2014

Dana Villa, "Postmodernism and the Public Sphere", in *American Political Science Review* 86, No. 3, 1992, p. 719

Eugène-Emmanuel Viollet-le-Duc, *Discourses on Architecture*, tr. Benjamin Bucknell, Grove Press, 1959

Vitruvius, *The Ten Books on Architecture*, tr. Morris Hickey Morgan, Dover Publications, 1960

Vitruvius, *Ten Books on Architecture*, rev. ed., tr. & ed. Ingrid D. Rowland & Thomas Noble Howe, Cambridge University Press, 1999

Adolph Max Vogt, *Le Corbusier, the Noble Savage*, MIT Press, 2000

Otto Wagner, *Die Baukunst unserer Zeit. Dem Baukunstjünger ein Führer auf diesem Kunstgebiet*, 4th ed., Vienna, 1914

Otto Wagner, *Modern Architecture: A Guidebook for His Students to This Field of Art*. tr. Harry F. Mallgrave, Getty Center for the History of Art and the Humanities, 1988

David Wang, *A Chinese Philosophy of Architecture*, Routledge, 2017

Robin Waterfield, *Timaeus and Critias* (intr. Andrew Gregory), Oxford University Press, 2008

David Watkin, *Morality and Architecture: The Development of a Theme in Architectural History and Theory from the Gothic Revival to the Modern Movement*, Clarendon Press, 1977

Trevor Watkins, "Opening the Door, Pointing the Way", in *Paléorient* 37, No. 1, 2011. Néolithisations: nouvelles données, nouvelles interprétations. À propos du modèle théorique de Jacques Cauvin, pp. 29–38

Lawrence Weaver, *Lutyens Houses and Gardens*, Country Life, 1921

Alfred North Whitehead, *The Aims of Education and Other Essays*, Macmillan, 1929

Alfred North Whitehead, *Process and Reality*, The Free Press, 1978

Jay Wickersham, "The Making of Exeter Library", in *Harvard Architecture Review 7*, 1989, pp. 138–149

Bernard Williams, *Problems of the Self, Philosophical Papers 1956–1972*, Cambridge University Press, 1973

Bernard Williams, *Descartes*, Penguin, 1978

Bernard Williams, *Moral Luck, Philosophical Papers 1973–1980*, Cambridge University Press, 1981

Colin St John Wilson, *Architectural Reflections*, Butterworth-Heinemann, 1992

Colin St John Wilson, *The Other Tradition: The Uncompleted Project*, Academy Editions, 1995

Mark Wilson-Jones, *Origins of Classical Architecture*, Yale University Press, 2014

Rob Withagen and Simone R. Caljouw, "Aldo van Eyck's Playgrounds, Aesthetics, Affordances, and Creativity", in *Frontiers in Psychology* 8, July 2017

Ludwig Wittgenstein, *Culture and Value*, tr. Peter Winch, ed. G.H. Von Wright, Basil Blackwell, 1980

Rudolph Wittkower, *Architectural Principles in the Age of Humanism*, Alec Tiranti, 1949

Tom Wolfe, *From Bauhaus to Our House*, Farrer Straus & Giroux, 1981

Richard Wollheim, *Art and its Objects*, 2nd ed., Cambridge University Press, 1980

Frank Lloyd Wright, "The Art and Craft of the Machine", in *Brush and Pencil* 8, No. 2, May 1901

Lance Wright, University of Leeds, *Architectural Review Vol. CLV No. 923*, January 1974

Dan Zahavi, *Phenomenology the Basics*, Routledge, 2019

Peter Zumthor, *Thinking Architecture*, Lars Müller Publishers, 1998

List of plates and credits

Figure 1.1:   RIBA Collections

Figure 1.2:   Raphael, public domain, via Wikimedia Commons

Figure 1.3:   Nicolas Poussin, CC BY-SA 3.0 https://creativecommons.org/licenses/by-sa/3.0, via Wikimedia Commons

Figure 1.4:   Titian, Public domain, via Wikimedia Commons

Figure 1.5:   Karl Eduard Biermann, public domain, via Wikimedia Commons

Figure 1.6:   Karl Friedrich Schinkel, public domain, via Wikimedia Commons

Figure 2.1:   Benjamin Brecknell Turner, CC0, via Wikimedia Commons

Figure 2.2:   Louis Sullivan, public domain, via Wikimedia Commons

Figure 2.3:   Unidentified photographer, black and white photographic print, 8 in x 10 in, 1893, Smithsonian Institution Archives, public domain, via Picryl (http://siarchives.si.edu/) Accession no. 12137

Figure 2.4:   Saleh Masoumi, CC BY-SA 3.0 <https://creativecommons.org/licenses/by-sa/3.0>, via Wikimedia Commons

Figure 2.5:   Gustave Doré, https://creativecommons.org/licenses/by/4.0, via Wikimedia Commons

Figure 2.6:   Ebenezer Howard, public domain, via Wikimedia Commons

Figure 2.7:   M.H. Baillie Scott, public domain

Figure 2.8:   Skokloster Castle, public domain, via Wikimedia Commons

Figure 2.9:   Henry Fuseli, public domain, via Wikimedia Commons

Figure 2.10: University of Glasgow Library, Special Collections, Sebastiano Serlio, Architettura, Sp Coll S.M. 1971, CC BY-NC-SA 2.0, via Flickr

Figure 2.11: William Wilkins, public domain

Figure 2.12: © User: Colin/Wikimedia Commons

Figure 2.13: © Michael Heinrich

Figure 2.14: Edward Edwards, public domain, via Wikimedia Commons

Figure 2.15: T. Higham; Z. Martin, public domain, via Wikimedia Commons

Figure 2.16: Augustus Pugin, public domain, via Wikimedia Commons

Figure 2.17: Eugène Viollet-le-Duc, public domain

Figure 2.18: Canaan/Wikimedia Creative Commons

Figure 2.19: Martin Charles/RIBA Collections 105088

Figure 2.20: © Nicholas Ray

Figure 2.21: Charles Rennie Mackintosh, public domain

Figure 2.22: M.H. Baillie Scott, public domain

Figure 2.23: Henry van de Velde, unknown photographer, public domain

Figure 3.1:   Martin Zeiller, public domain, via Wikimedia Commons

Figure 3.2:   Gerd Eichmann, CC BY-SA 4.0, https://creativecommons.org/licenses/by-sa/4.0, via Wikimedia Commons

Figure 5.5–5.8: © Nicholas Ray

Figure 5.9: DACS/Fondation Le Corbusier

Figure 5.10: © Darren Stewart Capel

Figure 5.11–5.16: © Nicholas Ray

Figure 5.17: Alvar Aalto Foundation

Figure 5.18: © Nicholas Ray

Figure 5.19: Alvar Aalto Foundation

Figure 5.20: Alvar Aalto Foundation

Figure 6.1: © Maxime Turner

Figure 6.2: © Maxime Turner

Figure 6.3: © Nicholas Ray

Figure 6.4: University of Pennsylvania, Architectural Archives

Figure 6.5: © Keith de Lellis Gallery LLC /University of Pennsylvania, Architectural Archives/John Elstob photographer

Figure 6.6: David MacGibbon/ Thomas Ross, Public domain

Figure 6.7: © Maxime Turner

Figure 6.8: © Nicholas Ray

Figure 6.9: Philadelphia Museum of Art

Figure 6.10: University of Pennsylvania, Architectural Archives

Figure 6.11: © Maxime Turner

Figure 6.12: © Nicholas Ray

Figure 6.13: © Maxime Turner

Figure 6.14–6.17: © Nicholas Ray

Figure 6.18: © Maxime Turner

Figure 6.19: Rosenfeld Media, CC BY 2.0, via Flickr

Figure 6.20–6.22: © Nicholas Ray

Figure 6.23: © Maxime Turner

Figure 6.24–6.25: © Nicholas Ray

Figure 7.1: © Maxime Turner

Figure 7.2: DACS/Fondation Le Corbusier

Figure 7.3: DACS/Fondation Le Corbusier

Figure 7.4: From *Team Ten Primer*, copyright holder undiscovered

Figure 7.5: Andrew Curtis, CC BY-SA 2.0, via Geograph

Figure 7.6: Clare Hall archive, Carment Frankl

Figure 7.7: In possession of Nicholas Ray

Figure 7.8: Aldo van Eyck Archive © Aldo van Eyck

Figure 7.9: Aldo van Eyck Archive © Aldo van Eyck, Violette Cornelius photographer

Figure 7.10: Aldo van Eyck Archive © Aldo van Eyck

Figure 7.11: © Nicholas Ray

Figure 7.12: AHH, Amsterdam

Figure 7.13: © Nicholas Ray

Figure 7.14: AHH, Amsterdam

Figure 7.15: © Herman Hertzberger

Figure 7.16: © Nicholas Ray

Figure 7.17: Het Nieuwe Instituut, Amsterdam

Figure 8.1: Harry Lawford, CC BY 2.0, via Flickr

Figure 8.2: Staib, CC BY-SA 3.0, https://creativecommons.org/licenses/by-sa/3.0, via Wikimedia Commons

Figure 8.3: Edwin Lutyens, public domain

Figure 8.4–8.5: © Nicholas Ray

Figure 8.6: Robert Venturi, CC BY-SA 4.0, https://creativecommons.org/licenses/by-sa/4.0, via Wikimedia Commons

Figure 8.7: Smallbones, CC0, via Wikimedia Commons

Figure 8.8: Venturi, Scott Brown and Associates, Inc.

Figure 8.9: © Nicholas Ray

Figure 8.10: © Nicholas Ray

Figure 8.11: Tom Bernard, courtesy of Venturi, Scott Brown and Associates, Inc.

Figure 8.12: © Nicholas Ray

Figure 8.13: Courtesy of Michael Graves

Figure 8.14–8.16: © Nicholas Ray

Figure 8.17: JAHN

Figure 8.18: JAHN

Figure 8.19: Foster + Partners

Figure 8.20: Courtesy of Michael Graves

Figure 8.21: © Nicholas Ray

Figure 9.1: Léon Krier

Figure 9.2: Colin Rowe and Fred Koetter, *Collage City*, MIT Press, 1978

Figure 9.3: Colin Rowe and Fred Koetter, *Collage City*, MIT Press, 1978

Figure 9.4: Michael Dennis

Figure 9.5: Léon Krier

Figure 9.6: Léon Krier

Figure 9.7: Fred Romero, CC BY 2.0, via Flickr

Figure 9.8: Jean-Nicolas-Louis Durand, public domain

Figure 9.9: DACS/Fondation Le Corbusier

Figure 9.10:   Thomas Cole, public domain
Figure 9.11:   © Eredi Aldo Rossi
Figure 9.12:   Gabriele Pierluisi, via Flickr Commons, https://snl.no/Aldo_ Rossi, CC BY 2.0
Figure 9.13:   © Michael Moran, by kind permission of Rafael Moneo
Figure 9.14:   © Rob Krier
Figure 9.15:   © Eredi Aldo Rossi, Palladium Photodesign Barbara Burg + Oliver Schuh
Figure 9.16:   Imagery ©2022 Maxar Technologies, map data © 2022 Google
Figure 9.17:   Léon Krier
Figure 9.18–9.19: © Nicholas Ray
Figure 9.20:   Joe Shlabotnik, CC BY 2.0, via Flickr
Figure 9.21:   Zaha Hadid Architects, render by Negativ
Figure 9.22:   Taylor & Francis, used under the first factor of fair use legislation: educational purposes

Figure 10.1:   Peter Aaron/OTTO
Figure 10.2:   Copyright OMA
Figure 10.3:   Copyright OMA
Figure 10.4:   準建築人手札網站, Forgemind ArchiMedia, CC BY 2.0, via Flickr
Figure 10.5:   © Bernard Tschumi Architects
Figure 10.6–10.8: © Nicholas Ray
Figure 10.9:   © Bernard Tschumi
Figure 10.10:   © Steven Holl
Figure 10.11:   Steven Holl
Figure 10.12:   Steven Holl
Figure 10.13:   Peter Guthrie, by kind permission of Richard Murphy
Figure 10.14:   © Nicholas Ray
Figure 10.15:   Microsoft product screen shot(s), reprinted with permission from Microsoft Corporation
Figure 11.1:   patt, via Flickr, www.flickr.com/photos/ trevorpatt/28056784634, CC BY-NC-SA 2.0

Index

Aalto, Aino 121, 245, 259
Aalto, Alvar 4, 20–21, 64, 109,
  110–133, 154–155, 164, 177, 206,
  219, 223, 244, 245–247, 251n46,
  253, 258, 261, 268–270; National
  Pensions Institute 122–123;
  Paimio sanitorium 114–120,
  126–127; Säynätsalo 98, 121–123,
  126; scepticism 128–133; teaching
  experience 110, 266
Adler, Alfred 62
Adler, Dankmar 28–29
Adler, Victor 60
Adler House 135
Adorno, Theodor 232, 234
aesthetics 11–14, 22, 44, 51–54, 106, 225,
  232–233; *Aesthetics of Architecture*
  224; modernist 105, 154, 165
Alberti, Leon Battista 1, 35, 77, 157n26,
  158–159, 244
alchemy 22
allegory 16, 128
ambiguity: formal 193, 225, 257;
  literary 181n5; spatial 71–72,
  166–168, 169, 174, 257
Amsterdam 35, 92–93, 145, 166, 168,
  171, 175, 237; playgrounds 168
analysis: aesthetic 20, 232, 257;
  formal 97–98, 185n13, 226;
  psychoanalytical 61, 63; technical
  86, 131, 145, 187, 212, 216, 264–265
anarchism 32, 250–251
Anscombe, Elizabeth 6, 132n25
anthropology 15n29, 76, 106, 166, 233
anti-semitism 20n40, 60n6, 60, 234
antithesis 17
anxiety: existential 234, 267; as to
  future of architecture 5, 29, 37;
  political 52
Apollonian art 19, 52, 109, 252
a priori 10, 227, 269

architecture: alternative critical
  readings of 1–5, 13–14, 21–22;
  brutalist 77, 105; domestic 30–31,
  47–49, 70–71, 95, 121, 155, 178,
  217, 226, 232–233, 252–253, 255;
  education for 22, 24–25, 81–82, 107,
  265–268; essence of 18, 84, 114, 134,
  145, 232; formal analysis of 97–99,
  185n13, 226; futuristic 92; materiality
  of 4–5, 27–31, 41–42 (*see also*
  construction); philosophy, relation
  to 3, 180–181, 227, 262–263, 265, 267;
  theory of 1, 4–5, 53, 74, 77–78, 231,
  254; *see also* classical architecture;
  modern architecture; organic
  architecture; vernacular architecture
Aristotle 16, 18, 21, 57, 227, 232;
  Nicomachaean Ethics 18
art 14, 16, 18, 24, 40, 55, 70, 80–81,
  85, 168, 212–213, 224, 232; Aalto's
  view of 110–111, 115, 127, 128, 131;
  architecture as a form of 11, 87,
  93–94; Freud's view of 61–62,
  78, 268; Gropius's view of 84;
  Heidegger's view of 242–243;
  history of 12, 35; idealist theory
  of 19; Kahn's view of 155–156; Le
  Corbusier's view of 87, 92, 263;
  Loos's view of 71; museums and
  galleries 99–101, 107, 135, 145, 178,
  241; nominalist theory of 19, 21;
  relation to science 22; schools of
  46–47, 50; *see also* aesthetics
Artek 119, 127
Art Nouveau 35, 45–47, 50–51, 59, 63,
  66, 107, 261, 268
Arts and Crafts 33–34, 47, 49–50, 63,
  71, 85, 107, 181; Chicago society 30
aspirations: as distinct from ideals 18,
  20–21, 113, 132, 201, 269
Asplund, Gunnar 112–14, 251n46

association: stylistic 42–43, 52, 56, 239
astrology 22
astronomy 22, 26
axe-man problem 11

Baghdad University 83, 103
Baillie Scott, M. H. 33–34, 49–50, 51,
    184, 187, 226; *Houses and Gardens* 33
Bakema, Jacob 92, 93, 175
Banham, P. Reyner 1n1, 179n35, 260;
    *Theory and Design in the First
    Machine Age* 3, 105n40, 260
Barcelona 22, 34, 46, 63, 219
Barlow, William Henry 42, 261
Baroque 17, 35, 36, 56, 181–182, 189,
    212, 247
Bauhaus: credo 71, 106–107; criticisms
    of 98, 105–106, 114, 160, 212, 213,
    218, 258; Manifesto 79; teaching 81,
    83, 136n4; *Vorkurs* 81, 83
Beardsley, Aubrey 45
Beauvoir, Simone de 234, 270
beauty 12, 13, 52, 63, 157n26, 190
Beaux Arts: École 36–37, 107, 134, 138,
    139, 181; teaching 36–37
Beckford, William 43–44
Behrens, Peter 50–51, 85
Being, divine 16, 132
Being, existential 15, 22, 94, 232–234,
    243, 245–246
Benjamin, Walter 19, 226, 232, 234,
    239, 242, 254
Bergson, Henri 130
Berlage, Hendrik 35, 145
Berlin 40, 50, 57, 81, 94, 106, 160, 175,
    182; Haupstadt 176; IBA exhibition
    176, 219
Bernays, Edward 62n18
Bofill, Ricardo 209–210
Botton, Alain de 13
Broadacre City 34, 87–88, 92
Brutalism 77, 105
Buchanan, Colin 91–92, 220
Burke, Edmund 22, 51–52
butterfly house 49–50

Cambridge 40, 61, 96, 181n3, 208, 229,
    260; Churchill College 103–105,
    189; Clare Hall 163–164
capitalism 15n28, 53, 73, 76, 234,
    237, 264
Carlo, Giancarlo de 169, 179, 215, 249,
    251, 268
cars 28, 92, 254

Carson, Rachel 231n2
Carson Pirie Scott building 28–29
Cartesian grid 94, 235
Cartesian thought 36n21
Cassirer, Ernst 106, 232–234
cast iron 26–27, 45
Cerdá, Idelfonso 34–35
Chambers, William 35–36, 212
charrette 37
Charter of Athens 91, 159
Chartres 257
chiasm 245–246
Chicago 28–30, 73, 87, 138, 198, 260;
    Columbian World Fair exhibition
    29–30, 223
China 91, 239, 259
CIAM 91–94, 103, 109, 158, 176
circulation: within buildings 38, 97,
    122, 135, 138, 140–141, 187, 205;
    traffic 34, 92, 103
cities: developing 258; European 26,
    31–32, 35, 54, 55, 85, 91–92, 107, 160,
    177, 207, 236, 237, 255, 261(*see also*
    Garden Cities); medieval 27, 160
classical architecture 14, 38, 43–44,
    52, 94, 157
classicism 36
climate 15, 43, 260; effect on design
    43, 163, 179, 253, 257
Cogito 22
Cole, Thomas 213–214, 223
colonialism 5, 53–54, 166n11, 258–259
Colosseum, Rome 35
Colquhoun, Alan 50n39, 74, 196n30;
    Typology and Design Method 23,
    213–214, 215
construction: as component of
    architecture 21, 85; high-rise 29, 84;
    machine-made 26, 27; rationalized
    techniques 107, 261; timber
    frame 195; trabeated 31, 35–36;
    truthful 105
constructivism 79, 115, 241
consumerism 177, 202
convention: architectural 14, 52,
    70, 83, 98–99, 132, 207, 211, 214,
    261; human 227; ironic 192;
    philosophical 10, 19, 209
Cornell University 99–101, 189,
    204, 215
craft 18
Cretan Liar 17
critical theory 53
Crystal Palace, London 27, 28, 42

culture: European 13, 33, 36, 43, 52, 252; modernist 83, 85, 169; non-Western 166, 178, 207n4, 259; popular 181, 182, 201; Viennese 54, 59, 71, 75, 78
Curtis, William 2n6, 85n15, 108

Dan Dare 92
Darwin 129, 245n38, 254, 266
deconstruction: architectural 240–241; literary 157, 241
decor 1
decoration 35, 180, 189–190, 193–194, 196, 200–201; in Aalto's work 111, 128; in Kahn's work 156; in Wagner's work 66–67, 69, 73, 77
Deleuze and Guattari 54n47, 239n25
density, housing 32, 33, 86
Derrida, Jacques 156, 180–181, 241, 253–254
Descartes, René 9, 22, 130, 227, 261, 269
Dessau 81–82
determinism 23–24, 102–103, 169, 214
Dewey, John 21, 132, 228, 269
dialectics 17, 53
Dilthey, Wilhelm: *Weltanshauung* 15, 106
Dionysian art 19–20, 52, 252
disposability 28
Dom-ino system 31, 108
Doré, Gustav 31–32
dualism, Cartesian 22, 24, 265n22, 266, 269
Durand, Jean-Nicolas-Louis 37, 134, 211–212; *Précis des Leçons d'Architecture* 211–212
duty, ethical or moral 10–11, 15, 52, 86, 215, 245

eclecticism 35, 40, 56, 181, 193, 208n6; in Aalto's work 111
École Polytechnique 37, 211–212
Edinburgh 52
education, architectural 24–25, 82n7, 107, 110, 265–268
Einstein, Albert 12n17, 169
Eisenman, Peter 96–98; *Formal Basis of Modern Architecture* 96
empathy 13
empiricism 1, 10, 12
energy 28, 260
Engels, Friedrich 32, 60

Enlightenment 3, 22, 36, 75, 77–78, 107, 132, 180, 181, 234, 245, 253–255; split 22–24, 35, 78, 132
environmental performance 27, 260
existentialism
epistemology 3, 10, 12, 17, 21–22, 253–254
Erasmus 129
Erskine, Ralph 161–165, 168–169, 174, 179
equity 18n35
esquisse 37, 143
essence 14–15, 18, 134, 145, 213
ethics 10–11, 14, 18, 51, 265, 271; in architectural expression 11, 35, 42, 51, 77, 105, 124, 190–192, 242; virtue 11, 18
existentialism 231–232, 234, 244–245
expression: architectural 3, 13–14, 29, 42, 169; free 23–24, 214; material 50, 56; neurotic 64; personal 225–226; services 92n30, 140; social 173; structural 11
expressionism 62–64

façade 28–29, 102, 117, 119, 136, 182, 187, 190; decorated 66–67, 193, 209, 231; free 31
faith: architectural 2, 80, 179; religious 60, 129–130, 131, 266–267, 269
Feininger, Lyonel 80–81
female architects 4, 259
female philosophers 7
film 232, 235, 247
Finland 110–111, 121, 129–130, 132
First World War 50, 61, 81, 106, 181, 223, 264
Foot, Philippa 6
Ford, Edward 77n39, 144n14, 154–155, 157n28
formalism 9, 220
forms: architectural 8–9, 13, 47, 62, 91–95, 99, 127, 176, 207–208, 211–213, 215, 220, 242, 260; painting 85; Platonic 86, 244
Forth Bridge 30
Forty, Adrian 1n3, 9n6, 187n15, 259n9
fossil fuels 28, 78, 260
Foster, Norman 173, 174–175, 198, 199, 207
Foucault, Michel 127, 254, 266n25
Frampton, Kenneth 2n6, 8, 26, 179n34, 271

Freud, Sigmund 13, 53, 61–62, 78, 254, 268; on artistic creativity 268; *Civilization and its Discontents* 177

Friedrich, Caspar David 36

Fuller, Buckminster 3, 136, 142, 260

function 1, 29, 91, 93, 115, 127, 168–169, 182–183, 236, 239

functionalism 29, 71, 114, 179, 182n7, 224

Fuseli, Henri 36, 37

futurism 80–81, 92

Garden Cities 32–33, 86–87

Gaudí, Antoni 46–47

Gesamtkunstwerk 64

gender 5, 11, 259–260

Gestalt 13, 244

Gibson, J.J. 226–228, 230

Giedion, Sigfried 2, 17, 107, 109, 169, 187; *Space, Time and Architecture* 120, 141

Glasgow School of Art 46, 245

God 14–15, 19, 22, 130, 180, 227, 266

Gödel, Kurt 17

Goethe 13n22, 40, 129–130, 252, 270

Gombrich, Ernst 18, 214, 266

Goodman, Nelson 18

goodness 16, 18

gothic: revivalism 38–39, 40, 43–45, 52–53, 56, 80, 97, 193; style 43, 94

Gowan, James 4

Graaf, Reinier de 235, 263–265

Graves, Michael 180, 194–202, 213, 219

Greece 14, 16, 37, 242, 259

Greek etymology 210, 252

Greek revivalism 56

Greek temples 35, 38, 156, 242, 251–252

Gropius, Walter 4, 18, 64, 71, 79–85, 109, 190, 226, 258–259; as architect 50, 81, 83, 85, 91, 121; *New Architecture and the Bauhaus* 82–83; *Scope of Total Architecture* 83, 98; as teacher 83, 84, 99, 105–106, 178

Gullichsen, Harry and Maire 116, 119

Guyer, Paul 131, 190n19, 244

Häring, Hugo 93–95, 106, 127, 261, 268

Harvard: Graduate School of Design 22, 84, 98, 219; Yard 84, 121

Haussmann, Baron 34, 55

Hawking, Stephen 14

Hegel, Georg 10n8, 17–18, 53, 109, 210, 252n51, 266n25

Heidegger, Martin 14–15, 24, 228, 230, 232–234, 242–244, 247, 251, 252–254, 269n39; *Being and Time* 15n27, 234, 244

Hellerau 50, 76, 106

Hertzberger, Herman 166, 171–178, 219; Centraal Beheer 172–174

hierarchy 77, 124, 157, 182, 203, 208–210, 220, 255

Hill, Richard 21

history: of art 35; cultural 106, 233; Hegelian interpretation of 17; ignorance of 83, 99, 252; Marxist interpretation of 53; Nietzschean view of 238; preservation of 39, 248–249; typological understanding of 210, 214, 218

Hitler, Adolf 60, 82, 107

Hoffmann, Josef 63, 66

Holl, Steven 124, 245–247

Horta, Victor 46–49, 66

House for an Art Lover 47–50

Howard, Ebenezer 32–33; *Garden Cities of Tomorrow* 32

Hugo, Victor 5

Huizinga, Johan 168n14, 177

Humana Building, Portland 198–201

humanism: philosophical 63, 129n15, 129, 132, 165, 170, 176–179, 198; Renaissance 12, 98, 130

Hume, David 10, 12, 52, 132, 227, 257, 269–270

Husserl, Edmund 14n26, 232–234, 245, 251

iconography 103, 112, 201, 241, 256

idea: as design concept 8, 21, 38, 142–144, 214, 269; single and multiple 161; as source of knowledge 10, 16–18, 21, 227, 267

idealism 16–18, 53, 81n6, 143; definition 15; reactions to 130, 176, 177–179, 269

imperialism 53

inclusiveness 180

industrialisation 26–28, 31, 86–87

insolubility 7, 14

insulation, thermal 78, 256, 260

intention, architectural 21

irony: architectural 192–194, 241

irreducibility 17

Itten, Johannes 81

Jahn, Helmut 198–199
James, William 21, 228
Jeanneret, Pierre 85n16, 101–103
Johnson, Philip 182–184, 196, 196n31
Joyce, James 63n20, 176, 181, 267n30
judgment: aesthetic 2, 12–13; legal
    18n35; moral 12–13
Jugendstil 46, 50
Jung, Carl 13, 62

Kahn, Louis 17, 109, 133, 134–157, 168,
    181, 187, 194n27, 205, 251, 255n5, 261,
    263; European travel 134, 134, 139;
    form and design 141–142; houses
    135–136; influence 159–160, 173,
    181–182; institutions 134; ornament
    145, 157; served and servant space
    138–139, 155, 225
Kandinsky, Wassily 81, 267n31
Kant, Immanuel: aesthetics 12–13,
    225, 232; anthropocentricism
    255; epistemology 10; ethics 11;
    metaphysics 16, 254; politics 177,
    181, 232; sense and understanding
    10, 106, 253
Kaufmann, Emil 107, 267
Klee, Paul 81
Klein, Melanie 13
Klimt, Gustav 59, 64
Koolhaas, Rem 19, 235–240, 245,
    263; Congrexpo, Lille 237–238;
    S,M,L,XL 235–238; Villa Dall'Ava
    235–236
Kraus, Karl 60–61, 71, 210
Krier, Léon 57, 203–210, 222–223, 238,
    246; Poundbury 222–223
Krier, Rob 219–220; *Architectural
    Composition* 219
Kristeva, Julia 6
Kropotkin, Peter 32
Kuhn, Thomas 26n1, 132, 254

Labrouste, Henri 37
language: architectural 1, 3, 5, 14, 71,
    103, 196, 198, 210, 224–226, 257, 261;
    metaphorical 14; musical 62, 215;
    philosophical 14, 60, 128, 232
Lasdun, Denys 85n17, 179
Las Vegas 182, 235
Laugier, Abbé 35–36, 77, 78,
    108, 212; *Essai sur l'architecture*
    35, 212
law 13, 177; aesthetic 29, 46

League of Nations competition
    8–9, 81
Le Corbusier 4, 17, 30–31, 51, 73, 77,
    79, 82, 85–86, 88–98, 101–102,
    107–109, 113, 115, 158, 160–162, 171,
    259, 263; City for Three Million
    87–88, 108; *objet-type* 51, 213; as
    painter 127, 213, 259; reactions to
    118, 143, 165, 176, 181, 203–207, 216,
    236; *Vers une Architecture* 17, 85,
    89–90, 160, 213; Villa Savoye 17, 95,
    117, 206, 256–257
Leeds university 101–102, 104, 105
Le Havre 31
Leibniz, Gottfried 14, 267
Letchworth 32–33
Lethaby, William 43
light: artificial 127, 150, 155–156;
    natural 46, 127, 155–156, 245;
    perception 226; transcendental
    meaning of 26, 244, 265n22
Lincoln Cathedral 18
Liverpool 7, 21n8, 86, 111
Locke, John 10, 227
logic 7–9, 12, 130, 181, 245, 265–266
logical positivism 6, 254n3
London 32, 38, 60, 82, 165, 193–194,
    198, 215; County Council 264
Loos, Adolf 60–61, 64, 70–74, 77–78,
    84, 95, 210, 231; *Ornament and
    Crime* 70
Lutyens, Edwin 181, 183–188, 193,
    208n6, 259
Lyotard, Jean François 6

Macdonald, Margaret 46
McGilchrist, Iain 24n48
Mackintosh, Charles Rennie 46–47,
    49, 63
Mahler, Alma 64, 65
Mahler, Gustav 62
mannerism 17, 181, 187, 196, 225
marche 38, 138
Marcuse 177
Marx, Karl 18, 53, 177n26, 254
marxism 2, 15n28, 53, 232, 234
mathematics 16, 21
"Mathematics of the Ideal Villa" *see*
    Rowe, Colin
mechanization 26–27, 86, 261
melancholy 19–20, 60, 78,
    235, 254

Merleau-Ponty, Maurice 13, 132,
    244–245
metaphor 5, 14n25, 236
metaphysics 14–20, 106, 232–234,
    266n27, 267, 269; resistance to 131,
    212, 228
Meyer, Adolf 50, 79–80, 82
Meyer, Hannes 8–9, 81, 130–131
Midgley, Mary 6
Mies van der Rohe 34n17, 81, 106–107,
    141, 165, 182, 207
mirror neurons 13
misogyny 20
Modern Architecture: formal basis
    96; technical basis 26–27; theory
    of 1, 91
modernism 1–4, 62–77, 82–85,
    256–257; anticipations of
    44–50; criticisms of, aesthetic
    105–106, 142, 154, 161, 164, 168,
    173, 177, 182–192; criticisms of,
    environmental 163, 260–261;
    criticisms of, humanistic 114–115,
    158–160, 176; criticisms of,
    theoretical 130, 133–135, 207, 215,
    323; origins of 26–54; other arts
    59–63
Mondrian, Piet 81, 267n31
Moneo, Rafael 4–5, 21–22, 214n13,
    218–219
moral: criteria 42–45, 77; duty 52;
    judgment 5, 157n28, 255
Morris, William 30–32, 38–39, 49, 86,
    248; News from Nowhere 32
Murdoch, Iris 6
Muthesius, Hermann 49–50, 268;
    Das Englische Haus 49

Nagel, Thomas 24n47, 267n29, 267n32
National Gallery, London
    194–195, 241
National Romantic style 111–112
Nazi Party 81, 107, 232n10, 234
neo-classicism 17, 35–36, 50, 77,
    86n21, 108, 113, 211n7
Neo-liberalism 3, 264
neo-Platonism 12
Neue Sachlichkeit 81
Neutra, Richard 70
Newton, Isaac 22
New Urbanism 228, 238
New York 29, 63, 83, 107, 182, 193,
    196n31, 215

Nietzsche, Friedrich 19–20,
    24n48, 52, 54, 61, 78, 86, 234, 237,
    252, 254, 266; Birth of Tragedy 19,
    52, 252
nihilism 19, 63
Nolli 204, 216
nominalism 18–20, 21, 128
nostalgia 246, 252, 264; concern to
    avoid 163, 179

objectivity 7, 13n19, 14, 24, 54, 78, 81,
    106, 233, 236, 245
Oedipus Complex 61
Olgyay, Victor 260
optimism 19, 102, 235, 264n18; about
    technology 27, 102–103
order: aesthetic 31; classical 29, 96,
    214; mathematical 16n31; recall to
    36, 86
organic architecture 94
Otis, Elisha Graves 29

painting 4, 82, 95, 108, 117; Viennese
    63–64
Palladio, Andrea 36, 206, 211, 215, 251,
    257; misunderstandings of 251
Pallasmaa, Juhani 13n22, 132, 244, 247
paradigm 26, 132, 236, 265n23, 266n27
paradox: of architectural profession
    263–264; philosophical 17
Parker, Barry 33, 226
Parliament: London 38; Vienna 57
parti 37, 144
particulars 16, 16, 18
Pawley, Martin 3
Paxton, Joseph 27, 27
Pei, I. M. 83, 99, 100–101
Perret, Auguste 30–31, 85
personality: of architects 8, 15, 111,
    138, 178
pessimism 15, 106, 131, 177n26, 231,
    246, 262
Pevsner, Nikolaus 18, 18n36, 34, 39,
    50, 50n40, 183–184, 184n11, 194
phallocentrism 192n21
phenomenology 14, 14n26, 24, 232,
    234, 244–245, 265n22
philosophy: architecture, relation
    to 3, 180–181, 226, 262, 267, 270;
    definition 3, 7; Non-Western
    6n2, 254–255; terminology 6–24;
    Viennese 60
Picasso, Pablo 85, 127, 176, 181, 254n3

picturesque 52n43, 60n9, 216, 219, 229, 251, 268; pejoratively applied 216, 219, 230

piloti 97, 105, 108n50, 119, 167, 236

Plato 9, 12, 16, 16n30, 17–18, 21, 227, 232

play: importance of 168, 172, 177, 244, 254

poché 37, 139–140, 205–206

poets: influence 244; modern 267; Plato's suspicion of 18, 19

politics 51, 60, 105, 232, 234, 252n54; aesthetics, relation to 53, 267

polychromy 37, 169

Popper, Karl 18, 18n33, 18n37, 266, 266n27

Porphyrios, Demetri 127, 127n12, 203n1, 223, 223nn24–25, 225

positive scepticism 21–22, 131, 269, 271

positivism 6, 14, 85, 232, 245, 254, 261, 265n22, 267, 269

postmodernism: architectural 4, 180–202, 209–210, 240, 262; literary 4, 181

post-occupancy evaluation 8

practice: apprenticeship within 39, 268; architectural 3–5, 11, 24–25; contingent nature of 263–265, 268; ethical and metaphysical 18; everyday 178

pragmatism: ethical 41n31, 255; philosophical 15, 21, 132, 228, 230

prefabrication 26, 260

Prior, Edward 30n12, 49

prisons 11, 212

Prix de Rome 37, 63

projet 37

proportion 2, 12, 19, 29, 52n45, 60, 89, 114, 124, 155, 163, 192, 196, 200, 224–225, 258, 262

propriety 1, 77, 190

prototypes 8, 218

Pugin, A.W.N. 38n25, 39, 43–44, *45*, 51

Purism 85, 107

psychoanalysis 13, 55, 61, 78

psychology 8, 14, 61, 244; Gestalt 13, 244

quantitative: compared to qualitative 12

Quincy, Quatremère de 210–211, 218

race 5, 52, 131, 266

racism 20

railway 26, 28, 88, 113, 172

Raphael 16, *16*

rationalism 22, 45, 83, 107, 234, 261

rationalization: structural 28

realist 17, 24

Renaissance 1, 3, 12, 35–36, 56, 139, 267; style 57, 193

repair 39–40, 248–249, 260

restoration: of historic buildings 39–40

RIBA 1n1, 194n26, 210, 253

Riegl, Alois 74–75, 77

Rietveld, Gerrit 159–160, 171, 177

Ringstrasse, Vienna 35, 55–59, 64, 67, 76, 204

Riseboro, Bill 2

Rochester Unitarian Church 141–144

Rococo 35, 212, 247n42

romanticism 22, 86–87

Rome 59, 135, 181, 189, 204, 216, 259; Nolli's map of 204, 216

Ronchamp 101, *102*

Rorty, Richard 21–22, 132, 181, 228, 230, 269

Rossi, Aldo 203, 210, 215–219, 262, 268; *Architecture and the City* 215–216; Broni school 219, 221; Gallaratese housing 217–218; Teatro del Mondo 218

Rowe, Colin 57, 96–97, 138n6, 160, 203–206; *Collage City* 204; on Gropius 82n7; on Krier 203; "Mathematics of the Ideal Villa" 96

Royal Society 10

Ruskin, John 11, 39, 43–44, 51–53, 86, 107, 130, 248; *Seven Lamps of Architecture* 11, 39; *Unto This Last* 52

Russia 79, 107, 124

Saint, Andrew 264–265

Salk, Jonas 144

Salk laboratories 144–147

Sartre, Jean-Paul 234, 270

Säynätsalo 98, 121–122, *122–123*, 126

Scarpa, Carlo 248–249, *249–250*

Scepticism: definition 15; epistemological 12; melancholic 254; positive 128–132; Pyrrhonian 269

Scharoun, Hans 94, 127, 219

Scheler, Max 106

Schiele, Egon 64

Schindler, Rudolph 70

Schinkel, Karl Friedrich 22, *23*, 40

schizophrenia 14, 60

Schmitthenner, Paul 106, 120
Schnitzler, Arthur 61–62
Schönberg, Arnold 62–65, 71, 215
Schorske, Carl 55, 57, 61, 63–64
Schulz, Christian Norberg 244, 252;
    Intentions in Architecture 244;
    Meaning in Western Architecture 252
science: apparent objectivity of 15,
    75, 106; distinguished from art 22,
    23–24, 35, 75, 115, 130, 211, 232, 265;
    and falsifiability 266n27; successes
    of 17, 26, 255, 265
Scott, Baillie *see* Baillie Scott, M. H.
Scott, Geoffrey 11
Scott, George Gilbert 40, *41, 42*
Scott Brown, Denise 182, 189–190,
    191, 193, 195, 235, 259; *Learning from
    Las Vegas* 182, 189
Scruton, Roger 224–226, 228
Scully, Vincent 156, 251–252; *The
    Earth, the Temple and the Gods* 251
Secession 59, 64
Second World War 33, 101, 106,
    204, 234
secularism 132
Seinäjoki 111, *112,* 127–128, 155
Semper, Gottfried 59, 76–78, *76*
sense: common sense 226, 247, 266;
    contrasted with understanding 10,
    106, 130, 253, 257
Serlio, Sebastiano 36, *38*
sexism 259
Siena 8
Sitte, Camillo 57–58, 59, 76, 204, 268
Siza, Alvaro 111, 131
skiagraphy 38
Smithson, Alison 160, 165, 176
Smithson, Peter 1, 8, 165, 176
Society for the Protection of Ancient
    Buildings 39
Socrates 12
Socratic philosophy: post-Socratic 14,
    22, 24, 239; pre-Socratic 232
Solipsism 17
Sommerfeld House 79–80
Speer, Albert 106–107
Spengler, Oswald 106
spirit of the age 2, 11, 17, 109, 192
steel 26, 29–30, 46, 117, 121, 137, 152,
    155, 223, 240, 261
Steiner, Rudolf 267n31
Steinhof, St Leopold 66–67
Stirling, James 4, 166, 179, 208, 260

Stoics 12
Stokes, Adrian 13
St Pancras station 41–42, 53, 261
Strasbourg 40, 55; Cathedral 40
Street, George Edmund 38
structuralism 166, 177
structure: brick 29, 35; concrete 145;
    efficiency of 137; expression of 77,
    121, 124, 140; fictive 77; hybrid 67
style: Bauhaus 82; classical 14, 35;
    eclectic 41, 119; as game 85, 187;
    International 107, 179n34, 212;
    musical 62–63; period 33, 39–40,
    222; National Romantic 111; organic
    94; painting 81; personal 115, 132
stylelessness 47
subjectivity 13–14, 24, 106, 245
sublimation 61, 78
sublime 51–52, 88, 91
Sullivan, Louis 28–30, 46, 107, 111;
    Autobiography of an Idea 29
Summerson, John 1, 3, 8, 10, 14–15,
    93, 108, 187, 210, 253; *Classical
    Language of Architecture* 1, 210
sustainability: environmental 2, 5, 260
symbolism 9, 191, 198, 201–202,
    208, 237
synthesis: in Hegel 17, 265–266

TAC 83–84, 103, 105
Tafuri, Manfredo 2, 60
taste 2–3, 13, 40, 43, 181, 225;
    consumerist 202; Japanese 46;
    modernist 180, 201
Team Ten 8n4, 138, 158, 160–166, 171,
    175–180, 203, 215, 244, 249
Team Ten Primer 158, 160–161, 165, 179
temperature: as example of realism 24
tendenza 216, 218
terrace house 31
Tessenow, Heinrich 50, 106
theatre: Bayreuth 64; city as 40, 57;
    Teatro del Mondo 218; Werkbund 50
theory: absence of 101, 270; aesthetic
    12–13; of affordances 227–228;
    of architecture 1, 4–5, 75, 78,
    231, 254, 267; colour 81; critical
    53; Eurocentric 255; geometrical
    212; grand 254; of knowledge
    10, 265–266; of light 226;
    Marxist 54; picturesque 52, 252;
    psychoanalytical 62, 266n7; urban
    91–92; Vitruvian 190, 270

Theosophy 267
thesis: dialectical 17; geometrical
    96–98
Till, Jeremy 265
totalitarianism 18
townscape 108, 192, 229–230
trabeated construction 35
transcendental: in Kantian theory 10,
    21, 131; meaning of light 26, 265n22;
    philosophers 32
Trenton bath house 216
truthfulness: in architectural
    expression 11, 105; ethical 10–11, 233
Tschumi, Bernard 19, 239–243,
    252; Acropolis Museum, Athens
    241–243; on language 1n5; Parc La
    Villette, Paris 240–241
tuberculosis 32, 144, 176
Tyng, Anne 135–136, 140, 155–156, 259
typhoid 32
typology 21, 23, 29, 202–203, 210–214;
    formal 98, 256; of high rise offices
    29, 86; ideal 215; origins of 211;
    three types 213–214

understanding: embodied 231, 252;
    epistemological 3; existential 234;
    intersubjective 234
Unité d'habitation 91, 171
universals 15–16, 18
university campuses 79, 101, 144
Unwin, Raymond 33, 57, 226
USSR 54, 107; see also Russia
utilitarianism 10, 236

values: commercial 57, 73, 194, 229;
    ethical 10, 239, 252; human 129; of
    inherited buildings 39
van der Velde, Henry 46, 50, 81, 268
van Doesburg, Theo 81
van Eyck, Aldo 138, 158–160, 165–171,
    174, 176–179, 183, 209, 226, 240,
    246; orphanage, Amsterdam
    166–171, 209
Venice: hospital 162; Quirini
    Stampalia 250; school of
    architecture 134, 168; Teatro del
    Mondo 218
Venturi, Robert: Complexity and
    Contradiction in Architecture 182,

189, 192; Learning from Las Vegas
    182, 189; Mother's House 183
vernacular: buildings 50, 216; style
    117, 120, 173, 184, 187, 190
Vienna 55–80; city plan 57–58, 268;
    Postal Savings Bank 67, 68–70, 74,
    77; Wittgenstein house 231–232
Villa Mairea 114, 117, 117–120, 120–121,
    164, 271
Villa Savoye 17, 95, 117, 206, 255,
    256, 257
Viollet-le-Duc, Eugène 44–45, 46, 50,
    77, 134
Vitruvius, Marcus Pollio 22, 35, 190,
    244; De Architectura 1, 270
Voisin Plan for Paris 88, 94

Wagner, Otto: city planning 57;
    Modern Architecture 59; Postal
    Savings Bank 68–70, 74, 77
Wagner, Richard 62
Walpole, Horace 43, 43
Warburg Institute 13, 96
Watkin, David 271
Webb, Phillip 30, 38, 49, 264
Weber, Max 15, 76
Weimar 50, 79, 81; Republic 82, 106
Weltanschauung 15, 106, 253
Werkbund, Deutsche 50–51, 106
Whitehead, A. N. 16, 266, 269
Wigley, Mark 4
Wilford, Michael 4
Wilkins, William 40, 41
Williams, Bernard 10, 130
Winckelmann, Johann 20, 35, 37
Wittgenstein, Karl 64
Wittgenstein, Ludwig 61, 131–132,
    231–232, 254; Vienna house 61, 131,
    231, 254
Wolfe, Tom 107
Wren, Christopher 10
Wright, Frank Lloyd: Art and Craft of
    the Machine 30; Broadacre City 34,
    87–88, 92; Usonian houses 188

Yale: art gallery 135–140; Mellon
    Center 136; university 135, 137, 152

Zoroastrianism 81
Zumthor, Peter 5, 247–249